MW00806969

HIROSHIMA

ALSO BY M. G. SHEFTALL

Blossoms in the Wind

HIROSHIMA

THE LAST WITNESSES

Embers Volume I

M. G. SHEFTALL

DUTTON

DUTTON

An imprint of Penguin Random House LLC
penguinrandomhouse.com

Copyright © 2024 by Mordecai G. Sheftall

Maps courtesy of M. G. Sheftall

DUTTON and the D colophon are registered trademarks of Penguin Random House LLC.

LIBRARY OF CONGRESS CATALOGING-IN-PUBLICATION DATA
Names: Sheftall, M. G. (Mordecai G.), author.
Title: Hiroshima : the last witnesses / M. G. Sheftall.
Description: New York : Dutton, [2024] | Series: Atomic bomb ; volume 1 |
Includes bibliographical references and index.
Identifiers: LCCN 2024000705 | ISBN 9780593472255 (hardcover) |
ISBN 9780593472262 (ebook)
Subjects: LCSH: Atomic bomb victims—Japan—Hiroshima-shi. | World War,
1939-1945—Japan—Hiroshima-shi. | Hiroshima-shi
(Japan)—History—Bombardment, 1945—Personal narratives.
Classification: LCC D767.25.H6 S493 2024 | DDC
940.54/2521954—dc23/eng/20240325
LC record available at https://lccn.loc.gov/2024000705

Printed in the United States of America
1st Printing

BOOK DESIGN BY ANGIE BOUTIN

In honor of Seki Chieko (1932–2021), who made everything possible.

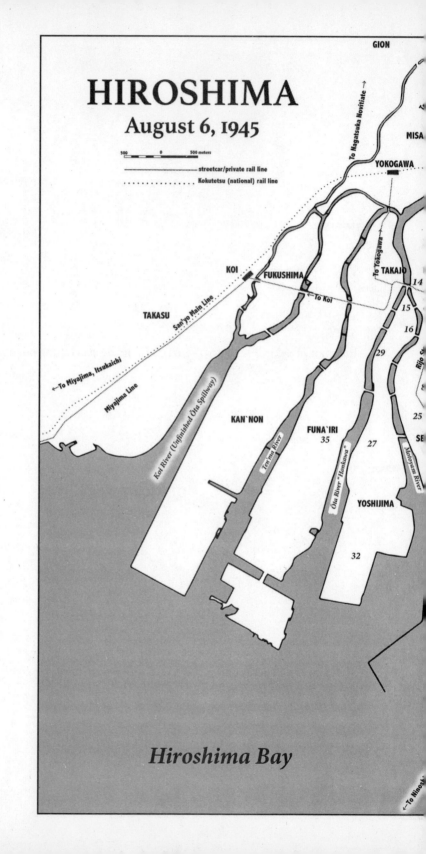

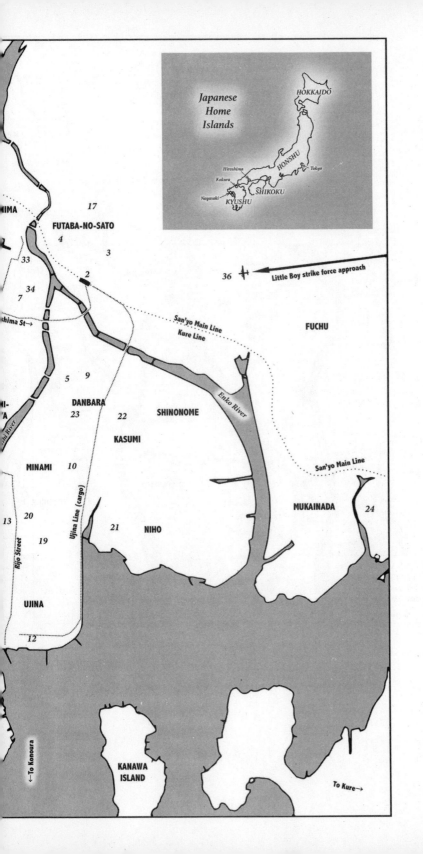

Japanese
Home
Islands

HOKKAIDŌ

HONSHU

Hiroshima
Kokura
Nagasaki   KYUSHU   SHIKOKU   Tokyo

17

FUTABA-NO-SATO

NIMA

4

3

33

2

34

7

36 ✈ ⟵ Little Boy strike force approach

shima St→

San'yo Main Line

Kure Line

FUCHU

5   9

Enko River

DANBARA

23   22   SHINONOME

KASUMI

MI-
A

u River

MINAMI   10

San'yo Main Line

MUKAINADA   24

Ujina Line (cargo)

13   20   19

21   NIHO

Rijo Street

UJINA

12

⟵ To Konoura

KANAWA
ISLAND

To Kure→

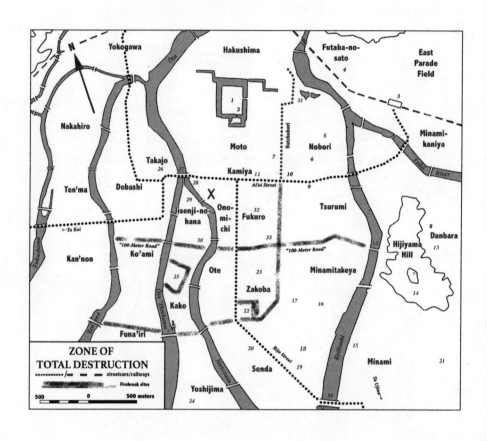

ZONE OF
TOTAL DESTRUCTION

•••••••••• /== ≡≡≡ streetcars/railways
▬▬▬▬▬ Firebreak sites

500   0   500 meters

What were those tens of thousands of people doing when they died? I wondered. . . . I did a lifetime of wondering in that fragment of a moment when we waited for the blast. And I've wondered ever since.

—*Abe Spitzer, B-29 radio operator, on Hiroshima and Nagasaki missions*[1]

HIROSHIMA

"HIROSHIMA . . . IT'S ALL GONE"

THE BOMBER

Fifty kilometers south-southeast of Iwo Jima
Dawn, August 6, 1945

AS THE REST of human civilization enjoyed the last few hours of its prenuclear innocence, a B-29 bomber named *Enola Gay* flew low and alone over a desolate stretch of the Pacific.

Even though the sun had just barely cleared the eastern horizon, the plane's pilot, thirty-year-old Colonel Paul Tibbets, had already had a very long day.

Some six hours earlier and twelve hundred kilometers to the south-southeast, *Enola Gay* had been parked on the tarmac at North Field, its Tinian Island base in the Marianas. Protected by a cordon of military policemen, the plane was illuminated by klieg lights, looking, in the words of its nineteen-year-old radio operator Richard Nelson, "just like the opening of a supermarket back home."[1] Swirling before this cordon was an excited commotion of Brownian motion that was a cross between a Howard Hughes Hollywood premiere and the Lindbergh landing at Le Bourget. The crowd pressing in on the plane consisted of well-wishers and gawkers of all ranks, including generals and admirals too numerous to count and a smattering of civilians one could have gotten arrested for asking the wrong questions.[2] Even though the main event that all had gathered to see was still a couple of hours away, it seemed that everyone who was anyone in the

Southwest Pacific Theater was already here. They had come to see off *Enola Gay*, its crew, and, if they were lucky enough to catch a glimpse of it, the top secret wonder weapon carried in the plane's bomb bay. According to rumor, it was supposed to shorten the war by months, if not end it virtually overnight.[3]

Among the select civilians in this throng who knew exactly what *Enola Gay* was carrying was a small, rumpled little man in a war correspondent's khaki uniform. This was William L. Laurence, a science correspondent for the *New York Times* and an early public cheerleader for the then new field of nuclear physics. But the professional credential that allowed him to be the only civilian journalist with security clearance to be on Tinian was his moonlighting occupation as a War Department PR man.

Laurence had witnessed the first test-firing of America's stupendously powerful, potentially war-ending new bomb in New Mexico three weeks earlier. As such, he was fully aware of—if not positively thrilled by—the historical significance of what he was witnessing there on North Field. However, he was also somewhat crestfallen. He had originally been cleared to fly as an observer on one of the B-29s in Colonel Tibbets' strike force, but a last-minute security-clearance snafu had bumped him from the Army transport flight out of California that was to be the first leg of his journey to Tinian. Nevertheless, Laurence was by nature a driven man.[4] If a second combat mission for the new wonder weapon were to prove necessary, he would be sure to find a spot on one of the planes next time.

In a ready room a short truck ride away, the crew members of *Enola Gay* and six other B-29 bombers were wrapping up their final briefing from Tibbets. In addition to being the *Enola Gay*'s pilot for the mission, the stocky, granite-jawed colonel was probably the Army Air Forces' top expert on the B-29, having been one of its original test pilots when Boeing was working the design kinks out of the aircraft. He was also the commanding officer of the 509th Composite Group— the specialist unit to which everyone in that briefing room and another eight hundred or so pilots, bombardiers, navigators, enlisted clerks, mechanics, and airmen on Tinian belonged. The 509th had been training in the tactics and deployment of their top secret weapon at a secluded base in the Utah desert for nearly a year before shipping out to Tinian the previous June. Today they would be using that weapon in combat for the first time.

At the end of the briefing, the assemblage stood with heads bowed and hands clasped in a special prayer for the occasion written and led by Captain William Downey, a young Lutheran minister from Minnesota presently serving as the 509th's chaplain.

"Almighty Father," Downey began, "Who wilt hear the prayer of them that love Thee, we pray Thee to be with those who brave the heights of Thy heaven and who carry the battle to our enemies."

Downey continued: "Guard and protect them, we pray Thee, as they fly their appointed rounds. May they, as well as we, know Thy strength and power, and armed with Thy might may they bring this war to a rapid end. We pray Thee that the end of the war may come soon, and that once more we may know peace on earth. May the men who fly this night be kept safe in Thy care, and may they be returned safely to us. We shall go forward trusting in Thee, knowing that we are in Thy care now and forever. In the name of Jesus Christ. Amen."[5]

With an echoed "Amen," the crews filed off to the 509th's mess hall, affectionately dubbed the "Dogpatch Inn" after the fictional Appalachian setting of the comic strip *Li'l Abner*. Although North Field was home to more than three hundred B-29s of the Twentieth Air Force, the 509th got special treatment and priority in all matters, from regularly replaced engines and extra-mile maintenance attention to (relatively speaking) sumptuous quarters and chow. To wit, for their preflight meal that night, their mess sergeant, Elliott Easterly, had put up paper decorations on the walls, prepared a spread of American comfort food, and made mimeographed menu cards keeping with the Dogpatch Inn's hokey "hillbilly" theme. While Tibbets tanked up on black coffee, tablemates tucked into "Sas'sage . . . We think it's pork," "Apple butter . . . Looks like axle grease," and other delicacies.[6] As with practically everything else on the island aside from the airplanes and their crews, these items had been shipped across the Pacific by the Twentieth Air Force's proprietary (for all intents and purposes) Merchant Marine fleet, tucked between the tens of thousands of tons of incendiary bombs and dozens of Olympic-sized swimming pools' worth of aviation fuel Major General Curtis E. LeMay's B-29s burned through every month raining hellfire on Japanese cities every night.

———

As Tibbets was getting up to leave the mess hall, he was pulled aside and quietly handed a small pillbox by the 509th's flight surgeon, Captain Donald A. Young. The pillbox contained twelve cyanide capsules—one for Tibbets and one each for the other eleven men who would be flying with him today.[7]

After being trucked to the personal equipment supply hut at the airfield, the crews were issued the rest of their gear for the mission: parachutes; "flak suits" for protection against antiaircraft shrapnel; survival and flotation gear; and .45-caliber sidearm pistols and ammunition, among other items.[8] It was at this point that Tibbets broached the subject of the cyanide capsules with the eight other members of his flight crew and the three special passengers for the day's mission. The latter were present at the behest of "Project Alberta," the code-named team of Tinian-based representatives of the Manhattan Project, the top secret Army Corps of Engineers program that had just spent nearly two billion dollars developing and producing four atomic bombs for America's wartime arsenal. One of those bombs—the one-off design its builders and minders had come to refer to as "Little Boy"—had been loaded into the bomb bay of *Enola Gay* earlier that evening.

The only person to take up Tibbets' cyanide-capsule offer was one of the Project Alberta passengers, Captain William Parsons. The lanky, balding Navy officer was a top-secret-clearance ordnance weapons specialist who knew the inner workings and mysteries of Little Boy as intricately and thoroughly as Tibbets knew the cockpit instruments and flight characteristics of a B-29.[9] It would not do for the Japanese to capture him alive, and the same went for Tibbets, who prudently stowed the pillbox in a pocket of his flight suit. Out of everyone who would be aboard the *Enola Gay* today, only Parsons and Tibbets had enough knowledge about atomic bomb technology and American plans for its use to reveal vital information about those ultra-top-secret topics in the unlikely—but still possible—event of their capture and interrogation (assuming an enraged mob of Japanese civilians did not beat them to death first—this was a real and ever-present danger for any Allied airman shot down over Japanese territory). In consideration of this risk, upon the 509th's posting to the Pacific earlier that summer, Tibbets had been grounded from flying over Japanese-controlled territory or waters for the specific purpose of avoiding just such a catastrophic security breach. This meant that he had not participated in any of the recon missions and practice bombing runs over Japan that the other B-29 pilots and crews of the 509th had been flying for the past month.[10] Today's flight to (and hopefully back from) Japan would be his first.

Conversely, the fact that none of the other crew members had taken up the cyanide offer was not necessarily problematic. Since there was no "need to know" about the Manhattan Project on their part in order to perform their individual tasks on the plane, none of them even knew yet that the special weapon they would be deploying today was an "atomic" bomb.[11] And anyone who had just spent nearly a year, as they had, in the draconian security environment at the 509th's training base in Utah and now on Tinian had long since learned never to engage in rumormongering or imprudent inquiry of any kind related to the unit's ultimate mission or decision-making above their pay grade and specific job assignment. As far as they were concerned, the only things they knew about "the gadget" or "the gizmo"—as they were wont to hear it referred to in briefings—were that it was top secret, that it was very expensive, and that it was going to make a very large explosion with a lot of fire that was going to kill a very large number of people.

At a briefing two days before the mission, Captain Parsons had talked to the assembled crews to give them some idea of what to expect—and what some Japanese city had in store for it—when "the gadget" exploded: "The bomb you are going to drop . . . is something new in the history of warfare. It will be the most destructive weapon ever devised. . . . We think it will wipe out almost everything within a three-mile area. . . . One bomb . . . one single solitary bomb will do all that. And maybe more."[12]

The math could not have been simpler, nor the consequences more stark: one plane, one bomb, one city gone.

If any of the crewmen harbored personal doubts about participating in such bloodletting, they could convince themselves that today's mission would not really be that different in terms of civilian casualties from one of Curtis LeMay's incendiary raids being flown out of North Field or his other Mariana Islands airfields on Tinian, Guam, and Saipan. As far as they were concerned, the most significant difference about the death and destruction they would be unleashing was that it would be accomplished risking only one plane and a crew of eleven instead of the typical mass formations of hundreds of bombers with thousands of men flying into harm's way. To the young men who had to face the enemy flak and fighters, destroying a Japanese city by putting only 1 percent of the usual number of American lives at risk to accomplish the same objective would have sounded like a bargain. From the perspective of their limited knowledge of the bomb that they would be using on the mission, this was not necessarily an unreasonable leap of moral logic. Nor were they alone in this respect.

In August 1945, not even the planners at the Manhattan Project and the decision-makers at the Pentagon and the White House had really given much thought about what Little Boy and its rotund atomic sibling, Fat Man, were going to do to human bodies beyond the usual effects one would normally expect to be involved when incinerating wooden Japanese cities. And as for making any moral distinction between "military" and "civilian" when planning attacks on Japanese targets, American air strategists had long since let that consideration—if it had ever really existed to begin with—fall by the wayside over four years of brutal fighting against enemies who seemed to resist more savagely, desperately, and stubbornly the closer they staggered toward defeat.

For the men in Washington privileged with a better grasp of the big picture, the frustration and desire to just get the war over with already would have been as palpable as those of the men in that Tinian Quonset hut listening to Captain Parsons describe Armageddon: Why didn't the Japanese just give up already and stop the bloodshed—and do so before the Soviets had time to join the fight against their country and do to half of Japan what they were doing to half of Germany?

Perhaps, the thinking went, Little Boy and his brothers would bring the Japanese to their senses.

———

Once on the tarmac at North Field, the crews of the other six B-29s participating in the day's mission headed off to their planes to attend to their final preflight checks and other preparations for takeoff. While all of this runway activity was happening behind them, Tibbets and his crew were kept standing in front of *Enola Gay*, where they squinted under klieg lights and were ushered this way and that to pose singly and in groups for cameras. As flashbulbs popped, the men fielded interview softballs from Twentieth Air Force PR types.

The first mission planes to depart were three weather reconnaissance B-29s. Nearly an hour ahead of *Enola Gay*'s scheduled departure, they took off from North Field, headed for the Japanese Home Islands. Once there, they would report back on weather and visibility conditions over three separate target option areas: The B-29 named *Straight Flush* would be headed for the mission's primary target, Hiroshima; *Jabit III* and *Full House* would be headed for the secondary and tertiary targets at Kokura and Nagasaki, respectively.[13]

The fourth B-29 to leave the field was an emergency standby replacement "strike plane" headed for Iwo Jima. Cheekily named *Top Secret*, it was equipped and crewed to deploy Little Boy in *Enola Gay*'s stead, for example, in the event of some major mechanical malfunction or the sudden disability of a key crew member.

As was well known to the American authorities on Tinian in

August 1945, there were still Japanese survivors of the battle for the island a year earlier who were holed up in the heavily wooded hills and jungles around North Field. If any of these holdouts had been watching the buzz of activity currently underway at the airfield, it would not take a military intelligence genius among their number to figure out that something very significant was afoot tonight. And if any of these lurking observers had access to a radio transmitter, Tibbets' strike force could be in for a surprise welcome party upon its arrival over the Japanese Home Islands.[14]

Regardless of this potential security risk—if it was even recognized as such by the Americans—the festivities continued unabated and spectacularly illuminated until finally, at 0220 hours, the no-nonsense Tibbets had had enough. After he shouted, "Let's get to work," he and the other crew members and passengers climbed up into their bomber and prepared for takeoff.

Seven minutes later, *Enola Gay*'s four engines coughed to life. To the applause of the gathered crowd and the whir and clicks of cameras, the plane slowly taxied out to its takeoff position 1.5 kilometers away, on the southwest end of North Field runway "Able."[15]

At 0245, on a signal from the North Field control tower, Tibbets redlined the engine throttles and released the brakes, and the overloaded *Enola Gay* rolled down the runway and off into the night.

Leaving behind all the klieg lights, cameras, and crowds on Tinian, *Enola Gay* returned, at least temporarily, to tense top secret anonymity. Along its route tonight, a rescue patrol line of Navy ships, submarines, and flying boats stretched from Tinian practically right up to the coastline of Japan itself. This knowledge provided some comfort to the crew as the B-29 flew low and alone over a vast and featureless Pacific Ocean.

While the plane might have appeared tiny and vulnerable on the scale of the western Pacific, up close—at human scale—it was a gleaming winged beast of menace and majesty. The cheering crowds *Enola Gay* had left behind on Tinian three hours earlier could have attested to as much, as could millions of residents of all the Japanese cities and towns that had been napalmed to ashes over the past half year by

LeMay's armadas of bombers like this one. For the latter group, a low-flying B-29 appearing overhead at incendiary-dropping altitude—scudding across the sky with its silvery skin, roaring engines, and high-keening turbochargers—was an apparition to inspire awe, horror, and loathing in equal parts.

STANDING BY

Strike force assembly point
Three thousand meters above Iwo Jima
0600 hours Tinian (0500 Japan)

SO FAR EVERYTHING was clicking like clockwork, and the mission was proceeding flawlessly. At its present position and heading, *Enola Gay* was ten minutes from the morning's rendezvous point over Mount Suribachi on the southern tip of Iwo Jima—a terrain feature made famous by the iconic photo of American Marines raising the Stars and Stripes on its summit during the battle for the island some five months previously.

Upon arriving on station over Suribachi at 0600, Tibbets banked *Enola Gay* to the left to begin a counterclockwise orbit of the area. He would maintain this "holding pattern" until joined by the other two B-29s in the strike force following up several minutes behind.

One of these planes, named the *Great Artiste*, carried telemetry instruments—"radiosondes" is the technical term—that would be parachuted over the target area to measure and provide data on the blast effects of the weapon *Enola Gay* would be dropping on a Japanese city a few hours from now.[1]

The yet unnamed third plane, code-numbered "Dimples 91" for the mission, was carrying photographic and motion picture equipment. This would record the event: for later analysis; for historical posterity;

and for convincing postwar politicians that the taxpaying American public had gotten its money's worth from the Manhattan Project.

Enola Gay had barely made one circuit around Mount Suribachi when the *Great Artiste* showed up, precisely on schedule, followed momentarily by Dimples 91.[2]

With the linkup over Suribachi successfully completed, the strike force resumed its northward heading, bound for one of three possible target cities clustered on the far western edge of the Japanese Home Islands.

Hiroshima was a key rail depot and military port on Japan's Seto Inland Sea, and the site of the Army headquarters where the defense of the entire western half of Japan would be coordinated once the anticipated Allied invasion of the Home Islands began later that autumn (assuming the atomic bombs were insufficiently convincing in conveying their message that further Japanese resistance was futile).

Kokura, on the far northern tip of the island of Kyushu, was the site of the Imperial Japanese Army's most important arsenal.

Nagasaki was a deepwater port on the East China Sea with historically and culturally significant connections to both China and the West. Related to that latter historical and cultural connection, it was home to the largest concentration of Roman Catholics in the Japanese archipelago. In its present incarnation, it was also home to the Mitsubishi shipyard that had produced the *Musashi*—sister ship to the legendary Japanese super battleship *Yamato*—and two major naval ordnance plants also owned by Mitsubishi.

It was no coincidence that all three of these potential targets for the first use of the atomic bomb were located far from Tokyo—at least six hundred seventy kilometers away for Hiroshima and nearly a thousand for Nagasaki. In one sense, this distance was merely the result of a process of elimination. By this point in the war, there was very little standing aboveground in terms of built-up urban concentrations virtually anywhere else in the country that merited targeting with one of the Americans' still scarce (and astronomically expensive) atomic bombs.[3]

Even emphasized with a stupendous explosion and a spectacular

mushroom cloud, the political and morale shock value of merely rear-
ranging the rubble in already ruined cities (or performing a demonstration shot off the coast of Japan, as some Manhattan Project
scientists had suggested) would have been negligible, as would the
return-on-investment ratio in terms of gleaning useful data when it
was time for technicians and planners in the Pentagon to analyze and
quantify the capabilities and effects of their new weapon technology.[4]
But far from the flattened urban ash heaps at the center of the country, there were yet relatively untouched, nearly fully populated cities
on its western periphery whose destruction would have been far more
convincing, it was surmised, toward moving the hearts of Japanese
leaders who otherwise seemed hell-bent on fighting to the bitter end.
Accordingly, once these cities had been placed on the preliminary
atomic target list by the joint White House / Manhattan Project / Pentagon "Target Committee" the previous April, they had been placed
off-limits to LeMay's Marianas-based incendiary campaign against
Japan's urban concentrations.[5]

Moreover, maintaining this distance from Japan's already almost
completely destroyed capital was prudent, as doing so would preserve
what was left of Japan's political nerve center. After all, if Emperor
Hirohito and those in his inner circle were killed by the bomb, there
would have been no one left alive with the authority to order and en-
force the country's surrender when the time came for such a decision.

This morning, August 6, *Straight Flush*, *Jabit III*, and *Full House*
would soon be signaling back their respective reports on weather and
visibility conditions over the target cities. If it was determined that
conditions over the primary target of Hiroshima were less than optimal, then depending on which of the alternate cities had the better
weather and visibility that morning, either Kokura or Nagasaki would
end up as Little Boy's target.

As the strike force formation continued northward and awaited
the final weather reports, the crew of *Enola Gay* performed its duties in
shirtsleeve comfort inside the plane's pressurized, climate-controlled
fuselage. Tibbets, as he was wont to do during long flights, had puffed

a pipe during much of his time in the cockpit this morning, and he had even delegated some stick time to the plane's autopilot system during the Tinian-to-Iwo leg of the trip, allowing him and his copilot, Captain Robert Lewis, to get a little shut-eye.

Such imagery aside, it would be a misrepresentation to suggest that Tibbets was "relaxed" this morning, as that is not normally an adjective one would use to describe the mindset of a man sitting on the equivalent of twelve thousand tons of TNT and headed into enemy airspace with a tin of worst-case-scenario cyanide tablets in his flight suit pocket. "Tensely confident" would probably be a better description of the state of his nerves at the moment. As a seasoned combat bomber pilot, Tibbets would have been all too familiar with the nervous tension inevitably involved when flying a large airplane full of gasoline and explosives into a combat zone. But he would have also been experienced enough to know how to prevent those "nerves" from interfering in the performance of his mission. Tibbets harbored little in the way of doubts as to his own ability to lead this crew and fly this airplane competently and skillfully this morning. And if he felt any fear creeping around the edges of his confidence to glower at him from the darkness, he could have banished it back to its abyss as he always did—by thinking about his mother, his oldest mentor and most earnest cheerleader, for whom *Enola Gay* had been named the day before (much to the consternation of Captain Lewis, the aircraft's officially assigned full-time pilot).[6]

Tibbets was supremely confident in his crew, at least half of whom he had handpicked personally for this mission. For the priority task of getting Little Boy where it had to be, when it had to be there, the two most critically important of these crew members were his navigator, Captain Theodore "Dutch" Van Kirk, and his bombardier, Major Tom Ferebee. Both men were widely regarded as being among the best at their respective jobs in the US Army Air Forces, both had been flying on Tibbets' personal aircraft since their Eighth Air Force B-17 days over Europe in 1942, and both had been among the first men whose personnel folders Tibbets had "pulled" to join him when he was forming up the atomic-attack-specialist 509th Composite Group in Utah the previous autumn.[7]

Also flying with Tibbets today were another two trusted companions from his old Eighth Air Force days: flight engineer Sergeant Wyatt Duzenbury and tail gunner Sergeant Robert Caron. The final four members of the crew were Captain Lewis; assistant flight engineer Sergeant Robert Shumard, who would help Duzenbury coax maximum performance out of the B-29's suite of four very powerful but also very temperamental engines; radar operator Sergeant Joseph Stiborik, who would assist Van Kirk with navigation or, alternately, bombardier Ferebee in target acquisition in the event of sudden inclement weather; and radio operator PFC Richard Nelson, whose primary tasks would be to monitor VHF signals from the weather reconnaissance planes over Hiroshima, Kokura, and Nagasaki, and to relay them between Tibbets, mission HQ in Tinian, and the 509th liaison on Iwo Jima for the replacement strike plane *Top Secret*.[8] Nelson would also stand by to receive a special coded "abort" signal from Tinian in the event that some miraculous diplomatic development resulted in Japan's surrender before *Enola Gay* reached its target.[9]

THE BOMB

THE ONLY ELEMENT of today's operation over which Tibbets did not have complete knowledge and authority was Little Boy itself. *Enola Gay* might have been Tibbets', but Little Boy was the purview of Captain Parsons and his two other Project Alberta "passengers": Army ordnance officer and Little Boy specialist Lieutenant Morris Jeppson, whose job was to assist Parsons in preparing and arming Little Boy; and a short, pugnacious Army radio countermeasures first lieutenant from Baltimore named Jacob Beser, whose primary mission responsibility today was to ensure that Little Boy's highly sensitive radar-based automatic-fusing system was not inadvertently set off by rogue Japanese radio or other electromagnetic signals.

Parsons was an Annapolis graduate and, at forty-three, the oldest man on the aircraft today by more than a dozen years. He had made a name for himself in the Navy as a math whiz and a technical engineer, and he had been the top ordnance researcher in the service when he was assigned to the Manhattan Project practically concurrently with its inception. His involvement with the specialist bombing unit that was to become the 509th Composite Group even predated that of its eventual commander.

As a Manhattan Project researcher, he had put in long months with Robert Oppenheimer and the rest of the atomic weapons development team of Nobel Prize winners and other world-class physicists at their main research laboratory in Los Alamos, New Mexico. Some three weeks earlier, flying over the New Mexico desert in an observation B-29, he had also witnessed "Trinity"—the successful test detonation of the first atomic bomb.

As the chief "weaponeer" for the mission, Parsons would have final judgment and say as to whether "his" bomb would actually be dropped on a target or not. As unforeseen events might dictate, he also had the authority to have Little Boy disarmed and dumped in the ocean, unexploded, if this proved to be necessary to save the plane and crew and/or to prevent it from falling into the hands of the enemy. Finally, he had the authority to order the bomb defused and disarmed in flight so that it could be flown back to Tinian for recovery or, under different circumstances, to Iwo Jima for reloading on *Top Secret*.[1]

Because Jeppson was Parsons' "assistant weaponeer," his primary jobs today would be to help his boss place firing charges in Little Boy after *Enola Gay* had safely taken off from Tinian (after all, nobody wanted an atomic bomb prematurely detonating in the middle of North Field); to check and recheck the complex electronic circuitry of Little Boy's triplicate layers of redundant fusing systems; and to replace a bank of three saltshaker-sized green safety plugs located in the outer casing of the bomb with three red firing plugs. This last step was required to close and activate the arming and fusing circuitry in the bomb, and it would be performed during the final approach to Japan.

At 0253, eight minutes after takeoff from Tinian and once at a safe enough remove from it to begin powering up Little Boy, Parsons and Jeppson crawled out of *Enola Gay*'s main crew compartment and went to work. After climbing a short ladder down into the plane's bomb bay, they began the first stage of arming the bomb—opening an access hatch near its tail to charge the firing mechanism with four two-pound bags of cordite gunpowder and a detonator.

For such an exorbitantly expensive weapon with such highly

sophisticated and complex electronic triggering systems, Little Boy's firing mechanism was surprisingly simple: a converted naval gun barrel running nearly the entirety of the bomb's length. This arrangement was, in a form-following-function sense, the reason for Little Boy's distinctive elongated shape.

At the breech end of this gun barrel was a projectile stack of uranium 235 (U-235) rings with a combined mass of some thirty-nine kilograms. These rings were backed, in firing configuration, by a tungsten carbide plunger disk, the propellant cordite bags, and the detonator, which was connected to Little Boy's electronic fusing. At the muzzle end of the barrel was a target slug of some twenty-five kilograms of U-235 sized to fit—with a tight squeeze—through the holes of the projectile rings.

Kept separate, the projectile rings and the target slug did not possess enough U-235 on their own to form a "critical mass" to create the kind of runaway chain reaction of nuclear fission that produced an explosion. In this state, the material was even radioactively weak enough for it to be handled with gloves (though inhaling or ingesting even a few atoms' worth of it would not have been advisable). Placed together, however, the rings and the slug would constitute a critical mass of U-235 that, upon its formation, would almost instantaneously undergo a chain reaction of catastrophically radioactive nuclear fission. Depending on how quickly the material was brought together, this chain reaction would either be stupendously explosive or it would just end up being a very "dirty" (and expensive) heat-generating lump fatal to any living thing in its vicinity as its shattering atoms of U-235 spewed out alpha and beta particles, gamma rays, and neutrons.

In terms of producing the desired "fast" chain reaction versus ending up with an undesirable "slow" one, the margin of error came down to a matter of microseconds. If the material was placed together with insufficient velocity, the result would be what the physicists at Los Alamos called a "fizzle." Using an analogy of the critical mass lump as a vigorously shaken bottle of Coca-Cola, a fizzle is what would happen if the bottle cap was very slowly and incrementally opened as opposed to popping it fully open all at once and getting the expected (and, in the case of this analogy, desired) vigorous geyser of carbonated sugar water. In an actual fizzle event, the colliding halves of the critical mass would leak away their combined explosive capacity as they traveled the final centimeters, millimeters, and micrometers separating them before they came into full contact with each other. There would still be an explosion, but it would be something equivalent in force to that of a conventional bomb—if even that—and it would diffuse the critical mass before it had a chance to exploit more than a minute fraction of its fissile capacity.

To get the "fast" chain reaction necessary to produce the desired massive, catastrophically violent nuclear explosion, a critical mass of U-235 had to be formed as quickly as possible—that is, before it had time to fizzle away the energy for its "pop." Physicists had crunched the numbers to get a ballpark idea of the minimal mass of U-235 required for criticality, as well as the minimum velocity required to result in a fast chain reaction versus a slow one. With the latter number in hand, they realized that a fast chain reaction could be achieved by using conventional chemical explosives to trigger a nuclear explosion. In the Little Boy design, this would be achieved by detonating the cordite firing charge in the breech of the gun barrel, propelling the projectile rings down the gun barrel to slam into the target slug at the speed of an artillery shell. There would be no time for a fizzle: the (for all intents and purposes) instantaneously formed critical mass of U-235 would undergo a fast chain reaction of violently explosive atomic fission in a matter of nanoseconds, producing heat at temperatures that had no business occurring naturally on earth, and destructive power that—even in the opinion of some of the world-class physicists who helped build the things—had no business in the hands of ordinary mortals.[2]

Pre–Manhattan Project US government scientists had known since at least 1941 that a U-235–based atomic bomb of this basic design could function if enough of the uranium isotope could be refined, isolated, harvested, and then thrust quickly enough into a lump of sufficient size to achieve explosive critical mass.[3] Figuring out the gun-barrel arrangement to reach the desired critical mass with sufficient speed had been the easy part. Getting enough U-235 for the job, though, had been a technical and logistical nightmare.

Over nearly three years, the Manhattan Project spent some 60 percent of its entire wartime budget trying to do just that. The problem was that only seven-tenths of 1 percent of naturally occurring uranium atoms consisted of the unstable U-235 isotope that was capable of undergoing nuclear fission—the rest of it was of the unfissionable U-238 variety.

Another method of harvesting fissile material was to convert U-238 into plutonium through uranium enrichment—intense neutron bombardment inside a nuclear reactor—but the technology for this was still several years away when the Manhattan Project first got underway. With the specter of Nazi Germany getting atomic bombs before America breathing down its collective neck, the Manhattan Project had to go with the technology it had, and considering what was at stake (or believed to be at stake—the Nazis never got anywhere near developing a functioning device), the crucial decision was reached to go big on uranium refinement.

At the time, scientists had no way of quickly and efficiently refining uranium to get a quantity of bomb-grade U-235 sufficient for a critical mass of the stuff. To overcome this engineering and scientific challenge, Brobdingnagian efforts and expenditure were sunk into building massive top secret facilities for uranium refining at Oak Ridge, Tennessee, as the first major project of the Manhattan Project. The undertaking eventually consumed some $1.2 billion of the Manhattan Project's total wartime expenditure of $1.9 billion.

From an engineering standpoint, the construction of the Oak Ridge facilities and the mind-bogglingly complicated machinery and other equipment used there was a stupendous accomplishment. From a scientific standpoint, though, anyone involved had to admit that Oak Ridge had turned out to be something of a boondoggle: After all that time, effort, and expenditure, by the time Parsons and Jeppson climbed down into *Enola Gay*'s bomb bay, essentially the entirety of the U-235 harvested by the United States over nearly three years was sitting in the repurposed naval gun barrel at Little Boy's core. And even that much had been gathered only barely in time for this mission.[4]

Having only one atomic bomb on hand would have been unacceptable in light of American strategic aims of ending the war without necessitating an invasion; once the Japanese had shaken off the shock of the first atomic bomb going off over one of their cities, they would have to be convinced that the Americans had an unlimited supply of the things and that they were prepared to use the weapons over and over again until Japan capitulated or, alternately, was wiped off the face of the earth.

Luckily for America (but unluckily for the city of Nagasaki), the Manhattan Project had not bet the entire farm on U-235 refining. Once Enrico Fermi demonstrated in late 1942 with the world's first nuclear reactor (what Fermi and his colleagues at the time referred to as a "pile") that chain reactions of uranium could be sustained and controlled, the key technology for the production of plutonium was at hand. Since 1944, a top secret and nightmarishly environmentally destructive facility on the banks of the Columbia River in the high desert of Washington State had been producing plutonium of bomb-grade quality.[5]

However, extreme challenges in developing the technology to induce explosive fast chain reactions in plutonium—the most significant being that the gun-barrel configuration did not work with this material—had caused extensive delays in the atomic bomb program. These delays saved Germany from being the eventual target of the first atomic weapons, but they would not save Japan from that fate. The technological problems had eventually been ironed out, and the plutonium-cored Fat Man atomic bomb design had been successfully detonated in the Trinity test on July 16, 1945, ten weeks after Germany's surrender. Now America was producing enough plutonium to make several Fat Man bombs a month. One of these was already on Tinian, ready to go, and more were on the way.

In the meantime, for the opening act of Japan's nuclear Götterdämmerung, the one-off weapon Little Boy would get its one and only day in the sun. At 0715 Tinian / *Enola Gay* time, after hours of preparation and circuit testing with Captain Parsons, Lieutenant Jeppson replaced the bomb's green safety plugs with red firing plugs, its internal battery power came online, and Little Boy winked to life. After the deed was done and reported to the cockpit, Tibbets got on the intercom and announced to his crew: "We are carrying the world's first atomic bomb."[6]

FAITH IN FINAL VICTORY

Chūgoku Military District Air Defense HQ bunker
Hiroshima Castle
0709 hours (Japan)

STRAIGHT FLUSH ENTERED Japanese airspace nine thousand meters over the Shikoku island port of Mugi, heading north-northwest toward the main Japanese Home Island of Honshu.[1] As part of its special weather recon mission on the morning of August 6, the lone B-29 was flying the same course the Little Boy strike force would fly an hour later if the skies over the primary target of Hiroshima were clear this morning.

Shortly after seven a.m. local time, as *Straight Flush* passed over Misaki Peninsula on the northern coast of Shikoku, it was picked up by a Japanese air defense observation post. The bogey contact was immediately reported by dedicated landline to Kure Naval Arsenal, the most important Imperial Japanese Navy base in the region. Concurrently, the bogey was also reported to Imperial Japanese Army air defense authorities in Hiroshima.

As part of the Army's *hondo kessen* ("final decisive battle for Japan") preparations to counter the Allied invasion of the Home Islands expected later in 1945, the entire ground war defense for the western half of the Japanese archipelago was going to be coordinated from Hiroshima. The command responsible for this mission was the Second

General Army, formed the previous April under Field Marshal Hata Shunroku.[2] The Second General Army was headquartered across the street from the Hiroshima railway station on the northern edge of the city; a sizable portion of its table of organization and equipment still existed only on paper and war-gaming tables. At the moment, however, its busiest daily mission was to oversee defense preparations for the southernmost Home Island, Kyushu—where the first Allied landings were expected and where the Japanese troops and tanks and artillery pieces waiting for them were quite real, indeed, and increasing daily in strength, reaching some 545,000 troops digging in and preparing to defend the island as of the beginning of August.[3] Given the high priority of this mission, the headquarters' location directly adjacent to Hiroshima Station, astraddle the main railway and communications trunk line in western Japan, was ideal. From this spot, the Second General Army could closely monitor the constant flow of military rail traffic to Kyushu and ensure that it was kept running as smoothly as possible.

Another aspect about the site that must surely have seemed ideal—if not too good to be true—was the fact that the Allies' bombers seemed to be completely ignoring the city during these long, slow, hot summer days of 1945.

A twenty-minute walk west of Hata's command was the headquarters of the Chūgoku Military District / 59th Army, housed on the grounds of the old samurai castle that had given Hiroshima its name nearly three hundred fifty years earlier. Like its parent organization, the Second General Army, the double-barreled name of this command was an idiosyncrasy of Japan's hurried *hondo kessen* preparations. Once actual bullets started flying in the streets of Hiroshima, the command, in its guise as the 59th Army under Lieutenant General Fujii Yōji, would be coordinating military operations against the Allied invaders in the old geographical designation of the Chūgoku region—an area encompassing the prefectures of Okayama, Hiroshima, Yamaguchi, Shimane, and Tottori, which constituted the westernmost third of the main Japanese Home Island of Honshu.

In the meantime, General Fujii oversaw the military governmental administration of this same geographical region as commander of the

Chūgoku Military District (CMD). At present, the CMD's primary activity was coordinating air defense measures in the area, with particular emphasis on its home turf of Hiroshima, where an ambitious campaign of firebreak construction was clearing long, wide swaths of mostly privately owned wooden housing and storefronts to protect key military and civilian government installations in the downtown districts from American incendiary raids. Thousands of Hiroshima civilians were assisting in this crash project, and many thousands— often the same individuals—were being "dehoused" as their homes were torn down to clear the firebreak lanes.

The administrative center of the Hiroshima Castle complex during daytime working hours was an old, late nineteenth-century building that had housed Emperor Meiji's Imperial General Headquarters (IGHQ) during the First Sino-Japanese War (1894–1895). Its 24/7 nerve center, however, was an underground concrete bunker facility built near the southern moat of the castle when the CMD had been designated and activated in June 1945. The primary function of the bunker facility was to coordinate air defense for the Chūgoku region. Army personnel in this hot, dank underground workspace monitored enemy aircraft activity on their western Japan beat around the clock, in shifts, dependent on radar and observation posts in the region as well as on civilian radio broadcasts from NHK stations around the country to serve as their eyes and ears on the outside world.[4]

Also working in the bunker were thirty-member-strong shifts— three per twenty-four hours—composed of mobilized students from nearby Hijiyama Girls' School. In their blue school uniform sailor blouses and Rising Sun headbands, and with their adorable pluck and uncomplaining enthusiasm, the girls were regarded with both fondness and respect by their military colleagues in the bunker.[5]

Perhaps aware, on some level, that part of the value of their work here also involved morale boosting, the Hijiyama girls invariably peppered their exchanges with their military colleagues with chipper patriotic exhortations—no doubt earnestly and sincerely felt—to keep up the good fight and do their best for a nation that had undying faith in final victory.[6] If any of the adults in their work environment were beginning to harbor personal doubts about Japan's fortunes at this point in the war, none of these morale-sapping sentiments seemed to have rubbed off on the schoolgirls.

Like millions of their age peers around the country mobilized to work in military facilities like this, toiling in munitions and aircraft factories, or helping to dig defensive earthworks at expected invasion sites around the archipelago, these girls—fourteen to fifteen years old—had barely seen the inside of a classroom for the past year. Of even more significance in molding their worldviews and mindsets was the fact that their age demographic had never known a Japan that was not engaged in, or at least preparing for, full-scale, all-out warfare utilizing the total physical, economic, political, cultural, and spiritual resources of the nation. This was the world they had known all their lives. They made sense of it and their place in it by counting themselves among the emperor's most ardent and loyal subjects. Their fighting spirit was nourished by a round-the-clock stream of daily media content drilling into their heads the notion that despite the fact that the Americans were now burning their country's cities to the ground every night (everywhere, it seemed, but Hiroshima), Japan's peerless spiritual strength would eventually prevail over the cowardly enemy's material superiority. As the girls marched to work for every shift, they often sang songs about being prepared to die to help make that happen. Before their shifts, they would form up to receive exhortative speeches from their teacher chaperones and officers from the HQ building before engaging in thirty minutes or so of mock bayonet drill with rubber-tipped *bokujū* practice rifle stocks. Belying any suspicions that their enthusiasm might have just been empty cheerleading, their age peers on Okinawa a few months earlier, and those on Saipan a year before that, had already shown that the ardor and resolve proclaimed in these scripted public displays were not always just an act put on for a captive audience of fellow Japanese slowly succumbing to malnutrition and being terrorized nightly under Curtis LeMay's incendiary bombs.

When the *Straight Flush* contact was reported shortly after 0700 on August 6, the girls in the command and communications room of the bunker went into action, manning phone desks where they received reports from observation posts along the bogey's route. They passed these reports through a small aperture in a concrete wall opening into the otherwise off-limits operations room, where one entire wall was occupied by a giant map of western Japan fitted with small electric lightbulbs at locations of each of the thirty-three air defense observation posts in the CMD.[7] When a contact report came in from any one of them, its light would be illuminated, and this information would assist in tracking the heading and likely target of any incoming enemy bomber formation.

This morning, the duty officer in charge was thirty-two-year-old Major Aoki Nobuyoshi, who appraised the incoming data on *Straight Flush*'s ingress and assessed whether the threat merited disrupting Hiroshima's work routines (i.e., war production) with either a *keikaikeihō* general warning alert or a *kūshūkeihō* full air raid alert, the latter of which would compel all civilians in the city to drop whatever they were doing at the moment and run for air raid shelters.

At 0709, Major Aoki decided that the lone B-29 did not merit a full air raid alert. Protocol did, however, call for at least a general-warning-alert order in such a situation, and this was duly issued.[8] In quick succession, the Hijiyama girls sent out calls to antiaircraft batteries and other air defense facilities in the region. Although the nation's force of fighter planes was for the most part grounded by this point in the war to conserve aircraft and aviation fuel for kamikaze use against the anticipated Allied invasion, notices went out to their airfields anyway.[9] Occasionally, in similar circumstances, a few desultory sorties might be sent up from these fields, perhaps more to buck civilian morale on the ground than to try to intercept B-29s that were in any case usually flying too fast and high for any Japanese fighters to reach. On this day, however, no planes would go up after the lone American B-29.

The girls also gave the NHK Radio Hiroshima announcer in the bunker instructions to begin broadcasting the alert, and relayed Major Aoki's order to sound air raid sirens throughout the area to the Hiroshima prefectural office.[10] There, the civil servant on duty at the Air

Defense Observation Post Bureau flipped a switch, and for the seventh time in ten hours, sirens began another low-moan-to-high-shriek crescendo that echoed through the streets of the exhausted city.[11]

According to civil defense directives, households with elderly family members and/or small children were to start moving off to their nearest bomb shelters in the event of a general warning alert, and across the city, *Keibōdan* air raid wardens and other professional and volunteer civil defense first responders (police and firefighters) made sure that standard operating procedure was followed. As it was only a general warning and not an air raid alert, though, all other able-bodied adults were free—if not encouraged—to go on with their morning routines, and this was just what most did.

It was, after all, only one high-flying plane.

THE CASTLE

THE GENERAL ALERT was an inauspicious beginning to another Monday morning of life during wartime for the residents of Hiroshima, as very few of them had been able to sleep more than an hour or two—if that—because of the incessant sonic barrage of air raid sirens throughout the previous night.

The sleep-ruining culprits had been two separate air raids by large formations of B-29s. The first had been against petroleum facilities in Ube, Yamaguchi Prefecture, about a hundred fifty kilometers to the west. The second was a B-29 incendiary attack against the textile-manufacturing town of Imabari in the Shikoku Military District, some sixty kilometers away to the southeast across the Seto Inland Sea.[1] Technically speaking, even though the latter was the closer of the two attacks, the Imabari raid had occurred outside of General Fujii's bailiwick, but the relative proximity and size of the enemy bomber formations and the constant flyover of the Inland Sea between Hiroshima and Imabari by American reconnaissance and command liaison aircraft had compelled Chūgoku HQ to err on the side of caution and stay on full alert. LeMay's bombers, after all, had been known to conduct feints during their raids, changing headings at the last minute to catch their targets' air defenses off guard. Accordingly, twice during the night, residents of the region had been roused from their futons by the sirens and directed by NHK Radio announcer Furuta Masanobu's broadcasts from the Chūgoku HQ air defense operations bunker to don their protective gear, shoulder their emergency bags, gather their family members, and head for the shelters—where they remained once for two and a half hours, and a second time for an hour and forty-five minutes.[2]

On the bright side, Hiroshima's luck vis-à-vis the B-29s had held up once again, but the downside was that the commuters shuffling into town along Hiroshima's dusty midsummer byways were even more exhausted than usual this morning.

In the parts of town closer to the waterfront, such as the Ujina Harbor District, residents had been kept awake not only by the warning sirens, but also by the sounds of actual explosions carrying over the water from Imabari. Thirteen-year-old Ujina resident Tominaga Chieko, a first-year student at Second Hiroshima Prefectural Girls' School, heard the Imabari bombs and secondary explosions from the burning town as distant rolling thunder. Despite being physically exhausted from working at an air defense firebreak-clearing site near city hall with her classmates on Sunday, she had been unable to sleep a wink—kept awake by the sirens, by having to run back and forth to her local air raid shelter, and by the bombing sounds carrying across Hiroshima Bay from Imabari.

This morning, as the sirens wailed throughout the city to alert citizens to *Straight Flush*'s incursion, Chieko was running a low-grade fever and afflicted with a bad case of diarrhea. Her condition was no doubt exacerbated by a combination of chronic exhaustion from sleep deprivation and physical fatigue from the firebreak work. But the real culprit behind the diarrhea was a crate of grapes the Tominagas had received the previous day as the gift of an uncle from neighboring Okayama Prefecture. The grapes were a luxury (and technically contraband) delicacy in late-war Japan, when most people were subsisting on a near-starvation diet.[3] Accordingly, Chieko's mother had originally planned to ration them out one at a time to family members to make them last as long as possible. But when the air raid sirens had started that night, they all agreed that it would be better to eat all the grapes while they still could rather than risk losing them in a fire. So Chieko and the other family members had stuffed themselves in an ecstasy of grape gorging.

Now, ten hours later, Chieko was doubled up with cramps on her futon. This did not stop her, however, from arguing with her mother's decision that the fever and diarrhea were reason enough to duck out of firebreak detail this morning. In this case, Chieko's strenuous objections were not motivated by a burning desire to work for a war she had long since stopped believing in. And her insistence on going to her firebreak worksite certainly did not arise from some unrequited love for Hiroshima. In fact, it was closer to the truth that she hated the city. She hated that her elite Mitsubishi executive father had been transferred here to manage Ujina harbor operations for the Army. She hated the provincial mindset and the bumpkinish way people talked here, and the way her neighbors and peers laughed whenever she opened her mouth and they heard her well-educated Tokyo accent. At school, she hated the lockstep conformity, patriotic naivete, and general ignorance of her classmates and the way that they constantly dropped references and comments betraying the resentment they held toward this Tokyo interloper. She hated that they thought she was a snob and a city slicker softy who wasn't pulling her weight for the war effort because she had a piano and live-in servants and two flush-toilet bathrooms in her big Ujina house. She wanted to go to the worksite this morning because she wanted to prove her classmates wrong. And her intention to defy her mother and go to work today was only intensified when her older sister, Machiyo, a student at nearby Hiroshima Prefectural Women's Teachers College, teased her about letting down the war effort on account of a little tummy ache.[4]

———

After the "All Clear" for the Imabari raid had been sounded at 0215, the staff of CMD HQ was kept busy keeping an eye on (but not sounding alarms for) a third B-29 raid—this one against Nishinomiya,

Osaka, in neighboring Chūbu Military District. When the last American planes connected to the raid cleared Japanese airspace sometime after four in the morning, General Fujii gathered his headquarters staff, thanked them for their hard work on this long night, and dismissed them to go home to their quarters with orders to return to work by 1030 instead of the usual 0800. A skeleton crew of two field-grade officers—a lieutenant colonel and a major—was left on duty to mind the HQ offices, and Major Aoki was left in charge of the operations room in the air defense command bunker. If any more sirens were going to be sounded in the Chūgoku region this morning, it would be on his orders.

One kilometer southwest of where Aoki had been keeping his wee-hours bunker vigil, his young family—wife, Fumi; four-year-old daughter, Yoshimi; infant son, Nobumi; and sister-in-law—slept, or tried to sleep, in their Army-rented home in the district of Fukuro-machi.[5]

—————

Hiroshima Castle was a symbolically appropriate site for Chūgoku HQ. It had been a traditional locus of regional political authority and military power since the sixteenth century.

In the late 1580s, when the Japanese islands were still racked by power struggles between rival warrior clans, samurai warlord Mōri Terumoto was looking for a new fortress home. When he was surveying potential sites for the construction of a castle in his western Honshu domain of Aki, his eye soon fell on the broad fan delta of the Ōta River as a potential location. The seven streams (the Ōta and six tributaries) cutting roughly north to south through the seven-kilometer-wide delta here offered excellent potential commercial access to a bay fronting on the Inland Sea. Moreover, as these bodies of water formed a deep, naturally multilayered moat that provided defense against potential attackers—an occupational hazard for any samurai commander at the time—this particular piece of real estate offered clear military advantages, as well.[6] This last point might have been the deal sealer for Mōri. Not long after his tour of the site, his surveyors laid

out a plot for the new castle almost precisely at the geographical center of the delta.[7] In 1589, ground was broken on the project.

The design and construction of the castle followed the architectural norms and expectations for the headquarters of an ambitious
youngish warlord on the make. They might have even been a bit on
the ostentatious side. At the center of the castle's layout was a keep
surrounded by a square moat. The keep was built on an elevated
earthen table walled in by large boulders and ringed with wooden
ramparts. The most prominent feature of the keep was a thirty-seven-
meter-tall *tenshukaku* donjon of wood, plaster, and elegantly gabled
metallic gray roof tiles. This stately donjon would go on to dominate
the skyline of the delta for the next three and a half centuries.

At the dedication ceremony for his castle, Lord Mōri christened
both his new home and the delta at whose center it sat "Hiroshima"—a
name purportedly inspired by the resemblance of the delta's tributary-
ribboned and islet-striated topography to a wide archipelago.

In the decades following the Meiji Restoration (1868), when Japan
began flexing its muscles as an up-and-coming regional power, Hiroshima quickly evolved into a major command and logistical nexus for
the new Imperial Army.

The town grew by leaps and bounds during the Meiji era, really
coming into its own during the First Sino-Japanese War, when both
the Imperial General Headquarters and Emperor Meiji himself picked
up stakes in Tokyo and set up camp on the grounds of Hiroshima Castle for the duration of the conflict.

During this war and the Russo-Japanese War (1904–1905) and
continuing for the next half century, public funds via direct Army expenditure or money from military manufacturing contracts for the
Mitsubishi Shōji Co., Ltd., corporation and other private enterprises
transformed Hiroshima into the Imperial Army's most important
embarkation point for men and matériel headed to and from the
Asian continent and, later, the South Pacific. By 1929, some 28 percent
of usable land area in the city had been set aside for military use.[8] This
growth was particularly impressive in the harbor district of Ujina on
the south-side waterfront of the city. Here, both activity and real

estate were dominated, by the start of the Second Sino-Japanese War (1937–1945), by the Imperial Japanese Army Shipping Command. This organization—basically the Japanese Army's proprietary Merchant Marine fleet centered on the operations of troop transports and supply ships—was more commonly known in local and military circles as the Akatsuki ("Rising Sun") Command. The Akatsuki Command was also responsible for transporting Allied POWs to and from far-flung Japanese Army camps around the empire aboard what would come to be known in postwar war crimes tribunals as "hell ships." These vessels were infamous for their high ratio of in-transit POW fatalities due not only to atrocious onboard conditions, but also because of sinking by American aircraft and submarines.[9]

Concurrent with, and connected to, the evolution of the Ujina Harbor facilities, Hiroshima became one of the most important regional cargo and maintenance depots in the national railway system. By the onset of the Second World War, it had become the Seto Inland Sea's hub for both land and maritime military transportation. The city's population grew around this core of military-driven economic activity to a peak of nearly 420,000 in 1942. By August 1945, however, a nationwide civil defense policy of evacuating elementary-school children and select categories of adults not engaged in essential war labor from air-raid-vulnerable urban concentrations had seen the population fall to 245,000.[10] By this point the city's residents consisted primarily of those either too young or too old to endure evacuation; their caregivers; adolescents and adults engaged in war work; municipal and prefectural government employees; and some forty thousand Imperial Army soldiers.[11]

WEATHER REPORT

Hiroshima City
0709 hours (Japan)

ALTHOUGH HIROSHIMA HAD so far been spared one of Curtis LeMay's city-killing fire raids, his B-29s had been passing overhead constantly for the past six months. By night, this traffic mostly consisted of roaring, low-flying armadas headed to and from the incineration of some unlucky neighboring city or to and from seeding the Seto Inland Sea with anti-shipping mines. In daylight hours, the uninvited visitors tended to fly in barely visible and only faintly audible singles, pairs, or trios, and at speeds and altitudes far above the reach of any Japanese flak artillery or fighter interceptors.[1] But whether by day or night, these gigantic silver aircraft never dropped so much as an empty beer bottle or anything more lethal than propaganda leaflets on downtown Hiroshima, with the exception of a single stick of bombs mistakenly dropped on the business district in April. This is why it was not an event of much urgency or concern in the CMD air defense bunker on the morning of August 6—beyond the issuing of a routine general alert order—when *Straight Flush* made landfall about sixty-five kilometers to the east, banked hard left, and began flying in a beeline toward Hiroshima.[2]

Since early summer, when the American capture of Okinawa had put the Home Islands within range of smaller tactical aircraft, the

B-29s over Hiroshima had been joined by B-24 and B-25 bombers and even the occasional sweeps of prowling P-51, P-47, or P-38 fighters. These attacks were also occasionally joined by carrier-based American naval aircraft. Unlike the stately but heretofore innocuous B-29s, however, these smaller planes occasionally strafed targets of opportunity in Hiroshima Bay and other military facilities around the area. These strikes, which seemed to be mainly done as afterthoughts, used machine-gun ammunition left over after raids on Kure Naval Arsenal, fifteen kilometers to the east. The marauders would shoot up some fishing boats or lighters in the harbor or perhaps a warehouse or storage tank on the waterfront before winging off to the southwest and their Okinawan sanctuary.

In July 1942, three months after suffering the humiliation of the Doolittle Raid on Tokyo, the Army Ministry issued a legal directive to all commands stating that since Allied aviators were dropping bombs on targets that did not meet strict criteria as being military in nature, international law did not require their proper treatment as prisoners of war. The directive gave ground commanders the authority to hold courts-martial and summarily execute for "war crimes" any Allied aviators captured in their jurisdiction.[3] After February 1945, amended directives were issued delegating authority to execute captured airmen without even paying lip service to legal proceedings.[4]

Luckily for the crews of those few American aircraft otherwise unlucky enough to have been shot down over Greater Hiroshima, it was not the policy of the CMD to summarily execute captured enemy fliers. Instead, standard procedure called for them to be detained in downtown Hiroshima for initial interrogation and processing at Chūgoku Military Police HQ before being sent to more permanent POW facilities, such as the infamous Camp Ōmori in Tokyo, whose more notable residents included renowned Marine Corps ace "Pappy" Boyington and Captain Louis Zamperini, the former US Olympic team runner.[5]

When the general alert sirens began wailing for *Straight Flush*, thirteen American airmen were being held by military police authorities in Hiroshima. Ten B-24 crewmen and three naval aviators—all shot down in late-July raids on Kure—were locked up in holding cells either at the Chūgoku Military Police HQ or at other CMD commands in the Hiroshima Castle district of Moto-machi.[6] All were mere hundreds of meters from the Aioi Bridge, which *Enola Gay* bombardier Tom Ferebee would be using as his aiming point an hour from now if Hiroshima ended up being Little Boy's final destination.

The occasional high drama of an impromptu waterfront strafing or an even rarer enemy shoot-down aside, flyovers by single or small groups of American aircraft had become so frequent in recent months that the people of Hiroshima barely paid attention to them anymore.[7] Moreover, civil defense authorities not only in Hiroshima but everywhere else in the country had become hesitant to squander war production man-hours by issuing air raid alerts that would send workers to bomb shelters unless it was beyond doubt that a large-scale attack was imminent.[8]

The approach of smaller elements of singles, pairs, or trios of B-29s or other enemy planes would merely get a general warning alert. This lower-urgency-level alert was basically a heads-up to the populace to prepare to make a run for the shelters in case these planes proved to be advance recon elements or pathfinders for a larger raid force following up from behind. Preparations in such a case would include dousing open flames and turning off gas lines; getting elderly family members and/or neighbors and small children moving toward shelters; and donning steel Army-style helmets, padded cotton *bōsaizukin* ("disaster prevention hoods"), or any other protective clothing at hand.

Under the original stipulations of the National Air Defense Law of 1937, able-bodied adults in cities or factories under air attack had been legally obligated to stand their ground—either as individual homeowners or organized into neighborhood or workplace volunteer fire brigades—to cooperate in firefighting and other civil defense efforts. In August 1943—scant weeks after upwards of fifty thousand residents of Hamburg had died in firestorms ignited by British incendiaries and fanned by American high explosives—the Home Ministry published millions of copies of a pamphlet titled *Essential Knowledge for Air Defense* and distributed them through schools and neighborhood associations. True to its title, the pamphlet included ostensibly useful instructions for constructing simple air raid shelters in house floors or gardens; making smoke-inhalation or gas masks from common household items (including smaller versions for toddlers and infants); and putting out small incendiaries with buckets, mops, and handheld bamboo-pipe water squirters. As a redundant reminder to the civilian populace of what was expected of them in the service of emperor and state, the frontispiece of the publication featured an exhortation titled the "Air Defense Creed for Final Victory," which read:

> *We are all warriors defending our nation;*
> *We shall remain at our posts even at the cost of our lives;*
> *We shall fight on until the end, with faith in final victory;*
> *We shall make all possible preparations, and train until we have*
>   *full confidence in our abilities;*
> *We shall follow all orders, and not act selfishly;*
> *We shall cooperate with one another to bring all of our strength*
>   *and abilities to bear in our air defense efforts.*

After a March 1945 raid in which a hundred thousand residents of Tokyo had been killed in a single night, the authorities had been compelled to rethink the stand-your-ground policy for civilian urban residents. Now the issuing of an air raid alert—announced through sirens and radio broadcasts—legally obligated every person in the affected area (with the exception of official first responders) to evacuate immediately to the nearest prepared shelter, regardless of individual circumstances, the hour of the day, or weather conditions.[9] Many Japanese civilians complied with this law by digging shelters in their own homes, going right through their tatami matting and floorboards to do so. If they were well enough off to afford the luxury of backyards, they dug trenches and typically covered them with logs and sandbags. But experience in real air raids had proved that these homemade shelters more often than not turned out to be crematory tombs for their occupants. A much safer option, if available, was to evacuate to

steel-reinforced concrete buildings—such as schools or public offices—
or, best of all, to professionally constructed communal shelters, which
were typically dug into hillsides or railroad embankments.

Somehow, though, for all of the mental and physical preparations,
false alarms, and civil defense drills its residents had endured, Hiroshima had yet to be visited by a full-scale air raid. East, west, north,
and south of the city, Curtis LeMay's gleaming armadas of B-29s had
by this point burned down nearly every urban concentration on the
Japanese archipelago with a population of more than fifty thousand.
In the process, they had killed hundreds of thousands of Japanese civilians and, in the term preferred by American strategic bombing
planners, "dehoused" millions more.[10]

But why was Hiroshima being spared?

The authorities had no firm idea as to the reason for this, but
optimists among the general population came up with various theories to explain the city's luck so far. Some attributed it to divine intervention, pointing to the fervent Jōdo ("Pure Land") Buddhist faith
traditionally observed by the majority of its residents.[11] Others ventured that perhaps the Americans were not bombing the city because
so many Japanese Americans had ancestral roots there, or because of
the city's important Christian community.[12] One of the loopier conspiracy theories making the rounds held that Hiroshima was being
spared because, for some reason, President Truman's mother was living in the city incognito.[13]

Pessimists, on the other hand, saw something more ominous in
Hiroshima's so far being spared an American torch. Perhaps, as German Jesuit Hubert Cieslik overheard some of the parishioners of his
Nobori-chō church saying, the enemy was saving the city for something truly awful.[14]

But for optimist and pessimist alike, the constant state of tension
in waiting for LeMay's other shoe to drop was taking mental and
physical tolls. By early August, the residents of Hiroshima had spent
several long, hot summer months of sleepless nights and exhausted
days going through a seemingly never-ending routine of shelter evacuations (closely and strictly enforced by neighborhood association

busybodies doubling as air raid wardens) and preparations for conflagrations that might come any night—or never at all.[15]

On the off chance of catching a good, or at least a better, night's sleep in the midst of their state of chronic exhaustion, many women and small children living in the central districts—where the air raid sirens were loudest and the air raid wardens most numerous—were leaving the city each night to stay with friends or relatives in outlying suburban or rural districts. Those not fortunate enough to have countryside acquaintances simply packed up bedding and carted it out of town to sleep rough in the farming fields or on the heavily wooded mountainsides ringing the city.[16] Then, a few hours later, the urban exodus would be played back in reverse: The yawning sleep refugees—bedrolls and babies slung across their backs, toddlers in tow—would pour back into the city, clogging the streets and the picturesque bridges over Hiroshima's waterways.

Among these rush hour pedestrians, perhaps the most hurried and harried were the housewives and mothers who had to get back to their kitchens to cook breakfasts and prepare lunch pails for their menfolk and adolescent children to take to their war labor worksites. On this first Monday morning of August, these wives and mothers would be especially busy, as they would be preparing lunches for some eight thousand twelve- and thirteen-year-olds—nearly the entirety of Greater Hiroshima's seventh- and eighth-graders—newly mobilized to do firebreak work in the downtown district.

In the standard operating procedure for firebreak clearing, teams of adult males with carpentry knowledge / skills would begin the process of toppling a wooden house or storefront on a given worksite by sawing through a key support beam on one corner of the structure. Ropes would then be strung around the roof, and large teams of chanting volunteers would pull repeatedly and rhythmically, like a tug-of-war team, until the entire structure collapsed into a pile of timber and a cloud of dust. As the final stage in the process, cleanup teams would follow up to pick through the resulting pile of rubble and divide it up into recyclable building materials (e.g., ceramic roof tiles, corrugated metal, pipes, electrical wiring, intact lumber beams, etc.).

These sorted materials would then be stacked for later retrieval by trucks or carts. It was in this last task, the cleanup, that the city's junior high school students would prove useful, as it required little in the way of physical strength and not much more than youthful energy, a positive attitude, and a naive belief in the inviolability of their cause—all qualities the children had in spades.

Tasked with overseeing the firebreak construction for the city was Major General Kotani Kazuo, local commander of the Hiroshima Military District (HMD) branch of the CMD.[17] At the moment, his most pressing responsibility was to mobilize labor resources in the prefecture for the project and coordinate with local civilian authorities to do so. In short order it became quite clear among all concerned that the general was particularly insistent about getting the firebreaks finished as quickly as possible and intolerant of anyone who dared to get in his way.[18]

When Kotani had first pushed his proposal to put schoolchildren to work on the firebreaks, there had been understandably vociferous initial resistance to the idea among the city's teachers and parents. The matter came to a head in mid-July 1945 during a meeting at the prefectural office, where Kotani, CMD chief of staff Major General Matsumura Shū'itsu, and other assorted HMD and CMD staff officers had gone to discuss what they saw as unsatisfactory progress on the city's firebreak-construction work. Assembled to hear the Army's demand for more mobilized civilian labor were prefectural and municipal bureaucrats and also principals and other faculty representatives from every educational facility in the city.[19]

The Army insisted that the only solution to picking up the pace on the firebreak project was to put the city's heretofore underutilized (in their opinion) seventh- and eighth-graders to work on the clearing sites. The assembled school representatives, however, countered this by pointing out the obvious danger of having thousands of their prepubescent charges working out in the open, vulnerable to an air raid that might come at any time, and with no nearby place to seek shelter in such an event.

The military representatives responded with shouted accusations of insufficient patriotism and dedication to the war effort, insisting that the firebreak work had to take priority over such concerns as individual safety, and that it could not be completed in time without this extra student labor. The civilian faction finally folded when one of the military men—probably Kotani himself—emphasized the Army's position by banging his sword scabbard on the floor. As face-saving salve for the defeated educators, the prefectural and city bureaucrats promised to fund more faculty chaperones for the student work teams, and managed to get the Army to agree to let the children go home every day two hours earlier than their adult "volunteer" co-workers.[20]

At 0724 hours (local), *Straight Flush* arrived over the Hiroshima city after an uneventful ten-minute-long simulated bomb run across Hiroshima Prefecture.[21] Nary a fighter had scrambled and only a couple of desultory whiffs of hopelessly short antiaircraft fire had greeted the plane during its sixty-kilometer-long ingress over dry land. The spot directly over Hiroshima where Tom Ferebee would line up the Aioi Bridge in his Norden bombsight crosshairs and press a button to hand control of the aircraft over to the device and begin a sixty-second automatic-drop procedure was actually far off in the eastern suburbs of the city; forty-four-hundred-kilogram Little Boy would begin its drop from ten kilometers up and moving with an initial horizontal velocity matching *Enola Gay*'s four hundred fifty kilometers an hour. Falling in a long half parabola, it would traverse about four kilometers of Hiroshima ground distance before reaching "Air Zero"—its designated detonation point some six hundred meters above the Aioi Bridge.[22]

Seen from nine thousand meters up, Hiroshima was like a school science fair diorama of a densely populated river delta. Dominating the terrain were five islets, none much wider than a few hundred meters or much longer than five kilometers. Laid side by side in slightly skewed north–south orientation, each of these was separated from the next by either the Ōta River or by one of its six tributaries fingering their way down and out to Hiroshima Bay. There were patches of green here and there—parks, many in strips along the waterways, and some small-scale agriculture—but most of the dry land of the Ōta River's alluvial plain was covered cheek by jowl with tens of thousands of wooden houses and neighborhood factories with their traditional gunmetal-colored ceramic-tiled roofs. Slashing this mauve-gray mass of human habitation were hundred-meter-wide, ruler-straight light gray bands that Twentieth Air Force aerial photoreconnaissance had identified as firebreaks cleared around key military and civilian authority facilities.

At present, visibility over the city was marginally cloudy, and this was sure to improve as the hot August sun burned off the rest of the morning haze later on.

At his radio operator's desk aboard *Straight Flush*, Staff Sergeant Pasquale Baldasaro encoded and then began tapping out the Hiroshima recon mission's weather report.

A SLOW MORNING

Aboard Enola Gay
0715 hours (Japan)

FIFTY MINUTES OF flying time south-southeast of *Straight Flush*, Private Richard Nelson was sitting at his radio operator's station aboard *Enola Gay*, with Tibbets looming over his shoulder, when Baldasaro's coded signal started coming in. Nelson wrote out the message: *Y-3 . . . Q-3 . . . B-2 . . . C-1.*

Using the special cipher sheet issued for the mission, Tibbets decoded the message that Nelson wrote out: *Low, middle, high cloud cover less than three-tenths at all altitudes. Bomb Primary.*

"It's Hiroshima," Tibbets announced to the flight deck.[1]

Kurashiki Aircraft Corporation
Yoshijima Plant
Yoshijima District, Hiroshima City
3.7 kilometers south of Ground Zero
0715 hours (local)

About five hundred meters west of where Tominaga Chieko had gone back to sleep in her well-appointed Ujina home, seventeen-year-old

Chai Tsong Chin and his Kōryō Junior High School classmates heard the high, faint engine drone of *Straight Flush* over the city. Assuming it was just another "mail plane," as they jokingly called the solitary B-29s that constantly flew over Hiroshima at all hours of the day and night, they barely gave it a second thought.

It was, after all, only one plane.

When the All Clear for the solitary intruder was sounded at 0731, Chai and his classmates were walking to work at the Kurashiki Aircraft Corporation. The company was a former textile manufacturer that had traded in its looms for lathes and was now doing subcontracting work making aircraft engine parts for the Japanese military. The factory—a typical wartime-expansion rush job of hastily and cheaply erected wood frame and corrugated metal—was located in Yoshijima, another one of Hiroshima's waterfront districts, two islets west of Chai's school and Tominaga Chieko's house. It was conveniently located near the Ujina Harbor facilities and warehouses, and was directly adjacent to a half-finished Navy airstrip under construction on a long stretch of landfill poking almost a kilometer and a half out into Hiroshima Bay. Chai and his classmates had been working at the factory for several months now.

Chai had been the pride of his family back in Taiwan when he passed the entrance examination—rigorous even for a native Japanese speaker—for Hiroshima's prestigious Kōryō Junior High School as the first step toward becoming a doctor. The plan had been for him to attend Kōryō, where he would cram for an entrance exam to a medical school in the Japanese Home Islands. The residents of Taiwan had been imperial subjects—Japanese, at least on paper—since their island had been annexed into the Empire of Greater Japan (*Dai-Nippon Teikoku*) after the First Sino-Japanese War. Therefore, there would have been no legal or institutional barriers to Chai getting a Japanese medical license if he graduated from such a school. Doing so would allow him to practice medicine back in Taiwan, in Mainland Japan, or anywhere else in the empire.

When Chai arrived in Hiroshima in April 1943, he'd had a bright future ahead of him. But in the meantime, Japan's military situation had not developed favorably in terms of his plans. In fact, he had barely seen the inside of a classroom since the Student Mobilization Law had been passed the previous year, after the fall of Saipan gave the Americans the first of their long-dreamed-of Pacific B-29 bases within striking range of the Japanese Home Islands. Now Chai had neither the time nor the energy to study for medical school or, for that matter, to study anything at all, aside from slipshod on-the-job training at various war labor worksites, with the most recent of these being the Kurashiki factory.

Aircraft engine work at the plant was a travesty; the hundred twenty Kōryō third-year boys working there had little idea of what they were doing, and there were not enough skilled Kurashiki full-time employees on hand to properly supervise everyone's work. On their first day on the job, the Kōryō boys had gone straight to work, turning piston cylinders on the lathes and casting aluminum engine blocks in green sandboxes, with only over-the-shoulder instructions and occasional screams of exasperation or alarm from full-timers to guide them. This was a situation repeated at thousands of other war plants throughout the empire in the summer of 1945. Too many of the country's experienced skilled workers had been taken away by the Army, and the labor force of adults in nonessential industries who might have been hastily trained to replace them had long since been maxed out. Things were so bad and stretched so tightly that the critical war work of assembling combat aircraft engines—normally a task that would have been at the very apex of the industrial machinists' trade—was being done by children, and both the quantity and the quality of production were suffering.

Work in the Kurashiki plant was noisy, arduous, and dangerous. Moreover, the Kōryō boys were not being paid for it. Along with the honor of being given this opportunity to contribute to the war effort, the free meals they received from the company were supposed to suffice as compensation for years of sacrificed schooling and youth they would never get back. Chai could have complained, but there were worse types of work he could have been doing today. If he had been two years younger, he would have been one of the four hundred Kōryō first-graders who were in downtown Hiroshima this morning, out in the brutal sun, doing the grueling work of firebreak clearing a few blocks east of Tominaga Chieko's class.[2] At least in the factory, Chai would have a roof over his head. And as today was a regularly scheduled *denkyūbi* (literally, "electricity holiday") brownout—a power-grid-rationing measure—for most of the factories in the city, none of the heavy machines would be operating, so that meant he had a relatively easy work shift ahead of him. It could have been a bit cooler, but that aside, it was turning out to be a nice, slow morning.

INGRESS

Niho-machi, Hiroshima
4.7 kilometers east-southeast of Ground Zero
0731 hours (local)

WHEN THE "ALL CLEAR" sirens in the city sounded at 0731, twelve-year-old Lee Mi Cha was playing in front of her house in Niho-machi, a working-class residential and agricultural neighborhood about 4.5 kilometers southeast of the Aioi Bridge aiming point, and about the same distance, due east, from Chai Tsong Chin's workplace at Kurashiki Aircraft Corporation.

Mi Cha was born near the southern Korean city of Daejeon in December 1932. A few months after her birth, her father moved his young family to seek his fortune in Hiroshima—part of the great migration (whether voluntary, cajoled, conned, or coerced) of Korean laborers to the Home Islands after the annexation of their homeland by Japan in 1910. The Chūgoku region—with its concentration of industries involved in military production—was a popular destination for these workers. By November 1944, the Lees were among the nearly eighty thousand ethnically Korean Japanese subjects living in Hiroshima Prefecture.[1]

Mi Cha's father had worked hard over the years, including a stint in the National Railroad, some part-time farming, and other business ventures. His efforts had paid off and he was able to support his family at the level of a middle-class Japanese family—owning a home and a small field for farming. The Lees were now among the better-off families in the small Korean community in Niho. The farming side business meant there was always food on the table—one way or another—which was more than many of their neighbors, Korean or Japanese, could say. There was enough money for the older children of the household to attend junior high school—also no mean feat for a Korean family in Hiroshima. In their home neighborhood, Mi Cha and her younger siblings had no problems fitting in at the local public elementary school, where they got along with their Japanese class-mates and endured little, if any, of the anti-Korean prejudice and bul-lying that happened in other parts the city, and in Japan in general. One reason for this, in the Lees' case, was that they followed official directives about refraining from using the Korean language or wear-ing distinctive Korean clothing in public—so as to better blend in (at least visually, if not culturally) with their ethnically Japanese counter-parts in their daily lives. They also made sure their children used *tsūshōmei* (Japanese-sounding "passing" names) outside of the family home. For example, at school and among the neighborhood children, Mi Cha used the name "Hashimoto Kazue."

Mi Cha's daily life was relatively carefree—at least as much as could have been expected in a wartime Japanese city that had not fallen victim to American incendiaries. But school authorities were not taking any chances on the city's luck holding out much longer in that respect. Japan's secondary tier of regional cities had begun to feel the wrath of Curtis LeMay earlier in the summer, and as part of a nationwide civil defense policy applying to such jurisdictions, most of the elementary-school fourth-, fifth-, and sixth-graders in Hiroshima had been evacuated in class groups to the outskirts of the city. In the case of Niho Elementary School, the children had taken up evacua-tion residence at two Buddhist temples in Saeki Ward, deep in the mountains on Hiroshima's far-western edge.[2] Here, they received room and board and a modicum of classroom-type instruction from their teacher chaperones.

Although participation in these evacuations was ostensibly mandatory, exemptions were available for children who, for health or other reasons, were deemed unsuited to being separated from their families. In Mi Cha's case, her parents—possibly worried about heretofore suppressed intercultural friction with classmates flaring up under the stress of a lengthy evacuation—had made a formal request for an excusal, and it had been granted. As a result, she had spent most of the spring and summer of 1945 playing with her younger siblings at home and around the neighborhood while her junior-high-student older brother worked days doing mobilized labor on the Ujina Line—a private railway that carried cargo, soldiers, and civilian passengers between the Army's harbor facilities and Hiroshima Station.

Now and again she and her siblings helped their father with a lotus root bog he worked near their home. Occasionally, Mi Cha and the older *zanryūgumi* ("stay behinder") children in the area who had been excused from the school evacuations were corralled by neighborhood association types and coerced into doing volunteer work. Just this morning, a work group pushing carts loaded with picks and shovels had stopped in front of her house and tried to lure her away to do firebreak work with them in the city center. Finally managing to beg off with some excuse, she watched as the work band of neighborhood adults and older children pushed their carts away to the north. She would never see them again.

———

When the Little Boy strike force crossed the coast of Shikoku to enter Japanese airspace, Mi Cha had long since resumed playing in front of her house. Nine kilometers to the south of her home, on the island of Etajima in Upper Hiroshima Bay, the soldiers of the Akatsuki Command's Tenth Army Maritime Training Battalion were just wrapping up their morning calisthenics.

The outfit was commonly known as the Saitō Unit, after its commanding officer, Major Saitō Yoshio. Like its training and support cadre, its rank and file was composed mostly of newly minted and mostly teenage corporals who had recently finished an intensive training course on the nearby Inland Sea island of Shōdoshima, where they had learned how to crew the Akatsuki Command's aging fleet of Daihatsu infantry landing craft. As the Japanese Army's glory days of amphibious assault operations were already a fond yellowing memory by the time these boys had enlisted to participate in this training in early 1945, they shared a comforting understanding that as long as they had to be in uniform anyway, there were far worse places they could have been stationed and duties they could have been performing. This matter was rarely discussed openly, but its basic wisdom was reconfirmed every time the newspapers and the radio blared headlines about yet another wave of mass kamikaze attacks off Okinawa or yet another garrison fighting gloriously to the last man on some forlorn Pacific outpost, surrounded by Allied ships and submarines and cut off from supplies or evacuation to the Home Islands.

However, these there-but-for-the-grace-of-the-gods thoughts were short-lived.

In July, the new corporals had been posted en masse to the Akatsuki Command Annex Base at Kōno'ura, a cove on the north shore of Etajima. Upon their arrival, they had been informed that their primary duties here would no longer involve operating landing craft. Instead, the exigencies of Japan's war effort being what they were, the boys were being assigned to what the Army called its Wakashio ("Young Tide") Force, and their first order of business in preparation for this assignment was to begin training as pilots for a one-man Toyota-truck-engine-powered motorboat that was officially designated the "Type 4 Thin-skinned Attack Craft." In the Akatsuki Command, the motorboat was commonly referred to as the *Marure*.

In September 1944, Kōno'ura had become the Akatsuki Command's center for *Marure* training, logistics, and organization—hosting Wakashio units not only for the defense of Upper Hiroshima Bay and the western end of the Inland Sea, but also for combat deployment later in the autumn in the Philippines, then in Okinawa and Taiwan in early 1945. But rumors in the ranks had it that the *Marure* boys who had been dispatched to these war zones had been utterly obliterated by enemy defenders, and that they had achieved little in the way of combat results to show for their ultimate sacrifice.

On paper, and officially, the pilot of a *Marure* boat was supposed to get as close as possible to an enemy ship—preferably a troopship loaded down with enemy infantrymen—to inflict maximum casualties. Once alongside the target, the pilot would stomp on a pedal to release a two-hundred-fifty-kilogram explosive charge before flooring the throttle to try to escape before the detonation of the weapon, which was time-fused for four seconds. This, at least, was the official Navy version of how the *Marure* was to be used in combat. It soon came to be acknowledged by all involved in the program that, official stances aside, the *Marure* was, in fact, a waterborne kamikaze weapon. Its deployment would of necessity involve the destruction of machine and pilot alike—regardless of whether or not it got anywhere near its intended target.

One of the Saitō Unit's new *Marure* pilots, seventeen-year-old Corporal Tsuchiya Keiji, had been a latecomer to Kōno'ura. During his last days at Shōdoshima, he had come down with a nearly fatal case of dysentery that had laid him up at an Army animal quarantine facility and hospital on Ninoshima—another island in Upper Hiroshima Bay, just north of Kōno'ura. One day during his three-week convalescence, the island had been showered by leaflets air-dropped from a B-29. These warned residents of the Hiroshima area to evacuate the city, as it would soon be the target of a massively destructive air attack.[3] While the dropping of such leaflets on Japanese cities was a standard American psychological operations tactic by this point in the war, scuttlebutt in the hospital had it that the Americans had something special in store for Hiroshima. A well-educated orderly in the hospital who had befriended Tsuchiya told him that he had heard rumors that the Americans had developed a special weapon—a single *shingata bakudan* ("new-type bomb") of unimaginable destructive power—and that Hiroshima was to be its first target. However, after arriving at Kōno'ura and being confronted with the details of his new duties as a *Marure* crewman, Tsuchiya—now with far more immediate personal-survival concerns on his mind—forgot all about the leaflets and the special-bomb-rumor episode. He was also incredibly busy, particularly so on this morning, as today was to be his turn to perform the solemn duty of bringing his platoon leader's breakfast tray up to the headquarters shack.

—————

Sometime around 0750 hours local time, Chai Tsong Chin and his classmates settled into work at Kurashiki Aircraft.

In Ujina, Tominaga Chieko had been asleep since losing her argument with her mother about missing her school's firebreak detail this morning.

In Niho-machi, Lee Mi Cha was still playing alone in front of her house.

In Kōno'ura, Tsuchiya Keiji was mentally rehearsing the lines he would speak when he delivered his platoon leader's breakfast tray a little less than half an hour from now.

Nine thousand meters over Misaki Peninsula, on the northern coast of Shikoku, the Little Boy strike force had reached attack altitude and was heading out over the Inland Sea.

A few minutes before the force reached the coast of Honshu to assume its attack heading for Hiroshima, the photography plane dropped back and entered a three-hundred-sixty-degree turn to put distance between itself and the other two planes. After a circuit over the Inland Sea, it assumed a westerly heading parallel to the one the *Enola Gay* and the *Great Artiste* would take as they approached their target over land. It was, of course, important for science, for politics, and for posterity that what was going to happen in Hiroshima approximately ten minutes from now was to be photographed; to ensure that both those photographs and their photographers survived the event, it had been deemed prudent to put a generous margin of error, distance-wise, between the cameramen and their subject.

On board *Enola Gay*, which was still flying on autopilot, Tibbets and the rest of the crew donned heavy armor-lined flak suits and readied their parachute gear in preparation for beginning their bomb run. Parsons and Jeppson made last-minute checks on Little Boy's circuitry before Parsons completed the arming sequence. Van Kirk crosschecked his navigation with Sergeant Stiborik's radar imagery of the outline of the fast-approaching Honshu coastline. Beser—forgoing his detested flak suit—monitored his ECM gear to make sure no Japanese radio or radar activity on any of the four electromagnetic frequencies intefered with the range-finding radar in Little Boy's firing circuitry using these wavelengths.

Each workstation gave its report to Tibbets. Weapon, clear. Navigation, clear. ECM, clear.[4]

———

Whether intentional or not, the approach of the Little Boy strike force was timed perfectly for catching Hiroshima's air defense during a lull in its alert and response capability as the graveyard shift at CMD HQ was being relieved by the daytime shift. Most of the Hijiyama girls getting off the graveyard shift were away from their communications tables, eating their customary meal on the Army's dime before going back to their dormitory on the castle grounds to sleep and rest up for the following night's work shift. From LTG Fujii Yōji on down, all of the senior and middle-ranked officers at CMD HQ who had pulled semi-all-nighters had gone back to their quarters around four in the morning, leaving Major Aoki in charge of the air defense bunker and two other field grade officers to mind the store in the main headquarters building.[5] General Fujii and the other senior officers had not been roused to return to duty during the *Straight Flush* incursion.[6] Most were probably sleeping through the last minutes of their lives.

As *Enola Gay* and the *Great Artiste* bore down on the city, the Hijiyama girls coming in for the day shift were outside on the castle grounds. After standing in formation to receive their morning motivational speeches, they engaged in "bayonet" drills with their wooden *bokujū*. Their shouts and exhortations would have been audible through a small window high in the concrete of the northern wall of the air defense bunker, where three of the Hijiyama girls—Itamura Katsuko,

Nishida Toshie, and Ōkura Yoshie—remained at their phone desks in the command and communications room.

On the other side of a concrete wall, Private First Class Furukawa Yoshio manned a radio set in the wireless room. Next to him, the table for the NHK announcer night shift team was empty, as these civilians had left to return to their office in Nagarekawa-chō shortly after the *Straight Flush* All Clear.

Meanwhile, and perhaps most crucially in terms of the chain of events that was about to unfold, Major Aoki had also temporarily left the bunker to confer with the two graveyard shift field-grade officers in the two-story main CMD building, several hundred meters away beside the castle keep. Two junior NCOs were left in charge of the bunker's operations room. This meant that there was now no one present in this crucial information and communications center with enough rank to call the prefectural office and tell them to begin sounding air defense sirens if enemy contacts appeared over the city. The Navy's air defense people at Kure Naval Arsenal could—and would, some minutes later—call NHK Hiroshima with an air raid warning. However, in terms of sirens—the population's primary early-warning system—their jurisdiction did not extend past Kure city limits.

At 0806, an air defense observation post sixty kilometers east of Hiroshima phoned CMD HQ and Kure Naval Arsenal to report two high-flying enemy aircraft passing over their position on a northwest heading.[7] Simultaneously, the lightbulb for the Matsunaga-chō post lit up on the operations room wall map. While this was happening, precious minutes were squandered as the two NCOs who had been left to mind the store debated whether this contact was actually the same aircraft that had triggered the earlier general alert simply circling back to take another harmless pass over the city. Failing to reach a conclusion and/or unwilling to take the responsibility for a potential citywide false alarm, they sought out Major Aoki to make the decision for them and determine whether this newest bogey—whatever it was— merited another round of air raid sirens. With their departure, Private Furukawa was now the highest-ranking individual in the bunker.

THE BOMB RUN

Aboard Enola Gay

Approximately twenty kilometers due east of Ground Zero

0807 hours (local)

THROUGH THE GREENHOUSE-LIKE plexiglass canopy encasing *Enola Gay*'s flight deck, the mountain-ringed, island-speckled bay of the target area was just beginning to come into view on the distant western horizon.

"Do you all agree that's Hiroshima?" Tibbets asked the crew members in the forward area of the fuselage.[1] The query was answered affirmatively. All had studied the geography and topography of the Hiroshima area (as well as Kokura and Nagasaki) so thoroughly and for so long that they could have easily drawn accurate maps of their targets blindfolded.

As the seconds ticked down to the Little Boy strike force's scheduled 0814 hours arrival at Tom Ferebee's aiming point, reports from the field continued to come in to the CMD HQ operations room. The light for the Itaki observation post near Saijō-chō, twenty-some kilometers east of Hiroshima, lit up on the bunker's wall map, and a report came in of a small high-flying formation of B-29s headed west. Minutes later, the wall map light for a searchlight battery at Nakano, fewer than twelve kilometers to the east, lit up, and another report of approaching aircraft came in. Both the phoned-in reports and the winking wall map now clearly showed that the contact—whatever it was—was heading directly toward Hiroshima.[2]

———

At 0812 hours, the Little Boy strike force began its final bomb run, precisely on schedule. Aboard *Enola Gay*, Tom Ferebee assumed his position at his bombardier station and began feeding data into his Norden bombsight. Tibbets reminded the rest of the crew to put on their special dark Polaroid-lensed protective goggles to protect their eyes from the expected atomic bomb flash.[3] At 0813 hours, Tibbets said, "It's yours," and handed over control of the plane to Ferebee and his Norden.[4]

———

At Kōno'ura, Corporal Tsuchiya carefully balanced his platoon leader's breakfast tray as he walked from the mess hall up to the command shack.

———

At Yoshijima, one of Chai Tsong Chin's classmates ran into the work area of Kurashiki Aircraft and said "Hey, someone just said the plane from before is coming back. . . ."

———

In Ujina, Tominaga Chieko was lying on her futon, nursing her stomach, while her father sat in the foyer of their house wrapping Army-style canvas gaiter straps around his calves as he prepared to head off to work in the harbor.

———

In Niho-machi, Lee Mi Cha heard the drone of aircraft, high and faint, somewhere to the north.

"Are those airplanes?" she asked an adult neighbor working in front of his house.

The neighbor answered affirmatively.

Mi Cha looked up and caught the sun glinting off a tiny silver speck moving across the northern sky.

⸻

At 0813, the air defense bunkers at Kure Naval Arsenal and CMD HQ simultaneously received a coded air raid alert.[5] Kure Naval Arsenal was on the ball, immediately setting off the Kure City sirens and calling in the report to NHK Hiroshima.

In the air defense bunker at CMD HQ, the aperture connecting the operations room to the command and communications room slid open and someone—whose identity has never been determined—handed Ōkura Yoshie a slip of paper reading *0813 Hi Ya Ke Ha* ("0813, air raid alert for the Hiroshima and Yamaguchi areas").

However, with no one in the bunker authorized to issue an alert order to the prefectural offices, the city's sirens remained silent. Moreover, most of the radios in the city would have been off, their owners assuming that on this particular weekday morning, as on any other, NHK would have been on its daily "broadcast recess" from eight a.m. to ten a.m. (another late-wartime electricity-saving measure).[6] In the command and communications room, the three Hijiyama girls took the only action they were authorized to take under the circumstances: While Itamura and Nishida called the Yoshijima airstrip, the Ujina antiaircraft battery, and Shikoku Military District HQ across the Inland Sea in Zentsūji, Ōkura called other locations in the city, including the NHK office in Nagarekawa.

⸻

With their radios turned off, and far beyond earshot of Kure's now wailing sirens, Hiroshima's residents went about their daily business, blissfully unaware of what was approaching.

The city's sirens never sounded.

———

At 0814 and seventeen seconds, Ferebee called out, "I've got it," as he acquired the Aioi Bridge in the crosshairs of his bombsight.[7] He flipped a switch and *Enola Gay* began broadcasting an electronic tone to the *Great Artiste* and Dimples 91 to signal that Ferebee's Norden and the plane's automatic pilot were now in control. Sixty seconds later, the bomb bay doors on the two B-29s snapped open; the long, cylindrical gray coffin of Little Boy fell from the belly of *Enola Gay* and the *Great Artiste*'s three radiosondes were parachute-dropped to begin their telemetry measurements. The moment their respective mission payloads were free and away, Tibbets and Major Charles Sweeney immediately put their planes into the designated 155-degree-turn escape maneuver that they had been practicing for months—*Enola Gay* banking hard to the right and the *Great Artiste* to the left. If the planning calculations were right, the maneuver would put the planes some twelve kilometers away when Little Boy detonated six hundred meters over the target.

———

Like everyone else in Hiroshima, Lee Mi Cha was by now well accustomed to seeing lone B-29s flying high over her home in daylight. But the B-29 she was watching now suddenly did something she had never seen one of the gargantuan bombers do before: It made a sharp, diving turn like a fighter plane. She kept her eyes fixed on the plane to track its path across the sky, slowly turning her back toward the city as she did so.[8] Approximately thirty seconds after she saw the surprising maneuver, the distant growling, almost grinding sound the plane's engines had made powering through the turn finally reached Mi Cha on the ground some nine kilometers below.

When Little Boy broke free from *Enola Gay*, a static line wire-tethered to an attachment point in the bomb bay pulled loose, cutting the electronic tone that had been sounding in everyone's headsets, and activating a bank of circuit-breaking timers in the bomb. These ticked off fifteen seconds before closing the first row of active firing circuits—a step that engaged Little Boy's range-finding radar to begin looking for something flat, hard, and large at the designated detonation distance of six hundred meters. This time lapse ensured that *Enola Gay* would be far enough away from the bomb that the radar would not mistake the receding aluminum bomber as its target.

After the bomb passed below an altitude of 2,133 meters, a barometric-altimeter-pressure fail-safe switch closed the final arming circuitry. Now everything was up to the range-finding radar. When any two of the four radar antennae agreed that the detonation altitude of six hundred meters had been reached—roughly seventeen seconds later—an electrical firing signal would be sent to the detonator in the breech of Little Boy's naval gun core. This would fire the gun, and milliseconds later, the explosive chain reaction of a supercritical mass of U-235 would occur.

This nuclear catastrophe was barely ten seconds away when the engine growls of *Enola Gay*'s and the *Great Artiste*'s respective escape maneuvers reached the ground, causing people all over the city to turn their eyes to the sky.

On the street outside the NHK office in Nagarekawa, a dozen or so citizens with broken radios patiently waited in line for these to be repaired.[9] On the second floor of the office, NHK announcer Furuta Masanobu and the rest of his night shift crew had just returned from Hiroshima Castle and had barely settled down at their desks when the phone calls from Kure Naval Arsenal and CMD Air Defense came in.

The NHK phone operator handed the alert memo to Furuta, who scanned its contents as he ran to the broadcasting studio across the hallway. Reaching the studio, he approached the microphone. At that very moment, anyone in Hiroshima who had forgotten to turn their radio off would have heard a studio buzzer clank on, cutting off the broadcast recess static, then Furuta Masanobu managing to get out, "Alert from Chūgoku Headquarters! Three enemy planes have been sighted over western Saijō—," before the signal suddenly stopped.

===

At that instant, some combination of Little Boy's four radar range finders concurred that detonation altitude had been reached. A firing signal was sent to the explosive charge in the gun barrel's breech, and an explosive supercritical mass of U-235 was achieved some six hundred meters above Shima Hospital in downtown Hiroshima. The Norden bombsight—probably due to wind drift—had placed the bomb less than two hundred meters east of the Aioi Bridge aiming point.

At the NHK office in Nagarekawa, the command and communications room of the CMD air defense bunker, the second floor of the CMD HQ building, the Kurashiki Aircraft plant in Yoshijima, the Tominaga home in Ujina, the Lee home in Niho-machi, and the command shack of the Saitō Unit on Etajima, Furuta Masanobu, Itamura Katsuko, Nishida Toshie, Ōkura Yoshie, Aoki Nobuyoshi, Chai Tsong Chin, Tominaga Chieko, Lee Mi Cha, and Tsuchiya Keiji, respectively, saw a flash of purplish white light brighter than a thousand suns.

===

Less than two seconds after the flash, the NHK Hiroshima office was shaken to its foundations and Furuta Masanobu, midsentence in his air raid broadcast likely heard by no one, was thrown to the floor of his windowless studio in a cloud of concrete dust.

===

Less than three seconds after the flash, the Hijiyama girls were hurled against the northern concrete wall of the CMD air defense bunker by the blast and briefly knocked unconscious. Luckily for them, there was no window aperture facing south. The concrete in the southern wall and the earthen defilade on the south side of the bunker shielded them from the heat flash and the initial radiation shower of gamma rays and neutrons emitted by Little Boy at the instant of its explosion. Wavering in and out of consciousness, Nishida Toshie heard a deep wooden groaning and cracking as the keep of Hiroshima Castle wobbled, toppled, and collapsed into a pile of plaster and timbers that was already ablaze by the time it hit the ground.

———

Perhaps half a second after Little Boy's blast wave hit the bunker, it blew in the windows and south wall of the second-story office in the CMD HQ building where Major Aoki had been conferring with two colleagues. These two other officers were killed instantly, while Aoki was blown out of the room and down a stairwell, coming to rest on the first-floor landing, where he was discovered by rescuers a few minutes later. He lived until the end of August before succumbing to radiation sickness—long enough to learn that his entire family in Fukuro-machi had been wiped out.

———

Some thirteen seconds after the flash, the corrugated metal roof and the northern wall of the Kurashiki Aircraft plant collapsed on Chai Tsong Chin and his classmates. Two of the boys were killed instantly by falling debris; Chai was saved by the heavy steel lathes he had fallen between when the roof came down.

———

Nearly simultaneously, two islets east of Chai, Tominaga Chieko's house was shaken as if by a sudden gust of typhoon wind, and all its windows blew in from the north in a swarm of flying glass and wooden window frame splinters. Her father received a deep cut on one of his shins from glass shards from the front door, but the sturdy canvas of his gaiter wrappings saved him from more serious injury.

In Niho, Lee Mi Cha was lifted off her feet and thrown several meters through the air by a powerful gust of wind that arrived with the loudest sound she had ever heard. A few seconds later, stunned but otherwise uninjured, she stood up to shake the sand out of her hair (which was likely slightly singed on the back of her head). She looked to see that her house was now crooked on its foundations and missing all its windows and doors. She then turned around to face the city and saw a giant red fireball and a roiling column of smoke that began climbing into the sky at high speed.

On Kōno'ura, there was a brief commotion in the Saitō Unit command shack as the officers and men present wondered what had caused the flash they had just seen. Lightning? A bomb? If so, where was the blast?

The soldiers were just beginning to return to their morning routine when Tsuchiya Keiji cleared his throat and ceremoniously lifted the platoon leader's breakfast tray to eye level. He had just managed to get out, "Good morning, Lieutenant Takakura, sir. The corporal has brought—," when a sudden gust of some kind rocked the wooden command shack and blew in the windows from the north. This was accompanied by the loudest sound any of the soldiers had ever heard.

Air raid sirens on the base began to wail as Tsuchiya and his comrades in arms shook off the shock of the explosion and ran outside to see what had happened. At first, nobody seemed to know what to do. Then Tsuchiya became aware of a general flow of other soldiers down toward the waterfront to the north. The khaki-clad throng began moving in a walk, then broke into a run before stopping at the shoreline, where the quays and concrete ramps for their *Marure* boats were located. Here and there, a comment arose from the crowd: "What in the hell is it?" . . . "Japan is done for." . . . but most of the soldiers, including Tsuchiya, could do no more than stare in stunned silence at the mushroom cloud still roiling and rising over the city, with flashes of light in every hue visible to the human eye poking out from gaps in the brownish gray smoke. Across nine uninterrupted kilometers of water, various sounds emanated from the dying city: a long, continuous thunder roll that seemed to be produced by the cloud itself; a static crackling as tens of thousands of wooden structures on the far shore of the bay simultaneously collapsed and began to burn; and floating above it all, a high, faint sound, barely perceptible, that Tsuchiya incredulously perceived as human screams.

———

When the Hijiyama girls in the bunker came to their senses, their first instinct was to go outside and see what had hit them. As they emerged from the dugout, they saw that everything—all of the trees that had been in front of the entrance; the Shintō Shrine for the War Dead (*Gokoku Jinja*) to the left of the entrance; the central keep and the surrounding buildings in the castle grounds—had been reduced to splinters and burning wreckage.

Holding a handkerchief over her mouth, Nishida Toshie struggled to breathe the dusty, smoky air as she ran to look for help at the main CMD HQ building. But when she arrived where this structure was supposed to be standing, all she saw was a pile of masonry rubble and smoldering, shattered timbers. Strewn before her on the ground in front of this wreckage were the girls from the incoming day shift who had been formed up here doing bayonet drills a few minutes earlier. The faces of most were burned beyond recognition. All were dead, holding their *bokujū* in death grips.

To the south lay a vista that no one in Hiroshima had seen for centuries; standing here on the rubble piles covering the castle grounds, Itamura Katsuko could see all the way to the bay. There were no obstructions—natural or man-made—to the view. Everything had been blown down and/or blasted apart and was now in the process of burning up. The city was gone.

Ōkura Yoshie saw a soldier yelling, "They've hit us with one of those new-type bombs!" This briefly snapped her out of her own shock long enough to bring her mind back to her duty. The news of what had just happened to Hiroshima had to be reported to some authority outside the area. She remembered the dedicated landlines running out of the bunker; these were buried for security purposes, unlike the typical pole-strung civilian telephone lines that, as of this moment, no longer existed in Hiroshima. Stepping over smoldering wreckage and bodies, she made her way back to the command and communications room in the bunker. Incredibly, the landline phones still worked, and she was able to get through to the Western Military District headquarters in Fukuoka. She then had a longer exchange with an officer in Fukuyama—the city in eastern Hiroshima near where the Little Boy strike force had wheeled into its attack run less than thirty minutes earlier.

"Hello? Hello? Something terrible has happened," she said. "Hiroshima has been destroyed by a new-type bomb."

"A new-type bomb?" the officer in Fukuyama shouted back over the line. "You mean, it landed right on top of the division?" (He was referring here to the Fifth Division, which was normally headquartered in the facilities now occupied by CMD HQ.)

"No, I mean Hiroshima," Ōkura answered. "It's all gone."[10]

PART TWO

INTO THE FIRE

COSMIC FIRE

WILLIAM "ATOMIC BILL" LAURENCE was a small man with a penchant for lobster-bib-sized neckties that were as flowery and flamboyant as his prose. His most distinguishing physical feature, though, was a face that was a cross between that of rock impresario Bill Graham and a deflated football—a mug that would have looked more at home on an aging Brooklyn bantamweight or a Dick Tracy villain than on a man of letters. The pièce de résistance tying the whole look together was a nose—by appearances squashed flat enough to impair normal breathing—that Laurence claimed had been mashed in "by the butt of a Cossack rifle" during a youthful flirtation with anti-czarist politics in his native Russian-occupied Lithuania.[1]

After his encounter with the Russian rifle butt, Laurence's life course had followed a classic turn-of-the-century, Ellis Island, up-by-his-bootstraps storyline. He had immigrated to America in 1905 at the age of seventeen; dropped his foreign-sounding birth name for one that would have looked right at home on the *Mayflower*'s passenger manifest; taught himself English and acquired an education (that included non-degree-awarded stints at Harvard University); and served in France with the Signal Corps in World War One. After returning

home from the war, he finished his bachelor's degree and then acquired a law degree from Boston University before embarking on a
career move into journalism that landed him in New York City. There
he got his start with the infamously "yellow" *New York World* before
jumping ship in 1930 to join the *New York Times*, eventually inventing
a niche beat for himself there as a science correspondent.

The 1930s were an exciting time for the hard sciences—
particularly the new(ish) field of nuclear physics—and Laurence, true
to his job description, stayed current by reading scholarly journals
and attending academic conferences, at one of which he once waylaid
a not-yet-household-name J. Robert Oppenheimer with a request for
an impromptu personal tutoring session on the finer points of nuclear
fission. His burgeoning interest in the topic first garnered widespread
attention on May 5, 1940, when the *Times* ran a front-page article of
his under the headline "VAST POWER SOURCE IN ATOMIC EN-
ERGY OPENED BY SCIENCE." Following this—which for the average
American newspaper reader in 1940 must have sounded like a line from
a Buck Rogers serial—were equally breathless subheadings: "Relative
of Uranium Found to Yield Force 5 Million Times as Potent as Coal /
GERMANY IS SEEKING IT [with special screaming ALL CAPS] / Scientists Ordered to Devote All Time to Research—Tests Made at Columbia."[2] Four months later, an article he wrote for *The Saturday
Evening Post* titled "The Atom Gives Up" made a similar splash as well
as attracting the attention—and warranting the concerns—of the
War Department, whose censors soon put in place a policy of ban-
ning, in the interest of national security, any further media mention
of the uranium isotope until the Hiroshima story broke, nearly five
years later.[3]

With the ban in place, it might have seemed at that point that
Laurence's professional relationship with U-235 had come to an abrupt
end. In fact, it had yet to start in earnest, though this second act would
have to wait for the final months of the conflict for its curtain to go
up. In the interim, Laurence gradually worked himself into the good
graces of the War Department (and collected a little side income)

writing middlebrow, techno-jargon-inflected feel-good pieces about the boys at the front getting everything they needed and American know-how and ingenuity winning the war.[4]

Uranium 235 came back into Laurence's professional life in the spring of 1945 when he was recruited by Major General Leslie R. Groves, the Army Corps of Engineer officer in charge of the Manhattan Project, as a sort of embedded journalist / unit historian. The always media-savvy Japanese military had been proponents of "embedded journalism" at least since the 1930s; they perfected it in cloyingly sentimental late-war coverage of the activity and atmosphere around the various Army and Navy air bases feeding hundreds of boys and young men a day as kamikaze pilots into the aerial crematory over the American fleet at the peak of the Battle of Okinawa. But the embedded journalist role was still relatively novel in the American military at the time, and the ground rules for what Laurence's job entailed and what he could and could not do seem to have been largely made up on the fly. One ground rule that was firmly established, however, in his case, came with an ironic twist: Because of the top secret nature of what he would be observing, it would be months before he would be allowed to publish any pieces about the Manhattan Project and its technological magic (or sorcery, as the case might have been) in the *New York Times*. From here on out and for the duration, he was a member of Groves' PR team first and a journalist second.

One of the first tasks Laurence was given when he joined up with Groves was to help draft PR copy for the occasion of the first bomb being dropped on some unlucky Japanese city sometime later that summer, when the existence of this fearsome new weapon and the American justification for its use would have to be explained to the American public and the world at large (including the Japanese).[5] One of Laurence's early efforts toward this end, written in May 1945, was a proposed radio address to be delivered by President Truman after the first bombing. "Today marks one of the most important days in the history of our country and of the world," the draft began, with typically breathless Laurencian flair:

Today, as the result of the greatest scientific and engineering development in the history of mankind, our 20th Air Force has released upon Japan the most destructive weapon ever developed by any nation. . . . [Used] in the new weapon . . . [is] the greatest source of cosmic power ever to be tapped by man, utilizing the unbelievable quantities of energy locked up within the atoms of the material universe. . . . This new development, which brings this "Cosmic Fire" down to earth for the first time, just as Prometheus, father of civilization, brought ordinary terrestrial fire down to earth from Olympus, marks the opening of a new era in our civilization. . . . One cannot fail to see the hand of Providence in the fact that it was our people that Almighty God saw fit to give this weapon to us first.[6]

Although Atomic Bill's draft made (and makes) for great reading, all this talk of "Prometheus" and "Cosmic Fire" was apparently a bit too long-haired for Groves and the rest of the White House / War Department / Pentagon atomic bomb decision-makers' loop. "After it became clear he was incapable of writing a press release that sounded like anyone's voice but his own," historian Alex Wellerstein writes, "Laurence was given a new task better suited for his talents: writing stories about the Manhattan Project and what it had accomplished."[7] He was gradually nudged out of the front office to concentrate on fieldwork—which he was happiest doing anyway—while day-to-day Manhattan Project PR duties primarily became the purview of Arthur W. Page, an assistant to Secretary of War Henry Stimson. In peacetime, Page had been a seasoned wordsmith who had gotten in at the birth of the New York / Madison Avenue advertising industry. Later, as chief communications officer of AT&T, he had been the first professional PR man to sit on the board of directors of a major American corporation.[8] He was a natural for the job.

As for Laurence, his refocus on field duties did not mean that the eccentric newspaperman was on the outs with the Manhattan Project—just that his daily schedule and deadlines were less pressing. He was kept on in his unique role as an embedded journalist, only now at somewhat of a remove from the center ring tightrope of the Washington media circus. Now free to follow his craft and secure his place in history on his own terms, Laurence happily traded in his crumpled suits and garish neckties for a war correspondent's khakis, and headed west to rub shoulders with Oppenheimer, Enrico Fermi, and the other physicists applying the finishing touches to the Fat Man plutonium bomb design at Los Alamos. In this capacity, he was the only journalist allowed to observe the first successful test detonation of this design at Alamogordo, New Mexico, in the wee hours of July 16, 1945.[9]

Soon after his New Mexican sojourn, he shipped out to Tinian to see out the rest of the war directly embedded with the 509th Composite Group. Arriving on Tinian just in time to witness the takeoff of the Little Boy strike force, he was too late to actually fly on one of Tibbets' B-29s. He might have missed out on what would certainly have been a Pulitzer-winning opportunity to witness (and to write more breathless, mythology-inflected prose about) history's first atomic bomb dropped in anger, but he would be sure not to miss out on the second.

———

Some sixteen hours after Little Boy had exploded over Hiroshima, Harry Truman was crossing the Atlantic aboard the cruiser USS *Augusta* on his way home after the Potsdam Conference, which had been held in Allied-occupied Berlin to redraw the maps of Europe and determine the fate of the postwar world.[10] The president received the news during a photo op lunch with the captain and some crew members in the galley of the warship. Reading the short Hiroshima report placed into his hands by a staff officer, Truman supposedly leapt to his feet and exclaimed, "This is the greatest thing in history!"[11]

In addition to his expressed elation/astonishment, the president must certainly have also experienced relief in the moment; for one thing, now that the bomb had been used against an enemy, it would not have to be explained away as a $2 billion boondoggle to American taxpayers and voters with congressional midterms coming up in 1946 and his own presidential campaign to worry about two years after that. And now, with proven atomic bombs in his arsenal and the Soviet Union mere days away from fulfilling its Yalta Conference promise (reaffirmed by Stalin at Potsdam) to enter the war against Japan, it might mean the invasion of Japan that the Pentagon had been planning and staging for months would no longer be necessary.

The academic and historical question of how many human beings— both Japanese and American—were saved by that invasion being unnecessary has never been definitively answered; neither has the moral question of whether avoiding that invasion merited the sacrifice of a hundred forty thousand human beings on August 6, 1945, and seventy-five thousand in another city three days later. These issues— particularly the matter of Americans inflicting mass civilian casualties—saw brief frenzies of spirited discussion in the forum of American public opinion: once in the immediate aftermath of the first breaking of the atomic bomb news, and again when the *New Yorker* magazine published John Hersey's *Hiroshima* in 1946. But the Manhattan Project / War Department PR machine was successful in smothering both lines of discourse. In any case, in the short run, it was certain that Truman was off the hook militarily and politically. It also meant he had a very, very big stick to wave at the Soviet Union if Stalin had designs on encroaching on more of the globe than what he had taken away from the Nazis in Europe.

One time zone to the west and a full day's sail away for *Augusta*, a modest number of beat reporters were passing a sultry Washington Monday morning in the White House press room.[12] At eleven, Truman's assistant press secretary, Eben A. Ayers, walked in, announced, "I have got what I think is a darn good story," and began handing out three-page copies of an official presidential statement on the Hiroshima bombing.[13]

"Sixteen hours ago an American airplane dropped one bomb on Hiroshima and destroyed its usefulness to the enemy," the release began. "That bomb had more power than 20,000 tons of T.N.T.... It is an atomic bomb. It is a harnessing of the basic power of the universe."[14]

It is not difficult to imagine the assembled reporters, after encountering the phrase "atomic bomb," already beating a path to the telephone banks without reading another line of their mimeographed handouts. Within three minutes a bulletin on the story was already beaming around the globe via the Associated Press wire service and twentieth-century electromagnetic broadcast media.[15]

In the wake of this world-shaking news bulletin, many Americans in uniform—and their loved ones back home—wept with joy and relief. Other Americans were filled with patriotic pride at their nation's victory on "the battlefield of the laboratories," as Page's press release had somewhat disingenuously put it, framing a feel-good narrative justifying America's development and deployment of the atomic bomb before its enemies could do the same, as if the race had ever even been close (it had not).[16] Still other Americans—including many professional clergy members and even some Manhattan Project scientists—were filled with a sense of tragedy, moral outrage, and ominous foreboding.

Whatever their individual emotional reactions at that moment, everyone who heard the news knew that, after today, their world would never be the same.[17] Mere mortals were now tampering with fundamental forces of nature that had once been the exclusive purview of the gods.

THE BASIC POWER OF THE UNIVERSE

WHILE IT IS likely that Arthur Page's formal physics education ended when he was a turn-of-the-century Harvard undergraduate, his vaguely deist (and very Laurencian) basic-power-of-the-universe sound bite was actually a respectably accurate layman's summation of what had just destroyed Hiroshima. Specifically, this basic power is the "strong nuclear force," which, in addition to gravity, electromagnetism, and the weak nuclear force (responsible for radioactive decay), are the four known fundamental forces that mediate the interaction of energy and space-time in the physical universe.

Although the existence of the strong nuclear force had been postulated earlier, it was first mathematically formulated in 1935 by Yukawa Hideki, a twenty-eight-year-old Japanese assistant professor of physics at Osaka University. A former graduate student of Enrico Fermi—the legendary Italian physicist, Nobel Prize winner, and eventual member of the Manhattan Project research team at Los Alamos—Yukawa would follow in his teacher's footsteps to become a Nobel laureate in 1949 primarily in recognition for his work on the strong nuclear force. A jaundiced interpretation of this honor might point out the irony that a Japanese physicist's research indirectly helped to make possible the development of the atomic bomb; a more generous interpretation, however, is that his formulation of the strong nuclear force was a key step toward understanding the mechanisms by which energy becomes matter (and vice versa) and, as a result, makes possible gravity and space-time itself.

The strong nuclear force performs its function in our universe by reining in electromagnetic forces in the nuclei of atoms. Without its presence, positively charged protons in the nuclei would mutually repel one another and fly apart, making the formation of matter impossible. If the strong nuclear force had not emerged at the birth of the universe, all of the energy created by the big bang would have been expended in a spectacularly large but ultimately inconsequential electromagnetic event—an incalculably powerful burst of photons in the form of gamma rays and X-rays that would have never managed to coalesce into the frozen state of potential energy we are more familiar with as solid matter.[1]

The idea of matter as energy (temporarily) frozen in a potential state is what is expressed in Albert Einstein's famous formula $E = mc^2$. In the normal and profoundly stable state of matter as it exists anywhere outside of a nuclear reactor, the core of an exploding nuclear weapon, a black hole, or the churning nuclear-fusion furnace of our sun or any other star, the strong nuclear force keeps the mass of "matter" firmly and stubbornly in place, doing what it is supposed to do and existing in the only place where it is able to do so—within the confines of the intact nuclei of atoms.

In one way of looking at it, the nucleus of every atom in existence is a battery containing potential energy—in the form of the strong nuclear force—originally bound up into it in the first million seconds (about eleven earth days) of the big bang.[2] What the Manhattan Project spent two billion 1940s dollars on, then, was the development of the means of tapping into these "batteries" to unleash this potential energy as explosive kinetic energy.

As per Yukawa's work, much of the basic theoretical heavy lifting had already been done for this long before World War Two. A key conceptual breakthrough toward theorizing the existence of the strong nuclear force and then trying to figure out a way to get at it was achieved in 1932 when British physicist James Chadwick discovered that protons share their homes in the nuclei of atoms with particles of nearly identical atomic weight, which he named "neutrons" because of their "neutral" (i.e., lack of) electromagnetic charge.

If it were possible to observe an atom at a scale small enough to see what is actually going on inside it, we would see that its internal structure is almost entirely empty, and the atom's size and shape are defined by the orbit of electrons in its electron shell(s).[3] The only physical matter contained therein is the tiny kernel of the atom's nucleus, located at the precise center of this hollow sphere of otherwise empty space and taking up about $1/100,000$ of its diameter (envisage a green pea in the middle of an Olympic opening ceremony venue). Although it is the protons and neutrons clumped together in the nuclei of atoms that give matter mass—what we experience/interpret in the physical world, with the interaction of gravity, as an object's weight—it is the negatively charged and nearly massless electrons orbiting and protecting the physical integrity of those nuclei and encasing the empty space around them that give matter what we experience/interpret in the physical world as an object's three-dimensional size and solidity.

In another way of looking at it, when someone walks into a brick wall, what causes the resulting painful impact is the negatively charged electron shells in the atoms of their body being repelled by (and, vice versa, repelling, as per the laws of electromagnetism) the negatively charged electron shells in the atoms contained in the wall. If, through some technological magic, a switch could be thrown that would temporarily dial down to zero the electromagnetic charge of all the electrons in our careless pedestrian's body when they came into contact with that wall (without every atom in their body disintegrating instantly), they would be able to walk right through it.

Continuing our crude metaphor, what Chadwick discovered in the neutron—which was impervious to electromagnetic charges, whether positive or negative—was something that could literally walk through walls (up to a certain thickness and provided they were not made of lead). Using the neutron first as a probe, then as a battering ram, *Homo sapiens* were now at the gates of the atomic nucleus, and it was only a matter of time before they weaponized the strong nuclear force.

In 1934, Fermi—four years away from his defection from Fascist Italy to the United States—began a series of experiments employing a process he referred to as "neutron activation." In this technique, using a small lump of radioactive radium as a neutron source, Fermi observed and measured the effect of the collisions of these particles with the nuclei of various elements to see whether and how their makeup or characteristics would be changed.[4] In the words of Fermi's research colleague I. I. Rabi, what was observed was that

> *when a neutron enters a nucleus, the effects are about as catastrophic as if the moon struck the earth. The nucleus is violently shaken up by the blow . . . A large increase in energy occurs and must be dissipated, and this may happen in a variety of ways,* all of them interesting [emphasis added].[5]

One of the "interesting" methods of energy dissipation displayed by these nuclei—now heavier and thus knocked off-balance by the added mass of the single neutron they had absorbed—was that they had become radioactive; in their attempt to return to their natural state of equilibrium vis-à-vis either their electron shells or their now lopsided neutron-to-proton ratio, they had shed subatomic elements such as alpha and beta particles via the weak nuclear force. As a byproduct of this shedding process, gamma rays—a manifestation of energy at the highest, most powerful end of the electromagnetic force spectrum—were also released. What Fermi's neutron-activation-experiment process had created, observed, and measured, then, were two ways—initial radiation (neutrons and gamma rays) and residual radiation (alpha- and beta-particle contamination)—by which atomic bombs would be sickening and killing human beings in Hiroshima and Nagasaki eleven years later.

Though Fermi's aimed neutron streams had banged up his target nuclei and gotten them leaking a bit, so to speak, they maintained their basic structural integrity. None had yet shattered or split. The

weak nuclear force had been goaded into activity as a restorative measure to the unbalanced (i.e., now mildly radioactive) nuclei, but the
strong nuclear force—or what would eventually be known by that
name—remained elusive and aloof, its existence suspected but un-
confirmed, locked up and cloaked in its seemingly impregnable nuclear fortress.

With Yukawa's mathematical formulation of the strong nuclear
force and Fermi's experimental probing of its boundaries putting
practicable flesh on the thirty-year-old theoretical skeleton of $E = mc^2$,
the way was now open for physicists to visualize the strong nuclear
force as a potential fuel (or explosive) source, and to understand that
the way to tap into it was to get it to snap—somewhat like the abrupt
rupture of an overstretched rubber band—when the nucleus it normally held in its atomic death grip (and vice versa) was broken or split.
Physicists also understood that the best possible way to achieve this
was going to be through more neutron activation—in this case, getting a neutron to collide with the nucleus of an atom, break it into two
or more pieces, and unleash (i.e., cause it to lose) some portion of its
strong nuclear force as a result of the fissure. Even though this $E = mc^2$
conversion would not be total—there would be debris remaining, after all—the power released would still be orders of magnitude beyond
any that humankind had ever accessed before.

The catch here was that one could not simply put any old atom in
front of a stream of fast neutrons and get it to give up its strong nuclear force. As Fermi had found, the nuclei of the atoms in most forms
of matter are far too stable, their strong nuclear force locked away too
tightly and securely, for this to work. Under neutron activation, they
will become radioactive—after which they will, in turn, emit "ionizing radiation" that can and does kill living cells (and their hosts) primarily by disabling DNA molecules—but this radiation does not
provide any kinetic energy beyond a release of the weak nuclear force,
which may be enough to make a watch dial glow in the dark (or give
someone cancer), but it is not going to turn an electrical turbine or
blow things up.[6] If mankind was going to put the atom to work as a
fuel source—or as an explosive—the strong nuclear force had to be

accessed by causing atomic nuclei to split or disintegrate. And the trick for getting at such power would be to find an atom with a nucleus fat, wobbly, and rickety enough—that is, one that is ever on the verge of splitting under its own instability anyway—and just to help that process along with a little nudge from a loose neutron.

Fermi's neutron activation work in the mid-1930s pointed research in the field in the right direction, identifying U-235—the isotope of uranium that is still the primary fuel source of the world's nuclear power plants in the twenty-first century—as the best candidate for inducing this kind of reaction. By the end of the decade, with the clouds of the second global war in two decades gathering on the horizon, world-class physicists like Fermi, Niels Bohr, Werner Heisenberg, Lise Meitner, and others were scrambling to find a way to split the nuclei of U-235 atoms and, in so doing, tap into the strong nuclear force.

At this point, researchers were only one key conceptual step away from realizing fission and, from there, understanding the mechanism of a nuclear chain reaction.

In January 1939, scientists in Nazi Germany succeeded in causing a tiny amount of U-235 to undergo nuclear fission.[7] It was soon figured out that this process entails an "(n,2n) reaction," in which a loose, flying neutron (n) collides with and is absorbed by a U-235 nucleus, which then loses two (or more) of its own neutrons under the impact, like a rack of pool balls flying apart after a break shot. These freely caroming neutrons can now potentially collide with the nuclei of neighboring U-235 atoms, causing them, in turn, to undergo fission, and so on, and so on—in a chain reaction—with each (n,2n) reaction contributing its own tiny burst of released strong nuclear force to the ongoing explosion of energy. Once this understanding of a supercritical chain reaction became clear, the theoretical gates to weaponizing the strong nuclear force opened wide.

When the significance—and the danger—of this development was explained to Franklin Roosevelt in the summer of 1939 by physicist Leo Szilard (with the explicit endorsement of Albert Einstein), the president immediately green-lit a crash research program—which eventually grew into the Manhattan Project—to ensure that

Americans managed to weaponize this new science before the Nazis (or anyone else) did.

Looking back with privileged hindsight at the chain of events set in motion by Roosevelt's decision, one can fairly assume that the whole point of weaponizing the strong nuclear force was never to give the enemies radiation sickness and cancer, nor to cause birth defects in their in utero children, nor even to carbonize their bodies and flay their flesh with temperatures as hot as the surface of the sun.

The scientists who eventually developed the weapons; the engineers and technicians who built them; the military men who planned, trained for, ordered, and carried out their deployments; and the politicians who signed the checks to pay for it all seem to have done so in the grip of a mindset, akin to religious awe, that was simultaneously terrified and intoxicated by visions of cities, fleets, and armies—either ours or theirs—instantaneously blasted out of existence. The goal of cracking uranium atoms to access the strong nuclear force had always been the theretofore unimaginably powerful explosions this could make possible. It would seem that the radioactive evils of the weapon—when they were acknowledged at all—were expediently tolerated as collateral damage in the urgent enthusiasm of the moment.[8]

Explosive power, whether produced by conventional or nuclear means, is a by-product of the breaking or transformation of bonds between subatomic particles and the heat rapidly generated by this process. In any conventional explosive, from the caps used in a child's toy gun all the way up to the GBU-43/B MOAB bomb used by the US Air Force today, the power released by the explosion is the result of the abrupt rupture of chemical bonds—that is, bonds between electrons joining atoms together in the violently combustible molecules of whatever explosive compound the device uses, e.g., gunpowder for the cap gun, a mix of TNT and RDX for the MOAB, jellied gasoline for a napalm bomb, etc. When these bonds are ruptured in a chemical chain reaction set in motion by an initial ignition/detonation (via fuse, blasting cap, electrical spark, etc.), their potential energy is converted into kinetic energy—in this case, heat—with literally explosive rapidity. When this sudden generation of heat—what chemists call an "exothermic reaction"—slams into the surrounding air (or any other physical matter adjacent to it), some portion of this kinetic thermal energy is siphoned away to perform the mechanical work of compressing and pushing this air (or water, for a torpedo or sea mine; or soil, for a land mine) out of the way very quickly and violently, generating blast effect.

In any other kind of fire or combustion process, the heat generated is the result of the same rupturing of bonds between electrons, albeit at a much slower speed (alternately, the explosion of a conventional bomb may be regarded as an extremely fast fire). And this rupturing at an even slower speed is what makes possible the metabolism of nutrients in the digestive tracts and of oxygen in the lungs of living creatures.

Because electrons are, again, for all intents and purposes (though not completely) massless, in each of these three cases of ruptured-chemical-bond heat exchange—explosions, fires, and metabolism—the amount of matter that is converted to energy and flung back into the cosmos from whence it originally came, as per $E = mc^2$, is infinitesimally tiny—somewhere on the order of billionths of the original mass of the combustible material.[9]

Strong-nuclear-force bonds, in comparison, are some *ten million times* more robust—that is, that much more resistant to disruption and thus locking up that much more potential energy—than their electron-mediated chemical counterparts.[10] Under theoretically ideal conditions of detonation, an atomic bomb harnessing/unleashing the potential energy of strong-nuclear-force bonds would see a perfect one-to-one $E = mc^2$ matter-to-energy conversion; every atom in the bomb's fissile material would cease to exist as every quark in every neutron and proton of its nucleus disintegrated and was converted into pure kinetic energy. As William Laurence put it in one of the vivid illustrative examples for which he was known, if every atom of the mass in a single dime—an American ten-cent coin—could be perfectly and completely converted into kinetic energy in this manner, the resulting explosion could handily and instantly wipe a modern city off the face of the earth.

"VAPORIZED"

HIROSHIMA AND NAGASAKI discourse in English has long used the word "vaporize" to describe what the heat and force generated by Little Boy and Fat Man were supposed to have done to human bodies. If you are someone who desperately wants to believe that the bombs were justified, it is a very conveniently antiseptic word, almost evoking imagery of waving a magic wand over people, and then, presto change-o, watching them disappear with a nice, clean, painless "poof." In short, it is a word that lets the bomb droppers off too easily, and it is one with which my research colleague Dr. Tomonaga Masao (Nagasaki University School of Medicine) has never been comfortable.

I am pretty sure that I first heard the word "vaporized" in the summer of 1970. As an eight-year-old tail-end baby boomer living in a New York City apartment building with those creepy black-circle-and-yellow-triangle fallout shelter signs by the entrances, I was already quite familiar with the idea that nuclear weapons were objects of ultimate terror. But the TV documentaries I watched that summer around the twenty-fifth anniversary of V-J Day provided me with a new vocabulary item to put flesh on the bones of my theretofore vague concept of what being killed by a nuclear bomb would entail. I can remember being darkly comforted by the thought—possibly reinforced by a narrator's commentary—that being "vaporized" would be a physical process that would play out so quickly that it would all be over before I even had an idea that anything was happening. There would be no time to feel anything. If there were no warning sirens or panicked dashes for building basement fallout shelters, there would not even be time to register any fear.

Likewise, there may be readers who cling to some cold comfort in the notion that the people who were killed in Hiroshima died "instantly," having been vaporized by Little Boy. But the reality is considerably more grisly. The people killed closest to and in direct, open line of sight to the Hiroshima and Nagasaki fireballs were not so much vaporized as they were "carbonized." The bombs' six-hundred-meter detonation heights—calculated for maximum blast effects over the targets—guaranteed that every one of their victims suffered at least a second or so of (literally) searing agony. This would have been true even for people standing in the open directly under the fireballs. These hypothetical precise-geographical Ground Zero victims would have had just about time in the final second or two of their lives to begin registering hellfire pain, hear their own skin begin to sizzle, and perhaps take in a deep gasp of air for a scream before the supersonic shock wave—the impact, at this close range, arriving ahead of the sound of the explosion coming up behind it—literally blew them to pieces, delivering as much as eleven tons of pressure to every square meter of surface with which it collided.[1]

If you are going to defend these weapons' use, it is morally imperative that you own that image. Turn it around in your head a bit. Imagine it happening to ten thousand children or even just a single child.

Imagine it happening to *your* child.

People within the zone of total destruction (ZTD) who were partially or fully shielded from direct line-of-sight exposure to the shock wave and the three-second burst of flash and thermal rays from the fireball were not necessarily better off; if anything, their suffering before their inevitable deaths was worse because it was prolonged. If they had not been dashed against a concrete wall, or crushed under a house or building collapsed by the shock wave, or burned to death when firestorms consumed the resulting tangled wreckage in which they were trapped, then acute radiation syndrome (ARS)—typically in combination with thermal ray burns—killed them anywhere from hours to two weeks or so later.

Individuals who happened to be inside particularly sturdy structures (or basements—which were in any case rare in prewar Japan) located within the ZTD sometimes escaped immediate or near-immediate death, but in almost all these cases, the end result was the same, and few lived to see September 1945. One case of a group of otherwise ostensibly "sheltered" individuals within the ZTD was that of the occupants of the Hiroshima Bankers' Club, some two hundred fifty meters south of Ground Zero.[2] Although the building itself stood up surprisingly well to the physical trauma of the explosion, suffering only a "depressed" roof and "serious cracking of slab and beams," its primarily wood-and-plaster-lathing interior was completely consumed in the firestorm that swept the area after the blast.[3] As for its forty-eight occupants at the time of the event, twenty-five died "instantly" (i.e., by contemporary Japanese medical standards, within twenty-four hours of the fatal event). These fatalities were almost certainly the result of blast effects (including being crushed by collapsing building material and being struck by rubble, glass shards, etc., ballistically propelled by the turbulence of the shock wave) and/or fire / thermal radiation.[4] Another twenty-two who had somehow managed to avoid these more immediately fatal injuries nevertheless succumbed over the following eighteen days, either from burns, blast injuries, ARS, or, as with most ZTD victims, some combination of all three. One person who had been on the first floor of the building when the explosion occurred was still alive at the time of the United States Strategic Bombing Survey (USSBS) team's investigation of Hiroshima damage in 1946.[5]

Little Boy's nuclear core contained some sixty-four kilograms of U-235. Luckily for Hiroshima, and probably for the planet, this particular lump of matter did not undergo complete $E = mc^2$ conversion. In the first milliseconds after the triggering of the bomb's firing mechanism, approximately one kilogram (the mass equivalent of five hundred of Laurence's dimes) of this material underwent incomplete fission before the uranium in the rest of the core was spread too far by the explosion to sustain supercriticality and was instead dispersed over Hiroshima as an aerosolized mist of radioactive matter.[6]

As the nuclei of approximately 2.5 trillion trillion atoms in this kilogram of U-235 underwent fission, each splitting into what became nuclei of newly formed atoms of krypton and barium and losing (through the [n,2n] reaction) two or three neutrons in the process, the portion of the strong nuclear force that had been holding those two or three neutrons firmly in place was suddenly rendered homeless. But this enormous amount of potential energy did not simply disappear along with its nuclear home. It was compelled by the law of conservation of energy to take alternate form. In this case, this was by undergoing $E = mc^2$ conversion into the kinetic energy equivalent of fifteen thousand tons of TNT.[7] If this single kilogram of U-235 had been completely converted from mass to energy as per $E = mc^2$, the explosion would have yielded the equivalent of some 21.5 million tons of TNT—21.5 megatons—putting it in a class with some of the most powerful hydrogen bombs ever detonated.

For the first nanoseconds before Little Boy's kinetic energy began colliding with nonfissioning matter—the heavy tamper block of U-238 nestled around the core, the steel casing of Little Boy itself, and the air and other airborne atmospheric matter surrounding the bomb—it was expressed in a burst of *initial radiation*. A tiny fraction of this force was siphoned off to do the mechanical work of propelling neutrons and other subatomic debris let loose by the shattering U-235 nuclei out and away from the detonation point (at close to the speed of light); the rest of it emerged as a speed-of-light shower of the purest and pound for pound most powerful kinetic energy known to science, the stuff from which the big bang was formed: gamma rays and ultraviolet radiation at the most highly energized end of the electromagnetic spectrum.[8]

If, rather than exploding over Hiroshima, Little Boy had been detonated in an environment completely devoid of air or any other physical matter—for example, in outer space—the kinetic energy it released would not have resulted in any thermal radiation beyond a shower of the stuff about a millionth of a second in duration and the heating the heavy U-238 tamper around the core and the steel outer casing of the bomb itself would have undergone as they were literally atomized by the three-hundred-thousand- to one-million-degree-Celsius thermal energy of the chain-reacting U-235 during this same unimaginably brief time span. With the airless explosion being over in an infinitesimal fraction of an eyeblink, there would be no scorching, blinding, seconds-long fireball typically seen in the detonation of a nuclear weapon—only the briefest camera flashbulb–like burst of light in the narrow visible band of the electromagnetic spectrum.[9] Nor, again, in the absence of air, would there be any blast-effect shock wave or sound. With no transfer of kinetic energy siphoned off to perform the mechanical work of moving air or other matter out of the way (and heating up same), the vast majority of the energy generated by the detonation would remain in its initial pure form of unleashed neutrons and electromagnetic pulse (EMP)—still capable of killing, through ionizing radiation, and of wreaking havoc on electrical systems, but it would not be a form of energy capable of carbonizing organic matter and flattening cities.

But Little Boy, of course, did not detonate in outer space. It exploded in particulate- and moisture-laden summer morning air six hundred meters above Hiroshima. And in a purely mechanical and thermodynamic way of looking at that event, it was that very air, in a lethal embrace with the U-235 supercriticality in Little Boy's nuclear core, that leveled the city and burned to death most of the people who died as a result of the bomb's detonation.

It has been calculated that of the total kinetic energy released by Little Boy's detonation, some 50 percent was used up in moving that air, via blast effect. Of the remaining 50 percent of Little Boy's energy, some 35 percent was expended as heat and intense UV and visible light, and 15 percent consisted of initial (aka "prompt") and residual ionizing radiation.[10] These three categories of energy expenditure were roughly reflected in the breakdown of bomb-related Hiroshima fatalities by the end of 1945: More than 50 percent of these eventual hundred forty thousand victims died as the result of flash and thermal radiation from the fireball, or through burning structures / wreckage ignited by the same; some 30 percent died from ionizing radiation (either initial or residual); and 18 percent by blast effect.[11]

As soon as the initial burst of kinetic energy from Little Boy's detonation came into contact with the atmosphere, three roughly simultaneous catastrophic processes were set in motion:

1. Neutron Activation / Ionization

- Speeding neutrons and gamma rays collided with the atoms of the air immediately surrounding the bomb (and everything suspended in it), ionizing this material.
- Much in the way that water molecules are agitated and heated in a microwave oven, the electromagnetic radiation in this initial burst of energy turned a roughly spherical volume of air around the bomb into a super-compressed, superheated plasma balloon, forming a fireball (see process 3 below).
- Atoms in this fireball ionized by neutrons became radioactive, shedding alpha and beta particles via the weak nuclear force (adding another source of gamma radiation to the mixture, albeit a relatively small amount relative to that released in Little Boy's supercriticality/explosion itself) in an attempt to regain equilibrium (as per the matter ionized in Fermi's neutron activation experiments).
- Atoms in this fireball ionized by gamma rays, in turn, released ionizing gamma radiation of their own (via Compton scattering), which caused hazardous (e.g., highly carcinogenic) radiolysis reactions in the tissue[12] of living beings—both fauna and flora—below through the ionization of molecules in their cells (most commonly—but not exclusively—water molecules).
- Neutrons and gamma rays that found their way to solid ground also ionized and/or (in the case of neutrons) rendered radioactive the atoms of anything (and anyone) they encountered there.

2. Formation of Fallout Debris

- Much of this radioactive matter on the ground—soil, dust from pulverized building materials, ash from vaporized/ carbonized organic matter—became airborne from the shock wave of the explosion a second or two later, and was then lofted high into the atmosphere by subsequent thermals rising from the now superheated ground.
- This column of radioactive dust and other airborne debris rocketing skyward from the ground became the material visible as the "stem" of Little Boy's iconic mushroom cloud.
- Ionization caused microscopic bits of matter surrounding the explosion to become charged and mutually attractive, fusing together into heavier-than-air particles in the heat of the fireball that then joined up with the column of additional ionized material rising up from the city.[13]
- Linking up with moisture suspended in the atmosphere, now including large amounts of water from the various rivers and waterways in the city evaporated by the intense heat of the explosion, this combined mass of humidity, smoke, dust, and other debris formed a cloud of precipitation (the "black rain" mentioned in so many Hiroshima—and Nagasaki—survivors' testimonies) that began falling some forty-five minutes after the explosion and returned to the ground as nuclear fallout.

3. Generation of the Fireball

- In the initial hundredths of millionths of the first second of Little Boy's detonation, "more than 95 percent of [its] explosive power" was released as a burst of high-intensity electromagnetic energy in the form of gamma ray and X-ray radiation mediated by photons invisible to the human eye at this wavelength.[14]
- Little Boy's fireball, which was responsible for the lion's share of Hiroshima's devastation, was formed when these photons collided with the atoms and molecules in the surrounding air and began surrendering their energy—in the form of heat transfer—with each collision; as the

photons' energy was steadily leached away by this process, they shifted down into lower-energy (longer and eventually visible) wavelengths of the electromagnetic spectrum.

- Each successive wavelength band of energy on this spectrum spewed its own characteristic form of destruction from the fireball—the roiling, roughly spherical bubble of super-pressurized, superheated plasma in the immediate vicinity of the detonated bomb: first, from gamma rays to slightly lower-energy (longer-wavelength) but still ionizing X-rays; then down into the burning bands of the spectrum, starting with ultraviolet light; then through the narrow (and in this case blinding) band of light visible to the human eye; and from there down into infrared and microwave thermal radiation.

In the first microseconds of its existence, Little Boy's fireball was twenty-six to twenty-eight meters in diameter, had a core temperature of between three hundred thousand and one million degrees Celsius, and was orders of magnitude brighter than the sun in terms of lumen output.[15] Before it exploded outward in a shock wave, the air pressure in this superheated core was some hundred thousand atmospheres.[16]

After 0.3 seconds, the surface temperature of the fireball cooled to seven thousand degrees Celsius—some fifteen hundred degrees hotter than the surface of the sun.[17] At one second, the fireball had swollen into a radiation-spewing, incandescent heat lamp the size of three football fields, and it cooked the ground and everything else below it out to about a radius of one kilometer into the three-thousand- to four-thousand-degree-Celsius range for as long as three seconds.[18] Within this one-kilometer-radius circle, the fireball bathed every surface it touched with some 23.2 calories of thermal radiation per square centimeter (three calories per square centimeter is sufficient to cause organic material to combust).[19] Metal and even the surfaces of concrete and granite building materials and ceramic roof tiles melted. Anything made of wood or other organic materials was nearly instantaneously carbonized.

Even two kilometers away, human skin directly exposed to the flash and thermal energy from the fireball was destroyed by third- and fourth-degree burns. Hair and clothing burst into flames.[20] Out to a distance of up to three thousand meters from the point of explosion, the fireball inflicted skin burns upon: 84.3 percent of people caught out in the open in direct line of sight of the fireball; 27.3 percent of people who were outdoors and shielded in some way from direct line of sight of the fireball but still burned by the superheated air surrounding them; and 13 percent to 14 percent of people who were indoors (caught near open windows, etc.).[21]

DR. TOMONAGA

THREE DAYS AFTER Little Boy destroyed Hiroshima, a two-year-old boy named Tomonaga Masao was taking a nap on the second floor of his family's Nagasaki house when the plutonium Fat Man device exploded two kilometers away to the north. The Tomonaga house and its residents were shielded from the bomb's burst of initial radiation, thermal rays, and line-of-sight blast force by a nearby mountain. However, this terrain feature offered no protection from the momentary tremendous displacement of air over the city caused by the explosion. The violence of this sudden expulsion of atmospheric volume—followed by another shock when all of this displaced air quickly rushed back in to fill the resultant vacuum—was of sufficient force to dislodge the second floor of the Tominaga house and send it and its toddler occupant crashing into the garden below.

If the chain of events that played out in the next few seconds were gamed on a Monte Carlo simulation computer program, there would probably not be one run in a hundred in which Baby Masao was not crushed to death under a pile of wreckage. But while his mother's flower beds might not have made it, the child was a bit luckier. If it hadn't been for a sort of tepee framework of wooden beams that just happened to fall into place directly over Baby Masao, shielding him from the cascade of roof tiles and rafters crashing down all around him, I would not be speaking to him seventy-one years later, almost to the day, in the coffee shop of a Nagasaki hotel.

My first impression of Tomonaga-sensei is that he has been giving directives—and expecting them to be complied with immediately and unquestioningly—for most of his adult life. His overall demeanor reminds me of those of the Imperial Military Academy and Imperial Naval Academy graduates I interviewed many years earlier in another (but ultimately related) research project; he's a take-charge type fairly representative of his generation of Japanese man—crusty but basically benign, with lingering notes of old-school male privilege. His speech switches seamlessly back and forth between Japanese and English; it is also very direct, occasionally to the point of bluntness, though this effect is less conspicuous in his use of his second language than it is in his use of his far more protocol-bound native tongue. The more I learn about his history and background—for instance, that he is a third-generation Nagasaki Medical College graduate and the scion of a fine old family of Nagasaki samurai retainers who traded in their katana swords for stethoscopes after the Meiji Restoration—the more sense these observations make. The doctor is descended from a long line of men accustomed to being listened to and obeyed.

Tomonaga-sensei is also a permanently busy man, so the niceties in our self-introduction discourse are dispensed with quickly, even curtly. It is, after all, atomic-bombing memorial, symposium, and media interview season—the busiest time of year for him. Moreover, he still doesn't know me from Adam, and for all he knows, I may be just some hack looking for a quick lead so I can swing for the fences on a sensational bomb story. In that case, I will not be worth sharing any more time with than it takes to drink an iced coffee, leave a business card, and part ways with "Don't call me. I'll call you."

But he will give me a chance to make my case.

He opens our interview with a stunning left jab: What, he asks in so many words, makes me any different from all of the other researchers or journalists who are always coming down to Nagasaki and pestering *hibakusha* (atomic bomb survivors/victims) for heart-wrenching stories and juicy scoops?

My ears hear polite if somewhat brusquely delivered questions from the doctor, but in a dark, self-doubting corner of my mind, I am hearing, *Who do you think you are, an American stomping roughshod around Hiroshima and Nagasaki, making old people dredge up and share horrible memories? What makes you think you are qualified to take up such an important, painfully sensitive, and even sacred topic?*

I wrestle my inner voices of self-doubt into submission and compose myself to work up a long answer (I do not now recall whether this was in English or Japanese). I begin by explaining that, unlike a journalist or someone else who puts food on the table solely through their writing, I will not be working under a tight deadline. I can take as long as I need to on this to do it right. If necessary, I can research it until the Ministry of Education makes me retire in 2028, though I would prefer to think my project will not take that long. I would like the hibakusha who will cooperate with me to be able to see the project reach fruition—a book or perhaps even two. As I am speaking, I realize that this project—in one way or another—will probably never really end for me.

I watch Tomonaga-sensei's face as I make my pitch. It is impassive, and I can feel its owner studying me intently. There is still a little tension in the air, but it no longer feels challenging.

I explain the research I did in the aughts with survivors and bereaved family members of Japan's kamikaze units in World War Two—a highly sensitive and potentially minefield-strewn topic for any academic researcher in Japan foolhardy enough to take it up. This seems to impress Tomonaga-sensei somewhat. A little more tension unwinds.

Finally, I tell him about my trip to Hiroshima the previous May to witness Obama's visit to Peace Park, and about my epiphany there in front of the Children's Peace Monument the night before. I confess that this occasion marked the first time I ever really allowed myself to grieve and shed tears over the bombs, leaving myself open and vulnerable with no "Yes, but" equivocation to dull the pain. I also tell Tominaga-sensei that I do not think the agony (repressed or not) in America's soul about the bombs can ever begin to heal until all my countrymen—regardless of whether or not they agree with Truman's decision to drop the bombs—have allowed themselves that experience, if only once. If I can help other people—again, especially other Americans—accomplish that with my writing, then my scholarly mission will have been a success.

In the middle of this pitch, I am mortified to feel my throat tightening, my voice hitching, and my eyes beginning to water up.

Then I notice Tomonaga-sensei has grown silent. I look up from my interview notebook and into his eyes, which are now a little red and wet behind his glasses. Tomonaga-sensei nods slowly, any hardness that was in his facial expression before now gone. He says nothing. He does not have to.

I have a new research colleague.

ZHEN SU BING

===

Tri-Service General Hospital
Taipei, Taiwan
March 2019

EVERY MARCH, A team from Nagasaki University's Atomic Bomb Disease Institute (hereafter "Genken"—the common abbreviation of its Japanese name) visits Taiwan to conduct free health checkups and medical interviews for hibakusha who repatriated to their homes on the island after the war. The two-day annual sessions are held at Tri-Service General Hospital—a huge ultramodern medical complex administered by the Taiwanese military on the eastern edge of the capital city of Taipei. The Taiwanese hibakusha checkup program is funded as a joint venture by Genken, Nagasaki Prefecture, the Japanese Red Cross, and the Taiwanese government (although the Japanese Foreign Ministry is kept in the loop, diplomatic considerations vis-à-vis the People's Republic of China preclude more open official involvement). A sister program for South Korean hibakusha is conducted every December as a joint venture with the Korean Red Cross. Both programs are the brainchildren of Genken professor emeritus Dr. Tomonaga Masao.

Dr. Tomonaga's survival through a fluke of American disorganization, weather patterns, and a fortuitous entanglement of collapsing roof beams is something that has haunted him throughout a life lived, in many ways, in the shadow of Fat Man. But this experience has also imbued that life with an unwavering sense of purpose—a determination to help other hibakusha less fortunate than himself, and to do all he can to ensure that something like the bombings of his city and of Hiroshima never happen again. And although he could never be accused of being someone who shuns a reporter's microphone or camera, his entire curriculum vitae, from his time as a medical student in the 1960s on, is incontestable proof that the doctor walks the walk as well as he talks the talk: as a world-famous, second-generation (following in the footsteps of his father, Tomonaga Masanobu) atomic-bomb-related-leukemia epidemiologist at Genken; as the director emeritus of the Japanese Red Cross Nagasaki Genbaku (Atomic Bomb Survivors) Hospital; as a member of the Japan branch of the International Physicians for the Prevention of Nuclear War since its inception in 1980; as a cofounder and now director of the medical clinic of the Catholic Archdiocese of Nagasaki–administered Megumino'oka Atomic Bomb Survivors Nursing Home; as a regular participant in the Pugwash Conferences on Science and World Affairs—an international consortium of intellectual grandees who work on issues of nuclear disarmament; and finally, since he has worked long past the age when one might expect a doctor to begin enjoying golf and junkets to Tuscany, as the third-generation general practitioner of the family hospital that his grandfather established in the downtown Nagasaki neighborhood of Tamazono-machi a century ago.

Since our first meeting in 2016, Dr. Tomonaga has been an invaluable mentor as well as collaborator for me with my research. Two years later, he and his Genken colleague Professor Mine Mariko were instrumental in helping me secure a second Ministry of Education grant to continue my research on Japanese war memory, now focused on hibakusha experiences. Now, in 2019, Dr. Tomonaga has used his considerable influence to get the Taiwanese government, the Nagasaki prefectural government, and the Japanese Red Cross to allow me to participate in this year's Taiwan expedition.

Of the dozen or so Taiwanese hibakusha registered with and recognized as such by the Japanese Ministry of Health and Welfare who are still alive in 2019, seven of them have come to see Dr. Tomonaga (and his mysterious American research colleague) on the gray but mild March Taipei morning when we arrive at Tri-Service General Hospital for our interview sessions.

This morning, the hospital staff has been kind enough to give me an interview room directly adjacent to the office where Dr. Tomonaga is examining and interviewing hibakusha. As per my request, my room is equipped with a table for spreading out the large-scale maps of Hiroshima and Nagasaki I always use as memory-jogging aids and narrative-tracking tools when hibakusha are sharing their testimonies with me.

After a round of niceties and business card exchanging with the military doctors and nurses in this wing of the hospital who have helped make all of this possible, it is time for my interviews to begin. According to the list of interview subjects with which I have been provided, first up this morning is a ninety-one-year-old male, a Hiroshima hibakusha named Zhen Su Bing. In the remarks column on the list, there is a note indicating that Mr. Zhen has some Japanese ability.

There is a knock, and Zhen appears in the doorway to the room, smiling broadly. He is in a wheelchair pushed by a female Taiwanese Army nurse. His middle-aged son Lu Xi and his personal caregiver, a Filipina in her thirties, have also come along to listen in.

As Zhen is quick to tell me in surprisingly serviceable Japanese, the wheelchair conveyance is more hospital protocol than practical necessity. He could get up and walk around if he wanted to, but he is afraid the nurse would get angry. When he comes to the Army hospital to do the hibakusha health check every year, he tells me, they make him sit in this thing.

"Shō ga nai," he says. *What are you gonna do.*

As our interpreter translates these remarks into Chinese with blinding speed, Zhen's broad smile flashes again, and a titter flits around the room, shared by all present, including the Army nurse, who takes this as her cue to leave. She will be back in an hour to collect Zhen and bring the next interview volunteer, Chai Tsong Chin—like Zhen, another nonagenarian Hiroshima hibakusha.

Although the room is, at least to me, quite warm and the Taipei morning balmy, Zhen is bundled up in multiple layers of clothing, topped off with a submariner's snorkel jacket and a soft peaked hunting cap pulled down tight and low over his eyes, pushing his ears out. The bundles of clothing and the hat make him look tiny—like he is about to be swallowed up by his wheelchair. But his eyes are twinkling with excitement, and his smile is beaming. He is full of energy, raring to start the interview. I surmise that he is happy to be out of the house for an outing in the big city, enjoying an opportunity to encounter new faces. I get the feeling that he does not get to do this as often as he might like. It must be tough, I think, to be a superannuated extrovert when your loving but overprotective family treats you like you are too old and frail to be out and about as much as you would prefer.

We make a round of introductions. Zhen's son is in his early fifties—a few years younger than me. His English is quite good, as is the caregiver's. Our interpreter is also from Taiwan originally, but she has been living in Nagasaki for decades, since marrying her Japanese husband. She does freelance translation work for the Nagasaki prefectural government, which is paying her way for this trip.

I tell Zhen that I am from New York, but that I have been in Japan most of my life. He is surprised to hear that I am a professor in the Japanese public university system ("They let foreigners do that?") and that I am doing research about hibakusha.

I steer the conversational thread around to Hiroshima. Up to this point, I have assumed that Zhen, like so many other of his countrymen in 1945, was in Japan as a semicoerced laborer doing war factory work.

"No," he says. "I was a soldier."

"Army?"

"That's right."

"What unit were you in?"

Zhen replies, but it is garbled. Wa-wa-something-or-other. I look at the interpreter, and she gives me a shrug.

"Even though we were in the Army," Zhen says, "we were trained on boats."

My ears perk up at this.

"Did you say 'Wakashio'? You were in the Wakashio Unit? Special attack motorboats? Akatsuki Command?"

"That's right. Akatsuki."

I get a quick rash of goose bumps on my arms. In the excitement of my little eureka moment, I almost forget to turn on my digital sound recorder.

———

Zhen was born in Taiwan in 1928 as a subject of the Empire of Japan. Like their colonial counterparts in Korea at the time, the Taiwanese were also—again, at least on paper—"Japanese" citizens and, in their case, had been so since 1895, when their island had been ceded to the empire by Qing China after its defeat in the First Sino-Japanese War. Japan's victory in this conflict marked its debut on the world stage as an up-and-coming major power—a reputation it would cement with its shocking defeat of Imperial Russia ten years later (soon after which the Korean Peninsula was also annexed into the Empire of Japan).

Although the Japanese government's efforts to marginalize the local culture were not pursued as enthusiastically as they were in Korea, it was long recognized among the emperor's Taiwanese subjects that learning their rulers' ways and language was a prerequisite for a young person with ambitions for any future career more promising than menial labor. Accordingly, Zhen's relatively well-off merchant family made sure that he received elite schooling that would put him in good stead when it was time to move on to secondary school and then university or a teachers college. Throughout his scholastic career, approximately half of his curriculum consisted of classwork conducted in Japanese, and by the time he reached adolescence, he was thoroughly fluent and literate in the language. Nevertheless, the next desired step in his academic journey—to attend an elite commercial high school in Taipei where the curriculum as well as the entrance exam was entirely in Japanese—presented particularly daunting challenges for him. His parents had to order special exam prep textbooks from Tokyo bookstores for him to have any chance against the elite Japanese sons of high-ranking military officers, colonial administrators, and entrepreneurs stationed and/or based on the island who would be his main competition in the entrance test. Eventually, Zhen's hard work (and his family's investment) paid off, and he was accepted into a commercial school. But developments in the outside world were about to put detours in his career path.

Despite their legal status as imperial subjects, young Taiwanese men had traditionally been exempt from service in the emperor's uniform, outside of the small number of applicants from the island who were accepted into the Imperial Military Academy or the Imperial Naval Academy each year. This changed, however, in 1942, when developments in Japan's war with the West saw the beginning of official encouragement for Taiwanese—either aboriginal natives or, like Zhen, ethnic Han Chinese whose ancestors were originally from the mainland—to enlist in the Imperial Army. By 1944, however, when Zhen was in his third year at the commercial school, it was becoming clear—at least to anyone paying attention—that Japan's military fortunes were taking an increasingly dire turn. Rumors began making the rounds on the island that it would not be long before the Army began drafting Taiwanese. By the end of the war, some two hundred seven thousand islanders served with the Japanese armed forces, with approximately eighty thousand of these serving in uniform and the remainder as contracted civilian employees; some fifty thousand were eventually killed or ended up missing in action.[1]

Sensing the direction in which the winds of war were blowing, one of Zhen's teachers advised him that because the Army was going to get him sooner or later anyway, it would be better for him to go into the service as a noncommissioned officer. This route—a common one among adolescent boys of high academic or athletic ability across the empire in the last year of the war—would involve applying to and taking an exam for one of the Army's specialist NCO training schools; for Zhen, the teacher suggested the Imperial Japanese Army (IJA)'s Maritime NCO School on the island of Shōdoshima in the Seto Inland Sea, near Hiroshima. The operant logic here would have been readily apparent to Zhen or any other young man staring down the barrel of imminent conscription, as attendance at such a course would mean that he would have to face hazings, beatings, and other abuse for only a few months instead of for a full year, which was the typical fate of normal buck private conscripts, who occupied the absolute lowest position on the military cultural food chain. And duty on a landing craft or a transport ship would certainly be less arduous—and less potentially fatal—than crawling through the mud with a rifle on some godforsaken battlefield or flying a kamikaze mission in an airplane.

Zhen was convinced of the soundness of his teacher's advice. He applied to and was accepted into the same Akatsuki NCO school class as his future Saitō Unit comrade Tsuchiya Keiji, coming in just under the wire to miss the commencement of the military draft in Taiwan. He shipped out for Japan on an Akatsuki passenger freighter in January 1945. After several stops in Mainland Chinese ports on the way, ostensibly to take on freight, wounded soldiers, and other military personnel in transit, the ship arrived at Ujina in Hiroshima. It was Zhen's first experience of genuine winter weather—he had never known any in the near-tropical climate of his home island—and he was unpleasantly shocked at the bitterly cold temperature as he and his fellow recruits disembarked from their ship to be in-processed directly into the Akatsuki Command right at the waterfront.

Before Zhen and the other Taiwanese recruits would ship out to Shōdoshima to begin their training, however, they were first sent to an Army quarantine station on Ninoshima, where their final pre-enlistment medical examination procedure involved being made to wade into a neck-deep pool of disinfectant normally used to ensure Army horses and pack mules returning from continental Asia did not bring back any souvenir cases of hoof-and-mouth disease.

Despite being literally treated like an animal upon his arrival in the land of his colonial rulers, Zhen remembers, with considerable nostalgic pride, that he felt like a true Japanese when he donned his Army uniform for the first time.

TSUCHIYA KEIJI

Home of Tsuchiya Keiji
Kasaoka City, Okayama Prefecture
August 4, 2018

WHEN ONE WRITES about summertime travel in Japan, it borders on cliché to comment on the heat, but on the August afternoon that I am scheduled to interview Akatsuki Command veteran and Hiroshima hibakusha Tsuchiya Keiji, the intensity of the sunlight in the small fishing harbor of Kasaoka brings to mind the Nafud Desert scenes from *Lawrence of Arabia*. Decorum has necessitated that I wear my long khaki trousers today, but I mentally kick myself for my ill-advised overconfidence the night before as I explored Kasaoka on Google Maps in the cool comfort of my hotel room and decided I would skimp on taxi fare by walking the two kilometers from the train station to Tsuchiya's house. I am saved, more or less, by the day's low humidity and the plentiful beverage vending machines located along my route, but just barely.

My sweat-drenched appearance shocks Tsuchiya a little when he greets me at the doorway of his home. He hurries me into an air-conditioned side room he has prepared for our interview. He virtually pushes me onto a sofa and presses a tall glass of iced barley tea into my hand. He makes a face of comical surprise when I tell him that I have walked from the station.

"You may be younger than me," he scolds in the gentle but firm manner that comes naturally to this beloved retired schoolteacher. "But you're not *that* young."

We share a quick laugh.

Settling in, I am pleased to see that Tsuchiya has prepared for our interview by laying out several albums of yellowing sepia-toned photographs on the coffee table between us. I ask for and receive permission to take pictures of the photos as he is explaining them to me.

About half of the items pasted into the albums are professionally prepared postcards showing Shōdoshima NCO school scenes—happy, healthy, smooth-faced sixteen- and seventeen-year-old boys enthusiastically participating in various training and sports activities, wearing uniforms, outfits, and gear appropriate for same. There are shots of kendo fencing, calisthenics, and wrestling matches circled by spectators caught up in genuine ardor, excitement, and hilarity. Other shots show staged amphibious exercises with the boys, now stern faced and bundled up and buttoned down in life preservers and steel helmets, learning how to operate Daihatsu landing craft.

Tsuchiya tells me that the postcards were printed up and sold in sets by a civilian concession on the island, presumably being marketed to the boys in the NCO program. I imagine them sending the cards home to reassure their families that they were in good hands, and to show everyone what fine young men they were growing into. Thumbing through the cards, I also imagine being an anxious but proud parent getting one of them in the mail, and I wonder how many who did eventually receive notices from the Army, always beginning with the salutation "Congratulations," that their son had died gloriously in the service of the emperor. I also wonder how many of these bereaved families ever had any inkling at all that their sons had perished not heroically storming some beach in the first wave of an amphibious assault force, but drowning along with the other crew members and prisoner passengers on some fetid, stinking Akatsuki POW hell ship torpedoed by an American sub, or being cut to shreds by American machine guns and blown to pieces during their futile final sorties in flimsy plywood kamikaze motorboats.

Looking at the postcards in this light, I wonder if their intended use was not only as memorabilia but also for potential funereal purposes—visual narration for lives too short to have generated much original content of their own. They might have been displayed at wakes, laid out on a table in front of a carefully and ceremoniously cotton-wrapped ossuary box, compliments of the Army Ministry and a grateful emperor and nation. The box would have been empty of contents, save for a slip of paper calligraphy-brushed with the boy's name and maybe a handful of gravel to add convincing weight and a rattling sound when the box was handled.

The other items pasted onto the brown backing paper of the albums are shots taken by Tsuchiya, his comrades in arms, family members, and friends with their personal cameras. Photos from before and after Shōdoshima NCO training show Tsuchiya Keiji's transformation from pudgy schoolboy to lean soldier; only his round-lensed Tōjō-style eyeglasses and buzz-cut head remained unchanged. Another picture is a formal studio photo of Lieutenant Takakura, to whom Corporal Tsuchiya was delivering breakfast on Kōno'ura when Little Boy exploded thirteen kilometers away. There is a shot of Tsuchiya's father as a fifty-year-old "retread" Army Reservist lieutenant, looking sharp—if a bit long in the tooth—in his uniform with its peaked cap, high collar, and spit-shined knee-high boots. Near this is a magazine cutout of a famous photo of Navy lieutenant Seki Yukio and some of his enlisted pilots—the first aviators to make organized kamikaze attacks named and celebrated as such in the Japanese news media at the time. Seki and his men, posthumously, were hero-worshipped by the nation in the last year of the war—the contemporary Japanese equivalent of rock stars. The media blitz launching their story paved the way for thousands of boys like Tsuchiya Keiji to follow them into death carrying out kamikaze missions, not only in aircraft but also in motorboats and manned torpedoes.

In the margins of the album, there are notations that are variously proud, sentimental, and/or humorous. Much of this marginalia involves doodles and hand-drawn diagrams. As was the case for me nearly twenty years earlier during interviews with kamikaze unit veterans for another book on Japanese war experiences, I am surprised anew at the realization that even as the nation ran out of food, medicine, clothing, and ammunition, even low-ranked enlisted men had the wherewithal and means to equip themselves with cameras and film and go around taking pictures of everything.

As I look at Tsuchiya's photos, I get a quick rash of goose bumps thinking of how close he came to being killed seventy-three years ago, instead of surviving into the second decade of the twenty-first century to become the ninety-year-old man sitting in front of me. If he had enlisted in the Shōdoshima program only one class cycle earlier and had been sent with his motorboat to Okinawa, it is almost certain he would never have returned. I find this thought somewhat jarring contrasted with Tsuchiya's animated countenance and voice at the moment, and with the obvious nostalgia he is experiencing as he takes me on a guided tour down the memory lane of what seem to have been, based on his tone and demeanor as he recalls them, the most exciting and dramatic six months of his life.

Outside of occasional trips to Tokyo and a couple of speaking engagements in America in his seventies and eighties, Tsuchiya has spent almost the entirety of his life not more than fifteen kilometers— half a day's hike—from his birthplace on the outskirts of Fukuyama, Hiroshima Prefecture. Even including his three months on Shōdoshima and the four years he spent after the war attending Hiroshima University to study marine biology and get his junior high school science teacher's license, the radius of his lifeworld barely extends farther than a hundred kilometers—an hour's drive in a car obeying the Japanese highway speed limit.

Tsuchiya was born in 1928 as the second son of a wealthy agricultural landowner. The family home sat on an elevated, stone-walled mound in the middle of a vast sea of rice paddies that had been in his family for generations and that were worked primarily by sharecroppers. Among his earliest childhood memories are fond ones of watching the tenants on his family's lands go through their rent-paying rituals at the appointed times in the annual agricultural calendar. In a traditional ritual unchanged in centuries, the farmers would carry straw-rope-bound *tawara* bales of rice up the long, ramped earthen walkway to the Tsuchiya house, then present their "rent"—the fruits of their labors and the Tsuchiya land—to be recorded in a logbook before being stored in a mud, lath, and plaster *kura* storehouse on the property. Tsuchiya remembers watching all of this with great pride because he realized that his father was the man to whom *tawara*s were carried rather than one of the men who did the carrying and bowing. Such thoughts and feelings were already well on their way to becoming taboo in early 1930s Japan, being detrimental, after all, to the efficacy of a nation-state, society, and economy retooling and gearing up toward the breathtakingly egalitarian enterprise of waging twentieth-century industrialized "total" war. But cultural shifts stage-managed from Tokyo (which was not yet armed with the culture-leveling media-blitzkrieg weapon of television) often took a while to filter down and out into the rural cultural space of the rest of the archipelago, where traditions—and traditional worldviews—tended to cling on long past their official shelf life.

Still, neither social directives from Tokyo nor changes in the outside world at large could be kept forever at arm's length from rural Fukuyama—surrounding seas of rice paddies, inconvenient location and distance from the nation's power center, and local cultural stubbornness and inertia notwithstanding. Nor would the needs of empire. In the 1930s, following the Imperial Army's seizure of a vast area in Northeast China and Outer Mongolia in the wake of the Manchurian Incident, the national government undertook a policy to seed this newly won territory with Japanese civilian settlers. Toward this end, the government established what it called the *Manmō Kaitaku-dan* ("Manchuria/Mongolia [Manmō] Pioneer Youth Corps"). This would serve as the vanguard of a "Go west, young man" campaign of a sort to set up what amounted to a picket line of Japanese kibbutzim on the far-flung steppes of Northeast Asia. Specifically, the organization of the youth corps program would entail recruiting young people long on ambition and dreams but perhaps short on familial obligations or promising prospects in their hometowns; giving them military training and crash courses in agriculture and/or animal husbandry; and arming them and sending them to Manchuria or Mongolia. There they would set up and defend fortified village settlements surrounded by fields and pastures—snatched away from the local natives by hook or by crook—that they would proceed to work not only as professional farmers sending foodstuffs and needed raw materials back to Japan, but also as paramilitary frontier guards on the ever-expanding edges of the Japanese Empire.[1]

This, at least, was the plan. In the last days of the war, tens of thousands of these would-be Japanese yeomen—many now with young families in tow—would end up cut off from escape and overrun by Soviet tank armies, with the survivors of this blitzkrieg sent off to Siberian captivity. Most never made it home to Japan.

To set up the program, the central government in Tokyo relied on regional recruiting and grassroots organizational efforts, working largely through local Army Reservist Association branches and the agricultural bureaucracy at prefectural and municipal levels. In eastern Hiroshima Prefecture, a man like young Keiji's father was a natural choice to recruit, train, and lead the local Manmō Pioneer Youth Corps expedition: He was a seasoned agribusiness professional and a figure of influence, prominence, and long familial pedigree in the community. When he was approached with the job, the times being what they were, Tsuchiya Senior had no choice but to accept. He would not return to Fukuyama until he was called back in the early 1940s, after the war was already underway, and then only to be shanghaied back into the Army, commissioned as a lieutenant (at age fifty), and given command of an engineer platoon in Kure (most likely engaged in construction of ground defenses around the naval arsenal; Tsuchiya's older brother had an identical job, also as an engineer lieutenant, in Chiba Prefecture along the approaches to Tokyo during the last summer of the war).

During the years Tsuchiya Senior was away on the Asian continent, Mrs. Tsuchiya and her children had to run the farm largely by themselves. It was tough going, but the family's passage through this period was helped by its wealth and standing in the community, and its wherewithal provided their second son, Keiji, with an environment stable enough for him to proceed apace with his studies—a relative luxury in wartime Japan. Following in his family's footsteps, he eventually passed the entrance exam to the elite Seishikan Prefectural Junior High School in Fukuyama.

Nevertheless, the understanding that he would someday shoulder the honorable burden of military service was never far from his mind. This was not a possibility; it was an inevitability—even with the protection of superlative family connections. Like everyone else in his demographic cohort born during the first decade of the Shōwa Era, young Keiji grew up never knowing a Japan that was not actively fighting or at least preparing to wage total war. When he was born, the Imperial Army was already neck-deep in domestic coup plots and brushfire conflicts in Manchuria and Mongolia. Since he was an elementary-school third-grader, Japan had been at all-out war with China. In his second year at Seishikan Junior High, Japan's death match with the West had ensued with the attack on Pearl Harbor— the news of which Tsuchiya remembers listening to on the family radio with a sense of creeping dread.

In 1944, sixteen-year-old Keiji's education was put on hold when the Japanese government decreed that the nation's schoolchildren aged twelve and over, both boys and girls, would forgo their classroom learning for the duration of the conflict and be mobilized as war production labor. With this order, Keiji and millions of other adolescents began working either in munitions/weapons factories or food production or, in the last months of the war, helping to dig and prepare fighting positions and underground storage facilities throughout the archipelago in preparation for the anticipated Allied invasions.

In Keiji's case, he and a group of his junior high classmates were sent away to a shipyard on the Inland Sea, where they were minimally trained before being put to work hammering sheet metal into smokestacks and other ship components. Tsuchiya has tinnitus to this day from the incessant clanging on the shop floor that he had to endure during his ten months on the job. At night, the boys were put up in a company dormitory, where they were given little to eat other than rice mixed with soybeans or soybean waste products from the tofu-making process. The fare was difficult to digest and it played havoc with the boys' gastrointestinal tracts. Keiji, who had something of a delicate constitution, was constantly plagued with diarrhea—an ailment that would hound him on and off not only for the rest of the war, but for the rest of his life.

When Keiji entered the Akatsuki NCO program in January 1945, despite the hazing and harassment his classmates and he had to endure, it was almost an improvement over the living conditions he had known during the ten months he had spent at the shipyard; the food, for one thing, was far superior (although his GI tract continued to howl). And while a few of the sixteen- and seventeen-year-old boys in the program eventually suffered nervous breakdowns—with a few even running off into the mountains behind the NCO school facility, never to be seen by their classmates again—Keiji managed to stay on a relatively even keel. At Shōdoshima he kept his head down and his mouth shut—always a safe policy when finding oneself stuck in any kind of institutional situation involving uniforms and shouting superiors—and at times he even enjoyed his training; his only hiccup during the course was being laid up in an Army hospital on Ninoshima in Hiroshima Bay for several weeks after coming down with a nearly fatal case of dysentery in the final days before his graduation.

HURRY UP AND WAIT

WHEN KEIJI—NOW Corporal Tsuchiya—was sent to the Saitō Unit at the nearby Akatsuki Annex Base at Kōno'ura in July, Corporal Zhen and his other Shōdoshima classmates had already been training there on the *Marure* special attack motorboats for several weeks, and were all aware of the true nature of the weapon. After spending the immediately previous several months at Shōdoshima learning how to operate infantry landing craft that no one expected would ever be used in combat again, Tsuchiya, like his classmates several weeks earlier, was somewhat taken aback, to say the least, when he was brought up to speed on what he would be riding into battle when emperor and nation called upon him. But neither Tsuchiya nor his comrades were as shocked as someone in the twenty-first century might expect they were; for practically the entirety of their lives, these boys had been marinated in media and pedagogical content glorifying—if not literally apotheosizing—the idea that it was not only perfectly natural but unequivocally honorable and glorious for young Japanese men to willfully and enthusiastically allow themselves to be killed, without hesitation, in the execution of a military operation. The boys were human, after all, possessing natural, biologically hardwired survival instincts that would certainly have resisted the notion of such a fate (regardless of wartime media claims to the contrary), but such thoughts could be willed into submission. The most effective method immediately at hand for accomplishing this was to drink deeply of the *dulce et decorum* kamikaze Kool-Aid constantly thrust into their hands by every adult and media organ in their environment.

As Zhen Su Bing recalled, seventy-four years after the fact, the *Marure* kamikaze assignment was essentially forced upon him and his Shōdoshima classmates when they arrived at Kōno'ura. After being assembled to have this special duty explained to them, they were sent back to their plywood barracks with printed survey sheets, which Zhen remembers filling out on his bunk while all of the boys around him scribbled on theirs. The boys were to circle one of three responses:

1) I WILL DO THIS.
2) I DON'T WANT TO DO THIS.
3) I DON'T CARE EITHER WAY.

It would have been difficult—bordering on the impossible—for a young Japanese man in uniform in this situation to circle any response but number one, particularly with the Americans now burning the nation's cities to the ground every night. To do otherwise would have been to appear a coward or malingerer in the eyes of superiors, peers, and family back home. No one wanted to be the only sissy to raise his hand and say, "I quit," under such circumstances. No one *dared*.

If contemporary media depictions of such scenes were to be taken at face value as accurate interpretations of the late-war Japanese zeitgeist, then a proud, anxious nation expected nothing less of its young stalwarts. It is not unreasonable to assume that this framing of the kamikaze tactic—and philosophy—was welcomed by the Japanese public at the time not only because the vast majority of its members were utterly loyal to the state and naively trusting of the content continuously spewed forth by its technologically advanced media machine, but also because they were desperate for hopeful news, even if this reassurance was bought at the cost of the lives of thousands of their own and others' children. But one wonders if the stories would have been as readily consumed and desperately believed if the nation's parents had been given a chance to be flies on the walls of a kamikaze unit's barracks for a night and to listen to the boys softly sobbing into their pillows, tossing and turning in their bunks, muttering, "I'm sorry, Mom," or "I don't want to die." One wonders if those parents would have thought all of this was too much for the state to ask of boys who were not even old enough to shave, and if perhaps at least a few would have even raised their voices to express opposition to this willful expenditure of their sons' lives. But nothing like this ever happened, and it would seem that nary a peep of protest was ever officially or publicly raised against the Japanese military's kamikaze policy from the day of the tactic's spectacular media debut right up to the hour of the emperor's surrender broadcast on NHK Radio ten months later.[1]

In the meantime, the boys on Kōno'ura were kept too busy and exhausted to discuss seriously among themselves the option of ducking out of their inevitable kamikaze motorboat missions when the American troopships and landing craft eventually showed up in Hiroshima Bay. Everyone understood what their fate was going to be, and most, at least within sight and earshot of others, seemed to accept it.

When the Akatsuki Command's newest class of incoming *Marure* pilots woke up to begin another day of training on the morning of August 6, 1945, its members assumed they were another day closer to their scheduled collective fate of glorious immolation at the helms of their kamikaze motorboats.

———

Several hours passed after Little Boy's explosion before Zhen, Tsuchiya, and the other rank-and-file soldiers in the Saitō Unit at Kōno'ura received instructions from their higher-ups any more concrete and productive than some version of "Hurry up and wait." The commanders of some platoons left their soldiers—Tsuchiya and Zhen being among this group—on the waterline, where they watched the giant mushroom cloud across Hiroshima Bay grow to stupendous size, then deaden in color and eventually dissipate into a diffuse brownish gray pall, its lower surface glowing orange with the flames of a city burning end to end. Other platoon leaders sent their soldiers back to their barracks during this interlude. Many of the soldiers were practically asleep on their feet by this time, having been up all night running drills in the *Marures*; these soldiers had had to go straight into their normal morning training routines around the time *Straight Flush* set off sirens in the region during its weather recon flyover. But like almost everyone else in western Japan this morning, even the soldiers lucky enough not to have pulled training all-nighters had been kept awake by the incessant air raid sirens of the night before.

In the meantime, the Saitō Unit officers and radio operators on duty in their now windowless headquarters shack tried to get a grasp of the situation via their higher-ups at Akatsuki HQ in Ujina. Seven and a half kilometers closer than Kōno'ura to the hypocenter of the blast, HQ had suffered extensive physical damage and casualties, and they were just as much in the dark as the rest of the chain of command about what had happened in Hiroshima and what—if anything—they were expected to be doing about it. The state of overall confusion took a considerable turn for the worse about an hour after the blast when the first horrifically injured and disfigured victims from the city center began to stagger onto Ujina Wharf. This stream of suffering people had come to a stop at Akatsuki HQ perhaps not so much because it was their destination as because the path of their moaning forward motion away from the fires had been stopped in its tracks here by the natural obstacle of Hiroshima Bay. Fleeing the flames in the city, the procession of victims had followed Rijō Street—the city's main north-south *denshadōri* streetcar thoroughfare connecting Hiroshima Castle and Ujina. The major hospitals along the way—Red Cross Hospital (1.2 kilometers from Ground Zero) and Army Mutual Aid Hospital[2] (three kilometers from Ground Zero)—had long since been swamped to overflowing with the dead and dying and were now forced to turn the walking wounded away. As a result, most of the victims who had managed to reach Ujina had walked three or four kilometers over scalding-hot rubble- and corpse-strewn asphalt to get there. Many had made this journey barefoot, either because the bomb had caught them unshod in their now collapsed and burning wooden houses or because they had been outdoors in their customary wooden *geta* sandals, which might have been blown off their feet by Little Boy's shock wave or lost somewhere during their panicked exodus from the burning city. Exhausted by this trek, many fell where they stopped, never to get up again.

Akatsuki Command did not fall under the jurisdiction of CMD HQ or even the Second General Army; the organization was directly answerable only to the Army Ministry and Imperial General Headquarters in Tokyo, and for this chain of command to be able to issue any orders more relevant and substantial than "Stand by and await further instructions," Tokyo had to have some concrete idea of what was going on in Hiroshima. But on this morning of chaos and confusion, such information was slow in coming. Throughout much of the morning, it was unclear who—if anyone—was in charge in Hiroshima. In terms of governance conditions, the confusion was citywide—at least as far as it could be said that the city still existed as a political/ administrative entity.

For some hours, the only news coming out of the city had been the phone call to the Western Military District headquarters from Ōkura Yoshie in the CMD HQ's air defense bunker at Hiroshima Castle. In addition, around the same time, a coded message sent by Kure Naval Arsenal to Imperial General Headquarters in Tokyo reported that the large mushroom cloud filling the sky some ten kilometers to the west of their position was apparently from a large explosion of unknown origin that had occurred in Hiroshima. CMD HQ itself, any Fifth Division outfits in and around Hiroshima Castle, the Second General Army HQ near Hiroshima Station, and any other major Army commands north of Akatsuki's jurisdiction in the harbor district were not responding to attempts to contact them. Nor were any civilian authorities.[3]

As far as anyone knew, there were still thousands of soldiers in or at

least closer to the center of the city, and it had to be assumed that those
military personnel closer at hand—no doubt in conjunction with Hiroshima police officers, firefighters, and *Keibōdan* personnel—must certainly have been on-site, attending to rescue and recovery as needed. No
one at Akatsuki HQ yet suspected anything like the true scale of the
death and destruction to the north; they would not learn for several
hours yet that the entire organizational infrastructure of civilian and
military administration in the city had been essentially obliterated by
the explosion they had just seen. Neither did they know yet that most of
the soldiers anywhere near Hiroshima and anywhere else in the city
center were now dead, dying, or otherwise completely incapacitated. As
the morning progressed, initial intelligence reports began trickling in
and the victims of the bombing—living and dead—piled up on Ujina
Wharf. It was gradually becoming clear that Akatsuki Command was
not only the last functioning Army unit in the city; it was the last functioning official institution/organization in the city of any kind.

Adding to the morning's overall confusion, many of the Akatsuki
officers were missing—including several of the general officers in its
chain of command.

It was customary on the first Sunday of every month for Akatsuki
officers with homes on the mainland to be given a day's leave to spend
with their families; then they reported back ready for duty Monday
morning at a more leisurely hour than usual.[4] Before they could enjoy
this privilege, however, they were expected to attend professional-
development seminars held at the Akatsuki Operational Training
Section, located on the grounds of the Daiwa Textile mill in eastern
Ujina. This training organization was under the command of Lieutenant General Yoshimura Masayoshi, a gloriously Kaiser Wilhelm-
mustachioed career infantry officer and 1915 graduate of the IJA
Military Academy. Among his various assignments before transfer-
ring to maritime transport, he had served as a staff officer with General Matsui Iwane's Central China Area Army and Prince Asaka
Yasuhiko's Shanghai Expeditionary Force during the Nanking campaign in 1937–1938.[5]

When Yoshimura had been promoted to lieutenant general and

taken up his posting to Akatsuki HQ in 1941, his family had joined
him in Hiroshima, moving into quarters in Koi on the western edge of
the Ōta Delta.[6] The family seemed to have adjusted well to the move,
with their daughter Mieko passing the entrance exam for relatively
competitive Hiroshima Municipal Girls' School (Ichijo) in the spring
of 1945. On the morning of August 6, she left home to go to a downtown firebreak worksite with her Ichijo classmates.[7] It was the last
time her family saw her alive.

For the occasion of the August 5, 1945, seminar, the junior accounting lieutenant in charge of organizing the monthly events had
invited physicist Mimura Yoshitaka of Bunri University (Hiroshima
University of Literature and Science) to give the month's lecture.
Mimura chose a topic he must have thought would be stimulating—
even provocative—for his audience: recent efforts in the Japanese
physics community regarding the theoretical and practical possibilities of developing an atomic bomb.

During the Q and A session after the lecture, a lieutenant colonel
named Katō asked the professor, "Just what is this 'atomic bomb'
thing, and can we get one ready in time to use it during this war?"

Mimura drew up a quick concept sketch on the blackboard, explaining, "The matter has been under investigation by a research
team at Tokyo University under Professor Nishina. They have found
that although such a weapon would have an unimaginably destructive capacity, there is no way that it could be developed in time to use
in the current conflict."[8]

Katō seemed relieved by the professor's answer.

"Just to give some idea," the professor continued, "if a single
weapon with a nuclear core the size of a caramel were exploded over
Hiroshima, the entire city would be completely destroyed."

After the seminar broke up for the evening, some officers went
back to Ujina, Kōno'ura, or other Akatsuki facilities in Hiroshima Bay,
while others—taking advantage of their customary first-Sunday-of-
the-month leaves—went off for their monthly visits with their families. Among the latter group was Major Saitō, who headed off to his
family home in Nakayama, in the northern foothills of the city, and

left his executive officer, Major Tomita Minoru, and a skeleton crew of other officers to hold down the fort at Kōno'ura. They were still on duty the next morning when Saitō said goodbye to his family for what he must have assumed would be another long month, and headed off on foot for Hiroshima Station. From there, he would have caught the Ujina Line private railway to Ujina Wharf, checked in for accountability and new directives at Akatsuki HQ, and then taken an Akatsuki ferry to return to his command.[9]

Saitō took his customary shortcut to Hiroshima Station over the Ochigo Pass. En route, he heard maybe two or three B-29s passing overhead at high altitude. He found it odd that no sirens were going off—especially considering that they had gone off all over the city just half an hour or so before for a single plane. In any case, he decided not to leave anything to chance and began looking for an air raid shelter or any kind of defilade that would serve the same purpose. He soon found a nearby shelter entrance dug a little ways up into the heavily wooded hillside behind the Ochigo Municipal Crematory. He was joined there by two civilians.

Scanning the sky through the overhanging foliage, Saitō caught a silvery glint in his peripheral vision, and shifted his gaze toward it just in time to see a high-flying B-29 in a hard right turn. Ochigo Pass was only about 1.5 kilometers from the ground location directly beneath Little Boy's release point, so when viewed from Saitō's position, *Enola Gay*—at its ten-kilometer altitude—would have appeared to be almost directly overhead. He also saw the *Great Artiste*'s radiosonde parachutes floating down some kilometers away, high over Fuchu on the eastern edge of the city.

He was watching this scene when the sky turned blinding white.

Little Boy's shock wave arrived about ten seconds later, shaking the pine trees and bamboo groves lining the mountain pass like hanging laundry in a stiff wind. Saitō and his shelter companions were sure that some huge bomb or naval shell had just landed nearby. This was the first thought of just about everyone who experienced the event anywhere in the city: that what they had just heard was either enemy ordnance exploding or some catastrophic industrial accident happening virtually right on top of them. No one who initially experienced the explosion firsthand—with the possible exception of Professor Mimura—could have imagined that what they were seeing and hearing was simultaneously being seen and heard with equal or greater intensity for kilometers around in all directions by hundreds of thousands of other people, as well.

Parting ways with his shelter mates, Saitō crested the pass and began making his way down to Hiroshima Station. It was from here that he began to get an inkling that he had just had a close encounter with something more significant than a near miss from an ordinary shell or bomb. As he descended the slope toward the more built-up area near the station, the destruction only increased in magnitude. He began to encounter people with horrible burns and other injuries of inexplicable natures and severity. The major did what he could to help, but there were too many injured and suffering, and he had nothing to aid them with save his own hands. By the time he arrived at the half-destroyed Hiroshima Station, the front of his uniform tunic was covered in other people's blood.

The explosion had knocked all of the trains and streetcars in the city out of service, so Saitō had to cover the remaining five kilometers to Ujina on foot. His route followed the Ujina Line tracks running along the east side of the city, which the Kyōbashi River was protecting against the conflagration now consuming the downtown district. But although he was safe from the direct threat of the fires, he was not spared the horrible sights of the thousands of scorched people first running and later staggering out of the burning districts, many so charred and coated with ash and dust that it was impossible to tell their age or sex.

Saitō finally arrived at Ujina around 1000 hours to find Akatsuki's wharf teeming with civilian and military bomb victims. After wading through this sea of suffering to reach the Akatsuki HQ building, he was told that the radiomen were in contact with Kōno'ura and that there was no serious damage on the base beyond shattered windows, and there were no injuries beyond a soldier who had cut his hand on broken glass. He was also told that Akatsuki HQ had just relayed

Akatsuki commander Lieutenant General Saeki Bunrō's order to Major Tomita to prepare the Saitō Unit to stand by to have every landing craft and any other vessel on hand make its way across the bay to Ujina to commence rescue, relief, and recovery operations once the final orders came down. Saitō then caught a ride on the next Akatsuki motor launch to Kōno'ura/Etajima. The vessel was crowded with bomb victims, both quick and dead, who would be dropped off at the Army quarantine facilities on Ninoshima before the ferry reached its final destination of Kōno'ura and then headed back to Ujina to take on more of this miserable cargo. Eventually the ferrymen were so overwhelmed by the volume of corpses that they began tying them together with ropes and towing them behind their overloaded boats.[10]

Saitō reached the Kōno'ura headquarters shack around 1100 hours; there he was likely filled in on what the men on the base had seen that morning: soldiers outside and facing north when the explosion over the city occurred had been temporarily blinded by an incredibly bright purplish white light and felt an instant of intense heat on their faces simultaneous with the flash. Half a minute later, the sound and the shock wave of the explosion reached the base. Soldiers outside had had their service caps blown off by the blast. The HQ shack and the two-story soldiers' barracks had been shaken to their foundations and any north-facing window glass had blown in.

When the shock wave had reached Kōno'ura, the first thought of many was that the Saitō Unit's fuel dump on the north shore of the island had gone up, and they had started running down to the waterline to confirm this. In the HQ shack, Major Tomita wondered aloud if the big acetylene plant in Ujina had exploded. Whatever had just occurred, it soon became clear that the entire city was now ablaze. Moreover, no communications signals had either gotten through to or come from the city until Akatsuki HQ radioed in General Saeki's initial standby order around 1000 hours.[11]

Shortly after 1100 hours, Saeki's formal mobilization order came in over the wireless: "Hiroshima has been nearly obliterated by an enemy strike. . . . Cease all training operations at once, and gather all means at your disposal to go into the city to begin rescue and recovery operations."[12] Bugles sounding assembly were soon echoing around the base, and the soldiers—most still wearing the T-shirts and shorts of their calisthenics uniform—began to form up in their respective company areas.

Tsuchiya's company was told that the rest of the day's scheduled training was canceled; then they were sent to eat lunch about an hour earlier than usual. When the soldiers reached their respective company mess halls, they were surprised to be served something they had never seen before. Through some logistical windfall, the Saitō Unit had come into a huge consignment of horsemeat the previous day. As with most military personnel stationed in the Home Islands, the Saitō Unit's soldiers typically ate rather well—certainly in comparison with their civilian compatriots. But this feast was unprecedented; since the mess halls did not possess sufficient refrigeration equipment to preserve the meat, it was all going to be eaten today. Not being in a position to question the provenance of these veritable mountains of meat—which might have come their way via the largesse of colleagues at the Akatsuki animal quarantine facilities on Ninoshima—the soldiers gorged themselves. There was so much meat, the mess staff did not even bother boiling up the customary vats of rice. Although no one was aware of it at the time, this would be the last decent food any of them would see for at least a week.

"MIZU . . . MIZU . . ."

Akatsuki Command Annex Base
Kōno'ura, Etajima Island, Hiroshima Bay
Thirteen kilometers south of Ground Zero
1130 hours, August 6, 1945

AFTER NOON MESS, Tsuchiya and his company mates—who were still in their PT kit of T-shirts, shorts, and canvas sneakers—were issued gas masks, shovels, pickaxes, long-poled grappling hooks, and first aid stretchers. They were then ordered to mount up onto their Daihatsu landing craft, seventy men to a boat. No one told them what they were doing or where they were going. When all had boarded, the loading ramps on the boats' bows were pulled up and bolted shut.

The Daihatsu engines were started up and the boats pulled out of their moorings, headed north toward the smoke and fires still blazing across Hiroshima and loaded with boys who had no idea what was waiting for them twelve kilometers away. The Saitō Unit used every vessel at its disposal for the expedition; not only the Daihatsus but also smaller motor launches and even *Marures* overloaded with personnel and gear were soon churning up Hiroshima Bay. With their complements of soldiers armed with cutting implements and spearlike poles, the boats would have looked less like twentieth-century landing craft and more like Roman infantry galleys at Actium.

Tsuchiya's Daihatsu reached Ujina in fifteen minutes, a little after twelve noon. The wharf was already teeming with wounded and dying civilians and soldiers from the city, most covered in blood. Corpses were lined up in rows. Screams and moans filled air that was acrid with the odors of singed hair and charred flesh. Many of the Saitō Unit boys became nauseated as soon as they stepped off their boats; some were so overcome by the sights, sounds, and smells assailing their senses that they fainted on the spot. The fainters were lucky; they were sent back to Kōno'ura, their descent into Dante's Inferno temporarily and mercifully postponed.[1]

While Tsuchiya, Zhen, and the other psychologically sturdier soldiers capable of functioning in this new environment unloaded their gear and formed up into squads and platoons on the wharf, Major Saitō and his officers conferred with the Akatsuki Command staff in their nearby HQ building—a handsome three-story Art Deco–style brick building officially known as the Ujina Hall of Triumphant Return.[2] Here it was decided that the fifteen hundred or so soldiers of the Saitō Unit—with full logistical support of Akatsuki Command and its engineering specialist troops—would make their way into the burning city in two separate task forces.

One task force would take advantage of the Saitō Unit's shallow-draft landing craft and motor launches (including their *Marures*, now bereft of their concrete-filled practice barrel bombs), using these to ply through the waterways of the delta to rescue survivors who would no doubt be gathering along the riverbanks in search of aid. These efforts held out some measure of hope for success as, since the beginning of LeMay's firebombing campaign half a year earlier, the civilian population of Hiroshima had conducted multiple air raid drills based on a worst-case scenario of three hundred B-29s making an incendiary attack on the city.[3] Toward this end, the civil defense bureaus at both municipal and prefectural government offices had constructed and placed rafts along the banks of the seven waterways that ran through the city, with the idea that one avenue of escape from a furiously burning Hiroshima would be for residents to use these rafts to float out into the waterways and wait there either until boats rescued them or at least until the fires subsided enough to allow a return to dry land. As a backup, these civil defense authorities had borrowed some two hundred thousand life preserver bags from Akatsuki Command and distributed these to city residents. Akatsuki had this huge supply of life preservers on hand because they were no longer necessary for its primary mission; its oceangoing troop transports and freighters were now largely bottled up in harbor or otherwise prevented from accessing Hiroshima by Allied submarines, roving carrier-based planes, and the multitudes of air-dropped sea mines that now filled the approaches to the Seto Inland Sea.[4] In addition to the life preservers, rowboats and motor launches had also been borrowed from Akatsuki and moored at key points along the waterways, ostensibly to be operated by hastily trained city hall and prefectural office employees.

The second Saitō Unit task force would make its way into the city overland by borrowing Akatsuki Command's thirty-truck fleet, which was normally used to ferry cargo and personnel between Ujina and the Fifth Division / CMD HQ in Hiroshima Castle, as well as to the Army railhead at Hiroshima Station.[5] This task force would be further divided into two elements, each of which would take a different route to approach the ZTD; one of these would follow the Kyōbashi River up its relatively less damaged eastern bank to Hijiyama, the heavily wooded hill that dominated the topography of the eastern side of the city. Thousands of bomb victims and other evacuated people had been reported to be seeking refuge there from the flames. The task force would link up with a nearby Fifth Division communications regiment to set up a first aid station on the hill.

The other and larger force—which included Tsuchiya's and Zhen's respective companies and the Saitō Unit HQ staff—would take Rijō Street into the city as far as the fires would allow; that force's objective was to help set up a forward command post and another first aid station as a base for rescue and recovery operations near Red Cross Hospital. Earlier in the morning, Lieutenant General Saeki had ordered a special Akatsuki reconnaissance expedition to be sent into the city on foot; it was tasked with reestablishing contact with the hitherto unaccounted-for civil and military authorities in the downtown district, then reporting back observations and assessments of the range and degree of destruction from the cataclysm. This force had ultimately been unable to locate any civil or military chain of command worthy of the name anywhere near the furiously burning ZTD, but they had made it nearly three kilometers up Rijō Street, then crossed over onto the west bank of the Kyōbashi River before fires spreading from the city center had reached the area and temporarily cut off their line of retreat. There, while battling the flames threatening their position, they linked up with survivors of the Akatsuki Communications Battalion quartered at Senda Elementary School, just behind the main office and carbarn of the Hiroshima Electric Streetcar Company (Hiroden) on Rijō Street. The two units set up a temporary field headquarters at this spot, using it as a forward command post and staging area to mount rescue and recovery efforts deeper into the ZTD as such forays became possible. In the meantime, they did what they could to take on spillover capacity from Red Cross Hospital across the street, even as the communications battalion survivors were pulling their comrades out from under the wreckage of the wooden school buildings qua barracks that had been collapsed by the explosion blast and were now beginning to succumb to the flames.

As Zhen Su Bing recalls, soon after his company landed at Ujina around 1200 hours, they were assigned to the Rijō Street / central city ground element and told to make their way to this forward post at the Hiroden streetcar company office. Physically, aside from a lot of broken glass, Ujina and its immediate environs did not give the impression of a city that had just been destroyed. Only the moaning, gradually swelling throngs on the wharf had given the Saitō Unit and other Akatsuki troops arriving on the headquarters quay any heads-up toward psychologically steeling themselves for what they were about to encounter to the north. But before they would get anywhere near there, they were first going to have to help cut a way through mountains of detritus farther up Rijō Street.

One of the soldiers' most urgent tasks in the initial phase of their mission was to begin clearing away the tangles of utility poles, wires, wrecked vehicles, structural rubble, and corpses that were impeding the Akatsuki trucks' progress up this key thoroughfare; under current conditions, spreading flames from the city center meant the trucks were cut off on the opposite bank of the Kyōbashi River from the streetcar company command post in Senda, and the soldiers could now make their way on foot only as far as the Miyuki Bridge, a streetcar and vehicular crossing that spanned the Kyōbashi some three kilometers north of Ujina Wharf and that was not even halfway to the hypocenter of the explosion of whatever had just destroyed Hiroshima. Everything beyond the western foot of the Miyuki Bridge— including the immediate surroundings of the command post—was on fire and knee-deep in wreckage. Beyond the command post location, everything was knee-deep in wreckage and corpses.

As the central ground element commenced its advance up Rijō Street to approach the Miyuki Bridge, the road surface became increasingly indistinguishable from the shattered structures lining it because it was buried under debris—still mostly roof tiles and window glass by this point—that had been thrown by the blast. Increasing numbers of corpses, strewn across the roadway or sometimes in burned-out vehicles, were encountered.

On either side of the Rijō Street streetcar railbed, the soldiers passed a seemingly unending stream of bloodied, blackened, and dust-covered survivors headed in the opposite direction, ever southward, in long, staggering lines. Many were naked or nearly naked, having had their clothing blown or burned off by the blast and the subsequent fires. The hair of anyone who still had any after the fires stood straight out from their scalps like that of electricity-shocked cartoon characters, and it was hardened into fright wigs by a shellac of dust and blood. The thermal-radiation-singed or flash-burned outer epidermal layers of many of these victims hung off their bodies— most conspicuously from their bare arms—like curtains of filmy cream-colored cloth.

Ostensibly, these streams of walking wounded had just been turned away from the already hopelessly victim-swamped Red Cross Hospital and were headed toward the equally swamped Army Mutual Aid Hospital, which was located on Rijō Street about halfway between the Miyuki Bridge and Akatsuki HQ. Failing to gain admission at these hospitals, they had no choice but to walk, crawl, or be carried to Ujina Wharf. As the soldiers had neither medical equipment nor medicine on hand, about all they could do to help the victims was to point them south with promises of relief in Ujina and the choice of either walking under their own power or waiting for a ride on one of the Akatsuki trucks plying the two or three kilometers of Rijō Street that were traversable by vehicles at this point. In the meantime, the column of soldiers pressed on north by northwest, its ranks slowly but steadily burgeoned along the way by police officers and Keibōdan types in various stages of able-bodiedness, stranded from their organizations and looking for some way to pitch in and help. Ad hoc "interagency" task forces forming up like this around Saitō Unit / Akatsuki elements would carry out the brunt of relief, rescue, and recovery work in the shattered city for the next week.

The Saitō Unit's central ground element reached the Miyuki Bridge by early afternoon, but the flames on the west bank of the Kyōbashi were still too intense to allow further progress into the city. Soldiers from the Akatsuki Communications Battalion quartered nearby, along with their police and Keibōdan reinforcements, convinced them not to attempt to go any farther north, so the main Saitō Unit element stood in place, sharing the space with crowds of survivors milling about on the bridge, presumably waiting to reach homes or aid (perhaps not aware that none was forthcoming at Red Cross Hospital) farther into the city. The condition of the survivors Tsuchiya and his comrades encountered there was increasingly dire, with many seemingly lacking the ability or perhaps simply the will to join in the lines of people seeking refuge and aid to the south; many of the victims on the bridge who were still ambulant seemed to use this ability only to walk around in circles, alternately zombielike or screaming.

Eventually, the Saitō Unit detachment was waved through by the bridge guards and cleared to continue on its way up Rijō Street, and it reached the streetcar company command post sometime after one p.m. Beyond a certain point on the avenue, outside of the command post and the immediate environs of the heavily damaged but still functioning Red Cross Hospital, there was practically no sign of life at all. Everything within sight was blasted, smashed, burning, or smoldering. The ground in many places—especially the partially melted surfacing on the asphalt-paved Rijō Street—was almost too hot to walk on. This was especially so for those Saitō Unit soldiers still wearing their calisthenics sneakers, for whom standing in one place out in the open for too long in Senda-machi ran the risk of having the soles of their footwear melt into the ground.[6]

When Major Saitō himself reached the streetcar company around three p.m., following that afternoon's Akatsuki commander's conference in Ujina, a wood-plank signboard had been painted to announce the location as the "Saitō Unit Headquarters." Activity here began to assume a semblance of organization, but just barely. Chaos still reigned and would until the fires at last began dying down on August 7. But before that could happen, a night of hellish, seat-of-the-pants firefighting still lay ahead.

After their own arrival at the streetcar company earlier on the afternoon of August 6, Tsuchiya, Zhen, and the other Saitō Unit soldiers on-site had been immediately put to work performing three tasks simultaneously: continuing to clear Rijō Street so the Akatsuki trucks could start making it farther up into the destruction zone; fighting the fires still threatening the streetcar company position and Red Cross Hospital across the avenue; and helping to set up the sprawling aid stations being readied adjacent to the streetcar company on the campuses of Senda Elementary School and the nearby Hiroshima Engineering College and then to start bringing wounded to those locations.

Once the Saitō Unit soldiers began attempting to tend to the needs of the victims gathering in their aid stations, it was immediately apparent that the first aid gear and supplies that had been brought from Kōno'ura were completely inadequate. They had no painkillers or antibiotics, and nothing else in the way of medicine except for some antiseptics—mostly Mercurochrome and tincture of iodine. But these went quickly, given the sheer number of burn victims and, of course, the fact that none was coming across the avenue from Red Cross Hospital, whose own medical stores were also being rapidly depleted. After these meager supplies ran out, vegetable oil rationed from the nearby Ujina Army Food Depot and petroleum motor lubricants from Akatsuki's and Hiroden's stores were brushed onto the burn victims in an attempt to sooth their pain and, it was hoped, to help prevent infection (which would have been fatal in most cases, given the completely collapsed state of the city's health care system during this time of total destruction and chaos).

First aid stretchers were another item in woefully short supply. At some point, someone came up with an ingenious two-birds-with-one-stone partial solution to the predicament: Wooden planks salvaged from the ad hoc firebreak-clearing efforts around the perimeter were put to use, augmenting the purpose-built canvas-and-bamboo-pole stretchers the soldiers had brought with them because these stretchers were now completely inadequate for dealing with the unending stream of victims who had to be carried to the aid areas.

The wounded and dying were laid out on any cleared spaces on the school campuses. These soon filled up with these victims, some in such excruciating pain that they asked the soldiers to shoot them to put them out of their agony. Almost all of the victims were also desperately begging for water repeatedly, the voices of many so weak and cracking that they could manage ony a barely audible croaked whisper.

There was a belief common in Japan at the time that you were not supposed to give water—even the tiniest sip—to a severely injured/wounded person, as it would supposedly prove fatal. This belief seems likely to have had its origins in contemporary Japanese-military-combat first aid doctrine, which held that a gunshot victim should not be rehydrated, as this could accelerate blood loss and, thus, hasten death.[7] The idea possibly reached its way into awareness/acceptance among the general population via neighborhood civil defense training, or possibly just from conscripts returning to civilian life after their Army stints were finished. In any case, this mistaken belief that the restriction-of-water policy should hold true for any victim of a serious wound/injury—shrapnel- or bullet-perforated peritoneum or not—led to unnecessary additional suffering for blast, burn, and radiation victims of the atomic bombs in Hiroshima and Nagasaki, their agony compounded by the maddening thirst nearly all of them experienced as they lay dying in the final hours or days of their lives.

One of Tsuchiya's indelible memories of the afternoon and evening of August 6 was of a burn victim stretched out on the Senda Elementary School athletic grounds begging him for water "even if it kills me." This plea was so desperate and pitiful that Tsuchiya temporarily wavered from the first aid doctrine of his Army training and, looking around first to check if he was being observed, surreptitiously slipped the man a sip from his canteen. He then watched as a peaceful expression came over the agonized victim's face just before his head lolled off to the side and he drifted away.

Tsuchiya is haunted to this day by this memory, and he is still not sure that he did the right thing.

MISSION SHIFT

Senda-machi, Hiroshima City
Two kilometers south-southeast of Ground Zero
Night of August 6–7, 1945

THROUGH THE LONG first night after the bombing, Saitō Unit and other Akatsuki soldiers, able-bodied municipal first responders, and civilian volunteers joined in with hand-operated water pumps, picks, and shovels to fight pitched battles against the fires fingering their way down toward the harbor districts from the still blazing city center. Fanned by northerly and westerly winds sweeping in from the mountains ringing the city, the flames now threatened Red Cross Hospital and the Saitō Unit first aid stations and command post, all of which were teeming with victims, who were unlikely to be able to endure rapid evacuation if and when the fires arrived on-site (even if there had been enough first responders on hand to carry out such an evacuation—and there were not). This potential secondary humanitarian disaster on Rijō Street was averted by the valiant efforts of the firefighting soldiers and volunteers and, perhaps more critically and decisively, by winds that, early on the morning of the seventh, shifted with the rising of the sun to blow the flames back up toward areas they had already burned and west toward the natural firebreak of the Motoyasu River. Though the city was still smoldering on the morning of the seventh and would continue to do so for days to come, the worst of the conflagration was over. The flames would not venture this far south toward the harbor districts again.

During the day and night of high drama and terror they had just experienced, the soldiers and others engaged in firefighting, first aid, and other emergency response operations had at least been able to feel that they had had some agency in their circumstances; they could endure what they had so far by being comforted in some small degree by the sense that they had been helping others . . . that their efforts and energies had been directed toward visible, tangible exigencies that might yet be defeated, stopped, averted, fixed, pulled from the wreckage, bandaged up, washed, salved with vegetable or motor oil, and rescued. But the trials and tribulations of the city's first responders were about to enter a new stage, passing from a long twenty-four hours of chaos and desperation to a seemingly interminable week of dull horror, stomach-turning stench, sleep deprivation, and slow, soul-strangling despair. They were also about to begin fighting a foe that could not be seen and that only a handful of scientists in the entire country would even be able to detect or measure.

=====

The day after Hiroshima's near-total destruction dawned soundlessly over the athletic grounds at Senda Elementary School. There was none of the usual happy morning bustling of abundant semitropical fauna one would have expected to hear on a summer morning in this part of Japan; the city's birds and insects had been swept from the skies the day before. And there was still another day or so before plagues of crows and carrion flies would begin swooping in from the surrounding countryside to replace songs and chirps with caws and buzzing while growing fat on this brownfield of human detritus and misery.

Corporal Tsuchiya roused from a fitful catnap of an hour or two to survey the scene where he had been performing first aid throughout the night in between shifts of desperate firefighting. In this darkly meditative moment, there was only deathly quiet. His next thought upon noticing this unnatural silence was that the moaning of the victims laid out on the field had stopped, as well. Not a single one of the victims he and the other soldiers had braved flames, wreckage, and horror to rescue the day before had survived the night. He would remember the despair and sadness that he experienced upon that realization for the rest of his life. More immediately, it would set the tone for the next phase of the Saitō Unit's rescue and recovery mission. From now on, focus on "rescue" would wither in direct proportion to the steadily burgeoning urgency of the task of "recovery"—namely, the collection and disposal of corpses.

With the fires in the city center beginning to subside, the way was now cleared for the Saitō Unit to begin forays deeper into the ZTD. Tsuchiya's squad was sent on these expeditions. Working their way up Rijō Street, the soldiers pushed into desolate areas yet untouched by other first responders. The streets here, buried under still smoking rubble, were completely devoid of life and even of color, the dun browns and mauves of Ujina and Senda replaced by uniformly monochromatic vistas of charred black and ashy gray.

Traversing this moonscape, the expedition members began to encounter the remains of people who had apparently been killed instantly the previous day. These corpses lay where they had fallen, frozen in their horrific final poses and positions. Many of the victims had been trapped and subsequently completely consumed by flames within burning structures. Some had been caught in streetcars and still occupied their seats—workaday commuters transformed into blackened, shrunken lumps only barely recognizable as having once been human beings. Other streetcars had caught the full brunt of the blast at a bad angle and been flipped on their sides, the trapped passengers within jumbled and tumbled into piles that were incinerated as the cars burned down to their metal frames.

Elsewhere, victims had been crushed under toppled trees torn out by their roots, collapsed masonry walls, even large ornamental rocks of the type used in traditional Japanese gardens. Blood had exploded from every orifice of these victims' bodies, drying in brown rivulets on their faces and in puddles around the spots where they had fallen.

Attempts were made to extricate these corpses using the soldiers' excavation tools or planks from the surrounding rubble as levers, but in many cases, the fallen objects pinning them to the ground were simply too massive to be budged. The bodies were left in place for the heavy equipment to take care of once it was brought up later on the Akatsuki trucks.

Always using Rijō Street as their main axis of advance into the city and keeping this as their primary rendezvous "panic azimuth" in case they got lost, the Saitō Unit soldiers of the city center element worked out a routine in which they would break off from their squads individually or in pairs to fan out into the neighborhoods flanking the avenue to look for survivors—a mission parameter that was still actionable (though with a very rapidly closing window) on Day Two of the catastrophe. During these forays, the soldiers would occasionally stop and lower their heads close to a pile of house wreckage if they thought they had heard movement therein. If they detected a sound, they would go to work prying and digging with their pickaxes, poles, shovels, and bare, ungloved hands.

During his farthest yet probe into the ZTD, Tsuchiya stopped when he heard a high, thin female voice under a large pile of charred house timbers. He pushed away some of the wreckage around the perceived source of the sound, then put his ear close to the ground. He heard the voice again and started digging with his shovel before hitting a hollow of some kind that let out a puff of hissing, pungent, and quickly dissipated white steam. After digging a little deeper and pushing away more charred timbers, he uncovered the naked, parboiled corpse of a young woman—ostensibly the one who had been alive and crying out in pain and despair mere seconds before. With as much decorum as the circumstances and his solitary strength allowed, he gently extricated the dead woman from the wreckage pile and laid her out on the ground. Having nothing on hand with which to cover her up, he had no choice but to leave her as she was to be picked up by one of the Akatsuki trucks now working Rijō Street for body collection.

At this point in Akatsuki's mission, it was still practical for bodies recovered from the city to be trucked down Rijō Street to Ujina Wharf, then ferried by Akatsuki motor launches to Ninoshima or Kanawa-jima island in Hiroshima Bay for disposal in industrial-capacity facilities originally designed to cremate diseased Army horses and pack mules. One reason for this was bureaucratic: Regardless of the reality on the ground that Hiroshima essentially no longer existed, air defense blackout regulations were still in effect, so outdoor light sources—including, in this case, crematory burn pits—were prohibited within the bounds of the city proper.[1] A second reason was logistical: Because large areas of the ZTD still remained inaccessible to vehicles due to lingering neighborhood fires and rubble-clogged roadways, there were huge numbers of unrecovered bodies in the city center that the Akatsuki teams on the ground forces did not yet know about. When they were still picking and shoveling their way into the ZTD one block at a time, the number of corpses they encountered was still relatively manageable, from the perspective of the need to continue ferrying these to Ninoshima. The final factor was temporal/biological: Through to the end of Day Two, advanced putrefication had yet to set in for the tens of thousands of corpses left in the wake of the bombing. However, this situation would change suddenly and drastically by August 8, Day Three, when blackout regulations were finally waived and the Akatsuki teams set up around-the-clock field crematories across the ZTD.[2] For the next five days, working these sites would become the primary mission for Tsuchiya, Zhen, and their Saitō Unit comrades.

———

On the evening of August 7, after being officially tasked by Tokyo with overseeing relief and recovery efforts in Hiroshima, Lieutenant General Saeki held a conference at his Ujina headquarters.[3] There he announced that he was dividing the city into three administrative sectors. The somewhat less densely populated areas west of the Ōta Honkawa were designated the Western Sector, which was to be overseen by Lieutenant General Kaji Hidetoshi. Everything east and north of the Kyōbashi River was the Eastern Sector, encompassing Hiroshima Station, the (now obliterated) Second General Army HQ on the old Fifth Cavalry Regiment grounds, Hijiyama Hill, and the rest of the eastern edge of the city all the way down to Ujina Wharf. This sector would be overseen by Major General Sawada Yasutomi, normally in charge of education and basic training for Akatsuki Command. The third and most important jurisdiction, sandwiched between the Honkawa and the Kyōbashi, was the Central Sector, which encompassed Hiroshima Castle, the main business district, the lion's share of the ZTD and, as would soon be determined, Ground Zero for the explosion of whatever had destroyed the city. Saeki assigned his best man for command of this area: Lieutenant General Yoshimura Masayoshi, normally in charge of operational training for Akatsuki troops.

On August 8, Day Three, Yoshimura set up his Central Sector field headquarters in the Hiroshima branch of Sumitomo Bank.[4] This was located on what was known locally as *ginkō gai* or "Bankers' Row"—the stretch of Rijō Street running through the district of Kamiya-chō.[5] It was only about three hundred meters east of Ground Zero,[6] so its interior had been completely burned out by the firestorm, but its concrete shell was still structurally sound enough for the general's purposes.

The location was perfect for coordinating Akatsuki operations in central Hiroshima, but the sights and smells in the vicinity were horrific and must have been so even for a hardened veteran like Yoshimura, who had participated in the siege of Nanking during the Second Sino-Japanese War. Even relative to other areas in the ZTD, the corpse recovery situation here was particularly dire, most likely due to the high concentration of commuters and firebreak workers in the vicinity when Little Boy detonated. In an attempt to accommodate the overflow of bodies in the area, the burned-out concrete shells of the nearby Asano Library and Fukoku Insurance Company buildings had been used as temporary morgues since Day Two. However, the Akatsuki truck relay system to Ujina had not been able to keep up with demand, and now the interiors of these buildings were piled with "mountains of bodies" that were rapidly putrefying in the heat and emitting stinking black streams of human effluvia that flowed out from the buildings to pool up in Rijō Street.[7] Compounded by the citywide onset of the blowfly plague on August 8, scenes like this finally compelled the authorities to lift the blackout-regulations ban on open flames and begin setting up large-scale round-the-clock field crematories in the city center.

As these crematories required relatively rubble-free sites with good traffic access, they tended to be set up on school grounds and parks near cleared roadways, and in areas along riverbanks. These latter sites had the added advantage of being accessible to boats that could bring in fuel for the pyres while actively engaged in the herculean task of recovering the thousands of bodies clogging the city's many waterways. In Yoshimura's Central District, two of the busiest of these crematories were along the Motoyasu River. One was on the northern tip of Nakajima Island, at a spot known as Jisenji-no-hana. The other was about three hundred meters south of this site, directly across the Motoyasu from Zaimoku-chō, the neighborhood where Yoshimura's daughter—missing for two days now—had been doing firebreak work with her Ichijo classmates on the morning of August 6.[8]

Since the afternoon after the bombing, Yoshimura had been allowing his staff officers with family in the city to take shifts searching for loved ones. Historical records do not reveal whether or not he afforded himself this privilege or if he assigned any of his staff officers or clerks to see to the matter. Considering the enormity of the responsibilities of his present situation, he personally did not have time to search for his daughter in the aid stations—or growing body piles—in his district. The leadership tenet that a commander should never allow personal sentiment to interfere with his duties—and that an officer could never, under any circumstances, display feelings (other than anger or pride) in front of subordinates—was part of an ethos that would have been drilled into his psyche ever since he had been a teenage cadet at the Imperial Military Academy. Until he was relieved of his duties, he would focus on the mission at hand, overseeing: (1) the various first aid stations that had been set up in his sector; (2) the distribution of food, blankets, and other relief supplies to survivors now that Akatsuki HQ had authorized the opening of the Army Food

Depot in north Ujina and the Army Clothing Depot south of Hiji-yama Hill for this purpose; and (3) the rapid recovery and cremation—with exponentially increasing urgency—of the tens of thousands of corpses that were still strewn across the city center and steadily piling up on the banks of the Ōta, Motoyasu, and Kyōbashi Rivers after being pulled out of the water by Akatsuki soldiers and civilian volunteers.

YOSHIJIMA

Yoshijima District, Hiroshima City
3.7 kilometers south of Ground Zero

THE INDUSTRIAL DISTRICT of Yoshijima occupies a long spit of landfill between the Ōta Honkawa and Motoyasu River that has been steadily extended out into Hiroshima Bay since the 1930s.[1] In 1945, it still lacked streetcar service, and was home to not much more than a couple of paper mills, Hiroshima Prison, an unfinished airstrip, and Kurashiki Aircraft Corporation.[2]

In the wake of the explosion, evacuees had at first trickled—then poured—into this peninsular cul-de-sac. The situation there unfolded similarly to Ujina's, with panicked crowds fleeing the ZTD toward the presumed sanctuary of points south, and more than a few ending up in the water en route when their burns became unendurable or when they lost what was left of their minds. Many had also been rained on by the mysterious brownish black precipitation that had been intermittently falling across the western half of the city since shortly after the explosion. Burn victims in particular, lacking any other water with which to slake their maddening thirst, had been lapping at this precipitation with their tongues, either as falling raindrops or puddles on the ground.

By the time the crew members of the *Enola Gay* were touching down to a heroes' welcome in Tinian, Yoshijima (and just about everywhere else around the periphery of the still burning city) was teeming with the dead and dying. The circumstances would soon necessitate on-the-fly development of a systematized routine for the registration, and eventually the disposal, of the utterly unprecedented volume of human corpses. But the dead would have to wait for the full mobilization of Akatsuki Command's response for that to begin in earnest.

A rudimentary aid station was set up in one of the surviving factory structures on Yoshijima within hours of Lieutenant General Saeki's first general rescue and recovery mobilization order.[3] When the first detachment of Akatsuki soldiers arrived on the site in their landing craft and motorboats in the early afternoon of August 6, they quickly enlisted every civilian they encountered to help get their relief operations up and running. In this regard, the employees and mobilized student workers at Kurashiki Aircraft factory presented a made-to-order labor pool on this otherwise rather sparsely populated patch of reclaimed land, and those deemed fit for duty were put to work immediately, no questions answered, no excuses accepted.

══════

Chai's injuries were insufficient to exempt him from the Akatsuki NCOs' ad hoc corvée of Kurashiki's walking wounded. After his cuts and lacerations were bandaged up, he was corralled along with everyone else into helping the soldiers with their work, tending to the wounded and dying once the aid station was set up.[4] As the day wore on, their duties included laying the rapidly increasing numbers of corpses from the aid station outside in neat rows, at a respectful remove from those victims still drawing breath, until orders came down regarding what to start doing with them.

Sheltered inside the aid station from the intermittent black rain squalls, Chai received seat-of-the-pants on-the-job training on applying Mercurochrome and tincture of zinc to the lacerated bodies of the blast victims. Many of these patients, in addition to suffering from the concussion trauma of Little Boy's shock wave, were also honeycombed with dozens or even hundreds of puncture wounds from flying concrete bits, wood splinters, and, most destructive of all, glass shards from shattered windows. Chai also learned how to apply machine lubricant oil—the only ostensibly emollient substance then at hand—from the Kurashiki shop floor to the horrific wounds of the burn victims, who seemed to be the majority of the cases arriving at the aid station and in more intense agony than the people who had suffered only blast injuries.[5]

From the earliest aftermath stages of the explosion, aid givers and other first reponders noticed that there seemed to be two main varieties of burn injury. One was a first-aid-textbook variety exhibiting the blistering or charring that one would have expected when human flesh came into direct physical contact with burning material—in this case wood and other building materials or the victims' own clothing or hair.[6]

People suffering from the second category of burn injury, however, looked less like they had actually come into contact with something physically aflame and more like they had been seared by unnaturally intense sunlight. In many of these cases, the patterns of these flash burns indicated in which direction the patients had been facing relative to the explosion, or if they had been partially shielded by a wall or tree trunk or windowsill, etc., at the instant that they had been exposed to the bomb. Any part of the body that had been facing away from the bomb—or that was in the shadow of any physical object more substantial than cotton fabric—would be injury-free, while any top layers of epidermis that had caught the full unobstructed brunt of the flash were, in the worst cases, charred. The flesh of others was blistered, peeling, and hanging off their bodies like the skin of a blanched tomato, revealing salmon pink layers of freshly exposed, raw dermis underneath that first responders and other caregivers quickly learned was hypersensitive to sunlight and heat.[7] This exposed skin was also hypersensitive to any kind of tactile contact—a symptom that became particularly salient in coming days with the arrival of the blowfly plague that would descend on the destroyed city.

Likewise, the outlines and compositions of garments could also leave their marks—or perhaps, more accurately, their shadows—on the bodies of their wearers. The lines where collars, rolled-up shirt-sleeves, shirt cuffs, trouser cuffs, and thong straps of wooden sandals stopped and bare skin began were all distinct.[8] This was especially the case when shirts or blouses were made of white or other light-colored fabrics.[9] Darker clothes—such as garments cut from the dun brown khaki omnipresent on soldier and civilian alike in wartime Japan and, worst of all, anything black (including the hair on victims' heads, as was the usual case)—seemed to afford the skin of their wearers no protection whatsover. Heat energy emitted by the bomb had been absorbed by dark-colored fabric—particularly cotton—to assault the flesh of the wearer underneath just as readily as if these victims had been naked. In the most severe of these types of cases, this heat seemed to have gone all the way through skin and deep into limbs to reach tendons, muscles, and connective tissue. Injuries of this latter nature were sometimes not apparent until a rescuer or orderly tried to lift up a patient or a corpse by the wrists or ankles and came away instead clutching a clump of meat and sinews that had come off in their hands like barbecued spare ribs falling off the bone.[10]

Attending to the needs of the most severely burned survivors dominated the attention and efforts of the aid stations around the city during the first twenty-four to forty-eight hours after the bombing. But with the first wave of mass mortality for the worst cases trickling off toward the end of this period, still exhausted but now relatively less harried health caregivers began noticing a third and, to this point, largely overlooked and unclassified category of patients: These individuals—some of whom were not even visibly burned or lacerated—began manifesting symptoms of acute and gradually worsening malaise, nausea, diarrhea, hair loss, and strange purplish skin mottling.[11] Later, when time and facilities made testing practicable, disastrously crashing white-blood-cell count was added to the list of symptoms of this mysterious ailment.[12]

In Yoshijima, these patients were comforted and cleaned up after to the extent that this was possible.[13] But with the first responders not knowing what to look for or what they were looking at when they encountered this symptom, there was not much they and, in coming days, specialist field hospital orderlies could do for those afflicted with this mystery disease, most of whom would be dead within two weeks or so.[14] In the immediate aftermath of the explosion, the treatment options for medical first responders were greatly hindered not only by the dire lack of drugs and other essential medical supplies, but also by this lack of knowledge regarding what they were dealing with, particularly in the case of the wasting-away patients.[15] Until nuclear physicists and medical specialists flew down from Tokyo on August 8 (landing at the Yoshijima airstrip)[16] to survey the damage and report their scientific findings back to Imperial General Headquarters, no one with boots on the ground in Hiroshima (with the possible exception of the now severely irradiated Professor Mimura) had any firm idea of what had just laid waste to the city. All anyone who had been in Hiroshima on the morning of August 6 knew with absolute first-hand certainty was that, whatever it was, it had generated a blast shock wave and heat of such force and intensity that, in the blink of an eye, it had flattened entire square kilometers of the downtown area, simultaneously ignited the wreckage of the same, and incinerated every exposed molecule of organic matter it touched, including the flesh of tens of thousands of people.

It had been common practice since the beginning of regular B-29 raids on the Home Islands in late 1944 for workplaces and households with radios to keep these on essentially around the clock. This was particularly true at night—when the enemy bombers usually came, if they were coming—to listen for the latest air-defense-related announcements. In the immediate wake of the atomic bombing, there were not many functioning radios left in Hiroshima, but the Akatsuki aid station on Yoshijima had one of them; it was hooked up to the same gasoline-operated field generator that powered the lights at night. In Chai's recollection, this was kept on primarily to follow broadcasts about enemy aircraft sightings from NHK stations in outlying prefectures, whose reports were more regular and reliable than anything coming through the local military radio grid at the moment.

It was through this radio, a few days after the bombing, that Chai and his classmates first heard official mention that a new-type bomb of unknown composition had been dropped on Hiroshima. Listeners were warned not to drink or ingest any water or foodstuffs that had been exposed to the elements at the time of the explosion, as they were contaminated with some kind of "poison gas" dispersed by the weapon's massive detonation. Accordingly, Akatsuki Command HQ kept the aid station on Yoshijima—as well as its other aid stations around the city—supplied with uncontaminated rice balls and water from the Army Food Depot.

EXPLAINING THE IMPOSSIBLE

Yoshijima District, Hiroshima City
3.7 kilometers south of Ground Zero

AS THE INITIAL terror and disbelief of the first twenty-four hours after the bombing transitioned to a longer haul of dull, exhausted shock amid the ruins, survivors without access to radios or newspapers began groping for some explanation for what had just happened to their world. Lacking reliable concrete information during this period of chaos in the aftermath of the disaster, these "explanations" often took the form of conspiracy theories and wild rumors that ran rampant.

This kind of storytelling often rushes in to fill the "vacuum of meaning" that results when a community's normally robust culturally and socially provided worldviews are suddenly rendered dysfunctional by unprecedented catastrophe.[1] In shattered communities across Hiroshima, the sharing of these stories might have been a grip-on-reality lifeboat for survivors providing comforting illusions of agency over personal circumstances that were in fact threatening to spiral out of control at any moment.[2]

In terms of this grip-on-reality lifeboat function, even outlandish narratives were preferable to none at all. For example, perhaps eager to deny that a loathed foe was in possession of the power to flatten a city in an instant, many survivors clung to the idea that the cataclysm was instead the result of some terrible but perfectly explainable accident. The possibility that the Hiroshima Gas Company works in Minami-machi (on the eastern bank of the Kyōbashi, near the Miyuki Bridge) had blown up was widely discussed among survivors, as were suspicions that it had been one of the big chemical plants in the waterfront district—as the Saitō Unit's executive officer, Major Tomita, in Kōno'ura had immediately suspected upon hearing the explosion across Hiroshima Bay.[3] An alternate narrative involving ammunition dumps at the Army Ordnance Depot southeast of Hijiyama Hill also gained early traction. This latter theory might have been particularly persuasive because of a tremendous accidental powder magazine detonation that had sunk the battleship *Mutsu* in Lower Hiroshima Bay two years earlier; the explosion was heard throughout the entire region and would have still been fresh in the memories of many in the city.[4]

For other survivors on the ground in Hiroshima, the glaringly obvious likelihood that the enemy had an active hand in the destruction just visited on the city also spawned its own theories. One held that the explosion had been caused by some new type of American incendiary bomb using magnesium—which would explain the frequently reported purple-tinged white color and the intensity of the flash. This particular speculation, however, was somewhat less convincing in accounting for the intensity of the bomb's shock wave. One of the more inventive theories—which took into account the mysterious greasy brown-black rain that had started falling shortly after the explosion—was that a cloud of aerosolized fuel oil had been sprayed over the city by the first B-29 that had flown over the area at seven thirty; then that cloud had somehow been ignited by the two B-29s that had flown over forty-five minutes later—perhaps by some kind of radio-controlled device in the parachutes seen over the city shortly before the explosion.[5]

Simply finding the will to get back on one's feet, to be up and moving again with some semblance of normalcy, was another characteristic of this early period of urgent psychological recovery work. Keeping busy—caring for others, cleaning up, foraging for food and water—helped traumatized survivors not to dwell too much on the otherwise unbearably dark philosophical implications of the catastrophe, at least for the time being. Most seemed to have instinctively sensed that temporary grief and shock could not be allowed to metastasize into more permanent despair. Almost all hibakushas, at some point, had to endure this struggle before they were able to get on with the rest of their lives. Not all succeeded.

Every one of the survivors who have made it to the twenty-first century—who are still alive in their nineties—have done so because they came up with a way to compartmentalize and process their fear, anger, sense of helplessness, and despair as hibakusha that was not self-destructive. But as with the experience of frontline combat veterans, no one escaped psychologically unscathed or without emotional scars. For some, seven decades later, this struggle is ongoing, with their old vacuum of meaning never vanquished but just an intermittently dormant inner demon. This demon can return to descend on them like a shroud of blackout cloth without a moment's notice—for example, when visiting a doctor for some health issue and dreading being told that it is bomb related. Even stimuli as seemingly innocuous as the faint smell of singed hair from the open door of a beauty salon or the odor of smoke from fire-roasted meat at a street festival food stall can summon PTSD symptoms.

In the immediate aftermath of the bombing, exactly when and how intensely each hibakusha experienced the first inklings of this kind of philosophical crisis seem to have differed widely by individual. Apparently, for most, the first onset of something like this appeared once the most urgently pressing concerns of personal day-to-day survival began to level off, leaving more downtime for reflection and introspection. For many survivors, their emergence from conditions of immediate peril (recovering from injuries, avoiding starvation, etc.) and the beginning of longer-term grief work (meaningful life rebuilding) coincided roughly with the psychological aftershock that they received upon hearing the news of Japan's surrender.

In memoirs written many years after the war, Father Hugo

Lassalle—a German Jesuit who experienced the bombing in the Catholic vicarage at Nobori-chō, 1.2 kilometers from Ground Zero—recalled scenes of his Hiroshima neighbors and parishioners experiencing something like an existential crisis as they gathered around radios to listen to Emperor Hirohito's surrender announcement at noon on August 15. "People were weeping when Japan's surrender to the enemy was announced," Lassalle wrote. "I was shocked to see people who had witnessed the terrible destruction of the atomic bomb nevertheless weeping upon hearing that the war had ended." He continued:

> Up to that point, their lives had been based upon a belief in the inviolable honor of their ancestral homeland, centered on an Emperor who stood over it all like a towering edifice. Of course, even before the atomic bombing, most of them had realized that the war was not going well, and that there was little chance left of winning it. Moreover, many realized that even if the war ended in an armistice, Japan would have to accept that it would never be the same country it was at the beginning of the war. Still, it appeared to me that the survivors experienced the announcement of the end of the war as if they were watching the towering edifice of the former Japan stomped flat into the ground, reacting to it as a shock at least as traumatic as—if not more traumatic than—the atomic bombing itself. People who had not been driven to tears by the bombing wept upon hearing the surrender announcement.[6]

The phenomenon Lassalle witnessed here was one experienced not only by survivors in the atom-bombed cities (although it was arguably worse for them), but by Japanese everywhere in the Home Islands and throughout the empire. The surrender broadcast impacted many of the emperor's erstwhile unquestioningly loyal subjects with the psychological violence of the sudden death of a loved one. The vacuum of meaning this traumatic event created in the lives of tens of millions of Japanese provided fertile ground for proselytizing opportunists of various theological and ideological stripes, both native and foreign, fishing for converts and followers during the postwar period.

More immediately, while the dust was still settling over Hiroshima, the authorities in Tokyo had to figure out how to break the news about the fate of the city to the rest of the nation in a way that would not sap the people's will to continue fighting and supporting the war effort. Ever since the 1930s, both civilian and military authorities had been keenly conscious of the importance of media control for news-cycle-narrative management. This was put to effective use in fanning and maintaining public enthusiasm for wars first in Manchuria (1931–1932) and China (1937–1945), then from 1941 against the Western powers in Southeast Asia and the Pacific. The keystone in this media-control apparatus was a news industry brought completely to heel to serve as an unquestioning mouthpiece blaring 24/7 support for state military policy. This was accomplished through: (1) appeals to corporate interest (e.g., uncooperative journalists and editors would be cut out of the government information loop); (2) a series of spectacular assassinations of important public figures (including media industry leaders) at the hands of militarist/ultranationalist fanatics in the early and mid-1930s; and (3) the sheer burgeoning momentum of sincere patriotic enthusiasm.[7]

This last element—the patriotism-on-steroids brain fever that Father Lassalle described watching disintegrate among his Hiroshima neighbors and parishioners—was by no means an exclusive characteristic of the Japanese people in the global zeitgeist of the 1930s and 1940s. During that dark period in the twentieth century, the addled acolytes of totalitarian ideologies fetishizing militarism and conquest had boldly and even joyfully marched in lockstep toward mass catastrophe in many other countries, as well. But it is not unreasonable to posit that this ideological dynamic came together in a perfect storm in Japan's case, even relative to the fanaticism of its erstwhile fascist allies elsewhere. Japan's particular brand of militaristic ideology was sustained by and among a populace deeply steeped over several generations in a morbid ethos that glorified the concept of death for emperor and nation. This, in turn, was underpinned and sanctified by ultranationalism, the post-Meiji belief system extolling the inviolability and divine nature of the nation, manifested in the person of the emperor and his ostensible blood connection with each and every one of his subjects, no matter how lowly of birth. And the Japanese news media had been utterly complicit in stoking the fires under all of this and keeping it at a boil from the early 1930s until right up to the last days and hours of the war.

The state's grip on the news media had been essentially perfected with the creation of the Dōmei News Agency in January 1936.[8] This was an officially sanctioned corporate monopoly for news coverage that served as a choke point controlling what and how much information about national policy and world affairs—and later about the progress of the war—reached the Japanese public. The engine at the heart of this system was a reciprocal arrangement by which exclusive daily "scoops" were spoon-fed by Home Ministry officials and military public affairs officers to Dōmei-dominated "reporter clubs," who then, in turn, wrote up this information in ways that would keep these authorities happy, therein ensuring that these journalists were kept in the loop for the next news cycle and so on. As long as this system functioned, the state got its desired messages out with near-perfect signal fidelity. The populace was largely shielded from "alternative facts" coming in from overseas sources (including rare servicemen surviving to return from combat theaters), and popular morale regarding the war could be sustained and controlled.

Understandably, the emperor's-new-clothes shell game of the daily news cycle constantly reassuring the public that Japan was still winning the war became more challenging to maintain once American bombers began flying overhead every night. Nevertheless, perhaps due in equal measure to the efficiency of this news-media-maintained information bubble and to the simple but powerful imperatives of mass psychology in times of communal stress, Japanese public morale regarding the war and the necessity of pursuing it to the bitter end remained surprisingly resilient, right up to Emperor Hirohito's surrender broadcast.[9]

One increasingly troublesome source of leaks in this otherwise essentially airtight control over news, however, was the medium of radio. This was not so much an issue during the first few years of the war, when the nearest Allied-occupied territory was still thousands of kilometers away. During this Japanese-information-bubble grace period, the only radios in the Japanese Home Islands that could pick up foreign broadcasts—including Japanese-language American propaganda content—were shortwave sets whose owners were registered with and closely monitored by the police and the hypervigilant civilian-snitch networks that acted as their eyes and ears on the ground in local communities. With the fall of Saipan in June 1944, however, the Americans on the island began to beam Japanese-language broadcasts directly at the Home Islands, where anyone who owned a normal commercial-bandwidth radio could listen in if they were willing to risk fine and/or imprisonment to do so. When Okinawa fell to the Americans in June 1945, the signal got only stronger and clearer.[10]

Japanese authorities attempted various countermeasures to prevent civilians from listening to these broadcasts, including not only the aforementioned threat of criminal prosecution, but also radio-signal jamming. To cover the Hiroshima region, a signal-jamming facility had been established on the grounds of a school in Kannon-machi, a neighborhood in the western part of the city (about 1.9 kilometers southwest of Ground Zero).[11] As this campus was completely destroyed by Little Boy's explosion and firestorm, it can be assumed that this jamming facility was also destroyed. In this case, anyone in Hiroshima who still had a functioning radio should, in theory, have been able to hear Japanese-language versions of the US White House's official statement on the destruction of the city that was issued to the world some sixteen hours after Little Boy's detonation, and that constituted history's first public acknowledgment that the weapon was an "atomic bomb."

Nevertheless, any audience in Hiroshima for such a broadcast on the night of August 6–7 appears to have been exceedingly small. Of sixty-five mentions of people listening to radios in the official Hiroshima municipal history of the bombing, there is only a single mention of anyone in the city hearing the White House announcement (followed by a Japanese-language explanation of what had just been said) in real time—an Akatsuki Command HQ soldier manning a shortwave set on his night watch radio monitoring shift who just happened upon the broadcast while scanning the airwaves with the tuning dial to pass the time.[12]

Outside of a handful of other military radio contexts, all the other sixty-four mentions of radios in this official history are about people in the city listening to NHK broadcasts as part of their daily (and nightly) routine of air-raid-alert preparedness up until the early morning of August 6, or they are of survivors listening to the emperor's surrender broadcast—typically in some institutional setting, such as a hospital ward, church facility, or military headquarters day room. This would seem to indicate that very, very few people in the devastated city—other than the aforementioned Akatsuki soldier—heard any radio broadcast mention of the term "atomic bomb" before the end of the war. The majority of privately owned radios in wooden houses would have been destroyed by Little Boy's explosion—by blast effect, by the electromagnetic pulse emitted by its fissioning uranium, or by the subsequent firestorm; this probably also accounts for the paucity of radio listening among Hiroshima civilians during the August 6–14 time span, even once electrical power was restored to most of the city mere days after the bombing.

Newspapers—which did not begin reaching Hiroshima in substantial volume until several days after the bombing—provided little information about what had happened in the city and what might have caused it. Thanks to a telegram from a reporter near Hiroshima who had managed to get a wire to its Tokyo headquarters, Dōmei News Agency had some concrete idea of the scale of the mass destruction in the city probably at around the same time as Imperial General Headquarters did—that is, within a few hours of the event.[13] But the authorities immediately made it clear to the media organs that, until instructed otherwise, news about Hiroshima was to be left as vague as possible. On the afternoon of August 6, editors from Dōmei and the nation's major daily newspapers were summoned to the office of the Information and Intelligence Agency—the branch of the Home

Ministry in charge of media censorship. There they were told in no uncertain terms to essentially sit on the story of Hiroshima's destruction on the ostensibly professional-ethics pretext that "the information about what had happened in Hiroshima was inadequate" (at that point this was, admittedly, true), and therefore "they should bury the news of the bombing in some obscure place, so that it seemed like an ordinary air raid."[14] Accordingly, the next day, the major national daily *Asahi Shimbun* carried a small notice, mixed in with news about conventional B-29 raids around the country, about a "small flight of aircraft" dropping "incendiary devices" on Hiroshima and causing "moderate damage."[15]

Around the time that the *Asahi* morning editions were hitting the presses on August 7, a more explicit report from the field arrived in Tokyo: The entire city of Hiroshima had been completely obliterated by a single bomb.[16] Perhaps realizing the futility of trying to keep a lid on such momentous news, IGHQ changed course on their media policy on the event. Taking the lead on breaking the story in the following days, they flipped the narrative to an atrocity angle—framing the Americans' willingness to cause such wholesale and indiscriminate destruction as all the more reason for the nation to continue fighting.[17] But even in these newer, "realistic" official accounts of what had happened in Hiroshima—which included acknowledgments that tens of thousands of civilians had been killed—the technological agent of that destruction was never referred to with any more specificity than the "new-type-bomb" phrase already being used in radio news broadcasts and public service announcements. Even though cabinet-level military and civilian decision-makers in Tokyo already knew with certainty by at least August 10 that an atomic weapon had destroyed Hiroshima, the Japanese public—including tens of thousands of survivors in Hiroshima and Nagasaki—would not hear the new-type bomb referred to as atomic through official media channels until the day after the emperor's surrender broadcast, in which Hirohito referred to the Hiroshima and Nagasaki devices as "a new and most cruel bomb" (*arata ni zangyaku naru bakudan*).[18]

Shortly after the bombing of Hiroshima, the Americans decided to augment their broadcasts out of Saipan and Okinawa to take their atomic "Resistance is futile" message more directly to the Japanese people and in a way that could not be signal-jammed or censored. Echoing President Truman's Potsdam Conference threat of "prompt and utter destruction" for Japan if it were to continue fighting, B-29s of the Twentieth Air Force began dropping leaflets containing the following text (in Japanese) over "47 Japanese cities with population of over 100,000," which "represented more than 40% of the total population" of the country:[19]

TO THE JAPANESE PEOPLE

America asks that you take immediate heed of what we say on this leaflet.

We are in possession of the most destructive explosive ever devised by man. A single one of our newly developed atomic bombs is actually the equivalent in explosive power to what 2000 of our giant B-29s can carry on a single mission. This awful fact is one for you to ponder and we solemnly assure you it is grimly accurate.

We have just begun to use this weapon against your homeland. If you still have any doubt, make inquiry as to what happened to Hiroshima when just one atomic bomb fell on that city.

Before using this bomb to destroy every resource of the military by which they are prolonging this useless war, we ask that you now petition the Emperor to end the war. Our president has outlined for you the thirteen consequences of an honorable surrender. We urge that you accept these consequences and begin the work of building a new, better and peace-loving Japan.

You should take steps now to cease military resistance. Otherwise, we shall resolutely employ this bomb and all our other superior weapons to promptly and forcefully end the war.[20]

Eventually, some six million of these leaflets—which also featured a photo of the Hiroshima mushroom cloud taken by a Little Boy strike force crew member—were dropped on Japan.[21] On the evening of August 9, three B-29s dropped an estimated twenty thousand of these leaflets on outlying areas of Hiroshima.[22] Some leaflets, reportedly, were even dropped on the ruins of Nagasaki, which were still burning from Fat Man's explosion over the city earlier that morning.[23]

THE BURN PITS

$$\overline{}$$

Ōte-machi District, Hiroshima
August 8

BY AUGUST 8, Day Three of the bombing aftermath, Corporals Tsuchiya and Zhen and their Saitō Unit comrades had worked their way deep into the ZTD up the left/east bank of the Motoyasu River. From this day forward, their primary mission shifted from searching for and attending to survivors (there were aid stations and field hospitals for that all over the city now) to body recovery and disposal. For the duration of this final phase of the Saitō Unit's mission, Zhen's squad was assigned to duties at field crematories on Jisenji-no-hana, and also by the foot of a partially collapsed bridge in nearby Ōte-machi. Tsuchiya and his squad mates rotated back and forth between burn-pit work at those sites and retrieving bodies floating in this stretch of the Motoyasu.

Except when extreme-weather events produce abnormally heavy rainfall, the currents of the Ōta Delta waterways are not very vigorous by the time they reach central/downtown Hiroshima on their way to the bay. Moreover, this close to the Seto Inland Sea (and thus the Pacific Ocean), these waterways become brackish estuaries that are subject to twice-daily tidal fluctuations in which the direction of their current is reversed. This specific topographical characteristic of the delta directly impacted the Akatsuki Command's body-retrieval mission because it meant that most of the thousands—perhaps tens of thousands—of corpses floating in the city's waterways in the aftermath of the bombing never made it all the way to the bay, where time and tide would have seen to their natural return to the elements; instead, the bodies became trapped in the delta's up-down tidal seesaw, floating down toward the bay at low tide, then back toward the city at high tide, all the time steadily putrefying in the sweltering summer temperatures. This produced an increasingly noxious miasma hanging over center of the city that the authorities quickly realized posed a major hygiene risk, and the retrieval of these floating bodies became a high priority.

Although Akatsuki boat crews had been out on the water engaged in this task since the first afternoon after the bombing, their capacity was nowhere near being up to the task at hand. When the decision was reached on August 8 to commence mass round-the-clock cremation operations across the city, retrieval crews like Tsuchiya's squad jumped in to help take up the slack, working the water's edge on foot and armed with poles and grappling hooks for snaring floating bodies.

In Tsuchiya's recollection, this job was as physically arduous as it was grisly. While performing it, he spent most of his time waist-deep—and occasionally chest-deep or even neck-deep—in the Motoyasu, out among the bobbing corpses. Almost all these waterlogged bodies were scorched red-brown and naked, with their facial features so thoroughly destroyed that it was impossible to tell at a glance whether they belonged to adults or children, males or females. The ability to make such distinctions had no direct bearing on the performance of Tsuchiya's mission parameters of grabbing the corpses with his pole and hauling them to shore, and the more mechanically and unfeelingly he could do this, the more efficiently his work could proceed. Still, no matter how determined he was not to do so, it was impossible not to occasionally wonder about—and experience stabs of empathy for—the human beings these tattered lumps had been when they jumped into the city's rivers to escape the agony of their burns. Tsuchiya and his squad mates eventually managed to lift the veil of anonymity cloaking the bodies at least partially when they learned that they could distinguish the gender of a corpse by the manner in which it floated: males inevitably facedown and females faceup.

"We guessed it had something to do with the difference in body cavity distribution," Tsuchiya explains during our interview seventy-three years later, performing a quick series of hand gestures to illustrate the anatomical details—downward thrusts with parallel-karate-chop hands over his lower belly, then circular motions over his chest. "Women have wombs, and men have bigger lungs. We figured that was the main difference."

Once the bodies were towed to shore, Corporal Tsuchiya and his squad mates had to haul them up onto the stone wall embankments that lined both sides of the river. There the corpses were arranged in rows for stretcher-bearers to ferry to the burn pits. These quays also became viewing galleries for family members who had come into the ZTD looking for loved ones. As this stretch of the Motoyasu had been teeming with junior high school students clearing firebreaks to protect the prefectural office on the morning of the explosion, many of these desperate family members were parents trying to identify these now missing children by facial features, personal items, or civil defense identification tags sewn on whatever scraps of clothing remained on their bodies. Throughout the day, this somber scene's ambient sounds of lapping river water, swarming blowflies, and crackling pyre flames would be pierced by the sudden wail of a mother or the sobbed masculine scream of a father who had just found their child in the corpse heaps.

Since the enactment of the National Air Defense Law of 1937, all Japanese civilians were, by regulation, supposed to have cloth personal identification tags sewn onto their clothing and portable belongings so that their bodies could be identified and returned to their next of kin, if possible, after air raids. Information written on the name tags included name, address, blood type (for transfusions in a first aid situation), and, if applicable, the school or other organization to which the individual belonged. Under the system as originally envisaged, it was expected that police and *Keibōdan* officers would suffice, in terms of manpower, to recover bodies in a bombed area, line them up in rows in some open public space like a park or schoolyard, and then record the personal information on the identification tags while waiting for surviving family members to show up and claim the bodies of their loved ones and see to funerary arrangements privately.

However, Hiroshima—like the hundred thousand people killed in a single night in Tokyo five months earlier—presented authorities with a mass-casualty situation on a scale no one crafting the Air Defense Law could have imagined in 1937. Moreover, the condition of many of the dead—particularly in the ZTD—made them impossible to identify because any clothing they had been wearing had been either blown off their bodies by Little Boy's shock wave or incinerated in the subsequent fires. Accordingly, when Akatsuki Command took over rescue and recovery operations for the shattered city, it had to come up with an ad hoc field crematory operating routine to deal with this unprecedented situation.

In a typical Hiroshima field crematory, such as the Ōte-machi and Jisenji-no-hana sites worked by Tsuchiya and Zhen, a routine was rapidly established under which bodies collected from the surrounding area would be stretchered in, then lined up by the burn pit. When standard-issue canvas stretchers were not available for carrying the corpses, rubble-scrounged sheets of corrugated metal and the like would be used as pallets for the purpose. When nothing like this was at hand, the soldiers would strip down to their waists and fireman-carry the corpses to the burn pit, the idea being that it would be easier to rinse the inevitable reeking effluvia resulting from this work off one's bare skin than out of one's uniform tunic (or calisthenics T-shirt, as the case might have been).

After being carried to the pit, the bodies would be given a final going over by clerks (soldiers if it was an Army crematory; *Keibōdan* or police officers in the case of a civilian crematory) for any means of identification, usually through the standard civil defense ID tags on clothing, but occasionally through wallet contents, school items, etc. When such information was found, it was recorded on manifest sheets by the clerks. Unidentifiable bodies—which were the vast majority—

were logged as John Does / Jane Does. After the ID'ing process, the bodies—as many per batch as possible—would be placed on top of a wooden pyre framework with a Jenga-like structure of interlocked scrap wood either salvaged from the river (all of the wood and other organic material on dry land anywhere near Ground Zero having been incinerated by the thermal flash and firestorm) or brought in by Akatsuki trucks or boats. Then the pyre and the bodies would be doused with diesel oil and set alight.

In the fairly uncommon case of on-site identification of a corpse at the burn pit by next of kin, these bereaved family members would be allowed the option of taking responsibility for the bodies of their loved ones. If they had the means and ability to do so, they would carry them away for private funerary arrangements. However, when this was not feasible, the crematory burn pit would be the site of the family members' final farewell to the deceased.

For Zhen Su Bing, one of the most searing memories of the five days he spent on the Ōte-machi field crematory crews was when a panicking woman showed up at the site, froze in front of a pile of dead junior high school girls just about to be placed into the burn pit, and began screaming, "That's my daughter!" As Zhen remembers of the moment, he imagined his own mother coming across the body of one of his sisters in a burn-pit pile. It was one of the few scenes he witnessed during his week of hell in Hiroshima that he allowed to move him to tears, and even now, he cannot recall the scene without shedding them anew.[1]

In the aftermath of the bombing, human bodies were not the only rapidly putrefying remains of which the Akatsuki Command was now responsible for cremating. As the Allied air and naval blockade, particularly in the last year or year and a half of the war, had cut Japan off from its vital overseas petroleum sources, the country had become increasingly reliant on horsepower—literally—to take up the transportation slack left by Japan's now largely idle civilian truck fleet. Hiroshima was no exception to this, and the daily logistical needs of the city's economy relied on large numbers of horse-drawn vehicles. The center of the city had been filled with these vehicles on the morning of August 6.

Among the many memories of Hiroshima that haunt Tsuchiya-san to this day, some of the worst are of the times he and his squad mates had to dispose of dead horses. At first, they attempted to cremate these animals, but their sheer bulk and weight—which could have been the equivalent of anywhere from five to eight adult human males (assuming an average wartime weight of about fifty to sixty kilograms)—soon proved insurmountable obstacles in this respect. Because of their huge mass, a commensurately large amount of fuel and burn-pit time would have to be expended if they were to be thoroughly/properly cremated. Moreover, this same problem of excessive mass meant that moving them from their point of discovery to the nearest field crematory burn pit by manpower alone was in almost all cases nearly impossible. Once this was realized, Corporal Tsuchiya and his squad mates began burying the horses where they were found.

Burying even a single horse involved an inordinate amount of time and effort. First, a minimum of two or three soldiers would have to dig a hole of sufficient depth as close as possible to the horse. Then, using their tools, poles, lengths of pipe, or other substitutes at hand as levers, they would push the horses over into their "graves." The work would have been hard enough for well-rested teams, but by Day Two or Day Three, the soldiers were already near to the point of dropping where they stood because of exhaustion and lack of sleep (and, later, the onset of low-grade to moderate radiation sickness).

This task became exponentially more arduous and grisly with time and the farther the Saitō Unit pushed into the ZTD. As full-blown putrefication set in, these three-hundred-to-four-hundred-kilogram lumps of scorched and now rotting animal matter emitted odors so stomach wrenching and hosted clouds of blowflies so thick that the soldiers—even with wet towels tied over their noses and mouths—could only work at the task for perhaps ten or twenty seconds before being overwhelmed with nausea. In the case of Corporal Tsuchiya's squad, there were not enough towels to go around, so they worked out a rotation routine; upon the command of the senior NCO or officer on-site, the team that had been working would hand their tools and towels off to their replacements before inevitably running off some distance to retch and returning a minute or so later to tie the towels back on and resume digging or pushing.

The Akatsuki soldiers who were sent into the city after the bombing were completely lacking anything in the way of what would today be called PPE (personal protection equipment). This was particularly true of the Saitō Unit soldiers from Kōno'ura, many of whom—like Tsuchiya and his squad mates—had still been in their PT kit when they landed at Ujina Wharf on August 6. For those assigned to corpse recovery/disposal duties—which after August 8, Day Three, was almost everyone—this meant each one of them having to manhandle dozens or even hundreds of corpses a day with ungloved hands and getting covered head to toe in putrefied bodily fluids of every variety. Beyond the psychological and physical fatigue involved in doing work like this day in, day out for nearly a week with almost no sleep, their contact with this huge volume of decomposing bodies also exposed the soldiers to numerous biohazards. And what neither these soldiers nor their doctors and medics knew during the course of the Akatsuki's mission was that these bodies were radioactive, either through Little Boy's initial gamma-ray-and-neutron burst or through the residual radiation that had formed around the bomb's fireball and then floated down over the Hiroshima area as fallout. The dusty air they were breathing and any rain or sitting water they came into contact with in the ZTD were also highly radioactive, particularly in the first few days of their mission. By the time the Saitō Unit was rotated back to Kōno'ura on August 13 to resume their *Marure* training in preparation for the Allied invasion, Tsuchiya, Zhen, and almost everyone else was suffering from classic symptoms of mild to moderate radiation sickness, including vomiting, bleeding gums, diarrhea, and epilation (hair loss).

During the course of his work at the Ōte-machi burn pit, Corporal Zhen and his squad mates began to develop severe rashes on their hands and forearms. When they finally had a chance to get looked at by proper Army doctors back on Kōno'ura, they were rubbed down with some kind of lotion and told that they were suffering from pto-maine poisoning of the skin and that they would recover. He never heard anyone in authority—medical or otherwise—ever mention anything about radioactivity during the remainder of his time in uniform. Although his hands and arms eventually cleared up, he was plagued for years afterward with various other ailments—throat problems, in particular—which he is convinced were radiation induced.

GOING HOME

ZHEN SU BING was repatriated to Taiwan in 1946, during that island's brief historical window as a province of a Mainland China still ruled by Chiang Kai-shek's Kuomintang. After attending university to train as an elementary-school teacher, he pursued this occupation for a few years before settling down for a long career as an accountant in the civil service.

In early-postwar Taiwan, Hiroshima was an unpopular subject.[1] This was not because Taiwanese were necessarily morally repulsed by the bombing itself, but rather because many believed that the Japanese were milking it for sympathy toward absolution for (or at least dilution of) their own country's war crimes and Imperial Era aggression. There were even rumors at the time that Hiroshima had been a hoax somehow cooked up by the Japanese toward this end. Moreover, many were averse to hearing stories of the suffering caused by Little Boy and Fat Man because, in the rapidly developing foundation myths of Taiwan, the bombs were seen as miraculous, deus ex machina bringers of newly won independence from Japanese colonial tyranny.

In the first decade or so after the war, there was also a prevalent belief in Taiwan (as well as in Korea and Japan) that hibakusha could pass on their bomb-related pathology to others through physical contact or even just proximity. When Zhen first became aware of this new urban myth, he feared the consequences of other people finding out he had been in Hiroshima immediately after the bombing. For the next sixty-five years, he did not tell anyone that he was a hibakusha—not colleagues at any of his workplaces, not his future wife or her family when he proposed marriage, not even his own family or children. His son found out only when his father told him during a visit to Hiroshima in September 2011.

On the occasion of this visit—his first time back to the country since 1946—Zhen was also able at long last to secure the *hibakusha kenkō techō* or "hibakusha health card" he had been trying to get from the Japanese government since 2003. Issued to hibakusha since the passage of the Atomic Bomb Medical Assistance Law (*Genshibakudan Hibakusha ni taisuru Iryō nado ni kansuru Hōritsu*) in 1957, the *techō* is a certificate of official Japanese Ministry of Health and Welfare recognition of the bearer as an atomic bomb victim, qualified as such to receive free medical examinations and medical treatment (for ailments judged to be bomb related) at public expense.

Although Zhen had kept quiet about his atomic bomb experience upon returning to Taiwan after the war, his Japanese Army service was already a matter of public record and family memory, so he did not bother trying to hide this aspect of his personal history. He had even participated, through international mail correspondence, in *Marure* veterans' association activities (receiving monthly newsletters, etc). It was through this group that Zhen, still in his early forties, first heard that the Akatsuki Hiroshima first responders were eligible for *hibakusha techō*.[2]

To receive one of these cards, an applicant must provide documentary evidence and/or corroborating-witness testimony to their atomic bomb experience—evidence any Saitō Unit veteran would have little difficulty coming up with. However, because it was an original stipulation of the Atomic Bomb Medical Assistance Law that qualification for a card applied only to Japanese hibakusha, the matter of Zhen's post-1945 nationality was apparently insurmountably problematic, as Zhen and the other tens of millions of Emperor Hirohito's

Taiwanese and Korean subjects had formally lost their Japanese citizenship after the post-occupation restoration of Japan's national sovereignty in 1952.

Because of the nationality issue, Zhen had originally abandoned any hope of getting a *techō* card. However, in the meantime, long decades of legal battles waged by both Japanese and non-Japanese activist groups such as the Citizens Relief Council for Korean Atomic Bomb Victims eventually began to chip away at the stone wall of the Japanese government's obstinacy on the matter.[3] In 1994, a lawsuit judgment in favor of the activists' cause resulted in getting the Atomic Bomb Medical Assistance Law amended to recognize and provide aid for foreign hibakusha residing in Japan.[4] This was still not good enough to help Zhen, living outside of Japan as he did, but he and thousands of other overseas-dwelling non-Japanese Hiroshima and Nagasaki survivors were finally vindicated by a subsequent courtroom victory in 2003 that opened the gates for their official hibakusha recognition from the Japanese government.[5] When Zhen heard about the court ruling, he began the application process for his *techō*, securing documentation of his Saitō Unit service and providing the required corroborating-witness testimony.

After eight years of tortuous navigation of Ministry of Health and Welfare red tape, Zhen finally received his coveted *techō*. Today he lives in Taipei with his family and full-time caregiver, and looks forward to getting out of the house and going to meet Dr. Tomonaga every March for his checkup at Taiwan Tri-Service General Hospital. I am grateful, as well as honored, that he agreed to share his precious time with me during his 2019 hospital visit.

———

Like Mr. Zhen, Tsuchiya Keiji has also endured on-and-off bomb-related health problems since his exposure to radioactivity in Hiroshima. He believes that one of his most harmful exposures was in the first hours of the Saitō Unit's rescue and recovery mission, when his squad's initial supply of drinking water ran out. On that first day,

Corporal Tsuchiya made use of the intermittent precipitation falling over and puddling in the city to wipe grime off his body. On numerous occasions, he also raised his face to the sky and stuck out his tongue to drink falling raindrops. Tsuchiya believes that this exposure to radioactive water—particularly the raindrop drinking—was responsible for giving him bowel cancer in 2005. As he has had a *hibakusha techō* since the earliest days of the system in the late 1950s, and his attending physicians and the relevant Ministry of Health and Welfare bureaucrats concurred that this cancer was, indeed, bomb related, the costs of his successful surgery and lengthy postoperative hospitalization were completely covered by the Japanese government.

Tsuchiya went to college after the war and, like Zhen, ended up teaching in public schools. After graduating as a marine biology major from Hiroshima University in March 1953, he was hired by the Okayama Prefectural Board of Education as a junior high school science teacher. In April 1961, the Okayama Board of Education moved him to East Junior High School in the small fishing community of Kasaoka.

In the Japanese junior high school teaching tradition, young(er) teachers are always given responsibility for supervising some extracurricular club activity for students. In Tsuchiya's case, he was assigned by his new school to become faculty adviser to the fisheries club. It was an assignment that ended up changing his life. As Kasaoka Bay has long been famous as a hatching environment for horseshoe crabs, he convinced his student charges that the club should make the study and protection of these peaceful creatures its main focus. Early-stage awareness among the Japanese at the time of the ecological/environmental costs of Japan's postwar economic "miracle," which were impossible to overlook for anyone living on the then increasingly polluted and despoiled coastline of the Seto Inland Sea, added weight to Tsuchiya's appeal that the club's research might make an important contribution toward saving the crabs—"living fossils," as he is wont to call them—from certain extinction.

Of immediately pressing urgency, local government officials were planning a massive land-reclamation project to turn the Kasaoka Bay mudflats into agricultural plots.[6] Tsuchiya and his club took the lead in an eventually successful local campaign to stop this project, which would have destroyed the Kasaoka breeding and hatchery grounds crucial to the crabs' life cycle, and to secure government recognition and protection of the crabs' natural habitat in the bay.

Tsuchiya eventually became a leading authority on Japanese horseshoe crabs, and he has published widely on the subject. In 1975, he became a charter founder of the Kasaoka Municipal Horseshoe Crab Museum. He has continued this research—and related environmental/wildlife protection activism in the Kasaoka community—since his retirement from the Okayama Board of Education in the early 1990s. Until recently, he has served as the chairman of the Japan Association for the Protection of Horseshoe Crabs (*Nihon Kabutogani wo Mamoru Kai*).

He has also been active in hibakusha activities for most of his life, having regularly attended annual August 6 memorial ceremonies at Hiroshima Peace Memorial Park since the facility's opening in 1954. From his forties, he has also been active in Hidankyō, the Japan Confederation of A- and H-Bomb Sufferers Organizations, serving until recently as the chairman of its Okayama prefectural branch. It was in this capacity that I made his acquaintance, on the occasion of the annual national Hidankyō convention held at a Tokyo hotel in June 2018.

At the end of the third and last day of the conference, a round of self-introductions—which received scant attention from the rest of the gathering—was made by each of the various prefectural and regional delegates in attendance. The microphone was eventually passed to a short, cue-ball-bald gentleman. In a booming parade field voice, he introduced himself as "Tsuchiya Keiji, a former maritime kamikaze motorboat pilot with Akatsuki Command." This did not seem to register much with the rest of the audience—perhaps they had heard it before. However, I was intrigued to see someone at a hibakusha gathering so openly (if not proudly) broaching the subject of their imperial military service, and I had a hunch this old fellow had some stories to tell. At the conclusion of the conference, I waited by the elevators to make sure to catch him on the way out. We exchanged business cards after my successful ambush, and I called him the next day. Two months later I was in his living room sipping barley tea and looking at his war albums.

━━━━━━

A week after the bombing of Hiroshima, Akatsuki Command handed off recovery operations in the city to police and civilian agencies and returned to its urgent Little Boy–interrupted mission of preparing to fend off an impending Allied invasion of the Seto Inland Sea. Corporals Zhen and Tsuchiya and the rest of their Saitō Unit comrades—mild to moderate radiation sickness notwithstanding—rotated back to Kōno'ura to resume their *Marure* training. Two days later, they were ordered to put on their best uniforms and lined up in formation in front of radios in their company areas to listen to the emperor's surrender broadcast. Tsuchiya recalls experiencing mixed emotions at the moment the meaning of His Majesty's message really sank in; he felt shame and despair at Japan's defeat, after all of the chanted oaths of fighting to the last man and bullet, but he also felt relief—an emotion left prudently unexpressed in real time—at knowing he would now most likely survive the war.

After the broadcast, the Saitō Unit changed back into their fatigues and returned to their usual *Marure* training. As was the case at many Japanese military installations in the Home Islands and throughout the empire, the professional officers at Kōno'ura must have been loath to accept the sudden and total invalidation of a lifelong, sustaining warrior ethos all on the say-so of a single static-scratchy radio broadcast. Instead, they chose to interpret the message from Tokyo as meaning "Stand by for more information and, in the meantime, keep training to die." The Akatsuki Command would spend the next eight days in this state of cognitive dissonance, waiting in an operationally murky twilight of combat readiness, only standing down from full alert on August 23, when Lieutenant Colonel (and imperial family "cadet branch" member) Prince Takeda Tsuneyoshi visited Ujina HQ as a special imperial envoy from Tokyo to make sure the surrender decision was being complied with at this important Army base.[7] During his visit, the prince was particularly insistent that all kamikaze training and preparations be halted immediately and that the soldiers involved therein should stand down as soon as possible. Upon orders from Ujina issued as a result of this imperial visit, the men in the Saitō Unit turned in their sidearms and other weapons, and burned their boats on the Kōno'ura waterline.

The Akatsuki Command's war was now over, but various exigencies of postwar chaos and Allied occupation convenience saw it hang on in a state of institutional life support for another eight months, during which time its proprietary freighter fleet helped repatriate the millions of soldiers and civilians stranded at war's end in the ruins of Japan's overseas empire. During this period, Akatsuki's daily operations continued to be run out of the headquarters building in Ujina, with everything still—somewhat incongruously—under the executive management of former lieutenant general (now, briefly, civilian bureaucrat) Saeki Bunrō and his staff. This arrangement continued until April 1, 1946, when fifty-six-year-old Saeki "retired" and authority over the Akatsuki's shipping operations was transferred to the First Repatriation Ministry in Tokyo, with Yokohama becoming the primary disembarkation port for Japanese returnees from overseas.[8]

———

Chai Tsong Chin was still at the Akatsuki aid station at Yoshijima, tending to patients and working the field crematory burn pit with his Kōryō classmates, when he heard the emperor's surrender broadcast. In his recollection, he and the other orderlies continued tending to their patients at the aid station as they listened to the regular NHK content leading up to the speech. But at the strike of noon, Chai faced the radio set and assumed a rigid military position of attention, which he and everyone else who could still stand maintained throughout the emperor's address.

Although seventeen-year-old Chai did not experience the kind of existential crisis Father Lassalle reported seeing among Japanese neighbors and parishioners in the wake of the surrender news, ninety-year-old Chai nevertheless remembers actually feeling a little let down by the anticlimax of the war's end. For nearly a year—since the fall of Saipan, at least—he and his Kōryō classmates had been told by every media channel at the disposal of the Japanese state to expect the war to end in a grand apocalyptic land-combat struggle against Allied invaders of the Home Islands. But after all that dramatic anticipation, after all the bombastic rhetoric—not to mention all of the reassuring "news" about the progress of the war that they had been hearing for years before that—it turned out that the whole thing was going to end with a single, forlorn radio broadcast.

As Kōryō's Ujina campus had been spared ZTD levels of devastation, the school was able to resume classes barely two months after the bombing.[9] However, Chai would not be rejoining his classmates. While the war had exacted minimal physical privations on Taiwan, the sudden severance of Japanese cash flow that the island had depended on for half a century plunged the local economy into chaos. This meant that Chai's parents could no longer send him money to continue his studies, so there was no choice for him but to repatriate to Taiwan. Returning to his hometown of Chiayi, in the southwestern part of the island of Formosa, Chai took over the family store from his ailing father and looked after it for the rest of his working life.

Although Mr. Chai ended up becoming a prosperous business-man, he has always harbored regrets about his dreams of becoming a doctor ending in the ruins of Hiroshima. Over the long first half century of the postwar period, he also often found himself looking back on the time he had spent in the city—not only the traumatic memories of the bombing but also some happy ones about his time at Kōryō—and wondering what had become of his old classmates. In 1993, he went back to Hiroshima to find out for himself, attending a

reunion held there on the fiftieth anniversary of his class's matriculation. There he learned that one of the other Taiwanese boys at the
school, a grade below his, had died doing firebreak work with classmates. Another classmate had survived and was still supposedly living in Taichung, but no one knew any more than that. More than
anything else, though, what was most eye-opening and moving for
Mr. Chai about his trip back to Hiroshima was seeing what a fine,
vibrant city it had become, risen from the ashes of his memory.

THE SUN SETS ON AKATSUKI

TODAY, A SHOPPING mall occupies the former Ujina campus of Kōryō Junior High, which became a three-year high school under the post-war Japanese educational reforms, and moved out to the far northern suburbs of the city in the 1970s.[1] Just inside the main gate of the new campus, there is a tombstone-sized memorial to the thirty-six Kōryō students and two faculty member chaperones killed in the atomic bombing. The memorial is made of highly polished granite, with a shape that is somewhat evocative of an igloo or perhaps an archaic pottery kiln. It is a modest but handsome work of commemorative statuary of the kind that is found on dozens of other elementary, junior high, high school, and college campuses throughout the Hiroshima area, and that was erected in memory of students, faculty, and alumni killed by the atomic bomb.

Like most Hiroshima school campus bomb memorials, Kōryō's was primarily funded by its PTA and was erected during Japan's postwar period of high economic growth.[2] The timing here is significant for two reasons. First, this era saw the great majority of the postwar population finally emerging from the hand-to-mouth existence that had characterized the lives of most Japanese during the first decade after the war. This allowed them to begin using their financial resources toward goals beyond mere subsistence-level survival. As Japan's revitalized economy gained steam, average citizens could self-actualize through spending money on televisions, refrigerators, cars, and, in this case, memorial stones for events that had happened twenty years in the past.

The second operant timing factor was the advancing age of the parents who paid for the memorial. In 1965—when Kōryō's memorial was built—most of the bereaved parents of twelve- and thirteen-year-olds killed in 1945 would have been approaching sixty, give or take ten years. In our twenty-first-century era of hale and hearty seniors, sixty may not seem particularly superannuated, but to the Japanese in 1965, with living memories of a tuberculosis- and cholera-plagued prewar era when forty-five would have been considered "old," sixty to seventy would have felt like the cusp of terminal senescence and therefore high time to begin attending to (and thus spend money on) matters of eternity.

It is a universal aspect of human nature, when we reach the life-cycle milestone of rapidly approaching personal mortality, to begin thinking about securing what the psychologist Robert Jay Lifton has termed "symbolic immortality."[3] It is an age when we start to think about what vestiges and legacies of our lives, loved ones, and cultures we want to leave behind—safe, intact, and remembered—before we take our bows and make our final exits.[4]

Since the dawn of humankind, stone has been a time-proven favored artistic medium for materializing our desire for symbolic immortality. We go to great expense to erect pyramids, cathedrals, Mo'ai heads, triumphal arches, and totems made of the stuff as irrefutable physical proof of our existence and, of perhaps even greater importance, of the permanence of cherished beliefs and values. Statues, monuments, and gravestones are tactile manifestations of our insistent denial that the memories of heroes and lost loved ones are doomed to fall prey, Ozymandias-like, to the unstoppable march of time and the final, obliterating amnesia of death and dust.

Viewed in this light, it makes sense that public space from one end of Hiroshima to the other is veritably covered in memorial stones

and statuary commemorating what happened—and what was lost—
on August 6, 1945. This artwork constitutes a defiant, hopeful denial
of a narrative in which Little Boy obliterated a community and with it
any evidence that the tens of thousands of people the bomb killed
ever existed. It is an insistence not only on Hiroshima's symbolic immortality, but its literal immortality, as well. It says, in so many words
and in so much carved stone, "We are still here. We are still standing.
And we may forgive but we will never forget."

But if what Hiroshima's stones and statuary tell us is to be taken
at face value, there are some things—and some people—who have
been forgotten. There is a gap in Hiroshima's otherwise meticulously
and devotedly thorough commemoration in stone and bronze of its
communal atomic-bombing experience, and it is conspicuous if one
knows anything about the history of the city's recovery in the immediate aftermath of Little Boy. While there are a handful of Akatsuki
Command–related memorials in peripheral, inconveniently located,
and inconspicuous spots in the city—mostly concentrated in the
Ujina waterfront area—there is not a single memorial of any kind, in
any prominent central Hiroshima public space, for the Akatsuki
Command first responders to the atomic bombing.

Most of the Akatsuki soldiers who rushed headlong into the
burning city on August 6 were barely older than the thousands of junior high school firebreak workers whose corpses they collected and
burned over the next week. Personal opinions about the institution of
the Imperial Japanese Army aside, anyone making an objective historical and moral assessment of the conduct and sacrifices of those
young men must conclude that they were singularly courageous and
selfless and, moreover, that their contributions were instrumental in
the crucial initial stages of Hiroshima's recovery. Their presence in
the city gave hope and psychological comfort to its despairing surviving residents, and they likely saved the lives of thousands, often at
the sacrifice of their own (either immediate or through the eventual
consequences of radiation exposure). As such, their absence from conspicuous Hiroshima commemorative space may seem, at first glance,
an odd omission—odd, that is, until you realize that the legacy of this

selfless heroism is an inconvenient plot element in two explanatory narratives, one local, one national—that emerged in the early-postwar period to fulfill various symbolic, emotional, and political needs.

In the preferred reading of the first of these explanatory narratives—the favored local one—Hiroshima was a city of innocent civilians wiped out by American technology and cruelty as the explosive coda of a train-wreck chain of events set in motion by Japanese militarism—both "mistakes," as the words of the inscription on the Victims' Memorial Cenotaph in Hiroshima Peace Park intone, "which must never be repeated." As this narrative arc requires that one of its duo of central villains is wearing Imperial Army khaki, Akatsuki Command heroes do not fit in this story.

The almost total invisibility of the Akatsuki Command in Hiroshima's memorial landscape is also a vestige of a second, larger narrative encompassing the meaning of the war as a whole. Almost immediately after Emperor Hirohito's surrender broadcast, a story began taking shape in popular Japanese consciousness—initially pushed by the same Japanese media that had been cheerleading the war literally days earlier—in which blame for the nation's disastrous war experience was placed squarely on the shoulders of Japan's professional officer corps and the oversized ideological and political influence it had wielded since the Meiji Era. After the arrival of the bulk of the main Allied occupation forces in 1945, this narrative received a considerable and determined boost via conscious media message management through the offices of General MacArthur's Civil Information and Education Section (CIE).[5]

In broad strokes, this narrative depicted an otherwise honorable culture and innocent (if temporarily brainwashed) populace duped into the criminally hopeless catastrophe of the war by a cabal of sinister mustachioed militarists. This story was simple enough to be grasped even by schoolchildren, and it enjoyed a degree of historical, fact-based merit. To reap this story's psychological benefits and be absolved of one's war sins, all one had to do was to admit that it had all been a terrible mistake, and vow to honor its victims by never attempting anything like it again. From the perspective of the average war-weary (and Occupation-wary) Japanese, the story presented a golden opportunity to distance themselves psychologically, symbolically, and personally from a failed war effort in which almost everyone had been complicit and to which they had once been wholeheartedly devoted.[6]

Codified in Japan's new postwar constitution, given legal precedent in the verdicts of the IMTFE (International Military Tribunal for the Far East) trials for Japanese war criminals, sanctified in places like Hiroshima Peace Park, and, at least until the 1990s or so, taught to generations of Japanese schoolchildren, this narrative has had remarkable staying power. Even after seventy years of concerted, dedicated post–Occupation Era efforts by powerful Japanese conservatives to expunge it from the national soul, it remains surprisingly resilient— thanks in large part to the legacies of Hiroshima and Nagasaki—and it is the symbolic and psychological bedrock of postwar Japan's pacifism, at least in popular consciousness.

———

In the last years of his life, Saeki Bunrō looked back on the week his Akatsuki Command spent trying to save atom-bombed Hiroshima as "the last atonement of the Militarist Faction."[7] But in retrospect, that atonement—including his own—was only just beginning.

When Allied prisoners liberated after the war began recounting their experiences in Japanese captivity to official debriefing interviewers, a central element in their accounts was the suffering they had endured during sea transport to and from far-flung POW camps around the Japanese Empire. In contemporary American and British news media accounts, these transports—the majority of which were civilian merchant vessels chartered and commissioned by the Akatsuki Command—became infamous as so-called hell ships. As news stories about conditions aboard the ships began to circulate, there was a commensurate swell of public anger in the US, the UK, and other Allied countries calling for swift justice to be meted out against the Japanese military figures deemed responsible. Someone was going to have to answer for the hell ships, and it was certainly not going to be the emperor.

As the sole surviving Akatsuki Command commanding general who had been at least nominally responsible for the hell ships' operation, Saeki Bunrō turned out to be that "someone." In 1948, he was arrested by Allied authorities in his home city of Sendai in northern Japan and tried by the IMTFE as a Class B war criminal for what Allied POWs had to endure on the Akatsuki's hell ships, especially during the last year of the war. During his trial, Saeki never raised a word in his own defense.

His attorney, however, asserted that it was unreasonable to claim the conditions on the hell ships constituted a specific war crime against the POWs in question, because Japanese military personnel evacuating these regions had been on the same ships, ostensibly enduring the same conditions (although they probably at least got to go on deck for air now and then). But these entreaties moved no one on the tribunal bench. Saeki was convicted and sentenced to twenty-four to twenty-six years at hard labor in Sugamo Prison, Tokyo, which was also the postwar home of Tōjō Hideki, Koiso Kuniaki, Matsui Iwane, and other Class A war criminals.

After the end of the Allied occupation and the return of Japan's national sovereignty in 1952, Saeki, while still incarcerated, successfully petitioned the Japanese government to recognize all civilian ship crew members who died or were invalided as a result of their service on Akatsuki Command–contracted ships to qualify for *gunzoku* (civilians performing duties in direct support of military operations) public pensions and/or compensation funds for their bereaved families.[8] He was released in 1957, as part of the general trend of amnesty toward Allied-convicted Japanese war criminals championed by the new Liberal Democratic Party, which was dominating Japanese national politics by this point.[9] He died in obscurity in Sendai in 1967.

Today, on or very close to the location of the Ōte-machi burn pit that Tsuchiya and Zhen worked on from August 8–13, 1945, an approximately human-sized bronze statue of Kan'non-sama, the Japanese Buddhist goddess of mercy, stands in a quiet glade on the left bank of the Motoyasu River. The statue was built and erected in 1966, largely through the fundraising efforts and personal contributions of then Hiroshima City councilman Akita Masayuki, whose son Kōzō and 351 schoolmates at the nearby Hiroshima Prefectural Junior High School were killed in the bombing.[10] A small crypt in the statue's stone plinth contains bronze sheets on which are etched the names of some six thousand schoolchildren who were killed while clearing firebreaks in central Hiroshima. One of these names is Yoshimura Mieko.

On August 10, while making routine inspection rounds to check the progress of body disposal operations in the Central Sector (probably with his chief of staff, Lieutenant Colonel Nomura Kiyoshi), Major General Yoshimura chanced upon his daughter Mieko's body in a burn pile at one of his field crematories. It borders on the vertigo inducing to even contemplate the capacity for self-control Yoshimura would have needed to maintain his professional composure—something he, as an IJA officer and general, would have been utterly compelled to do in that setting—under the gaze of subordinates and other parents onsite looking for their own children. The only recorded remarks from this occasion were from one of his staff officers—again, probably Colonel Nomura—who pointed out how well preserved Mieko's face was compared to those of her classmates and the other bodies in the pile. Those present theorized that she must have gone into the river before the fires reached the spot.[11] They did not yet understand the nature of what had just exploded over the city, and thus would not have understood that most of the damage done to human bodies that close to Ground Zero would have happened in thousandths of a second. Mieko would have had no time to run, or probably even to finish her first and last scream, before she died, and her face had likely been preserved because it had been in the shadow of a stone wall or a tree trunk—or even a classmate—when the rest of her body was destroyed by Little Boy's thermal rays and shock wave.

The burn pit where Yoshimura Mieko was cremated was likely the Ōte-machi site, as this was the closest one to where Mieko and 543 of her Hiroshima Municipal Girls' School (Ichijo) classmates were working on August 6, clearing a hundred-meter-wide firebreak to safeguard the Hiroshima prefectural offices against the event of a large-scale incendiary raid on the city. Not one of them survived.

Today, the space the Ichijo girls were clearing is still open and still one hundred meters wide. It now encompasses a stretch of Hiroshima's showcase thoroughfare, Peace Boulevard.

PART THREE

THE FIREBREAKS

GRAND BOULEVARDS

Hiroshima
Present day

HIROSHIMA STATION IS located on the northeastern edge of the Ōta Delta, close up against the mountains that ring the city like a horseshoe. It has occupied this spot since the National Railways (*Kokutetsu*) system extended the San'yō Line to reach Hiroshima in 1894[1]—the *sine qua non* infrastructural quantum leap in the old samurai-castle town's rapid evolution into a vibrant modern city.[2]

Simultaneous breakneck development of the Ujina Harbor facilities, linked with the new station via a narrow-gauge railway, transformed the city virtually overnight into a key logistics and transportation hub for the IJA just in time for the First Sino-Japanese War.[3] That this transformation almost never happened is one of the many ironies in the city's history; if the San'yō Line had been extended to the far western tip of Honshu in the early 1890s, as originally envisioned, then Shimonoseki—not Hiroshima—would in all likelihood have become Japan's primary military embarkation port during the conflict. In this alternate timeline, if the emperor's ministers had opted to spend 1890s government funds on more western Honshu railroad track instead of more battleships and field guns, Hiroshima and its shallow harbor, inconvenient as it was for oceangoing vessels, would likely have played little more than an auxiliary role—if that—in this and Japan's subsequent wars of imperial expansion in Asia. As such, the city—assuming it ever really developed into one—might have received a desultory late incendiary campaign raid by LeMay's B-29s in the summer of 1945, perhaps with a high three- or low four-figure casualty count, and Hiroshima would be little more than a footnote in the chronicles of American airpower. But the San'yō Line was laid as it was, and the rest, as the saying goes, is history.

Throughout the 1890s and the first decades of the twentieth century, defense spending pumped investment capital into the city. Rail traffic running through Hiroshima Station kept apace of this growth, with the 1920s seeing the opening of three new rail lines with main terminuses in Hiroshima. The first of these was the Kure Line, which followed the rocky coastline of the Seto Inland Sea to connect the city and Kure Naval Arsenal with Mihara in the eastern part of the prefecture. Later in the decade, the western terminus of the Kure Line was joined at Hiroshima Station by the Geibi and Kabe Lines, both of which, following a textbook pattern of railway-driven Japanese urban sprawl, were built through valleys and passes in the mountainous terrain inland of the city to exploit this theretofore underutilized hinterland for new residential suburbs and industrial parks. The completion of these suburban lines would be the high-water mark of Hiroshima's transportation network for the next half century as the nation's coffers were increasingly drained by military expenditure through the 1930s and 1940s, then earmarked for rebuilding a war-wrecked country through the 1950s and early 1960s.

The next quantum leap in Hiroshima's transportation infrastructure occurred when the city became a stop on the San'yō Shinkansen "Super Express" Line in 1972.[4] Since then, this "bullet train" has been the prime people mover for the thousands of school trip participants and other tourists pouring into the city every day, primarily to visit atomic-bombing-related sites. Of these, the most popular destination is undoubtedly Peace Memorial Park, two kilometers west of the station, where Hiroshima spells out the official narrative of its atomic-bombing experience; this is done literally in the Peace Memorial Museum, and more symbolically through the powerful visual impact of physical objects such as the Children's Peace Memorial and, just across the Motoyasu River, the UNESCO World Heritage site Atomic ("Genbaku") Dome—the twisted skeletal ruins of the Hiroshima Prefectural Exhibition Hall, once the grandest European-style building in western Japan.

When tourists and the city's daily commuters detrain in Hiroshima, most of them exit the station on its south side. There many transfer to one of the myriad city bus and streetcar lines sharing a terminus at Hiroshima Station. If on foot, they proceed over picturesque prewar stone bridges and through utilitarian postwar tile-walled underpasses—one of the many infrastructure accomplishments of 1990s mayor Hiraoka Takashi—to workplaces, schools, or hotels/hostels in the downtown districts.

The area on the station's north side, in contrast, lacks any comparable feeling of optimistic bustle. Built over the old East Parade Ground of the Fifth Division—the Hiroshima Castle–headquartered IJA unit that called the city home from 1888 to 1945—this part of the city feels a bit neglected, despite the construction here in recent decades of some big hotels, shopping arcades, and other shiny, underutilized new facilities whose function is not immediately evident at first glance. Moreover, there is not much of it. Immediately behind this half-kilometer-deep belt of simultaneously physically cramped and culturally desolate urban buildup, there is little else but steep, heavily forested green hills and, between those, valleys packed cheek by jowl with single-family residences, schools, and the ubiquitous soot-streaked, stuccoed-concrete sixties and seventies Japanese apartment buildings.

Dominating this mountainous backdrop to the city is the 139-meter-tall Futabayama—a hill that is home to a Buddhist temple of the Nipponzan Myōhōji sect. From a distance, the temple's expansive cemetery—which is ingeniously terraced into the hill's steep slopes—has the appearance of a massive rock climbers' practice wall. To access a specific grave here, a visitor first uses a vertiginous, narrow concrete stairway to reach the corresponding terrace ledge. Once there, they must edge out onto their chosen terrace ledge along shoulder-width footpaths, with nothing but knee-high guardrails and the Buddha's mercy standing between them and, should they misstep, an assuredly bone-breaking—if not fatal—fall onto the headstones of the next terrace ledge below. I cringe imagining elderly people on canes or walkers trying to navigate these perilous precipices during the busy traditional Japanese *obon* grave-washing season every summer.

As per common Japanese custom, most of the grave plots here are the final resting places not of single individuals but of households. And rather than being deep excavations into the ground for skeletal remains, they are closer to small, shallow concrete crypts with a surface area about one meter square. In these crypts are placed small ossuary jars—about the size of an old-style Quaker Oats container—of cremated ashes for each deceased family member.

This is a practical and prudent use of precious real estate in a crowded country. But it is also a spiritually and symbolically weighty affirmation of the Japanese belief in the continuity of family obligation beyond the grave—a time-honored manifestation of filial piety in the finest tradition of ancestor worship in heavily Confucianism-influenced Japan.[5] Even in the twenty-first century, there remains in the culture a strong superstitious streak about the woes and misfortunes—known as *tatari*—that will befall the living if they disrespect the dead by not following this protocol. However, as storytellers, comedians, and bickering spouses here have acknowledged for generations—any fears of *tatari* and vengeful ancestral ghosts aside—contemplating spending eternity with their mothers-in-law in a concrete-lined crypt the size of an apple crate apparently evokes in some Japanese thoughts and emotions less comforting than the solemn pride of faithfully fulfilled familial duties.

Above this cliff-face cemetery, perched near the summit of Futabayama Hill, is the gleaming metallic bulb of the Hiroshima Peace Pagoda, which was erected in 1966 to comfort the souls of Little Boy's victims. Built by the Nipponzan Myōhōji Buddhist organization on the leveled former site of an antiaircraft battery, the pagoda is actually more of a stupa, in strict architectural terms, as it does not have an interior space for human occupancy. It does, however, feature a compartment containing a portion of ashes purportedly from the Buddha's actual cremated body—a gift from the people of Ceylon (Sri Lanka) and a consortium of Mongolian monks (the connection here is not explained on the visitors' information plaque). In recent years, perhaps in part due to the presence of this relic, the venue has also apparently acquired a reputation as a potent "power spot" among New Age types. This presumably adds to the visitor traffic to the top of Futabayama—although only the truly devout and/or delusional would make the pilgrimage on foot in the middle of a Japanese summer. One steamy August afternoon in 2018, I decide to give it a try.

After threading the death-defying staircase up through the cliff-face cemetery, sweating more out of fear than out of exertion, I reach the pagoda. It is a little before sunset, and I have the spot and the little park compound around it entirely to myself. The view is spectacular, offering one of the best natural panoramas in Hiroshima. The vantage point allows one to grasp at a glance how the basic plan of the city is channeled and defined by the waterways of the Ōta Delta, which from here resembles an extended right hand held flat, palm down.

The thumb of this hand—the Ōta tributary Enkō River—flows roughly west to east past the south exit of Hiroshima Station. It then takes a long, lazy curve along the eastern rim of the delta before emptying into the bay some five kilometers away. The remaining waterway "fingers" of our metaphorical hand follow straighter courses to Hiroshima Bay, dividing the rest of the delta up into its characteristically narrow, roughly north–south-oriented islets.

This topography of tributary waterways, islets, and landfill is stapled together with dozens of bridges—some of them Little Boy survivors still bearing ballistic debris pockmarks and thermal ray scorches. It is also crisscrossed by more straight, wide, and stately avenues and boulevards than one might expect in a city of otherwise fairly modest size. Several of these thoroughfares accommodate the old *denshadōri* and, like their prewar antecedents, still carry Hiroden streetcar traffic. The two most important and most heavily trafficked of these roadways are: Rijō Street, the north–south *denshadōri* connecting Ujina and Hiroshima Station, which we have already noted was the

Akatsuki Command's main artery into the burning city in the first
hours and days of rescue and recovery after the bombing; the other,
Aioi Street, an east–west *denshadōri*, traverses the downtown business
districts of Hatchōbori and Kamiya-chō, where its intersection with
Rijō Street—about two hundred fifty meters east of Ground Zero—is
home to Bankers' Row and, as such, generally considered to be the
financial heart of the city.

Most of the rest of these grand roadways, however, do not accommodate streetcar lines. Considering the comparatively light automobile traffic these thoroughfares carry outside rush hour, their
footprints take up what seems an unnecessarily excessive share of
real estate. Moreover, they appear to traverse and connect only modestly built-up districts along much of their length, with many stretches
fronted by ordinary wooden single-family houses.

If there seems to be no evident practical infrastructural or economic purpose for the existence of these apparent "highways to nowhere" in modern-day Hiroshima, it is because there is none. Most of
these grand boulevards crisscrossing and ringing the city center exist
as accidents of history: They are the firebreaks that were being cleared
by nearly thirty thousand adult civilian and junior high school "volunteers" on the morning of August 6, 1945.[6] Now they are paved over
with asphalt and fitted with traffic lights.

Of all of the former firebreaks, none is grander than the east–west
artery known since the early 1950s as Peace Boulevard. Because it is
nearly a hundred meters wide through most of its course, local authorities in the early postwar once seriously considered turning it into
a downtown single-runway airport before cooler heads prevailed and
then mayor Hamai Shinzō decided to turn it into the city's showcase
thoroughfare instead.[7] Today, it traverses over four kilometers of central
Hiroshima—streetcar-less for all but its westernmost 500 meters—
running from the foot of Hijiyama Hill in the east to Koi Station in
the west and crossing every waterway of the Ōta Delta (except for the
Enkō River) along its route. For almost the entirety of its length, Peace
Boulevard is lined on both sides with lushly verdant belts of park
space. These parallel parks are interspersed at regular intervals with

copses of trees and dotted with atomic-bombing-related memorial stones and statuary.

If one's eyes and antennae are attuned to such things, walking around Hiroshima can feel, in the words of one hibakusha, like taking a stroll through "a giant cemetery."[8] This applies not only to the immediate environs of Peace Boulevard, but also, to lesser degree, to just about anywhere in the city center. Physical monuments to Hiroshima's day of destruction and its victims are omnipresent and unavoidable; you will find them not only in showcase public spaces like Peace Boulevard, but also in schoolyards, next to playgrounds, on otherwise ordinary street corners, in office building lobbies—anywhere and everywhere.

Practices followed in the city for the postwar naming of public spaces and institutions are also thick with bomb-memory prompts. The most conspicuous of these is "peace"—*heiwa* in Japanese—a word whose use might have been encouraged by Allied occupation authorities as a way to help the people of Hiroshima forget or forgive Little Boy, but which for subsequent generations of postwar residents of the city is instead a reminder of that horror (assuming it has not long since decayed into semantically neutered white noise due to its utter ubiquity).

I often wonder if it affects its full-time residents psychologically to be surrounded in their daily living environment with so many reminders of death and catastrophe—of their community having been traumatized and physically savaged to the extent that it was and, moreover, at the hands of once loathed cultural and racial Others. I do know with certainty, however, what this memory-soaked environment can feel like from the outside looking in. When I visited the city for the first time in 1997, I remember experiencing this memory-haunted atmosphere not only with a feeling of deep sadness, but also, as a large, physically conspicuous Westerner, with a slightly paranoid sensation (probably more imagined than real) of being stared at and silently judged. And the place where I experienced this feeling most intensely was Peace Memorial Park.

"X" MARKS THE SPOT

PEACE MEMORIAL PARK is located at just about midpoint along the length of Peace Boulevard. It occupies the former site of Nakajima-honmachi—a district of temples, entertainment establishments, and private residences on the northern tip of Nakajima Island that was completely obliterated when Little Boy exploded almost directly overhead. The sharply pointed promontory here was traditionally referred to by locals as Jisenji-no-hana ("Jisenji Temple's Nose") after its distinctive triangular shape and the eponymous Buddhist temple that was once its most prominent occupant.

Although the neighborhood of Nakajima-honmachi no longer exists as an inhabited, living community, the promontory of Jisenji-no-hana still does, thrusting like the prow of a ship into the flow of the Ōta Honkawa, from which it pares off the tributary Motoyasu River.[1] Bracketed by the Ōta Honkawa and the Motoyasu, the park built upon the spot is a luxurious expanse of green against the backdrop of the bustling, noisy city that has grown up around it over the past seven decades. Standing in this serene space, I experience an emotional gut-punch imagining it blasted flat, scorched, and blanched of color, the surface of dry ground and water alike strewn with corpses as far as the eye could see. As unpleasant a task as it is, I believe that any visitor to the city is morally compelled to try to imagine this hellscape, and Peace Park exists to facilitate this.

The physical and symbolic epicenter of the park is the Victims' Memorial Cenotaph. Shrouded in a concave concrete dome evocative (to an American, at least) of a Conestoga wagon covering, the smallish box of the crypt houses special tomes on which the names of Little Boy's known victims are entered in artfully hand-brushed calligraphic script. Every August 4, the names of hibakusha who have died over the past year are duly reported in person to Hiroshima City Hall officials by representatives of Hidankyō and other hibakusha associations from around the country, who are in town then to attend the big annual August 6 memorial ceremony in the park. Once the relevant paperwork is checked and officially signed off on by city hall, the year's new names are hand-brushed into the tomes to join the rolls of the previously recognized dead in time for interment at the following year's memorial ceremony.

The Cenotaph is perfectly aligned with a reflecting pool and an eternal-flame installation framing the Atomic Dome in the distance, providing a visually powerful backdrop for the memorial gatherings held on the spot every year on the anniversary of the bombing. At these ceremonies, flowers, incense, and prayers are offered up to the spirits of the dead, and politicians make speeches that never stray far from the traditional rhetorical playbook for the occasion: grief and gratitude are expressed toward Little Boy's victims, whose collective sacrifice is explained as being responsible for the peace and prosperity of postwar Japan. At the climax of the ceremony, flocks of "peace doves" are released.

The park and its main buildings were designed by the renowned Tange Kenzō in the late 1940s, and the space is an architectural showcase imbued with a profound sense of symbolic weight. When you are standing in it—particularly before the Cenotaph—you experience an undeniable sensation of being at the center of something immortal and sacrosanct. Probably due to this atmosphere of physical and symbolic centrality, it is a common mistake for visitors to assume—as I did during my first visit—that the park occupies the location of Hiroshima's Ground Zero. The configuration of the park's main ceremonial plaza, with the Cenotaph at its nexus, has always seemed to me to suggest an "X marks the spot" significance for this space. But Ground Zero is, in fact, about three hundred meters to the northeast and across the Motoyasu River from the Cenotaph—much closer to the Atomic Dome ruins than it is to this spot. Today, as in 1945, Ground Zero is within the property boundaries of the most recent incarnation of the indomitable Shima Hospital, which is now surrounded by office buildings, luxury high-rise condos, and retail stores in the bustling business district of Ōte-machi.

Peace Memorial Park was built on top of the ruins of Nakajima-honmachi / Jisenji-no-hana instead of on Ground Zero primarily because of coincidence and convenience. In 1945, as it is at present, Jisenji-no-hana was easily accessed from the south by the hundred-meter-wide firebreak that is now Peace Boulevard, and from the north by Aioi Street via the T-shaped Aioi Bridge. These two wide thoroughfares were cleared of rubble within a day or two of the bombing, allowing them to be freely traversed by Akatsuki Command's trucks engaged in relief and recovery. This made the largely flat and empty space of post-bombing Jisenji-no-hana and other spots along the 100-Meter Firebreak ideal locations for high-volume crematoria, and they were used as such well into the autumn of 1945, after Akatsuki Command had handed their operation over to civilian authorities.[2]

Until the morning of the bombing, the temples and other structures built on Jisenji-no-hana were almost entirely of light wooden construction. When Little Boy exploded, its shock wave essentially blew these structures—and everyone in them—into the Ōta Honkawa. The firestorm of August 6–7 then burned up any remaining wood and other organic materials, leaving behind not much more than heavy ceramic roof tiles, metal piping, and tombstones.

Five weeks later, when the powerful Makurazaki Typhoon of September 17, 1945, swept through the region, storm winds and fast flood-waters completely scoured away what had been left on the ground here in the way of ashes and other light debris. Most of the still slightly radioactive topsoil and fallout dust here and everywhere else in the city was also blown away by the storm—a freak windfall in the midst of this disaster, which, in a cruel coda to an infernal summer, killed more than two thousand people in the city and surrounding prefecture.[3]

Photographs from October 1945 taken by *Chūgoku Shimbun* journalists surveying Little Boy's (and the typhoon's) effects on the ZTD show Jisenji-no-hana looking like the surface of the moon; its almost completely flattened desolation is conspicuously set apart from the more substantially built-up (and thus far more rubble-clogged) districts on the opposite banks of the Motoyasu and the Honkawa. In these photographs, there is little in the way of physical hints at what had occupied Jisenji-no-hana before the bombing. The concrete shell of a former fuel-rationing cooperative is one of the few standing relics, joined by a few carbonized, shattered stumps of some of the neighborhood's hardier trees.[4] At the very tip of the island, two heavy stone lantern pedestals that had flanked the Aioi Bridge–linked northern entranceway to the neighborhood somehow managed to remain standing.[5] As for Jisenji Temple, the only physical evidence that it had once stood there are the headstones (most but not all toppled by the blast) in its cemetery.[6]

In the first weeks and months after the bombing, this cemetery and the empty ground around it became the primary deposit point for boxes, buckets, and cloth bags of unclaimed cremated (or later, as the case might have been, simply ossified) human remains collected in central Hiroshima.[7] Most of these remains had been processed by the field crematories operated around the clock in schoolyards, along the riverbanks, and in other open spaces across the city in the days and weeks following the bombing.

In the standard protocol for body identification followed at these field crematories (partially explained in the previous section), when victims were identifiable by personal information patches sewn on any scraps of clothing that might have been remaining on their bodies, this data would have been recorded by an Akatsuki soldier, policeman, or *Keibōdan* officer before the corpses were stacked with others in a burn pit. This tabulated data was later posted for public viewing outside the local rescue and recovery command post (e.g., Lieutenant General Yoshimura's Central Sector HQ in the Sumitomo Bank building, the Saitō Unit's field post in Senda-machi, etc.) so surviving family members could search for information on missing loved ones. In the case of a missing loved one being confirmed from this posted data as having been cremated, family members would then inquire about how to claim remains.

This is not, however, to suggest that the ashes were individually processed and packaged for return. Such special treatment might have happened in rare cases for the remains of particularly important people, such as high-ranking military officers or government officials, but most victims were not treated with such decorum and ceremony. The urgent exigencies of public hygiene (and morale) called for the tens of thousands of rapidly rotting cadavers strewn across the city to be cremated ASAP and en masse—generally in burn pits containing anywhere from five to up to ten or even twenty bodies at a time.

When the incineration of one batch was finished, the ashes and bones gathered at the bottom of a burn pit would be shoveled out and into buckets, wooden boxes, or even cloth bags before the pit was refueled with scrap wood and diesel to prepare for the next batch. These ash containers would be tagged with reference numbers or some other markers corresponding to identified victims' lists for later retrieval. In the days after the bombing, family members went around to claim remains directly from the cremation sites or Akatsuki field posts. In subsequent weeks and months, clerks in the hastily reestablished temporary city hall used these rosters to notify assumed next of kin of the remains by mail or through *tonarigumi* neighborhood association networks.[8]

In either scenario, a typical transaction for the handing over of remains would have entailed bereaved family members showing up at the appointed location, where they were given a scoop of ashes and bone fragments—often in a paper envelope—from a large container corresponding to the recorded burn-pit data that might have held the remains of dozens or even hundreds of people. The bereaved had to console themselves with the possibility that there might have been a few chips or flakes of their loved one's remains contained in this scoop of otherwise anonymous ashes, dust, and gravel.

But just because the name of a cremated victim was known did not guarantee these remains would be claimed. In many cases, this was for the simple and brutal reason that any loved ones who might have sought the return of these remains had themselves also been killed by the bomb.

A second place where human remains were found was under deep piles of rubble amid the ruins of the city. If remains in such circumstances were not the subjects of dedicated and focused efforts by family members, colleagues, or classmates returning to the ZTD to search the ruins of known last locations, the discoveries of these bodies were largely haphazard and essentially had to wait until they were chanced upon by workers otherwise engaged in routine rubble clearing.[9] If these remains had already been reduced to bone by fire, exposure, animal ravaging, and/or time and natural decomposition, they could be readily collected, tagged with discovery-location information, and deposited at Jisenji-no-hana as they were.[10]

Remains that were not yet far enough along in their ossification for easy collection, however, posed different recovery challenges as the post-bombing period stretched from days into weeks and months. By the time many of these bodies were found, the well-organized and well-supplied field crematories were no longer up and running. Under the circumstances, it was simply not practical to prepare a spot, gather scarce fuel, and build a pyre for individual cremation every time an unidentifiable body or body part was encountered moldering in the rubble.[11] As a matter of expedience and, as might be surmised, because of simple exhaustion and burnout on the part of the city's otherwise valiantly toiling recovery workers, remains in such cases were often simply buried in place where they were found.[12] Interred either individually or in mass graves, skeletal remains like these were regularly discovered around the Greater Hiroshima area for decades after the bombing, typically during excavation work for new construction projects.

Even as the city's cleanup and revitalization proceeded at an admirable pace, the ZTD was still crunchy underfoot with smaller scattered bits of human remains for months after the bombing.[13] These body parts ranged in size from visually discrete ribs, vertebrae, and skull fragments, etc., down to bone chips and fragments barely distinguishable from pebbles or gravel. Their presence was particularly conspicuous in ZTD locations such as the former firebreak sites, which on the morning of August 6 had been jam-packed with people working out in the open, completely unprotected. Their bodies, in many cases, had been carbonized by Little Boy's thermal rays before being literally blown to pieces by its shock wave.

As with the accidentally discovered rubble-pile bodies, these skeletal fragments also posed recovery/disposal challenges, not the least of these being their utter ubiquity and small size. As such, they were as often as not brushed under the carpet, so to speak, in the midst of the breakneck pace and chaos of the ongoing cleanup. No one was going to be blamed and no one was going to complain—at least not yet— if a few corners were being cut to transform this city of the dead back into a city for the living as quickly as possible.

WHAT TO DO FOR THE DEAD

Nakajima-honmachi District, Hiroshima City

September 1945

NOT LONG AFTER the Makurazaki Typhoon, a recently demobilized twenty-one-year-old soldier named Kajiyama Senjun came home to Hiroshima from his final wartime posting on the nearby island of Shikoku, where he had been helping to prepare defenses on anticipated invasion beaches. He arrived to find "the normal fabric of community life" in his city ripped to pieces and his home neighborhood of Nakajima-honmachi wiped off the face of the earth—and his family along with it.[1] As for the temple on Jisenji-no-hana that his family had administered for generations, there was now only a wind- and water-scoured rubble field piled with mountains of human-remains containers that grew in size daily.[2]

No doubt decades ahead of the original family schedule for his eventual ascension to this inherited position, Kajiyama was now, by default, the new head abbot of Jisenji Temple. Sizing up the situation, the temporarily homeless young abbot gathered up salvageable building material from the site and built a small shack that would function as his new home and workplace. With no surviving parishioners and thus no other monastic duties to perform, he naturally gravitated toward the unofficial and unremunerated job of tending to and chanting sutras for the burgeoning mountains of human remains steadily piling up on Jisenji-no-hana. By late 1945, the ashes and bones of tens of thousands of cremated and/or otherwise ossified bodies collected from burn pits around the city or swept up from streets and rubble fields in the ZTD had been deposited on the temple grounds and the immediately surrounding area, which was also beginning to fill back up with living human inhabitants—in this case mostly day laborer squatters, many of whom had come from out of town to do recovery work. These newer Hiroshima residents either erected their own rubble-scrounged shacks[3] or else they simply dug ditches in the ground and covered these up with "roofs" of corrugated metal and boards or even logs and earth, somewhat evocative of dugout command posts in military trench works.[4]

Kajiyama eventually built a second shack in a valiant attempt to keep the bone-and-ash containers away from the elements, but the task quickly escalated far beyond the means and resources of the newly bereaved twenty-one-year-old. Clearly, something had to be done— and quickly—about Jisenji-no-hana. Political pressure soon mounted on the administration of the new mayor, Kihara Shichirō, to take action.

Kihara, the first mayor of postwar Hiroshima, assumed office some two months after the August 6 death of his predecessor, Awaya Senkichi. Kihara was the city's last unelected mayor, assigned to the post under the soon-to-be-abolished old system of direct appointment by the national government.

It did not take long after Kihara's appointment for the residents in Hiroshima to appreciate that the new mayor and his city hall administration were working themselves ragged to get the city back on its feet. With the immediate public hygiene hazard of the tens of thousands of corpses left behind in Little Boy's wake now basically behind them, those in city hall were free to concentrate their limited means and resources on bettering the lot of their living constituents. But as the community gradually came back to life, and the day-to-day struggle for basic survival became less of a direct, pressing concern for those constituents, the questions of what to do about and, just as important, what to do *for* the dead became increasingly salient political issues.

Nowhere was this issue more conspicuous than in the ongoing situation at Jisenji-no-hana, the "optics" of which, as a twenty-first-century PR type might put it, were unacceptable. First of all, in terms of quality-of-life concerns of the residents who had to pass the site in their daily comings and goings in the recovering city, the boneyard on the northern tip of Nakajima was a brutal, in-your-face confrontation with traumatic reminders of their own recent encounters with death, horror, and personal loss. It also stank. Moreover, now that Allied troops were patrolling the city—joined by a constant stream of foreign VIPs, Christian missionaries, journalists, and international aid workers pouring in daily—the Jisenji-no-hana situation was quickly becoming an unsightly and undignified embarrassment under the intensely felt alien gaze of Hiroshima's blue-eyed occupiers.

Above and beyond any of these concerns, though, the Jisenji-no-hana situation would have been considered a violation of hallowed cultural norms regarding treatment of the dead. Japanese culture—as has already been touched upon earlier in the text—is one in which exacting and dignified attention to the details of funereal and memorial rites has traditionally held a position of the highest importance in the ceremonial life and annual calendar of a respectable and responsible household. Moreover, the maintenance of ongoing relationships with the spirits of the dead in one's daily life—mediated through faithfully observed practices such as gravestone cleaning, offerings of food and incense on household altars, and regular prayer—is considered a solemnly cherished and even holy obligation for the living (with *tatari*, again, awaiting the careless and/or lazy). Although the people of Hiroshima would have acknowledged and appreciated the hard work and dedication that Mayor Kihara and his administration were putting into getting the city back to the business of living, there was also a growing consensus among Little Boy's survivors that "putting the bomb behind them" did not and should not mean simply throwing the dead away—both literally and figuratively—along with the rest of the rubble.

Dissatisfaction in this vein eventually manifested itself in public opinion and political action that varied widely in manner and degree across the precincts of the devastated city. Politically, this was essentially a nonissue in communities within the ZTD, such as Jisenji Temple's Nakajima-honmachi neighborhood, in which a potential demographic of disgruntled bereaved never had a chance to coalesce. This was either because almost everyone was dead or because the comparatively low numbers of survivors from such obliterated communities had given up on the city and moved elsewhere.

Many of these "Hiroshima refugees" eventually found solace—and a voice for recognition and compensation—in Hidankyō branches and other hibakusha support groups; this was especially true for those who had settled in big cities along the Tokyo–Fukuoka–Pacific Coast megalopolis, where they were statistically more likely to encounter fellow hibakusha and either form survivor communities or join already extant ones. But this was a process that in many cases took decades to play out.

In the meantime, the members of this refugee demographic did not participate in the early editorial-process stages of what would become the official or "master" narrative of Hiroshima-bomb memory—the story maintaining that postwar Japan owed its peace and prosperity to the sacrifice of Little Boy's victims. This is the same narrative, more or less unchanged after nearly eighty years, that millions of visitors to Peace Memorial Park see and hear every year, and from which Japanese politicians, when holding forth on the topic of the war and/or bombing, stray at their peril.

In comparison with the hibakusha-diaspora demographic, bereaved residents of Hiroshima neighborhoods and suburbs lying outside the ZTD were very actively engaged in these early efforts to craft a narrative of transcendent meaning out of the bombing. Later, as Japan's economy got back on its feet, a substantial segment of this cohort very skillfully employed this narrative as part of a long campaign for monetary compensation from the national government for bomb-related pain and suffering. The areas of Hiroshima from which most of these activists hailed were those that survived Little Boy's blast and firestorms relatively or completely physically intact, but from which

tens of thousands of commuters—office workers, civil servants, mobilized students, etc.—had come into the city for work on the morning
of Monday, August 6, 1945. When these tens of thousands of commuters never came home, their disappearance instantly created a deep
belt of grieving and, increasingly, aggrieved households surrounding
the ZTD. Many would soon unite into an influential and passionately
committed bloc of memory and political activism.

Initially, these new communities of the bereaved were understandably more preoccupied by their own personal "grief work" over their
vanished family members than they were with demanding official accountability for their fate. But once the bereaved came out on the other
side of this early period of confusion and despair to acknowledge the
finality of the deaths of loved ones, the last and permanent stage of
their grief work was to secure some kind of meaning for these deaths.
Toward this end, they began to engage in what historian Jay Winter
refers to as "memory activism," shifting their energies to a longer-term
campaign for official recognition of their pain and the sacrifices of
those they had lost.[5] The most obvious approaches were through direct
symbolic action in the form of memorial ceremonies, monumental
stones and statuary, and the like and through the crafting of an explanatory narrative of the bombing experience acceptable to the bereaved, the hibakusha, the general public, city hall, and, at least for
now, the Allied occupiers. For this to happen, local government was
going to have to sign off on political and financial assistance as well as
hands-on participation in the creative process for these efforts.

What decisively compelled Mayor Kihara to finally acknowledge
the moral responsibility (and the political expedience) in city hall taking the lead in this communal grief work seems to have been a letter
to the editor appearing in the December 24, 1945, edition of the local
daily Chūgoku Shimbun.[6] Penned by Mochizuki Yasuhiko—presumably
a bereaved family member—the piece appealed to the authorities to
take immediate action toward establishing both an official protocol
for mourning the city's dead and a central and symbolically expressive
venue for this purpose:

The tens of thousands of deaths suffered by our fellow citizens
when Hiroshima came under nuclear attack were sacrifices made
for the restoration of peace and should be cherished as such
[emphasis added]. At the time [of the bombing] we all heard the
gut-wrenching wails of those who were searching the city for the
remains of loved ones. We saw the drifts of bones piled up and
ignored on the sides of the roads. And who knows how many bones
are still buried under us, waiting to resurface someday? I propose
the erecting of a Memorial Pillar [kuyōtō] to assuage the spirits of
these bones and victims. As for a location, this should be built
somewhere near the epicenter of the bombing, and plaques in
Japanese and English should be displayed in front of it explaining
in detail what happened here, as I want the destruction caused by
the world's first atomic bombing to long be remembered. Moreover,
I think that it would be a gesture of profound meaning if every
August 6 were to be honored in the city as a Memorial Day on
which the souls of the departed will be mourned and prayers
offered up for peace. Let the spiritual [and/or psychological]
recovery of the citizens of Hiroshima emanate from the Memorial
Pillar day and night.[7]

In addition to being a sincere entreaty for communal action toward attending to the city's grief work, Mochizuki's letter is an interesting historical document in that it can give us some idea of how, and
from what point in time, the bombing could be publicly discussed in
early-postwar Hiroshima. Of particular interest is how Mochizuki
acknowledges—toes the official line on, one might even say—an early
version of the approved "They were sacrificed for peace" narrative for
assigning positive (or at least comforting) meaning to the deaths of
Little Boy's victims.

In Mochizuki's letter, we can see the broad strokes of the eventual approved narrative already taking form in Hiroshima barely four
months after the bombing, when much of the city would have still
been reeking of smoke and rotting organic matter. We cannot know
with certainty whether Mochizuki, in pushing the "sacrificed-for-

peace" message as conspicuously as he does here, did so as a true believer in this narrative, or if he was just trying to increase the chances that his letter would get past Allied censors and see publication to further his cause of getting a memorial built. In either case, the evidence of its publication belies the belief—long held in Japan—that censors in SCAP's CIE banned all mention of the atomic bombs in Japanese public discourse for the duration of the Allied occupation.[8]

In fact, in the press code issued by CIE on September 19, 1945, as a set of guidelines for Japanese media policy, there is no mention at all of Hiroshima, Nagasaki, or the atomic bombs that destroyed them.[9] Moreover, if one judges by the wide range of bomb-related media discourse and commemoration activities that the historical record shows were allowed to take place on CIE's watch, it would appear that SCAP not only tolerated but actively encouraged such activity, as long as its content, again, stuck to the approved sacrificed-for-peace narrative, refrained from openly criticizing the American decision to drop the bombs, avoided gruesome imagery, and did not delve too deeply into scientific/technological aspects of the bombs themselves.[10]

The catalyst for finally getting Hiroshima authorities to commit to an official public memorial ceremony commemorating Little Boy's victims (and a permanent venue for the same) was a visit to city hall in the spring of 1946 by one Kakihara Sei'ichirō of Ujina. In the recollection of then deputy mayor Hamai, the basic gist of Kakihara's entreaty was:

> *Of course rebuilding the city is important, but first there must be some kind of official public memorial ceremony for the victims of the war disaster. Surely, there are still many bodies all over the city buried under the rubble. These must be recovered and memorial ceremonies held for these victims before any other work to rebuild the city proceeds.*[11]

Kakihara—who appears to have been a building trades professional—offered to construct and erect a memorial marker, at his own expense, wherever city hall decided to put it.

At first, there were some deliberations over various candidate sites around the city that had already been long associated with war memorials, but all of these dated from the imperial period and venerated military war dead in some way. Their prewar provenance—and their implied valorization of the militarism and emperor worship that were now to be purged from postwar Japanese public space—effectively eliminated them as candidates for the location of an atomic-bomb-victim memorial.

Eventually, a solution was found when it was decided to erect Kakihara's carved wood totem at Jisenji Temple. This decision also led to Jisenji being chosen as the venue for Hiroshima's first official municipal memorial ceremony on the first anniversary of the bombing. The main venue of the ceremony was in front of Jisenji's new temporary ecclesiastical building, which doubled as the temple's ossuary and, on the day of the ceremony, as a convenient Potemkin village helping to block from the venue the view of the chaotic mushroom bloom of squatters' shacks that now covered Jisenji-no-hana behind the building.

The ceremony was attended by thousands of mourners, with rites conducted by the Hiroshima Council of Religions—an interfaith team of Buddhist monks, Shintō priests, and Christian clergy members.[12] The day's proceedings received wide and enthusiastic media coverage, and set the precedent for today's large memorial ceremonies held at this location every August 6. It also established the now customary practice at these events of observing a minute of silence—beginning at precisely eight fifteen a.m. (the time at which Little Boy exploded)—to the simultaneous accompaniment of fire department / civil defense sirens around the city.[13] According to contemporary accounts, the original 1946 minute of silence was observed not only at the ceremony venue, but in public spaces, workplaces, and private homes all over Hiroshima. Even street traffic came to a standstill from eight fifteen to eight sixteen, with people getting out of their vehicles to assume the traditional Buddhist standing funerary posture with heads bowed and hands brought together in a praying gesture.[14]

At the symbolic climax of the proceedings, Mayor Kihara rose to stand at a microphone set up in front of Kakihara's memorial totem and altars of flowers and burning incense. Following the traditional Japanese practice for a funerary orator, he would have stood facing not toward the mourners but rather toward the mourned, invisible but presumably floating in the ether with the incense smoke above the temporary altar and floral arrangements.

From the standpoint of the rhetorical situation at hand, Kihara had a particularly narrow messaging needle to thread. He would have to assign meaning to the deaths of a hundred forty thousand people killed by Little Boy before thousands of their grieving (and, it is easy to imagine, still very much-aggrieved) loved ones and under the scrutiny of members of the national media. He would also have to do so under the watchful eyes of SCAP, which would not take kindly to him, to his office, or to the idea of any further public August 6 commemoration if his message contained any criticism—even veiled or oblique— of the American act of dropping the bomb.

In any case, whatever Kihara—as the mayor of Hiroshima—said here on this day would have outsized and long-lasting influence toward determining, and cementing in the public consciousness, what would soon become the approved narrative of the city's atom bomb experience.

In the end, he opted to throw the Americans a softball.

"The sacrifice suffered by our city has encouraged the cause of peace throughout the world," Kihara began, ostensibly after the customary funerary-oratory boilerplate, "and secured the preservation of the Japanese people." He continued:

> *Even as we shed hot tears before the souls of our 100 thousand brethren who died here, we should remember that they did so that humanity might know eternal peace. Acknowledging this, we cannot but look back on that day without a profound sense of gratitude [emphasis added].*[15]

Reading these remarks nearly eighty years removed from their original utterance, we might be forgiven for assuming that they resulted in loud booing (if not an outright riot) from the thousands of assembled mourners hearing them in real time. But this did not happen. Instead, the assemblage took in the remarks in head-bowed, respectful silence, and that was it. The approved sacrificed-for-peace narrative was now a done deal—soon to be literally carved in stone all over the city—and the mayor's message was echoed approvingly in the following day's newspapers.

If the discourse of Hiroshima-bomb memory had still been somewhat fluid and contested until the moment Kihara stepped up to the microphone, he had now decisively shut it down, securing the unassailable high ground of the approved narrative of the city's bombing experience for generations to come. From here on out, anyone who dared in any way to challenge this narrative by suggesting that the city's dead were anything other than "noble sacrifices" (*tōtoi gisei*) for peace would have been committing apostasy (or, as the case might have been, political suicide), opening themselves up to immediate and vociferous criticism for inhuman insensitivity to the needs of Hiroshima's bereaved to believe that the horrific deaths of their loved ones had some transcendent—even holy—meaning. Ironically, this rhetorical sword—"How dare anyone challenge a narrative that brings comfort to the grieving?"—cut both ways, as it would be precisely the same messaging tactic employed after the end of the Allied occupation by conservatives, Imperial Era apologists, and war-bereaved family members who successfully clawed back a niche in Japanese public space for the veneration of the nation's wartime military dead—most conspicuously at Tokyo's Yasukuni Shrine, once one of the cornerstone facilities of Imperial Era State Shintō.

BUILD IT AND THEY WILL COME

Hiroshima City
Early-postwar period

IN TERMS OF pragmatic physical consequences for the city's recovery efforts, the most important legacy of Hiroshima's first public memorial ceremony was that it helped set in motion the ambitious municipal project that resulted in the construction on the site, five years later, of what is now the keystone of the city's tourism industry: Peace Memorial Park.

Funding for the park was provided by the Hiroshima Peace Memorial City Construction Law of 1949, which called for the former Imperial Army's vast landholdings throughout the city to be handed over to municipal authorities for resale liquidation to raise cash to be used toward ongoing recovery efforts.[1] Initially, the Japanese government was wary of setting a legal precedent for the private residents or local governments of other bombed cities (i.e., pretty much every municipality in the country with a population of more than fifty thousand or so) to demand similar national compensation for their losses of limbs, loved ones, livelihoods, and homes.[2] However, the Hiroshima proposal was popular with National Diet legislators of all stripes—probably not only out of genuinely empathic charitable sentiment, but also out of practical political interest (such a stance, publicly taken, would have been free "character reference" PR, after all, for candidates facing election fights). Moreover, what's good for the goose being good for the gander, the legislators also held out the hope (in vain, as it turned out) that their own home constituencies would shortly experience similar government recovery windfalls in recognition of, and compensation for, their own suffering under American bombs.[3]

From city hall's perspective, the construction of the park presented a kill-two-birds-with-one-stone solution to pressing problems it faced in the late 1940s. One of these was the ongoing Jisenji-no-hana situation—which had been somewhat ameliorated by Jisenji Temple's new building, but still lacked a fittingly substantial solution as to what to do with the human remains on-site. The other matter was the need to demonstrate, with tangible action and results, to Hiroshima's hundreds of thousands of surviving hibakusha and bereaved family members that city hall was committed to answering their nearly unanimously expressed desire for permanent public commemoration of the atomic bombing.[4]

There were American/Allied interests in play, as well. "In the world just after the war," as historian Monica Braw has explained the lay of the shifting landscape at the time, "the United States was widely regarded as the great savior from Nazism and fascism and the horrors they had brought. The wastelands of Hiroshima and Nagasaki were not consistent with this image of a humanitarian, altruistic America."[5] SCAP had a strong motive, then, from a PR / hearts-and-minds perspective, for supporting the Hiroshima Peace Memorial legislation. Construction of a prominent and politically neutral memorial facility in the heart of Hiroshima could affirm the approved sacrificed-for-peace narrative in an emphatic, tangible, and permanent manner. In this vein, it was not unreasonable to surmise that wanting to see the inconvenient optics of America's atomic handiwork swept under a narrative carpet of mutual forgive-and-forget largesse was behind SCAP's efforts to convince a hesitant Japanese national bureaucracy to get behind this bill and an equivalent one for Nagasaki's recovery.[6] The gesture would go far not only in terms of SCAP's relations with the Japanese people but also, as the US/Soviet Cold War rapidly heated up, in terms of America's standing in the court of world opinion.

In Hiroshima's case, according to the vision of Mayor Hamai Shinzō (who had assumed office upon popular election in 1947), the recovery law would lead to a revamped tourism industry by touting Hiroshima as a "Peace City."[7] In blunter terms, Hiroshima's recovery could be given a game-changing boost by promoting the city as a destination for curious tourists, both domestic and international, coming to see atomic-bomb-related sights.[8] Toward this end, a commemorative park space to be built over the rubble field of the former Nakajima District—encompassing Jisenji Temple and its ossuary—would be the spiritual and symbolic centerpiece of this Peace City vision.

A public contest announced by city hall for design proposals for the new park received 147 formal submissions from around the country.[9] The eventual winning proposal—announced on August 6, 1949, simultaneous with the passage of the Hiroshima Peace Memorial City Construction Law—was submitted by an up-and-coming young architect named Tange Kenzō.[10] Although the Tokyo Imperial University-trained Tange was not the most experienced architect to submit a proposal, he had made a name for himself during the war when he entered and won a design contest for a memorial commemorating the founding of Japan's Greater East Asia Co-Prosperity Sphere.[11] In an architectural irony that is not widely known, there are strong echoes of design and motif aspects of this wartime project (particularly the x-axis–y-axis layout of the central ceremonial plaza) in his successful Peace Memorial Park proposal.

In his 1949 design, Tange proposed that the park would encompass Jisenji-no-hana and all the rest of the islet of Nakajima north of the 100-Meter Firebreak (soon to become Peace Boulevard, also with funding from the 1949 recovery law), with the addition of a thin strip of embankment on the east bank of the Motoyasu River inclusive of the crumbling remains of the old Hiroshima Prefectural Exhibition Hall. These ruins were to be left intact as a physical testament to the violence the atomic bomb had visited upon the city.

The symbolic heart and dominant visual element of the park would be its ceremonial plaza, arranged around and along the alignment of the Cenotaph, reflecting pool, and eternal flame installation pointing toward the exhibition hall ruins / Atomic Dome in the distance. The park's functional heart—and its main visitor draw—would be a learning/conference center and a museum to reinforce the approved narrative of the bombing with emotionally powerful multimedia exhibits.

When construction for the park was green-lit in 1949, much of the real estate it was to occupy was still a brownfield of old 1945 rubble spottily covered with shacks. These dwellings were occupied by a mixed demographic of: (1) squatters from outside Hiroshima who had come into the city seeking work as day laborers on recovery building sites and/or to hustle in the city's thriving black markets; (2) Korean hibakusha who had been stranded in the city after the dissolution of the Japanese Empire and had been unable or unwilling to depart for newly independent Korea; and (3) surviving relatives of original area households—like young Kajiyama Senjun—who had returned to the neighborhood after the bombing to reclaim and rebuild upon their family real estate. More recently, the shacks of the Nakajima-honmachi shantytown had been joined by a smattering of slightly more substantial wooden homes and business establishments.

Before construction on the park could proceed, city hall would either have to evict or, as legalities necessitated, buy out these residents and businesses. After initially tortuous progress, these efforts were eventually successful. Public housing projects were constructed in districts west and north of the park, concentrated along the banks of the Ōta Honkawa in the neighborhood of Moto-machi. These were rented out to evictees who were legally registered Hiroshima residents. Landowners were bought out. As for the squatters, most simply broke camp and set up elsewhere—tending to seek out other river embankment patches of jurisdictional-gray-zone public land along the Motoyasu and the Ōta Honkawa or other real estate of yet indeterminate post-bombing ownership around the ZTD. The last of their settlements was not cleared by city hall until the early 1970s, with most of the evicted occupants also eventually ending up in public housing.

Once construction on the park finally commenced in 1950, the entire area was first buried under between fifteen and forty centimeters of earth and gravel trucked in to level off the park's topography completely.[12] The original scorched rubble of Nakajima was left as it was underneath this level of topsoil. A sample of this underlayer of debris can still be seen today behind a glass retaining wall along the descending stairway entrance to the partially underground Hiroshima National Peace Memorial Hall, which was built just north of the museum complex in the early 2000s.

The cremated remains of the tens of thousands of bomb victims that Jisenji and Zenhōji Temples had been storing on behalf of city hall eventually found a more respectfully fitting and permanent home in Peace Memorial Park. In 1955 an underground ossuary crypt / burial mound was excavated and constructed for the purpose next to Kakihara's memorial totem pole (which is still there) on the former Jisenji Temple grounds. In order to skirt the religion-state-separation provisions of Articles 20 and 89 of the 1947 constitution, which were under stricter public scrutiny in the early-postwar period than they are now, city hall set up an NGO—the Hiroshima War Victims Memorial Society—to fund, construct, and oversee the subsequent management of the ossuary privately.

As of October 2021, there were still 814 sets of identified cremated remains in the Peace Memorial Park ossuary awaiting return to next of kin.[13] The names of these victims are listed on posters that are regularly reprinted, distributed, and displayed in public facilities such as government offices, hospitals, libraries, and the like, not only in Hiroshima but around the country, as well. These remains are stored in jarlike containers on shelves in the ossuary, alongside other jars containing the remains of Hiroshima's seventy thousand John / Jane Does, which are marked only with the name of the district or neighborhood in which their bodies were found.[14] As there is virtually no hope of any of the unidentified victims ever finding their way back to loved ones and afterlife homes in family graves—even with modern DNA technology—the Hiroshima War Victims Memorial Society or, in the event of an eventual legal reinterpretation of the 1947 constitution's religion-state-separation stipulations, city hall will be responsible for these remains in perpetuity.

As for Jisenji Temple, after its first temporary relocation for the construction of Peace Memorial Park, it found a permanent home in 1973 in the harbor district's Ebasarayama Park—another one of the parcels of former Army land (in this case, a rifle range) handed over to city hall as a result of the 1949 recovery law.[15] Upon Kajiyama Senjun's death in 2019, at the age of ninety-six, his son Kenji became the new abbot of Jisenji Temple.[16]

THE MUTE MEMORIAL

ACROSS PEACE BOULEVARD from Peace Memorial Park, at the western foot of the Peace Bridge, stands the Hiroshima Municipal Girls' School (hereafter "Ichijo") Memorial. The stone originally stood on the former Ichijo school grounds in the south-central Hiroshima neighborhood of Funairi-chō, where it was unveiled in a memorial ceremony on August 6, 1948—the third anniversary of the bombing. It was moved to its present and highly prominent location on Peace Boulevard—sitting directly atop the Ichijo students' August 6, 1945, worksite on the 100-Meter Firebreak—in 1957.

The Ichijo Memorial somewhat resembles a speaker's podium in both shape and size. Carved in red granite by sculptor Kōchiyama Kensuke, the work was commissioned by an association of bomb-bereaved Ichijo parents. It is also an eloquent artifact of the lay of the land of bomb-related public discourse in Hiroshima under Allied occupation. To wit, on Kōchiyama's sculpture, there is a complete absence of wording or imagery with any connection to Japanese religion—elements an observer would normally otherwise expect to feature prominently on a Japanese memorial stone. A likely explanation for this is that it was designed to comply with SCAP guidelines prohibiting in Japanese public space any language, physical objects, or ceremonial practices associated with State Shintō—the nationalized, explicitly emperor-worshipping, nominally Shintō belief system whose diligent observation had been mandatory and all-pervasive in public life since it was invented by the new centralized Japanese government during the Meiji Era.[1]

SCAP's stated purpose for this policy was "to prevent a recurrence of the perversion of Shintō theory and beliefs into militaristic and ultra-nationalistic propaganda designed to delude the Japanese people and lead them into wars of aggression."[2] In short, SCAP wanted to eliminate State Shintō from the Japanese public sphere because it considered it inextricably and irredeemably intertwined with the militarist ethos the Allies were eager to see stay dead and buried in the ashes of defeated Japan. One would imagine this was a sentiment shared in the late 1940s not only by most East Asians, but by many Japanese, as well—particularly those who were unencumbered by a postwar psychic maelstrom of grief, guilt, and cognitive dissonance over having had a loved one die in the cause of, or simply as a result of, that ideology, and who were still going to bed every night with phantom air raid sirens echoing in their heads.

The official message, in any case, was clear: Japan's war dead could be mourned, but they were not to be venerated, and under no circumstances was any aspect of their wartime cause and/or the Imperial Era belief system to be publicly validated in any way, shape, or form. This meant that any terminology, visual imagery, or other symbolism evocative of that cause and that belief system was now verboten.

While SCAP had laid down the broad strokes of the purge of State Shintō (and any symbolism associated with it) from Japanese public space, the specific details of where to draw the operant boundaries of acceptable discourse for this were largely left up to Japanese interpretation.[3] For example, even though *eirei* ("heroic souls")—the standard wartime and prewar memorialization term for individuals who had died while performing military service—was not specifically mentioned in the SCAP guidelines, it was widely understood that the term was now unacceptable to use in public discourse.[4] Likewise, the similarly Shintō-inflected term *irei* ("soul consoling") was also considered taboo—ostensibly as it could have implied divine sanction of the sacrifice being commemorated—and thus off the table for inclusion in Occupation Era memorial activity. Instead of *irei*, the symbolically neutral, apolitical, and emotionally somewhat flat *tsuitō* ("mourning") was the preferred term, and this features prominently on other school grounds memorial stones erected in Hiroshima during the occupation.[5]

Kōchiyama might have been happy to get work at a time when many Japanese (including professional sculptors) still struggled to get three squares a day. But he was going to have his work cut out for him on this commission, as the exigencies of his clients' grief processes and the range of his artistic expression came up hard against the political realities of occupied Hiroshima. In this sense, he faced a rhetorical situation, as it were, similar to the one that had confronted Mayor Kihara at the first public August 6 memorial ceremony. On the one hand, he had to craft a message of appropriate emotional power that assigned meaning to the deaths being commemorated. On the other hand, he also had to make sure that neither the artwork—nor he himself professionally—fell afoul of occupation authorities keeping a watchful eye on any activity related to bomb memorialization. Complicating matters, the memorial the Ichijo parents wanted could not contain any mention of the atomic bomb that had killed their daughters, nor even of the fact that they had been killed by any external agency at all; it could impart only that the girls were dead and thus objects for appropriately apolitical public mourning in which the only acceptable emotions were melancholy, sentimentality, sadness, and, if the message could be shoehorned in, gratitude for Japan's new postwar peace and "freedom."

Kōchiyama's solution to his artistic dilemma was as bold as it was eccentric: He opted for eloquent silence. The only lettering that appears on the front surface of the memorial stone is "$E = MC^2$."

Einstein's formula is shown written on a box being clutched tightly to the breast of the central figure in a motif of three kneeling girls. The girl holding the Promethean boon (or Pandoran box) of atomic fire is frozen in prepubesecent time—the age at which most of the Ichijo girls died on their worksites along the 100-Meter Firebreak.

She wears the bobbed hairstyle and dowdy work clothes of wartime girl laborers—exactly what an Ichijo student would have been wearing on the firebreak site on August 6, 1945.

Somewhat anomalously, she has also grown angelic wings from her back—a strangely Christian trope to use in a memorial in this solidly conservative community with a traditionally devout loyalty to the Pure Land school of Buddhism. It is likely that Kōchiyama used the angel wings here as safely antiseptic symbolic shorthand for *This person is dead* in lieu of depicting her, more realistically, as having been burned and blasted to pieces. But the possibility that it was used ironically, in a sense of protest (*Look at the absurd ends to which we are compelled to go to say that our daughters were killed—OK, then let's see SCAP try to censor angels . . .*), cannot be entirely dismissed out of hand.

The slightly older girls flanking the central, box-clutching figure comfort and adorn her with flower garlands. The clear suggestion is that they are from the grievously sparse ranks of her few surviving Ichijo classmates. Aged appropriately for 1948, these comforting survivors are shown at the cusp of the full bloom of womanhood that the dead Ichijo girls would never know, and their long, braided hair, skirts, and bare legs and feet testify to the peaceful, comparatively carefree postwar lives similarly denied their dead classmates.

The only worded text on the memorial is to be found on its rear surface, which features an inscription carved after the brushed calligraphy original of its author, Miyakawa Masa'omi, who was principal in 1948 of the coed high school Ichijo became after the postwar national education reforms.[6] The inscription reads:

> *Rest in peace, comforted by your friends in this tranquil spot.*
> *August 6, 1948*
> *Miyakawa Masa'omi*[7]

On August 6, 2011, an NHK camera crew making a documentary filmed several elderly Ichijo survivors burning incense sticks in front of the memorial.[8] Responding to an NHK reporter's questions, the women acknowledged the artistic eccentricity of the "E = MC²" motif, while in the same breath they also appreciated the utility of the memorial in having given the bereaved family members a straw of hope to clutch toward taking some comfort in the idea—as thin a stretch though it might appear now—that their daughters' deaths had had some transcendent meaning and served some noble purpose by helping to usher in a brave new world of atomic marvels.

The elderly alumni also recounted their memories of being sixteen-year-olds attending the unveiling of the memorial on August 6, 1948, at its original location on the old Ichijo campus. Participating in the ceremony had been an ordeal for them not only because of the somber nature of the circumstances, but more than anything because they were ashamed of the fact of their own survival when almost all of their classmates had been killed. This survivor guilt and shame were especially acute under the gazes of the bereaved parents who had gathered at the ceremony, a few of whom actually confronted them to ask the question the girls most dreaded:

"Why are *you* still alive while *my* daughter is *dead*?"

ICHIJO WORKSITE

Ichijo firebreak worksite
Zaimoku-chō
Five hundred meters south-southwest of Ground Zero

SHORTLY BEFORE EIGHT A.M. on August 6, 1945, 544 first- and second-year Ichijo students had gathered at their firebreak worksite in Zaimoku-chō, a Buddhist temple and entertainment district just south of Jisenji-no-hana. As per their customary *chōrei* start-of-the-workday ceremony, the girls lined up in formation to have attendance taken and to receive the day's orders and special instructions. On this particular morning, these proceedings were capped by a motivational speech delivered by their principal, Miyakawa Zōroku.[1]

After his speech, Principal Miyakawa headed off to an appointment at the Prefectural Education Office of Academic Affairs near Hiroshima Station, leaving his students in the care of their faculty chaperones.

If Miyakawa had gotten his way earlier in the year, his students would not have even been in Zaimoku-chō this morning, or doing firebreak work anywhere else, for that matter. Ever since the government had ordered the mobilization of the nation's schoolchildren twelve years and older for full-time war labor a year earlier, the administration at Ichijo had walked a fine line between enthusiastic compliance with the exigencies of the nation's worsening war situa-

tion on one hand and on the other a desire to safeguard the physical
and moral health of its young charges.[2]

In light of the latter consideration, Miyakawa had initially balked
in 1944 at the idea of sending Ichijo's students to work alongside male
counterparts on the sweaty, dangerous factory floors of munitions
plants, which could themselves become bombing targets if and when
the Home Islands came within range of American warplanes. In lieu of
this, he had proposed to the Hiroshima Military District (HMD)—the
agency responsible for managing regional war labor mobilization—
that Ichijo turn half of its campus into a sewing factory to do piecework as an annex facility of the Army Clothing Depot in Deshio-chō,
just south of Hijiyama Hill. As a girls' school, Ichijo already had sewing machines on hand and instructors to bring their students up to a
reasonable approximation of military specs in their use, so any additional investment outlay to carry out the transformation of the campus into a factory for uniform work would be minimal.

After negotiations with the HMD and the clothing depot, the
proposal was accepted. On August 1, 1944, an official change-of-
command ceremony was held at the school marking the transfer of
the campus' sewing-floor facilities to the authority and administration of the clothing depot, and after two days of intense on-the-job
training, some three hundred twenty of the Ichijo girls officially began work as paid Army seamstresses.[3] Since the students were probably not yet skilled enough to cut and sew uniforms from new cloth, it
is likely that they were recycling worn uniforms brought into Ujina
from overseas combat zones, the processing and sorting of which—
also performed by student labor—was one of the main wartime tasks
of the clothing depot. After the bullet or shrapnel holes were stitched
up and the blood of their former wearers washed out, these recycled
uniforms would be almost as good as new again and ready to be reis-
sued to new recruits, thereby saving precious resources and man-
hours on the sewing floors.

In March 1945, however, Ichijo's sewing plant was ordered closed.
There were very few Akatsuki ships coming in from overseas anymore, so the uniform-recycling activity would have dropped off to

near zero. Moreover, in terms of the harsh realities of this stage of the war, from Japan's perspective, the HMD officer who issued the order for the closing succinctly encapsulated the new priorities when he stated that "bullets are more important than uniforms."[4]

In compliance with HMD's directive, most second-year and older girls were dispatched to the giant Japan Steel munitions plant in the eastern suburb of Mukainada. The first-year girls—considered yet too immature to endure the rigors of factory labor—performed unskilled volunteer day jobs in homeroom groups, doing farmwork, participating in scrap metal drives, or excavating shelters, trenches, and other underground military facilities in preparation for the anticipated Allied invasion. Since the city's most recent firebreak effort had begun in July, they had been working at firebreak sites, hauling and sorting dismantled construction materials for recycling.

Ichijo's student-labor routine was disrupted by an energy-saving *denkyūbi* power brownout scheduled for Monday, August 6, 1945. As the Japan Steel facility was in one of the districts of the city affected by the power outage, the second-year students who would normally have been working there were instead sent to the Zaimoku-chō firebreak site with their first-year schoolmates. The third-year and older girls were given a rare day off.[5] Those who were lucky enough to live in homes outside what would soon become the ZTD would live to see August 7.

NOGUCHI KAZUKO

Home of Noguchi Kazuko
Minami Takeya-chō
1.8 kilometers southeast of Ground Zero

IN 1933, CAREER bureaucrat Noguchi Ju'ichi was posted to Hiroshima by the Ministry of Agriculture and Forestry. A native of Sadogashima Island in the Sea of Japan, he was an expert in fishery development and had been sent in his professional capacity to help revamp Hiroshima Prefecture's marine industry—specifically its tuna and bonito fishing fleet. Hiroshima Bay had been famous for centuries for the quality of its oysters, and fishery efforts in the prefecture had naturally gravitated toward exploiting that highly profitable product. But from the standpoint of national food strategy, oyster farming did not compare favorably with deep-sea fishing and trawling as a high-volume source of animal protein—a precious and traditionally expensive commodity in Japan's livestock-poor, rice-intensive food economy. Moreover, the large, anchored rafts the oystermen floated in Hiroshima Bay did nothing toward showing the Rising Sun flag out on the high seas, nor could they be commissioned, in a wartime pinch, as coastline-patrolling, radio-equipped picket ships.

Despite Noguchi's efforts, however, local recalcitrance and the interruption of war prevented the retooling of Hiroshima's fishing industry out of its oyster-clogged inertia. But the prefectural fishing cooperative that he had helped organize in the 1930s was a success.

When Noguchi first arrived in the city with his then young family in tow, it is doubtful that he would have expected them all to still be there twelve years later. But that was where Ministry of Agriculture and Forestry wanted him, so that was where he stayed. And, all things considered, he had made a decent run of it. He had provided his wife, Haruko, and daughters, Reiko (b. 1930) and Kazuko (b. 1932), with a comfortable lifestyle in a sturdy Western-style house in Minami Takeya-chō—a central Hiroshima neighborhood tucked between city hall and the west bank of the Kyōbashi River.

Moreover, because he was a managerial-class national civil servant, Noguchi's position was imbued with a cachet of instant respect and status that also reflected upon his wife and daughters in this neighborhood of shopkeepers and tradesmen; Mrs. Noguchi, for example—despite starting out as an outsider in the eyes of her rather provincial Minami Takeya-chō counterparts—had naturally gravitated toward an influential role in the local housewife network over the years. Most recently, she had been in charge of a *Giyūtai* volunteer group composed of neighborhood women helping to clear one of the city's major firebreak sites in nearby Zakoba-chō.[1]

Reiko and Kazuko had also flourished here. The girls had both done well in their studies at Senda Elementary—the local district primary school located across Rijō Street, behind the nearby Hiroden streetcar headquarters. Upon graduation, Reiko had matriculated at the respectable private Shintoku Girls' School in 1942. Just the previous April, Kazuko, now twelve years old, had passed the moderately competitive entrance examination to Ichijo.

By any measure, the Noguchis had thrived in Hiroshima—at least to the extent that that term could apply to life anywhere in late-wartime Japan. And along with their Minami Takeya-chō neighbors and everyone else in the city, they could consider themselves lucky, cautiously, that their community had yet to be visited by one of the terrible B-29 fire raids that were burning the rest of urban Japan to the ground on a nightly basis.

But in mid-July, Reiko had suddenly taken ill after returning home from war labor work one evening. She died only a few days later, on July 17. The family never learned exactly what the ailment was, but the general consensus among doctors was that, whatever it was, she had probably contracted it at the Japan Steel plant in Mukainada, where she had been sewing parachutes all summer with her Shintoku classmates in sweltering heat and likely less-than-ideal sanitary conditions.

Reiko had been cremated after her death, and her ossuary jar now sat on a shelf in the family *butsudan* altar cabinet. The Noguchis would at some point see that the jar received proper interment in the family grave on Sadogashima, but for the foreseeable future, this was going to be extremely difficult. Travel between prefectures was discouraged for civilians not on official business. Moreover, train tickets for private use were nearly impossible to come by now that the national railway system was almost exclusively devoted to round-the-clock military traffic as the IJA rushed men and matériel to the anticipated next major battlefield in Kyushu. And if the summer's constant bedlam of air raid sirens, evacuations, and all-clear signals was any indication, any amelioration of the war situation was far from forthcoming. Reiko's interment would have to wait.

Given their recent bereavement, the Noguchis were taking no chances when Kazuko complained of a fever after coming home from her Ichijo firebreak worksite in Zaimoku-chō on the evening of August 5. Mrs. Noguchi sent her daughter straight to bed, and husband and wife took turns looking after the ailing girl through a night that ended up being sleepless for all three of them, not only because of the air raid sirens, but also because of Kazuko's worsening fever. When the family stirred to activity to begin their Monday on the morning of August 6, Mr. and Mrs. Noguchi decided that—the nation's desperate need for war workers be damned—Kazuko would not be joining her Ichijo classmates on the 100-Meter Firebreak in Zaimoku-chō today.

Mr. Noguchi was, in fact, so worried about his daughter that he made the decision—verily unthinkable for a national civil servant in late-wartime Japan, but understandable for a father who had just lost his other daughter to illness—to set off on his twenty-minute walk to work at the prefectural office a little later than usual today. He would stay behind to tend to Kazuko for a spell while Mrs. Noguchi went to Zakoba-chō that morning with her team of housewife firebreak workers. Still, he would not be able to put off going into the office indefinitely. Around seven forty-five, he left Kazuko's side for a few minutes to fetch his wife from the Zakoba-chō worksite and cajole her into coming home to take over tending to their daughter. The couple returned home together a little after eight and, standing over Kazuko's sickbed, decided on a caregiving routine for the rest of the day: Mr. Noguchi would go into work, after all, and in the interim, Mrs. Noguchi would periodically shuttle back and forth from Zakoba to check in on Kazuko. At the moment, they concluded that she needed some fresh water to hold her over while they were gone that morning. Mrs. Noguchi grabbed a bucket and headed out of the house for a moment to fetch some water from the neighborhood pump outside.

None of the three noticed the sound of high-flying B-29s approaching from the east.

ŌIWA KŌHEI

Home of Ōiwa Kōhei
Danbara Naka-machi
2.1 kilometers east-southeast of Ground Zero

ŌIWA TATSU'OKI SPENT the first half of his career with the *Kokutetsu* (National Railways) at various postings around his native Kyushu. Joining him along the way was his wife, Misaho, followed by their daughters, Naoko and Ayako, both born in the 1920s. The couple's only son, Kōhei—their third and last child—was born in 1932 in Kumamoto, the old samurai-castle town that was the family's final posting on Kyushu. The following year, another *Kokutetsu* transfer brought the Ōiwas to the important western Honshu railhead of Hiroshima.

As per the usual division of spousal labor in the household of a respectable executive in early Shōwa Era Japan, Mr. Ōiwa was expected to dedicate the full measure of his time and effort to his employer while Mrs. Ōiwa was expected to dedicate hers to everything else. First and foremost among her responsibilities in this regard was to see that their children attended schools appropriate to their status— and received educations appropriate to their gender—as the progeny of a management-level national civil servant.

Accordingly, Naoko and Ayako would be schooled and raised to become respectable, well-mannered young women with good marriage prospects. As was customary for a household of their station, any other personal aspirations that the girls might harbor for their respective futures were to be considered distantly secondary to the all-important, ultimate-life-course destination of getting married on time and to the right kind of young men.

The scholastic career of a daughter from such a background would have begun at an elementary school where she would rub shoulders with the right kind of schoolmates. If her home's zoned public school district did not provide such a venue, then her family would have to pay for one. This would often be at a Buddhist-affiliated kindergarten / elementary school. But it was just as often—and usually more prestigiously—at a Catholic- or Protestant-affiliated institution of nineteenth-century Western-missionary provenance. By the 1930s, despite their institutional origins, most Christian schools in Japan—if they wanted to stay in business and avoid harassment from the authorities and amateur ultranationalist zealots—tended to focus more on molding the moral character and bolstering the patriotism of their students than on attempting to convert them to the faith of their founders and faculty members.

The next—and probably final—step in our hypothetical well-bred Shōwa daughter's formal education would have been girls' school. This was the female equivalent of the four- or five-year junior high programs attended by middle- and upper-middle-class boys under the old Japanese education system. And as with their counterpart institutions for males, these schools also charged tuition, regardless of whether they were public or private.

Once enrolled at the right kind of girls' school, our Shōwa daughter would have followed a curriculum that was a mixed bag of scholastic subjects, white-collar vocational and teacher training, practical homemaking skills, and, from the 1930s on—perhaps anticipating the state's need for such skills on the home front in the foreseeable future—first aid and general nursing training.

With her formal education now at an end at seventeen or eighteen, our girls' school graduate's options would have widened slightly, and temporarily—but any final choice would still have been largely determined by parental (and probably also grandparental) input. If she wanted to pursue a postgraduation career for a few years before her inevitable and veritably compulsory marriage, she would have been permitted to do so as long as this was something like kindergarten teaching, secretarial work, or another occupation similarly acceptable for a girl of good breeding. But this would be tolerated only on the strict understanding that the daughter would not lose sight of her ultimate goal of marrying into a respectable and hopefully financially well-off family as the denouement of her brief season of relative personal freedom. With her nuptial endeavors accomplished—preferably in her early twenties—she would then be expected to dedicate the rest of her life to performing the same roles of wife, mother, and homemaker that she had grown up watching her own mother (who had likely married in the Meiji Era or the Taishō Era in her late or even midteens) perform selflessly, uncomplainingly, and unwaveringly.

If the girl had any brothers, the educational careers of these siblings were attended to and fretted over by the family at a different order of magnitude. This was especially true in the case of an only or oldest son, as he would bear responsibility for continuing and furthering the family name through honorable deeds and professional accomplishments and, literally, through the siring of progeny. This son would also be expected to care for his parents in their dotage—usually with them living under his roof, with their day-to-day needs and eventual end-of-life care attended to by his wife and whatever they could afford in the way of domestic servants.

Accordingly, no expense was spared, within reason and the upper limits of the household's financial means, to see that this male heir received an education that would optimally situate him for eventually taking on the mantle of these duties, while building up a network of personal school connections along the way that would help him further his future career and therefore augment his family's status. Ensuring that this life course was followed step by step was the responsibility not only of the heir's parents, but of his younger and/or female siblings, as well, in the sense that if the interests of these siblings regarding their own educational prospects conflicted with the heir's—for example, if the family could afford to send only one child to Tokyo or Kyoto to go to a top-level university—then the heir would get priority every time.

This Japanese version of primogeniture—like so many other pillars of the Japanese social order—had its origins in the Confucian ethical system that reached the archipelago via Chinese and Korean cultural influences in antiquity. Over long centuries, this practice had been followed by all classes/castes of recognized stakeholders in Japanese society, from its aristocracy and samurai down to the farmers, tradesmen, and shopkeepers who were its economic salt of the earth.

In its earlier, traditional guise, this practice had the desired outcome not of improving a family's station in competition with other households, but rather of maintaining and continuing that station. At the level of individual households—and individuals—this maintenance and continuity afforded the practice's faithful and competent observers a form of symbolic immortality through ancestor worship and the aforementioned siring of family-name-continuing progeny; at the level of community, the practice contributed to the preservation of harmony and the existing social order. Overall, this comported with a classically Confucianist worldview in which humankind was considered to be at its best when members of all castes, ranks, and stations knew their place, stayed there, and found peaceful satisfaction in this continuity/stasis.

For any stakeholder household in this static social order, no matter how humble, each generation's heir was the temporary custodian of his family's assigned hereditary status, which he would safeguard during his tenure as patriarch and then eventually pass on—hopefully undiminished—to his own heir. This meant that once the heir stepped into the patriarch role upon reaching mature adulthood, his life would be chained to his father's samurai clan, farm plot, workshop, or trade—regardless of whether or not the "family business" was suited to his individual personality, inclinations, or talents. Likewise, his own son would be destined—or doomed, as the case might have been—to an identical fate, and so on and so on down through the generations.

At least in broad strokes, this Japanese version of primogeniture survived the political, social, economic, and cultural upheaval of the Meiji Restoration. However, as the withering of the old system of hereditary caste and household status began to accelerate around the turn of the century, the traditional focus of Japanese primogeniture on cyclical continuity and social harmony was rapidly replaced by a Western-influenced, heavily capitalist-inflected ethos of doggedly pursued self-improvement. Unlike the old focus on harmony and continuity, the yardstick for success in this struggle was now ever-upward social advancement for households through the individual achievements of their sons in furious (if polite and sportsmanlike) competition with the sons of social peers. If a farmer's son could not go on to become a doctor, then at least he could acquire the biggest plot in his village. If a craftsman's son could not go on to become an industrialist, then at least he could build a bigger workshop and hire more assistants. If a shopkeeper's son could not go on to become an Army general or a diplomat, then at least he could build a department store.

In this hungry, aggressive New Japan, staid adherence to mere status quo and continuity were no longer admired ultimate ends in themselves; now they had about them the whiff of outdated mediocrity, if not actual moral indolence. And nowhere was this ethos of self-improvement and social advancement as patriotic duty pursued with more single-mindedly driven ardor than among the new class of educated and upwardly mobile professionals—men like Noguchi Ju'ichi and Ōiwa Tatsu'oki—who were the social vanguard of Imperial Japan.

Although Ōiwa Tatsuoki's Kyushu-boy-makes-good career as a national railway executive was exemplary of this Imperial Era meritocracy in action, he desired a better and more exciting future for his heir, Kōhei. Japan in the mid-1930s was not a place for young men of ambition and talent to seek the stability and security of desk jobs. With the IJA poised to dominate politics at home and to conquer half the world abroad, the national zeitgeist was electric with the frisson of unlimited potential and high adventure, both collective and individual. In this atmosphere, anyone could see that the armed services— in particular the IJA—were at the center of it all and that the best way for promising, forward-looking young men to meet and embrace the future was in His Majesty's uniform.

In this respect, the family's relocation to Hiroshima was fortuitous. No sooner had the Ōiwas arrived in their new home than Mrs. Ōiwa began reconnoitering the social and educational lay of the land to find the right schools first for Naoko and Ayako, but more crucially and importantly for Kōhei. These efforts paid off with a major coup when she secured admission for her son to the kindergarten program of the elite Seibi Gakkō.

Although this elementary school (and its kindergarten program) charged tuition, it was administered by Kaikōsha, the IJA Officers' Association, and its history in Hiroshima was almost as long as the Imperial Army's presence in the city. Moreover, the Hiroshima campus was one of only two Seibi Gakkō campuses in the country—the other being located near the Kaikōsha national headquarters in Tokyo. The significance of this distinction for Hiroshima was a reflection not of the city's importance as an urban or economic center, but rather of its history as a nexus of IJA culture and influence in western Japan.

The IJA's connection with Hiroshima began when the then castle town was chosen as the location of an important early military garrison soon after the Meiji Restoration, when the new regime in Tokyo established six such outposts around Honshu and Kyushu to oversee the transition of power and authority in this territory from localized feudal to centralized imperial governance. These garrisons were known as *chintai* (literally "subjugation bases"), and their most immediate and urgent mission was to demobilize the private armies of local samurai *daimyō* lords and their *han* fiefdoms as well as to absorb their political/administrative functions and—at least temporarily, until modern Japanese capitalism was fully up and running—their economic capacity.

Additionally, the garrisons performed the important symbolic role of projecting the power and prestige of the fledgling imperial regime to the far reaches of the Japanese archipelago. Along with the Tokyo-controlled nation-building media arsenal of major newspapers; the railroads; the nationwide network of state-managed Shintō shrines to promote emperor worship; and a centrally controlled system of compulsory education to teach the still largely functionally illiterate populace (particularly in the rural provinces) how to read and thus absorb government messaging (limited at the time to print media), the *chintai* garrisons helped to drive home the message to the residents of the archipelago that not only was there a new authority in the land—an "emperor" who had not previously been much of a presence in their daily lives—but also that they all now owed their loyalty and their lives to that emperor via a new identity as "Japanese."

Seibi Gakkō's Hiroshima branch was established in 1888, when the local *chintai*—headquartered in Hiroshima Castle—became the Fifth Division of the IJA.[1] Although the school was originally established exclusively for Army officers' children, in time, highly coveted entry spots in the elite school also became available to the children of locally posted national bureaucrats and civil servants. Eventually, the admission rolls were opened up to the children of movers and shakers in the local economy, as well, although these households were charged higher tuition fees than those paid by Army officers' and national civil servants' families.

While Seibi followed the standard national elementary-school curriculum dictated by the Ministry of Education, it never lost sight of its original charter of preparing its students for future careers as professional Army officers (or the wives of same). This grooming began for each new class year's students as soon as they toddled through the school's gates at the ages of four or five. By the time they graduated at twelve or thirteen, they had been thoroughly steeped in the ethos of "a new Japanese identity based on the ideal of self-sacrifice for the nation and emperor,"[2] bound up and supported by Imperial Era Japan's characteristic ideological iron triangle—firmly in place since the middle of the Meiji Era—of militarism, ultranationalism, and State Shintō.[3]

According to the plan plotted out by his parents for his own promising future, Kōhei would finish the course at Seibi, then attend a civilian junior high school of appropriate academic rigor for a year or two to prepare him for the entrance exam to the Hiroshima campus of the Imperial Military Academy Preparatory School (*Yōnen Gakkō*).

Spots at the IMA prep schools around the country were especially coveted, because acceptance into any one of them automatically secured subsequent admission to the Imperial Military Academy in Tokyo upon graduation. Non–IMA prep school applicants to the Imperial Military Academy had to take a highly competitive test at sixteen or seventeen—that is, as fourth- or fifth-year students under the old junior high school system.[4] Compared with their merely civilian counterparts, the boys who "escalatored" into the IMA from the prep school program had undergone an extra three years of professional officer ethos indoctrination, so they were considered an elite within an elite in the IJA, with a supportive old-boy network in the service that helped its members fast-track to eventual high military rank. Being a Seibi alumnus—either via Hiroshima or Tokyo—only added more prestige to the curriculum vitae of a future highflier in the Japanese military-industrial complex.

Beginning with his graduation from Seibi in March 1945, the initial stages of Kōhei's plan clicked into place in rapid succession. After he secured admission to Hiroshima Prefectural Junior High School (hereafter "Itchū")—one of the most prestigious secondary schools in western Honshu—he then sat for and passed the entrance exam for the Hiroshima IMA prep school in June 1945, at least a full year ahead of his original plan. From September 1, 1945, he would be living in a cadet barracks barely a thirty-minute walk from his family home in Danbara Naka-machi, a quiet residential neighborhood protected from the bustle of downtown Hiroshima by the abrupt topographical protrusion of Hijiyama Hill.

But before he would get to embark on his life-course-defining journey toward military glory, Kōhei had three more weeks of summer doldrums as a first-year Itchū student to get through. So far, he had passed this dreary season in an unvaryingly mind-numbing and backbreaking daily routine of shuttling between home and the Itchū campus and firebreak worksite in Zakoba-chō.

Although the work itself was grueling, boring, and beastly hot, the Itchū boys had it better than most students performing similar labor. As their worksite was directly adjacent to their Zakoba-chō school campus, their teachers had worked out an odd-even homeroom-number rotation schedule by which the first-year boys would spend every other hour on the firebreak, and the time in between ostensibly studying (without teacher supervision) back in their classrooms.[5] While the classrooms in the old wooden school buildings—especially on the second floors—were not much cooler than outside, having a roof overhead at least offered some temporary respite from the fierce summer sun. As an added bonus, the boys had all the water they could drink, as there were rows of concrete sinks with drinking faucets installed between the classroom buildings and the athletic field that occupied the southern half of the campus. All in all, it was a fairly enviable arrangement.

On a typical morning, Kōhei would have been up and out of the house before seven so he could make it to school and the day's work detail on the firebreaks on time with his classmates in Homeroom 1-6. But at seven o'clock on the morning of August 6, 1945, Kōhei was still at home in Danbara, where he had just finished a leisurely late breakfast with his mother, Grandmother Ōiwa, and a five-year-old cousin from the Harada family on his mother's side. The little boy had been staying with the Ōiwas since July, because his parents in heavily bombed and naval-gunfire-shelled Kagoshima thought Hiroshima would be a safer place for him to wait out the end of the war.

Mr. Ōiwa—whose usual workplace was in the *Kokutetsu* business office in Hatchōbori—would normally also have been at the family breakfast table on a typical morning, albeit perhaps an hour earlier. But today he was away on a business trip on the San'in Line, a national railway trunk deep in the mountainous hinterlands on the Sea of Japan side of Honshu.

The household's daughters were both long gone; Kōhei's older sister Ayako, a student at Hiroshima Prefectural Women's Teachers College, had been away for months now doing war work with her class-year group at a munitions plant on the Seto Inland Sea. His oldest sister, Naoko, had married a lieutenant from Akatsuki Command some years earlier. The Ōiwas did not get to see her much anymore since she had moved with her husband to his most recent posting—an

Akatsuki logistical depot deep in the mountains of neighboring Shi-mane Prefecture.

Today, Kōhei was at home instead of on his way to Itchū to join his classmates because he had felt some stomach discomfort and general malaise since waking up. Compounded by the air-raid-siren-harried and sleepless night they had all just passed, he simply did not feel he was going to be up to working in his present condition. With a little trepidation, he broached the idea of staying home to his mother.

"Well, it *is* going to be so hot out there," Mrs. Ōiwa replied, much to Kōhei's relief. "And it's not like you would be missing any class-work. . . . I don't think it's a problem if you take just one day off to rest up a bit."

An hour later, Kōhei was stretched out on a summer futon that his mother had laid out for him on the living room tatami matting. As he settled in to laze the rest of the day away, he contemplated the ser-endipity of his father being off on that business trip to the San'in re-gion today, because if he had been home instead, there was no way he would have allowed his son—the future professional IJA officer, no less—to take advantage of his mother's sentimentality and miss work like this while his more responsible classmates were resolutely per-forming their patriotic duty in Zakoba-chō.

Kōhei might have entertained a flicker or two of fleeting guilt about these matters as the hour bore down on 0815, but that train of thought would have soon been derailed by his continuing tummy rumblings and the shrill buzzing of the summer cicadas in the Ōiwas' front garden, where his little cousin—apparently also intent on pass-ing a carefree summer morning—was now happily playing alone around the flowers and bushes. Atop a table by the front door, the cloth-wrapped Bakelite bento lunch box his mother had prepared ear-lier in the morning for her son to take to his firebreak worksite sat in mute witness to the goings-on.

Perhaps if the cicadas had not been so loud, Kōhei might have noticed the sound of B-29 engines echoing off the steep slopes of Hiji-yama Hill just behind his house.

ITCHŪ WORKSITE

Hiroshima Prefectural Junior High School (Itchū) campus / Firebreak worksite
Zakoba-chō
Nine hundred meters from Ground Zero

WHILE ŌIWA KŌHEI and his first-year classmates at Itchū had been do-ing firebreak work almost every day since their matriculation, the school's older boys had been doing factory work alongside adults at weapons plants around the city. The most hazardous and exacting tasks were performed by the oldest boys, including the most recent (March 1945) graduates of the school, who upon the completion of their studies had been temporarily stuck in a sort of war-needs hu-man resources catch-22 limbo; on the one hand, since they had now graduated, they were no longer under the direct administration of their alma mater and thus the school could not officially mobilize them as war labor. On the other hand, they were still too young for conscripted military service. Still, every able-bodied person in the city was a potential munitions worker, and it would not do for this partic-ular group of boys simply to lie about at home, waiting for the war to end. Special orders were cut—ostensibly by HMD—designating this group a *teishintai* adult labor team.

In a rare example of Imperial Era interservice cooperation, these seventeen- and eighteen-year-olds were dispatched to the Kure Powder

Works to make gunpowder for the Navy. But whether working on a factory floor or temporarily lounging about at home, none of the young men expected to remain civilians much longer; with the "Decisive Home Islands Battle" against the Allied invasion[1] nigh, it was only a matter of time before there would be yet another emergency lowering of the draft age for Army service that would surely scoop all of them up and throw them into uniform. Few boys in the city from that age cohort—and in the rest of the country, as well—expected to get out of those uniforms alive.[2]

Of current Itchū students, the largest allocation of workforce—a roughly evenly divided mixed group of more than five hundred fifth-, fourth-, and second-year boys—was sent to do munitions work at the two Hiroshima-area factories of Asahi Manufacturing, Ltd. Most of the third-year students—the youngest at Itchū who had known any kind of "normal" student life before the national war labor mobilization of 1944—were doing munitions work at Tōyō Manufacturing, Ltd. (the present-day Mazda Corporation). The remaining third-year students—a single homeroom of fifty boys—worked with another hundred fifty second-year students, making airplane and engine parts at a subcontracted manufacturing facility the boys knew only by its Ministry of Munitions designation of "Aircraft Factory 7264."

As was the case with many other junior high schools and girls' schools around the city, the day's brownout for designated districts also affected the war labor schedule for Itchū's students on August 6. Specifically, Aircraft Factory 7264, located in the western suburban district of Takasu, was scheduled for a *denkyūbi* brownout, so manufacturing operations there would be suspended for the day. While many schools tended to give their students a precious day of rest when their workplaces were shut down for scheduled brownouts, Itchū's principal, Watanabe Toyohira, ordered the work groups affected by the August 6 brownouts to do firebreak work downtown on that day.

The affected third-year homeroom teacher complied and had his fifty-odd students working a stretch of the 100-Meter Firebreak in Dobashi on August 6. However, the Itchū chaperone for the second-year students at the plant, a young English teacher named Toda Gorō, told the hundred fifty boys in his charge to stay home for a "self-study day" instead.[3]

On August 6, nearly the entirety of the first-year students—more than three hundred boys, minus a handful fortunate enough to have been sick (or simply malingering) on this day—was at the Itchū campus in Zakoba, overseen by a skeleton chaperone crew of four teachers.[4] After the all clear from the *Straight Flush* weather recon flyover had sounded at around the end of the morning's *chōrei* ceremony, the odd-numbered-homeroom boys went out to the firebreak site across the athletic field at the southern end of the campus, while the even-numbered-homeroom boys stayed back in the school buildings to wait for the nine o'clock shift change.

In the second-story classroom of Homeroom 1-6, first-year student Honda Shigeo heard the B-29 engines and reflexively pulled his padded cotton *bōsaizukin* protective hood out of his backpack and put it on.[5] The boys in the class had all been trained to do this, but he was the only one to follow the protocol. The others had long since given up the practice after becoming inured to the sound of (so far) harmless B-29s over the city all summer. Besides, the hoods were hot.

Honda's classmate Takahashi Shigeru was in another corner of the classroom, reading *Shōnen Kurabu* and other *manga* magazines with some other boys.[6] Kodama Mitsuo was reading a textbook by a window on the south side of the building. Other boys in the class, including Hara Kunihiko, doodled in their notebooks or chattered, sotto voce, and otherwise enjoyed their unsupervised downtime sheltered from the day's already blazing sun. A few of the boys had run downstairs and outside excitedly to look for the B-29s when they heard the engine sounds, perhaps happy for the intrusion of a little drama and excitement upon the morning's ennui.

However, Homeroom 1-6's most academically talented student was conspicuously absent this morning. It was the first time the usually serious and hardworking Ōiwa Kōhei had missed school since matriculating the previous April.

Around 0815, Kataoka Osamu and his classmates in Homeroom 1-4 also heard B-29 engines for the second time this morning. This time, however—and somewhat ominously—there were no sirens. Some of the boys in the class ran to the hallway to look out the windows, searching the sky for the telltale silvery glint of high-flying American planes.[7]

DAI NI KENJO WORKSITE

Second Prefectural Girls' School (Dai Ni Kenjo) firebreak worksite
Zakoba-chō, south of city hall
1.1 kilometers from Ground Zero

SECOND PREFECTURAL GIRLS' SCHOOL (Dai Ni Kenjo) was established in 1941 as Hiroshima Prefecture's response to a nationwide move to expand secondary education opportunities for young women. Depending on how one looked at it, this effort was socially progressive—befitting the pedagogical policy of a modern nation in the mid-twentieth century. Alternately, it simply addressed the need for a new source of entry-level white-collar workers as Japan's military adventures steadily drained its supply of junior-high-graduate young men who would normally have occupied such positions. And although, according to its original charter, Dai Ni Kenjo should not have produced its first graduating class until March 1946, its war-accelerated, truncated curriculum allowed its first class of some eighty girls to graduate a year ahead of schedule. As with their age-group contemporaries at Itchū, the HMD required them to stay on in war labor, now as *teishintai* workers remunerated with a modest salary.

In addition to being new, Dai Ni Kenjo was also very small, with only two forty-girl homeroom class groups per grade year. Since it was not even large enough to merit its own campus, Dai Ni Kenjo was compelled to borrow classroom space at the North Ujina campus of the prefectural women's teachers college, with which it also shared the same principal and most faculty.[1]

Because of its minuscule student body, Dai Ni Kenjo would have been barely an asterisk on HMD's table of organization of Hiroshima-area civilian manpower. Nevertheless, in the nation's time of need, every able body counted, and the girls of Dai Ni Kenjo had been performing diligent and tireless war work, when and where they were told to do so, since the summer of 1944.

Dai Ni Kenjo was one of the comparatively few secondary schools in Hiroshima that had second-year students out on the firebreaks instead of working in factories, as was the case with, for example, Ichijo, Kenjo, and Itchū. Ironically, the school's administration had thought that war work in the munitions factories in the city's suburbs and hinterlands where older Dai Ni Kenjo students were already working would be too dangerous for the second-year girls not only because of the arduous conditions on the factory floors, but also because it was feared that these facilities—particularly the strategically significant ones like Tōyō Manufacturing, Ltd., Mitsubishi Heavy Industries, and the Mitsubishi shipyard in Ujina—would soon be American bombing targets.[2] Furthermore, as the B-29s had more recently begun to bomb cities only at night, it seemed to make sense that the firebreak work in Hiroshima's central business district would be comparatively safe, as it was carried out exclusively during daylight hours.

On August 6, the large Zakoba-chō firebreak that passed along the southern perimeter of city hall and Itchū's athletic field was packed with some three thousand firebreak workers, of whom 2,458 were junior high school and girls' school students.[3] Normally, and as had been the case just a day earlier, there would have been nearly one hundred sixty Dai Ni Kenjo students—two full class years—among their number. Today, however, there were only thirty-eight girls on the Dai Ni Kenjo firebreak detachment—all from Ms. Hata Yaeko's second-year West Homeroom. Along with Tominaga Chieko—at home that morning with a stomachache from eating too many grapes the night before—five other girls were absent on account of illness or injury.

The previous day, new directives from HMD had come down through the school administration. The Fifth Division's truck patch on the East Parade Ground needed weeding. HMD wanted it done on August 6, and tasked Dai Ni Kenjo with providing the labor. The school determined that the job would require students from three homerooms—about one hundred twenty girls—to be temporarily pulled from their usual war labor workplaces.[4]

As Dai Ni Kenjo's third- and fourth-year students could not be spared from their important munitions factory work, the school administration had decided to give their eighty or so first-year girls a break from the rigors of the firebreaks and send them to the East Parade Ground truck patch for the day. The other complement of students would come from one of the two second-year homerooms.

A round of rock, paper, scissors between the respective homeroom presidents determined which second-year class would get the easier duty for the day. West Homeroom president Hi'ura Ruriko lost. So the next morning, while the girls of East Homeroom were picking weeds with the first-year students at the foot of Futabayama Hill—some 2.5 kilometers north-northeast from what, in a few more minutes, would become Ground Zero—the West Homeroom girls, Hata-sensei, and Takahashi Ritsuko, a young probationary teacher, were toiling away at their routine slog in Zakoba-chō, barely a kilometer from where Little Boy would detonate.

As per their usual routine, Hata-sensei performed the key role of standing atop the rubble mound of whatever toppled wooden structure her group was working on as the hour approached 0815 hours. From her perch, which she shared today with Takahashi-sensei, Hata-sensei would constantly scan the pile of roof tiles, boards, metal pipes, and electrical wiring at her feet and decide what she was going to pick up next to hand off to the first girl in the bucket brigade line. Each girl in the line—which stretched off to the sorting piles along the side of the cleared roadway—would sing out a loud, high-pitched *"Hai!"* as she received her rubble item from the girl in front of her; then she would pivot to hand it off to the girl to her rear.[5] This cadence helped to break up the tedium of the task and maintained a momentum of mutual encouragement in the work teams. With the voice of the first girl in the line being echoed and multiplied by those from three thousand other throats also singing out *"Hai!"* every few seconds—and all those shouts punctuated every few minutes by a round of adult male heave-ho yells and a cracking, groaning wooden crash as yet another house was pulled down farther ahead—the ambient noise on this stretch of Zakoba-chō would have bordered on the cacophonous.

It was not, however, so loud that it drowned out the grinding of B-29 engines powering through a sharp turn, and this sound reached Zakoba-chō ten seconds or so before eight fifteen. At that moment, Hata-sensei called out, "It's a B! It's a B!" and pointed to a spot high over the northeast corner of the city.[6] While most of the West Homeroom girls followed the line of Hata-sensei's pointing finger and fixated on two tiny glinting specks in the sky, one of her students—Sakamoto Setsuko—did not.

All along the Zakoba-chō site, other children and adult workers on the firebreaks also looked up in the apparent direction of the engine sounds' sources. Cheers broke out among these onlookers when they mistook the three radiosonde telemetry devices parachute-dropped by the *Great Artiste* for crewmen bailing out of a stricken B-29.

TOMINAGA CHIEKO

Home of Tominaga Chieko
North Ujina
3.4 kilometers south of Ground Zero

TOMINAGA CHIEKO'S FATHER was born into an old family of Kyoto merchants. No one in the local mercantile community of his birth would have looked askance if he had simply eased into a position with the family business upon coming of age. But this was not the path he was destined to take. Instead, his family groomed him from childhood for a spot at the very apex of the new Imperial Era meritocracy—a journey that would take him far from the stifling traditions and limited life-course options of his hidebound hometown. The young man's talent and his family's investment in his education paid off when he passed the rigorous entrance exam for the Faculty of Law at Tokyo Imperial University.[1]

Upon graduation, young Tominaga was hired by corporate conglomerate Mitsubishi Shōji Co., Ltd., where he eventually became a specialist in shipping and harbor management. This professional niche was perfectly timed for an ascent through Mitsubishi's executive ranks during the 1920s and 1930s, fueled in large part by the IJA's voracious need for maritime warehouse capacity as it embarked on increasingly ambitious military adventures on the Asian mainland.

As per the classic life script of an elite Japanese executive of his era, Mr. Tominaga spent his career being shuttled between the Tokyo home office and various company branches—in this case, Mitsubishi port facilities around the country; he married and started a family along the way. Until 1942, these moves were always undertaken with his young family in tow. But on the occasion of his posting to Shanghai as the director of Mitsubishi's harbor operations in the IJA-occupied city, he and his wife thought it safer, given the ongoing war situation, to leave their daughters, Machiyo (b. 1929) and Chieko (b. 1932), behind in the family's home base of Tokyo with Grandmother Tominaga and their live-in maid.

In the spring of 1944, Mr. Tominaga was transferred back to Japan to head up Mitsubishi's extensive maritime facilities in Hiroshima. There, he would tend to the civilian end of warehouse management and other Ujina Harbor operations for the IJA's Akatsuki Command. In this capacity, he oversaw a small army of primarily Korean laborers employed under various degrees of indentured servitude.

Mr. Tominaga had always been proud of his status as an alumnus of Tokyo Imperial University—the most elite educational institution in the empire. As such, he was pleased to discover upon his arrival at his new posting that there was a tightly knit community of fellow alumni in the Hiroshima area. Among their number they counted leaders of local economic, educational, and bureaucratic/political life. Included in this latter group of individuals in early 1944 were Home Ministry–appointed prefectural governor Matsumura Mitsuma, as well as Hiroshima mayor Awaya Senkichi, with whom Tominaga was on backslapping, honorific-dropping terms as an old buddy and classmate from the Faculty of Law.

But while Mr. Tominaga might have been pleased with his new posting and the family was happy to be reunited after two years, not everyone in the household was content in their new environment. Although Mitsubishi had put the Tominagas up in one of the most enviably and luxuriously appointed houses in Ujina, Mrs. Tominaga thought her new neighbors were boorish bumpkins. Accordingly, she had as little to do with them as possible. This was not as little as she would have liked, however, since the national war labor mobilization policy had deprived her of the family's last remaining domestic servant—sent off in late midlife to work with teenagers on the floor of a munitions plant back in a hometown she had barely seen in decades. Now, like it or not (and she most certainly did not), Mrs. Tominaga had to line up with the other housewives when the *tonarigumi* neighborhood association distributed food or scheduled mandatory civil defense drills. Still, what was already an unpleasant situation was prevented from spilling over into certain intolerability by her husband's high status. Being the wife of the most important civilian in Ujina excused her from participation in the daily slog of "volunteer" physical labor around the city in which the other women in the neighborhood were compelled to participate as part of their contribution to the war effort.

Machiyo, now sixteen, and Chieko—a precociously intellectual and very headstrong thirteen-year-old—were not faring much better in the new environment. When Mrs. Tominaga set out to find appropriate schools for the girls in Hiroshima, she had been faced with something of a dilemma: Although there were schools in the city that might have been considered academically and, more important, socially suitable (if barely) destinations for her daughters, they were concentrated in the central business district, far from the family's Ujina home.

The Rijō Street streetcar line was only a few minutes' walk from their house, and this would have been a perfect conveyance—in peacetime—for the girls to use to commute to more prestigious downtown schools like First Prefectural Girls' School (Kenjo) or Hiroshima Jogakuin. But under the circumstances, it did not seem prudent to send the girls far from home every day. Although American bombers were not yet beginning to attack Japan proper, a man in Mr. Tominaga's position was well informed enough about the progress of the war situation to know that it was only a matter of time before this changed. Accordingly, he and his wife decided that the girls should stay within walking distance of the house, even if that meant having to rub shoulders with a rougher sort of classmate at local schools every day. In April 1944, Mrs. Tominaga secured a spot for Machiyo at Hiroshima

Prefectural Women's Teachers College, while Chieko entered Dai Ni Kenjo with a new class of first-year students. Both schools' campuses were adjacent to the Army Mutual Aid Hospital and barely a ten-minute walk from the Tominagas' house.

Although both Machiyo and Chieko shared their mother's overall aversion to their new social and cultural environment, personality differences between the sisters made for disparate experiences at their respective schools. The more generally agreeable and savvy Machiyo had an easier go of things, as she was the more adept of the two in the vital Japanese social skill of *kejime*—the ability to judge rapidly and bend with fluid social situations, masking one's inner thoughts and emotions when necessary or prudent to avoid interpersonal friction and/or undesirable attention as a suspected harmony disturber.

The headstrong Chieko, however, was an inveterate harmony disturber and, as such, faced significant obstacles to fitting in at Dai Ni Kenjo—not the least of which was that she constantly bristled at what were, in her opinion, ridiculously and unnecessarily spartan rules and customs at her new school, which imposed restrictions on her freedom of movement, expression, and personal appearance that she never had to deal with in the fancy private schools she had attended until now. Moreover, attendance at the school was a daily affront to her self-esteem. The ranking of personal attributes that were valued among the students at Dai Ni Kenjo could not have been more stacked against her own skill set; there, Chieko's budding talent as a writer had no formal outlet. Her overall scholastic ability—which was head and shoulders above those of nearly all of her classmates—meant nothing. Her cosmopolitan tastes and interest in Western literature and classical music were viewed by the other girls with a toxic mixture of suspicion, derision, and class envy.

In Dai Ni Kenjo's school culture, athletic girls with loud voices and ebullient personalities occupied the pinnacle of the social pecking order. This stratification was reinforced by teachers who saw in these go-getters—like Chieko's class president, Hi'ura Ruriko—soldierly virtues that the other students would have done well to emulate. Accordingly, they were invariably assigned to positions of responsibility and authority over their classmates, such as taking morning roll call and leading calisthenics, patriotic recitations and singing, and military drills.

Girls who did not fit this profile were expected to keep their mouths shut and fall into line behind the leaders. Most who were sorted out into this "follower" category accepted their station meekly and obediently. Girls who did not were shunned, and this was essentially Chieko's lot in life throughout her first year at Dai Ni Kenjo—where cultural norms of provincial insularity and knee-jerk suspicion of outsiders essentially mirrored the neighborhood of adults surrounding it, if not Chieko's new city of residence as a whole.

In her second year at the school, however, Chieko was rescued from her ongoing condition of near-total social alienation by the timely arrival of a new classmate named Tamekazu Michiko. Coming into such a school environment as a transfer student, in and of itself, would have seen Michiko automatically marked for ostracism that would have taken superhuman charisma and social savvy to come out from under. Unfortunately for the shy, bookish Michiko, she possessed neither of these characteristics. And adding yet another strike against her, she was, like Chieko, a cultural outsider vis-à-vis Hiroshima ways (including the local dialect of Japanese), having only recently arrived in the city when her father took over management of an ice plant in North Ujina.

Chieko and Michiko became fast friends. So much so, in fact, that Michiko soon began swinging by the Tominagas' fancy house every morning so the girls could walk to school together. From July 1945, the walks became considerably longer when every morning they had to trek nearly 2.5 kilometers to their firebreak worksites in Zakoba-chō—a journey made all the more arduous by the wooden *geta* sandals their ridiculous school regulations forced them to wear, instead of the lightweight rubber-soled *zukku* gym shoes students from most other schools were allowed to wear for the firebreak work.[2]

Early on the morning of August 6—before the weather reconnaissance B-29 *Straight Flush* set off a first round of air defense sirens around the city—Michiko came by the house to pick up Chieko for their long walk to Zakoba-chō. From behind a wooden *fusuma* door in a room where she was lying on her sickbed futon, Chieko heard her mother talking to Michiko on the *engawa* front porch of the house. This was a fairly routine occurrence, as it was often the case that Chieko would not yet be ready to leave when her more punctual classmate showed up every morning. On such occasions, her mother and Michiko would make small talk while Chieko made her last-minute rushed preparations to go to work or, perhaps once or twice a month, to school to see the inside of an actual classroom.

Today, however, the conversation sounded different. Chieko thought she heard something almost mocking in the tone of her mother's voice as she explained why her daughter would not be going downtown to work. When Mrs. Tominaga and Michiko shared a quick, tittering laugh over the word "diarrhea," Chieko felt a brief flash of shame and irritation—emotions that had already been simmering because a few minutes earlier, her sister, Machiyo, had teased her about playing hooky over a tummy ache before leaving for her duties at the teachers college.

Toward the end of the eavesdropped conversation, Chieko heard her mother mention how hot it was sure to be today out on the firebreak worksite. She then tried to convince Michiko to call in sick to school, too, so she could relax with Chieko, nice and comfortable out of the brutal sun.

Michiko politely refused the offer. Pausing at the front gate, she promised to explain everything to Hata-sensei, then set off alone for Zakoba-chō.

With the missed-workday decision now finalized, Chieko harbored embarrassment and relief in equal measure. Off the hook, in any case, she decided to make the best of her involuntary day off by rolling over on her futon and going back to sleep. Approximately seventy-five minutes later, she was still asleep when thousands of other people in the city heard the faint sound of high-flying aircraft engines approaching from the east.

Chieko sat up on her futon with a start when a flash of silent lightning illuminated her room. After a long ten seconds or so, there was a thunderous boom that rocked her house on its foundations briefly with something like a strong gust of wind. Accompanying the shake were a long, distantly echoing boom and, closer at hand, the sound of breaking glass, both inside the house and in the surrounding neighborhood. After a falling ceiling panel grazed Chieko's head, she bolted off her futon and ran to the kitchen, where her mother had been doing dishes.

At the moment of the flash, Mr. Tominaga had been sitting on the floor ledge at the *genkan* entranceway of the house, getting ready to go to work. He had just laced up his clunky Army boots and was winding his military-style canvas puttees around his shins when Little Boy's shock wave—weakened by distance but still packing a punch—clapped the house. A large broken pane of falling glass cut his leg, but the thick canvas duck of the puttees prevented the gash from being as deep as it might have been.

In the kitchen, mother and daughter were still holding each other when Mr. Tominaga called out from the front of the house, first to announce his not-unreasonable theory that an enemy bomb or naval shell must have just landed nearby, then to inform his wife that a piece of glass had cut his leg.

From her own room in the back of the house, Grandmother Tominaga checked in to report that the rattle had given her a start, but that she was otherwise uninjured.

While Mrs. Tominaga fetched Mercurochrome and a bandage for her husband's injury, Chieko went outside to check the damage done to the exterior of the house. But there was not much to see. The windows on the north side of the house were broken, but that was about it. There was no smoking crater in the ground or in the street, as one might have otherwise expected from the near miss of a bomb. Nothing nearby was burning or even smoldering. And damage to other houses in the neighborhood looked about the same: some paper shoji screens thrown ajar here and there; some roof tiles knocked loose; the same windowpanes broken on the sides of the houses facing north.

As Chieko surveyed the scene, she caught in her peripheral vision movement of something dark and coiling against the sky to the north. Turning to look at it, she saw a giant column of gray smoke rising over the city center, emitting a low, continuously rolling rumble during its rapid ascent into the sky, flecked and winking with flickers and billows of multicolored flame.

Now joined by her parents and neighbors who had also emerged from their houses, Chieko watched this inexplicable apparition in wordless awe as the already kilometers-high pillar of smoke and fire began to level off and flatten into a shape like an umbrella or the cap of a mushroom.

She was snapped out of this dark reverie when her father mentioned her sister's name.

Clearly something catastrophic had just happened in the city center. . . . Did Machiyo and her classmates at the teachers college have any business there this morning? No, Mrs. Tominaga assured her husband. When Machiyo had left this morning, she said that there was an assembly in the campus auditorium. She must be there.

Without another word and—at least for now—the gash on his leg completely forgotten, Mr. Tominaga set off as quickly as his fifty-something body could carry him to look for his daughter at the Prefectural Women's Teachers College.

Turning back to regard the ugly pillar of smoke rising above the city center, Chieko suddenly remembered where Hata-sensei and the girls of West Homeroom were this morning and that she was supposed to have been with them.

ŌIWA EXPLOSION

Ōiwa household
Danbara Naka-machi
2.1 kilometers east-southeast of Ground Zero

ŌIWA KŌHEI WAS on his futon in his living room, leisurely gazing out at the garden on the south side of his house, when everything suddenly turned white. The light was so intense that in the few seconds of silence that followed the flash, he had time to wonder if it were possible that the sun had somehow fallen out of the sky and landed right on top of his neighborhood.

Then something lifted him up and threw him across the room.

Like many other hibakusha who survived Little Boy at close range, Kōhei never heard its actual explosion. For a second or two, the bomb's supersonic shock wave created a kilometers-wide atmospheric vacuum over the center of the city that not only sucked the air out of the lungs of everyone in the ZTD, but also prevented the transmission of sound during its brief existence. By the time air from the surrounding area rushed back in to restore atmospheric equilibrium in the city, the shock wave was already well on its way out into the suburbs, where people like Tominaga Chieko in Ujina, Zhen Su Bing in Yoshijima, and the Saitō Unit soldiers on Kōno'ura—far enough away not to have been inside the atmospheric vacuum—heard Little Boy's explosion as the loudest sound of their lives.

Hijiyama Hill had shielded the Ōiwa house—and most of the immediate neighborhood—from the more horizontally oriented destruction of Little Boy's thermal rays and direct line-of-sight shock wave. But it had offered no protection against the violent displacement of such a huge volume of air over the center of the city. This rapid movement of air—first on the way out, then again when it rushed back in—had had the effect of blowing in every window in houses from various directions, propelling glass shards and splinters at shrapnel velocities, and stripping roofs of most of their heavy tiles. Hijiyama had likewise not offered any protection against destruction coming up from below. A seismic event—lasting only a fraction of a second—was caused when the surface of the earth centered underneath Little Boy's airburst had been momentarily deformed into a concave depression by the spherical shock wave impacting it. The effect was somewhat like what happens to the skin of a drum when it is struck with a stick. And similar to the atmospheric displacement, it also wrought two-cycle destruction: in this case, once on the downstroke, under the initial impact of Little Boy's drumstick smash, and then again when the ground snapped back up—in the expected equal and opposite reaction—to some approximation of its original position.[1]

Though brief, as well as shallow in terms of the distance it actually caused the ground surface to oscillate, this vertical seismic movement had been powerful enough to crack and dislodge the Ōiwas' roof. Viewed from the outside, the roof was not caved in, as would have been expected under the impact of an overhead airburst, but rather bent outwardly, convexly, as if some giant trapped inside the house had tried but failed to push its way up and out.

But the house itself was still standing.

As Kōhei came to his senses and the cacophony of his immediate environment quieted, he heard his mother calling from the hallway. His grandmother, shaken but apparently uninjured, answered from a room in the back of the house. His little cousin answered with a sob as he ran back into the house from the garden—obviously terrified but also apparently not seriously injured.

At the moment, Kōhei was curled up in a ball in the far corner of the living room, with his futon mattress now on top instead of underneath him. The same seismic drum slap that Colonel Tibbets and his crewmen experienced ten kilometers away as an echo off the earth's surface had likely lifted Kōhei (and his futon) up off the tatami floor, with the air turbulence then catching him—perhaps even in midbounce—to flip boy and futon over and toss both into a wall several meters away.

In the living room and the hallway that adjoined it, nearly everything—including the underside of the futon now covering Kōhei—had been pierced by bits and blades of flying glass. The floor and every horizontal surface in the room were covered with it, as well as by wood splinters, shattered picture frames, toppled tchotchkes, and other debris. And although his futon mattress had shielded Kōhei from the worst of the glass storm, the protection had not been complete: A piece had caught his left shin, and this spot was now bleeding—not heavily but still noticeably—though in his current psychological state, he was still hours away from registering any pain from the injury.

Next to the living room, Kōhei's mother had gone completely prone on the hallway floorboards in the instant of the initial flash—a quick reaction that was likely thanks to years of faithful participation in *tonarigumi* neighborhood association civil defense drills. When the atmospheric displacement shock wave hit the house, a wooden *fusuma*—the kind used to partition space in traditional Japanese interiors—had fallen on top of her, and its now shard-honeycombed surface had protected her from the worst of the window-glass implosions. Still, an errant sliver had nicked the corner of her forehead, giving her a cut that produced an amount of blood that, in the moment, looked worse than it actually was.

An hour or so later, when the Ōiwas began seeing the condition of people straggling into their neighborhood from the city center, their own injuries would seem very minor in comparison.

NOGUCHI EXPLOSION

Noguchi household
Minami Takeya-chō
1.8 kilometers southeast of Ground Zero

MRS. NOGUCHI HAD stepped back up into the house with a bucket of water for her sick daughter when the flash lit up everything in sight from all directions. Instinctively, she dropped the bucket and covered Kazuko with her own body an instant before the interior of the house imploded in flying glass, splinters, and falling ceiling panels.

Mother and daughter lay there together for a few seconds until Mrs. Noguchi got up to push open the now broken front door so the family could get out of the house. With Mr. Noguchi coming up behind them, the threesome—taking care not to cut their bare feet on the broken glass and other detritus on the floor—scrounged up some footwear from the now jumbled mess in the entranceway, and stepped out into the street.

Outside, the sky was dark with smoke and dust, but there was just enough ambient light to make out that every house in the neighborhood except their own had been knocked flat. The Noguchis regarded the scene in stunned silence until they heard voices and rustling in the clinking roof tile rubble and shattered lumber around them. Here and there, neighbors—not all but some—began emerging from under the piles of wreckage that had been their homes just a minute or so earlier.

At this point, Mr. Noguchi's executive instincts kicked in and he began shouting out orders for the survivors to form an evacuation party. Under his guidance, the group proceeded due west, eventually coming to a stop at the first spot they encountered that did not seem to be on the verge of bursting into flame—the broad but now scorched brown lawn of nearby Hiroshima Bunri University.[1]

Here, the Noguchis had their first opportunity since the explosion to catch their breath and assess their injuries. Mr. Noguchi had been standing near an open window on the north side of the house when the flash occurred; he received some burns on his face and arm, but he shrugged these off as not needing any immediate medical attention. Mrs. Noguchi, however, was in much worse shape, having been punctured by dozens of pieces of flying glass that she had taken in her daughter's stead when all the windows in the house had turned into shrapnel. Most of these pieces were relatively small, but a large shard had slashed one of her shins, and the cut was now bleeding profusely.

Kazuko, thanks to her mother's quick reflexes, was uninjured. As for her fever, the shock and drama of her current circumstances had pushed that far, far down on the list of things to be worried about at present. Like most other people in the city who were still able to move and function at this point, she would be numbed by shock and running on pure adrenaline for the next few days. The long grief work and trauma reckoning of digesting the catastrophe would come later. For now the all-encompassing immediate concern was physical survival. And at the moment, the primary antagonist in that struggle was fire.

WAKING UP IN HELL

Dai Ni Kenjo firebreak worksite
Zakoba-chō, south of city hall
1.1 kilometers south of Ground Zero

LITTLE BOY'S SHOCK WAVE knocked Sakamoto Setsuko unconscious. She never heard its explosion.[1] All she remembered of the last moment before she passed out was everything in her field of vision briefly turning white, then going black.[2]

When she came to, she did not know how long she had been out—maybe minutes, perhaps only seconds. But what had been a brilliantly sunny day under a cloudless sky a moment before was now a firelit hellscape under a canopy of night-dark sky. One block to the west, city hall and the groves of stately pine trees surrounding it were ablaze. Closer at hand, smaller tongues of flame licked up out of the wooden structures and rubble piles lining the cleared roadway of the firebreak.[3]

Purely by chance, Setsuko had been facing away from Little Boy at the moment of its detonation, and the shadows and defilade of her classmates' bodies had probably shielded her from the worst of the thermal rays and the shock wave of the explosion. As far as she could tell at the time, she had come away from her ordeal with only a burn on her upper-left arm and a smaller one on her right cheek.

But the ground around her was strewn with the bodies of classmates who had not been so lucky—and most of them were not moving. The faces of anyone who had been looking at the sky when the detonation occurred were now so badly scorched and smashed as to be virtually unrecognizable; some had been literally burned off—almost as if by a blowtorch—and were now barely more than featureless patches of brownish asphalt crusted over sightless eyes.

Some of these girls eventually managed to get back on their feet, screaming in pain and calling out for their mothers as they did so. The outer layers of their skin hung in filmy flaps and strips from their limbs—most conspicuously from their arms—with only scraps and tatters of clothing still clinging to their scorched and mostly naked bodies. Some of the girls would hang on to life for a few more hours or days, the more fortunate expiring before the inevitable acute radiation syndrome set in to compound their misery exponentially. Whether they knew it or not in the moment, they were already as dead as their classmates lying motionless on the ground.[4]

A few of the standing girls hobbled or staggered about in tight circles, perhaps trying to find a way of holding their bodies that would offer some reprieve from their agony. Others merely stood in place, shell-shocked and shivering. All appeared to be waiting—like the patient, obedient children they had been raised to be—for someone in authority to deliver them from their present circumstances.

As everyone else on the worksite still able to do so ran, shuffled, hobbled, or crawled for their lives to escape the fires closing in from all directions, the West Homeroom girls stayed put. But their immobility in the face of life-threatening peril was not solely a consequence of the girls' physical and psychological injuries. Student workers like the Dai Ni Kenjo girls had been trained to stay at their posts and within earshot of their faculty chaperones in any situation, whatever happened, until told by legitimate authority figures to do otherwise. And Hata-sensei's girls had been well trained.

Twenty-nine-year-old Hata Yaeko had a gentle and generous disposition that belied her physical appearance. She was large and powerfully built for a Japanese woman of her era—with a wide, round, rustic face that only added to her impression of wholesome strength and healthy vigor. She had always cut a physically charismatic figure in the flesh, whether standing in front of a blackboard, leading bamboo spear drills on the school athletic field, or handing down roof tiles from the top of a firebreak pile.

But as Setsuko saw Hata-sensei in this moment, framed against a backdrop of hell on earth, her teacher seemed almost colossal. Bent down to clutch Tamekazu Michiko and Sakai Tamie close to her body, and with her hair now starched stiff with blood and white with ash and dust, she looked like a statue of a giant bird shielding tiny chicks under her vast wings.

As Setsuko watched, Hata-sensei stood up straight and shouted, "Class dismissed!"[5]

With this command—her last official act as the teacher of second-year West Homeroom—Hata-sensei released her students to find their way to safety on their own. This was as per the worst-case workplace scenario they had trained for, in which their teacher was incapacitated and unable to lead them herself. And Hata-sensei was, indeed, incapacitated or close to it: Like everyone else (except Setsuko), she had suffered severe flash burns. She had also probably broken at least a few bones when she was blown off the top of the meters-high rubble pile by the shock wave. Nevertheless, she still found the strength to perform one final task for her girls while she was still capable of movement: Fighting through her pain and injuries, she hoisted Tamekazu Michiko up piggyback and, cradling Sakai Tamie in her arms, disappeared into the chaotic flow of evacuees surging down Rijō Street in the direction of Red Cross Hospital.

Setsuko and three other girls tried to follow their teacher, but they soon lost her in the chaos. Now completely disoriented, Setsuko's group ended up getting pulled into another stream of people—this one flowing due east through Fujimi-chō in the direction of the Kyōbashi River. The foursome held hands tightly as they were pushed and pulled along by the rushing crowd, the other three girls now completely dependent on Setsuko's still functioning eyesight to keep moving. They also had to make sure to stay on their feet, for if they fell, they would certainly be trampled to death by the panicking people coming up behind them.

During their exodus, Setsuko began feeling a burning pain on the soles of her feet and, cursing her misfortune, realized that, like her companions, she had been blown out of her wooden *geta* sandals back at the firebreak site. But at the moment, this was the least of her problems. Fires were spreading rapidly through the shattered buildings, houses, and mounds of wooden debris and rubble that now surrounded them, threatening to cut off their avenue of escape at any moment.

Looking for a way out of the city, Setsuko and her companions wandered through warrens of burning wreckage, having to constantly reroute when they reached dead ends. They also had to take frequent rest stops when their exhaustion and pain became overwhelming. As they did so, they were surrounded by scenes of human suffering with which their own—at least for now—paled in comparison. They passed children screaming for their mothers, and mothers screaming out the names of missing children—the desperate entreaties of both as futile as bird chirps in a typhoon. They passed concrete box firefighting cisterns stuffed with the corpses of people who—driven mad by their burns—had plunged headfirst into them and died in place, the upper halves of their bodies submerged in the water and their legs hanging out over the edges like skewers of meat on display at a street vendor's food stall.[6]

By this point, the conflagration consuming the city was evolving into its own weather system—a firestorm fueled by combustible organic material and superheated air that scorched the lungs of anyone trying to breathe it. Howling gusts of furnace-hot wind drove blizzard drifts of sparks and embers swirling over everything, including into the girls' hair and onto whatever clothes they still had on, which were constantly smoldering and on the verge of bursting into open flame. Several times when this actually happened, the girls had to douse themselves in cisterns—likely having to push and pull the dead and dying out of the way to do so.

Somewhere, Setsuko and one girl—the horribly burned and barely mobile Kitakoji Michiko—lost their other two companions in the chaos. Meanwhile, they ended up being pulled eastward again along with the mass of people making a beeline for the Kyōbashi—the waterway ostensibly holding out the sole hope for escape from the burning city.

But when the girls eventually reached their would-be sanctuary, they found that the conflagration they thought they had been running away from had long since beaten them to their destination, catching up from behind and closing a pincer of flame in front of them. Now the tightly packed wooden neighborhoods on the west bank of the Kyōbashi were one long, high wall of fire.

For a few moments of terror and despair, Setsuko and Michiko would have been presented with an awful choice: They could stand where they were and burn, or they could take their chances in the water, which was quickly filling up with the lifeless bodies of others farther upstream forced to make the same decision.

LD$_{50}$

Hiroshima Prefectural Junior High School (Itchū) campus
Northernmost classroom building
Zakoba-chō
Eight hundred eighty meters from Ground Zero

THE FIRST-YEAR BOYS in the even-numbered homerooms were knocked out by the shock wave a few seconds after they saw the flash. Most never regained consciousness. The few who did found themselves buried under the rubble of their collapsed school building.

In Homeroom 1-6, Ōiwa Kōhei's best friend, Takahashi Shigeru, had fallen between rows of classroom desks when he passed out.[1] Although the desks had banged his legs up pretty badly, they had also saved his life from the tons of falling debris that would have otherwise snuffed it out. Other than a few bruises and cuts, he did not seem to have any other injuries.

When his eyes adjusted to the low-light conditions, Takahashi could make out brighter spots in the murk—gaps and interstices in the jumbled Jenga pile under which he was trapped. While he tried to figure a way out, this task acquired a new urgency when he became aware of a steadily growing ambient crackling sound; the rubble around him was beginning to burn. Soon the air was so hot and acrid, it was painful to breathe.

Honda Shigeo had also fallen to the floor between desk rows after passing out.[2] When he came to, his arms and legs were in extreme pain, his mouth was full of dust and grit, and it was difficult to breathe. He struggled to crawl forward to get out of the collapsed building, but made no headway. He then tried to move in the other direction, toward his feet, where he found enough play in the rubble to allow him to make slow progress; he was showered with minor cave-ins of dust as he made his way toward the light.[3] All around him, he could hear his classmates, also buried under tons of shattered beams and roof tiles, moaning and whimpering in the darkness.

The rubble had also aligned favorably for Kataoka Osamu, who managed to crawl out relatively quickly through what was left of Homeroom 1-4.[4] Once free and clear, he found two other classmates who had also made good their own escapes, and the threesome promptly began chanting the "Imperial Rescript to Soldiers and Sailors" to try to buck up the spirits of the boys still under wreckage of the school. Here and there, feeble voices under the pile joined in the recitation:

> *The soldier and sailor should consider loyalty their essential duty.*
> *Who that is born in this land can be wanting in the spirit of*
>   *grateful service to it?*
> *No soldier or sailor, especially, can be considered efficient unless*
>   *this spirit be strong within him. . . .*[5]

When Kodama Mitsuo woke up under the rubble of Homeroom 1-6, there was a fifteen-centimeter-long carpenter nail sticking out of his shoulder.[6] As he was still in shock, he did not feel much pain yet. But breathing was difficult in the burning, dusty air. As with Kataoka Osamu in Homeroom 1-4, the rubble had also lined up favorably for him, and he seemed to have been one of the first boys in Homeroom 1-6 to make it out into the open air. Once he did so, he found the day dark as night, the air filled with smoke and dust, and everything within sight—including the wreckage of the Itchū school buildings—either aflame or smoldering.

Almost as soon as he had gotten back on his feet, Kodama doubled over and began vomiting. Although their old wooden Meiji Era school building and its sturdy tile roof had shielded the bodies of the hundred fifty or so first-year Itchū students sheltered indoors at the moment of Little Boy's detonation from the worst of its thermal rays and shock wave (the collapsed school building aside), it had done nothing to protect them from the intense burst of initial radiation released when the bomb's core of U-235 achieved criticality.

Decades later, Dr. Kamada Nanao, a renowned Hiroshima specialist in hibakusha-related medical issues, would estimate that the boys in the Itchū buildings received a whole-body instantaneous exposure of some 4.6 grays of direct radiation from the explosion, mostly in the form of neutrons and gamma rays.[7] This level of exposure closely corresponds with a figure American nuclear strategists and scientists since the nadir of the Cold War have referred to as "LD_{50}"—that is, the amount of radiation that proves fatal (LD = lethal dose) to 50 percent of an exposed group of human beings within thirty days of a nuclear event.[8]

The LD_{50} figure closely parallels the eventual fate of the even-numbered homeroom first-year students who had been in their school building at the moment of the explosion: Of the forty-six boys who managed to crawl out from under the wreckage of the collapsed school, only nineteen were still alive half a year later.[9] The other hundred or so boys in the even-numbered homerooms either died instantly from the building collapse or burned to death, trapped under the wreckage.

As for the other hundred fifty or so boys in the odd-numbered homerooms who had been outside on the Zakoba-chō firebreak, their own LD_{50} radiation exposure was essentially moot in the context of their catastrophic burns, blast trauma, and flying-projectile injuries. None lived to see the morning of August 7.

Like thousands of other initial survivors in Hiroshima who were concurrently beginning to experience the effects of ARS, twelve-year-old Kodama Mitsuo had no idea that he was vomiting because of exposure to an invisible form of energy that would eventually kill him. Similar to Sakamoto Setsuko's concurrent reaction to the cataclysm a hundred or so meters away, he assumed that by some kind of miracle, he had just dodged a catastrophe that had wiped out most of his schoolmates.

Fighting back his nausea as long as he could bear it, he helped a small group of boys who were trying to pull others out from under the rubble of the school. But the situation was not cooperating with the efforts of these would-be rescuers; as the flames both from the school and the surrounding neighborhood got higher and closer, the moans, whimpers, and resolute rescript recitation of the students still trapped under the school now turned into the high-pitched screams of children being burned alive.

At this point, Kodama's burgeoning panic became untenable. Telling his compatriots that he was going to try to find help, he ran off to the east and never looked back. Confronted with the desperate reality of his situation, with the entire city now engulfed in flame, he understandably opted to focus on his own survival. Skirting the encroaching fires, he continued heading eastward toward the Kyōbashi River.

REPRESENTATIVE OF THE ESTABLISHMENT

Home of Tominaga Chieko
North Ujina
3.4 kilometers south of Ground Zero

WHILE MR. TOMINAGA was away checking on Machiyo at the teachers college, a neighborhood man, sweat drenched and frantic with worry, barged unannounced into the Tominagas' home. He was carrying a terrified-looking girl of about five—presumably his daughter—whose arm had been cut by flying glass. The errant shard visibly protruded from its entry wound, which was bleeding profusely.

"Please help!" the man yelled. "They wouldn't even look at her at the Army Mutual Aid Hospital," he continued, in a thick working-class Hiroshima dialect. "You got any Mercurochrome?"

"Why won't they look at her?" Mrs. Tominaga asked, probably still too taken aback by the abruptness of the intrusion to take umbrage at this inherent breach of social protocol.

"Because they're swamped with wounded people," the man said. "An injury like this they won't even bother with."[1]

At that, the still nameless neighbor laid his now screaming and flailing daughter down on the tatami-matted floor of the living room. While he and Chieko held down the girl's arms and legs, Mrs. Tominaga pulled the glass shard out of the puncture wound, averting her eyes and grimacing as she did so.

After the injury was treated with Mercurochrome and bandaged, the man scooped up his daughter and went on his way. He never explained why after a ten-minute-or-so walk (or run) back from being rebuffed at the hospital, he had chosen this particular spot—out of all of the other houses in the neighborhood—as his daughter's sanctuary in his family's hour of emergency. The Tominagas knew the fellow only by sight, vaguely, as just another workingman from a neighborhood full of them, but they had had neither the occasion nor the inclination to interact with him in any significant way—not even to learn his name. Under normal circumstances, a man like this would never have darkened their doorway unless he had come to repair the plumbing or deliver a package.

Since the move to their scruffy Hiroshima neighborhood the previous year, the Tominagas had so far studiously avoided having anything to do with their new "neighbors." However, the morning's encounter with the frantic father suggested that, in the interim, their neighbors had nevertheless formed distinct opinions about the Tominagas. Specifically, it indicated that in the social hierarchy of the community, the Tominagas were regarded by their neighbors as *erai hito*—high-status representatives of the Establishment—and their grand home thus as a lifeboat of authority and stability in a crisis.

In the Japanese power dynamics operant here, *erai hito* were considered to occupy a different plane of existence from regular folk and were given a respectfully, even deferentially wide berth in normal times. They would be bowed to, at least from the neck up, when encountered in the street or in one's place of business, and spoken to directly only when invited to do so and always in one's best approximation of *keigo*—the highest honorific form of the Japanese language. But until the war began to shake up the old ways and to make extraordinary circumstances ordinary, an upper-class Japanese woman like Mrs. Tominaga might never have had the opportunity to appreciate the reciprocal flip side of the hierarchical privilege she had enjoyed all her life so far: In times of communal emergency, *erai hito* were expected—if not obligated—to lead from the front.

The unwritten rules governing this arrangement were as old as the days when samurai—the *erai hito* of a previous era (nevertheless still within living memory for any Japanese in 1945 over the age of eighty or so)—lorded it over an archipelago of (normally) obedient rice-farming serfs. Although widespread adherence to this kind of rigid social hierarchy would not survive long in the cultural upheavals of Japan's postwar period, it was still very much in place in August 1945, even after the inevitable social-leveling effect of seven or eight years of "total" war mobilization on the home front. And if the Tominagas had perhaps not fully understood all of this before their visit from the frantic father, they understood it in its wake. And they would receive more instructions as to the nature of their noblesse oblige in the coming days and weeks as they were compelled to allow the spacious living room of their luxuriously appointed Mitsubishi company house to be transformed into an auxiliary aid station for the neighborhood.

In addition to a newfound awareness of their previously unappreciated obligations toward their heretofore ignored neighbors, the injured-child interlude provided another revelation. The news about the dire situation at the Army Mutual Aid Hospital—the largest and best-equipped medical facility in Ujina—was Mrs. Tominaga's and Chieko's first intimation of just how bad things were under that ugly pillar of smoke still hanging over the city far to the north.

———

When Mr. Tominaga returned from the teachers college out of breath and in a visibly high state of anxiety, he was the bearer of good and bad news. The good news was that Machiyo was all right. Despite having been in the campus auditorium when the ceiling caved in, she had received nothing more than some contusions on her back and legs—of some concern, yes, but manageable.

The bad news was that the adjacent Army Mutual Aid Hospital was so swamped with grievously injured people pouring in from the city that the teachers college had been hastily transformed into an aid station to accept its overflow.[2] To staff this ad hoc aid station, Machiyo and her schoolmates—who had all received a degree of training for such duty—had been pressed into service as nurses and/or orderlies. Chieko's older sister would not be coming home for a while.

As the morning progressed, the Tominagas' neighborhood also began to fill up with injured people. Fleeing the now furiously burning city, these wretched refugees were streaming across the Miyuki Bridge with the fires hard at their backs. Having been turned away en route by both the Red Cross and Army Mutual Aid hospitals, they were now making their way down Rijō Street, ostensibly to seek medical attention at Ujina Wharf.

Mr. Tominaga was no stranger to catastrophe, and he possessed hard-won survivor's antennae finely tuned to recognize one underway when he saw it. He had been a thirty-year-old Mitsubishi man working in the company's Yokohama Harbor branch when the Great Kanto Earthquake leveled and nearly completely incinerated the Tokyo metropolitan area on September 1, 1923, killing some hundred thousand people. Although his wife and mother had safely ridden out the worst of the disaster in their house in Tokyo's Yamanote "High City" District, he still had traumatic memories of the long and horrific journey home he had had to make on foot that day through the devastated, burning metropolis, not knowing whether or not he was going to arrive home to find his family dead, injured, or at least homeless.

The family—its members by then including two small daughters— had also experienced the massively destructive Muroto Typhoon of 1934, when Mr. Tominaga had been posted to the Mitsubishi office in Osaka Harbor. This was one of the worst storms ever to hit the Japanese Home Islands, and Osaka had borne the brunt of its winds and catastrophic tidal flooding. The experience had been so traumatic for the family that Chieko even had a two-year-old's "flashbulb memories" of rising water swamping the first floor of the family house and of being carried on her father's shoulders as the family waded through flooded neighborhood streets to reach high ground.

This time, Mr. Tominaga was not going to wait for the disaster to reach his house before he evacuated his family to safety. He was becoming increasingly anxious about what he had seen at the teachers college, about the growing numbers of wounded people pouring into their neighborhood, and about the billowing clouds of smoke approaching from the north. Although the neighborhood was far from the city center, it was densely populated and occupied cheek by jowl by highly flammable wooden homes, warehouses, and industrial plants. He believed it was only a matter of time before the fires from the city jumped the Kyōbashi River and burned Ujina to the ground.

After a quick conference with his wife, Mr. Tominaga decided that the family would evacuate. One of his subordinates at the harbor management firm had a home and a small plot of farmland on Tanna Hill—high ground in an agricultural district in Niho, about two kilometers to the east. In previous workplace discussions, the manager had offered the Tominagas sanctuary at his place in the event that their own home in low-lying Ujina were ever threatened by one of the Ōta Delta's frequent floods or by fires from an air raid.

As present circumstances certainly constituted an emergency, the Tominagas would take the generous subordinate up on his offer. They packed up an evacuation bag of important documents and valuables and set out for Niho around ten in the morning. What should have been a forty-minute walk ended up taking some two hours on account of the frequent rest stops that Grandmother Tominaga demanded because of her arthritic knees. As a result, the family did not reach the house on Tanna Hill until after noon.

STACKING BODIES

Ōiwa household
Danbara Naka-machi
2.1 kilometers east-southeast of Ground Zero

LIKE ALMOST EVERYONE else in the city that morning, the Ōiwas assumed that a bomb had landed either on or directly adjacent to their house. But when they stepped outside to look at what they expected to be extensive external damage, they were surprised to find that other than their blown-in windows and a buckled roof, the house was still in pretty good shape. Looking around, they saw that all of the other homes in the neighborhood, nestled along the eastern slopes of Hijiyama Hill, displayed similarly moderate damage.

Kōhei and his mother had no explanation for what had just happened, nor for why the sky had gone dark—especially in the west. Neither did their neighbors, who were now also milling about outside their own houses, trying to figure out what was going on. Unlike the people in Tominaga Chieko's Ujina neighborhood two kilometers to the south, no one in Danbara (or anywhere else in or near the ZTD) saw the shape of the mushroom cloud because they were underneath its canopy. All they saw of it was the shadow it cast over their own neighborhood and the other central districts of the city.

Presently, a theory to explain the midmorning darkness began making the rounds to the effect that the IJA arsenal might have just gone up in nearby Kasumi-chō, the district bordering Danbara to the south. But this explanation did not jibe with what everyone was seeing in the sky, which was comparatively clear to the south in the direction of Kasumi-chō, but dark overhead and to the west, toward the downtown districts on the far side of Hijiyama. In any case, the theory was soon disconfirmed by people coming into Danbara from the direction of the arsenal.

Danbara enjoyed an interlude of hazy sunlight beginning about an hour after the explosion, when the morning's prevailing southwesterly winds dissipated the last of the dust pall that had been looming over the neighborhood.[1] But it was not long before its residents began to see black smoke rising up from behind Hijiyama Hill, from the direction of the central business district. Gradually, the sky returned to its former murky pall—false twilight in the middle of the morning—this time underlit with pulsing blushes of red and orange.

Roughly simultaneously with the redarkening of the sky, the first trickle of shattered survivors began cresting Hijiyama and descending upon Danbara Naka-machi in their exodus from the burning city center. Most of these people were naked or nearly naked, having had their clothing blown or burned off. Their exposed skin was a blotchy camouflage pattern of charred black and blood red. It was too painful for them to walk normally, as their burned arms would brush against their burned torsos if they did so. The predicament forced them to walk with their arms held out in front of them—these burned limbs invariably draping crepey curtains of translucent beige epidermis.

It was not long before the trickle of these walking dead became a stream, then a flood, coming up and over Hijiyama in staggering, stumbling, blind-leading-the-blind lines that wound their way down into Danbara. No doubt sensing relief upon arriving in the only part of the city that was not ablaze from end to end, these walking wounded would sit, lie, or fall to the ground, then never get up again. Some died quickly. Others lay there, lingering, moaning, begging for water or pleading for someone to kill them to end their suffering before they, too, inevitably nodded off dead.

Soon, the street in front of the Ōiwa house was so deep in bodies, there was barely any room to walk without stepping on one. Adding to the horror, the smell of burned human flesh was becoming more over-powering and stomach wrenching by the moment.

Amid the faceless masses of human suffering rapidly piling up on the street in front of the Ōiwas' house, one specific individual stood out. This person—whom Kōhei and his mother would thereaf-ter always refer to as "the Gentleman"—had entered the Ōiwas' gar-den through the front gate before collapsing into a crouch, wedged against the front-entrance doorway of the house. He was a very well-spoken and polite man about Kōhei's father's age—about fifty or so. Relative to the other victims filling up the scene—most of whom were barely identifiable as human beings—he was not nearly as badly burned. In addition to his sophisticated manner of speech, he had enough of a business suit remaining on his frame to indicate that he had been some kind of white-collar professional—perhaps an execu-tive or a high-ranking civil servant. At the time of the explosion, he had probably been in one of the reinforced concrete buildings in the downtown district; this could have explained why he did not have the monstrous appearance of most of the other survivors who had reached Danbara and who had probably been caught either out-side or in wooden structures of flimsy construction that had offered little protection against Little Boy's destructive wrath. Nevertheless, it was clear that the calamity had still wounded the Gentleman griev-ously. His overall condition suggested that he did not have much lon-ger to live—although, in the magical thinking people in shock-induced denial can sometimes display, he did not seem to be aware of his im-pending fate.

When Kōhei and his mother approached their uninvited guest, the Gentleman asked for water—his throat and mouth obviously scorched—and apologized for his impertinence in entering their prop-erty without permission. Politely denying the Gentleman's need for apology, Kōhei set off to fetch some water. Even though he had already heard—as most people in Japan had by this time—that you were not supposed to let injured people drink any kind of liquid, the Gentle-man's pleas were so plaintive that it seemed the lesser evil to grant what might have been the dying man's last request. Kōhei regretted only that he did not have enough water on hand for all of the moaning people sitting and lying down on the street in front of the house.

Although water mains in the neighborhood (and across most of central Hiroshima) had been broken by whatever had set fire to the city and killed or wounded all of these people, the Ōiwas' comfortably upper-middle-class home—unlike most houses in the neighborhood— was furnished with running water, and there was still a little of it left in the plumbing, slowly dribbling out of the kitchen faucet. Scrounging up an intact teacup from the piles of wrecked dishes and tableware on the kitchen floor, Kōhei filled this up with water from the leaking faucet and brought it out to the Ōiwas' guest. The pained expression on the Gentleman's face momentarily changed to one of peaceful relief as he gulped the offered water down. He then thanked his hosts profusely.

"Please write down your name and address," the Gentleman insisted, clearly envisioning a happier and healthier future for himself. "I would like to return here and thank you properly when I recover from my injuries."

"Oh, please don't worry yourself about that," Mrs. Ōiwa replied.

But the Gentleman was insistent, so Mrs. Ōiwa went back into the house to search through the wreckage for pencil and paper, then returned with the requested note. The moment she placed it in his hand, he took a deep, rattling breath. Then his eyes closed, his head lolled to one side, and he slumped over dead.

It was the first time thirteen-year-old Kōhei had ever seen a person die in front of his own eyes. He was shocked and frightened by the experience, but it might have prepared him, in a way, for what the rest of the day—and coming days and weeks—had in store.

———

The lead patrols of the Akatsuki Command first responders entered Danbara from the south sometime in the early afternoon. These were likely the Akatsuki HQ personnel who had been assigned to the ground-relief-force element making its way up the east bank of the Kyōbashi to establish an aid station on the southern foot of Hijiyama Hill. But as with the Saitō Unit soldiers on the west bank of the Kyōbashi concurrently struggling to make headway up Rijō Street, these troops first had to deal with the problem of clearing the roadways so that the Akatsuki trucks and other relief traffic could make it through. While the roadways in Danbara Naka-machi did not pose the same challenges as Rijō Street did in terms of knee-deep piles of structural wreckage and burning debris, they were covered with broken human beings, and no vehicular aid was going to be able to reach the neighborhood until these bomb victims were cleared.

As was the situation on Yoshijima, in Senda, and everywhere else in the city the Akatsuki soldiers were beginning to reach, there was not yet a standard operating procedure in place for the unprecedented scale of the most immediate and urgent task at hand—the process of body retrieval, clearance, and disposal. For the time being, the soldiers had to come up with a system on the fly. To begin clearing the roadways there in Danbara, the soldiers first had to distinguish the quick from the dead. The former were either walked or carried away to the aid station now up and running in a large air raid shelter on the slopes of Hijiyama; once trucks began reaching the area later in the afternoon, the most seriously injured of these victims were sent to Ujina, and thence ferried to Akatsuki quarantine facilities and hospitals on the Hiroshima Bay islands of Ninoshima and Kanawajima. As for all the dead bodies, until someone came up with a better idea for what to do with them, these were stacked up against the outer concrete block walls of the homes—including the Ōiwas'—that lined the streets. Even so, there were too many bodies and not enough soldiers to make any kind of headway at more than an unacceptably slow pace. To speed things up, the Akatsuki men began enlisting civilian bystanders to assist in the work.

Kōhei watched the grim goings-on in the street from the front gate of his house with a strange sense of psychological and almost physical detachment akin to an out-of-body experience. He was so numb with shock and overwhelmed by the horrors and tragedies he had already witnessed today that he had yet to begin registering physical pain from the deep and still bleeding laceration on his right shin.

Then he made eye contact with one of the Akatsuki soldiers.

"Hey, you," the soldier called out to Kōhei. "You're a junior high school student, right? Come over here and help us out."

Dutiful soldier-to-be that he was, Kōhei unhesitatingly did as he was told. Stepping out into the street, he proceeded to help the soldier stack bodies. The twosome quickly worked out a routine by which the larger, stronger soldier would lift the bodies up from under the armpits, while Kōhei provided stability and a little lifting power to the other end of the operation by picking up the corpses by their ankles.

Over the next two hours, they stacked dozens of bodies against the walls facing the street, slowly clearing space on the roadway. More times than Kōhei could count, the burned flesh and tendons of the corpses' ankles gave way and sloughed off in his grip, and he found himself holding on to bare bones. Starting from a normal psychological state, a thirteen-year-old boy suddenly thrust into such circumstances and performing such a task would have been forgiven for fainting on the spot—or at least constantly bending over to retch. In Kōhei's case, his psychic numbing was so profound by this point that he was able to perform the work without stopping, even as his own blood puddled around his feet from the shin wound. But while his mind could shut down its normal range of emotional responses to distance itself from psychological terror and physical pain, temporarily suspending its capacity for horror and empathy, its intellectual capacity continued to function, taking in and processing the environmental information his senses were feeding it.[2]

If there is a hell, he thought to himself, *certainly it must be just like this.*

RESCUING REIKO

Grounds of Bunri University
Senda-machi
1.4 kilometers south of Ground Zero

THE NOGUCHIS SAT on the scorched lawn of Bunri University with hundreds of other burned and bloodied people for hours, gazing off toward their neighborhood as it was gradually enveloped in flames. It was well into the afternoon when Mr. Noguchi suddenly remembered Reiko's ossuary jar. Dismissing his yet living family members' protestations, he stood up and double-timed off into the now smoke-shrouded precincts of Minami Takeya-chō.

Kazuko and her mother passed a long ten or twenty minutes before Mr. Noguchi eventually reemerged from the smoke, cradling his precious cargo. Now reunited, the four members of the Noguchi family watched from the relative safety of the Bunri University lawn as flames finally consumed the rest of their neighborhood—and their home with it—around three in the afternoon.

———

One kilometer northwest of the Noguchis' temporary sanctuary, Yamazaki Masutarō—a fifty-four-year-old widower and senior employee at Chūgoku Electric Power headquarters near city hall—was searching for his daughter Satoko, an Ichijo second-grader.

In the immediate aftermath of the bomb, he and his power company colleagues had been swept up in the same scrambling crowd streams that had carried Sakamoto Setsuko and other Zakoba-chō firebreak survivors away from the ZTD to the east and southeast. Thanks to the robust modern construction of his workplace, Yamazaki was far less seriously injured than most survivors this close to Ground Zero. This sustained him during both his initial escape, when he was understandably preoccupied with his own survival, and then again when he doubled back to look for his daughter in the city.

After six or seven hours, he finally managed to make his way into the still burning city center.[1] Working his way up through Ōte-machi on the east bank of the Motoyasu, he reached a spot directly across from the Ichijo worksite in Zaimoku-chō, a mere five hundred meters south-southwest of Ground Zero. Although the nearest bridge was down, the afternoon low tide meant that the water at this point in the river was shallow enough for him to wade across.[2]

Even after all he had seen during his hours in the ZTD, Yamazaki was still not prepared for what he encountered on the opposite bank of the Motoyasu. The burned, bloodied, and broken remains of hundreds of Ichijo girls littered the raised embankment and dry patches of the riverbed, and lay all ajumble down stone stairways that in happier times connected tourists and other perambulators along the embankment with access to pleasure boats or waterborne merchants hawking produce and wares.

When Yamazaki looked at the girls who had almost reached the river, it was not immediately apparent if they had been carried and laid out there by would-be early rescuers or if they had crawled there of their own volition, perhaps seeking water, before dying on the spot where they could crawl no farther. What was apparent, however, from the distribution and condition of the girls' bodies was that most of them seemed to have been killed instantly or close to it. There was perhaps a grim sort of solace to be garnered in knowing that their unimaginable suffering in such a scenario might also have been relatively brief.

But this was not true of all of the girls. An occasional slight movement could be seen in this killing field of otherwise immobile bodies—a twitch of a hand here, a foot there, a head briefly raised in forlorn hope of rescue (or perhaps just a last sip of water) before sagging back down under its now unsupportable weight. And hanging in the dusty air over all of this was a faint, almost mewling sound often described in Japanese Hiroshima or Nagasaki chronicles as *mushi no iki* (literally "the breathing of bugs")—the agonized, barely audible sighing and air gulping of people lingering on the edge of death who would otherwise have been screaming in agony if they had still had the strength to do so. But as miserable and pathetic as this "proof of life" was, it yet held out some glimmer of hope for Yamazaki: If some of the girls were still alive, it was possible that his daughter was one of them and that by some miracle she could be rescued.

And there was only one way to find out.

Yamazaki walked out among the bodies and began examining them one by one. Adding to the crushing despair of the scene—and in a final insult to the dignity of the dead and dying—the girls' work clothes had been nearly completely burned or blown off, leaving them naked under the smoke-filtered afternoon sun, their shredded bare skin scorched, as Yamazaki later recalled, "to the color of boiled octopus flesh."[3]

The condition of the girls' faces hampered Yamazaki's search efforts immeasurably. As was the case with so many victims who had been in the open this close to Ground Zero, the faces of the girls had been essentially erased by the thermal rays, blast, and flying debris produced by Little Boy's detonation. Moreover, the shock wave had slammed into some of the girls with such force that it had knocked their eyeballs out of their sockets, leaving them dangling by optic nerves and torn muscles.

With facial information thus removed—literally—from the equation, the only hope Yamazaki had for identifying Satoko lay in the fact that she was quite diminutive for her age and in the exceedingly thin odds of finding on a body a scrap of clothing or another personal item with her name on it.

Eventually, after examining untold numbers of corpses, Yamazaki came across the tiny body of a girl with an utterly destroyed face; she was scorched and had been blasted naked except for a little tatter of terry cloth belt that had somehow remained tied around her waist. Hanging from the belt was a cloth drawstring pouch with the four kanji ideograms for YAMA-ZAKI SATO-KO written on it. Too shocked and bewildered yet for grief, Yamazaki examined what was left of his daughter while he wondered what he was going to do with her body.

Suddenly, the body twitched. "Father," Satoko said in a tiny, raspy voice in the last words she would ever speak. "My throat hurts. . . ."

Yamazaki ran down to the river's edge and cupped his hands to scoop up some water, which he then trickled over his daughter's ruined face and into what was left of her mouth. He then lifted her up, slung her across his shoulders, and waded back out into the Motoyasu, which offered the only reliably fire-free pathway to escape from Zaimoku-chō.

As the borrowed room in nearby Tenjin-machi where he had been living with Satoko had been destroyed in the morning's explosion and fires, he had only one other option for an evacuation destination: the previous April, his older daughter, Takako—a fourth-year student at Hiroshima Prefectural Girls' School (Kenjo)—had entered a special advanced nurse training program at Second General Army HQ in Futabanosato.[4] To be closer to her new workplace, Takako had temporarily moved in with relatives living in suburban Ushita-machi, at the northern edge of the city proper. This location had been much more convenient than Tenjin-machi vis-à-vis commuting to Futabanosato, and the move would have had the additional benefit of getting at least one member of the family out of the city center every night, when everyone had expected fire-dropping B-29s to come eventually.

Yamazaki had not made it far upriver before he felt himself beginning to founder. The water was higher, up to his waist now, and his footing on the rock- and boulder-covered riverbed was uneven and treacherous. He was also dangerously close to a state of complete exhaustion. Just as he was beginning to give in to a new wave of despair and panic, mentally picturing himself losing Satoko in the river current, an Akatsuki motor launch putt-putted by, plying the Motoyasu to pick up survivors. Seeing Yamazaki's predicament, the soldiers in the boat pulled him and Satoko on board and ferried them to a stretch of the east bank in Ōte-machi where the fires were beginning to subside. This fire-free area was already filling up with victims in various states of injury seeking sanctuary from the roaring, swirling walls of flame still tearing through the rest of the central business district.

Amid this crowd of battered survivors, Yamazaki came upon a group of four or five of his colleagues from Chūgoku Electric. He sat down with them to rest for a while, needing to regain some strength for the remainder of what would be a long trek to Ushita-machi.

After a round of experience sharing about the day so far—anecdotes and testimony about the fates of absent colleagues and the newest information about evacuation routes—Yamazaki stood back up and, bidding the rest of the group goodbye and good luck, asked a coworker named Takemoto if he would help him lift Satoko back onto his shoulders.

What he heard next made his heart sink.

"I think you'd better put your daughter back down," Takemoto said.[5]

Yamazaki laid Satoko down on the ground and confirmed his worst fear. His daughter was dead.

The suddenly changed circumstances left Yamazaki with one final fatherly duty to perform for his daughter. While it was, of course, natural for a father to grieve over a dead child, it was also natural for a two-fisted, undemonstrative Japanese workingman of his generation to avoid at all costs doing so openly in front of nonfamily others. Accordingly, staying put with his colleagues to wait out the conflagration in their temporary sanctuary was not an option—certainly not now that his fight-or-flight adrenaline was ebbing, ceding ground to emotions about Satoko that must have been beginning to rise up in a slow boil. Moreover, if he stayed there with the Chūgoku Electric

group, there was a possibility of some team of Akatsuki soldiers coming along and insisting on taking Satoko's body away for disposal in
one of the stacks of charred and effluvia-oozing corpses already beginning to pile up around the area. Better to take his chances in the
fires than risk that. Whatever it took, he would get Satoko to Ushita-
machi to see Takako one last time. Then, and only then, would they
say goodbye to their daughter and sister. Satoko would get a proper
and respectful send-off—not a miserable one like the thousands of
other victims already anonymously stacked around the city like cords
of firewood.

Repeating his goodbyes and thank-yous to his young colleagues,
Yamazaki stood up, slung his dead daughter over his shoulders, and
headed toward Hatchōbori, where the subsiding of flames on Rijō
Street had opened up a new access route to the northern areas of the
city via the Tokiwa Bridge.

===

Back on the Bunri University campus grounds, the Noguchis discussed their options and determined that, at the moment, this place
was as good as anywhere else to ride out the fires while so much of the
city was still ablaze. They settled in as best they could to pass what
would be their second sleepless night in a row.

Kazuko had no idea yet as to the fate of her Ichijo classmates. Nor
did their parents, and by late afternoon, those who had survived the
day's catastrophe in yet ambulant condition were beginning to converge en masse on the Ichijo campus in Funairi-chō, demanding information about their children.

To handle these inquiries, the surviving faculty members at the
school set up a reception desk on the evening of August 6. As the campus buildings were now completely unusable due to bomb damage,
the desk was placed at the entrance of an air raid trench in the
schoolyard.

The faculty members—including Principal Miyakawa, who had
survived his bomb experience near Hiroshima Station to return to his

post—already knew that none of the Ichijo girls were coming back from Zaimoku-chō. But they were not prepared, at that point, to share this information with the parents. The best they could do was promise to send out search parties at first light the following morning to begin combing the city for surviving students and colleagues.[6]

As for the parents of Ichijo's first- and second-year students, those who had neither the heart nor the stomach to venture into Zaimoku-chō on their own would have one more night—for some, perhaps even another day or two—to hold on to and caress the hope, however thin, that their daughters might still be alive.

THE BAMBOO GROVE

Southeastern slope of Hijiyama Hill
Approximately 2.2 kilometers southeast of Ground Zero

WHEN SAKAMOTO SETSUKO reached the Kyōbashi embankment with the grievously wounded Kitakoji Michiko in tow, she was surrounded by evacuees running a gauntlet between towering curtains of flame on one side and the corpse-filled river on the other. Some of these people headed upstream toward the Hijiyama Bridge. This seemed a counterintuitive choice, as it would entail heading back toward the central business district and, therefore, the original direction of the morning's explosion. Others rushed downstream toward the harbor, perhaps instinctively headed for water but not realizing that this route, in fact, would expose them to far longer stretches of burning shoreline before they could cross over to the safer east bank of the Kyōbashi at the Miyuki Bridge. Many who took this route would never reach sanctuary and either became engulfed by flames en route or opted out of the situation altogether by jumping into the river—whether or not they were aware this would almost certainly end in their drowning.[1]

Setsuko was evidently levelheaded enough to rule out the water option and to realize that if she and Michiko kept moving along the embankment in either direction, they were bound eventually to reach a crossing. Fortuitously opting for the upstream direction, Setsuko pulled Michiko through the crowds until the girls reached and managed to push their way across the Hijiyama Bridge. When they made it across the east bank of the Kyōbashi, the abrupt mound of Hijiyama Hill would have floated over the smoky haze like a vision of cool green sanctuary from the fires they were escaping.

Although they were now out of the most immediate danger, it was not long before another major challenge presented itself: Michiko informed Setsuko that she was in so much pain that she could not walk another step. The exact verbal details of this exchange are lost to the ages, but it is not difficult to imagine that as a Japanese child of her era—drilled from birth with a martially inflected and utterly sincere ethos of self-sacrifice—Michiko would have pleaded with Setsuko to leave her along the road somewhere and concentrate on saving herself, instead.

Knowing what we know about her character from her actions so far, we can safely assume that Setsuko—imbued with the same ethos— did not consider even for a moment abandoning her ailing classmate to make good her own escape. Instead, she pulled Michiko up piggyback, just as she had seen Hata-sensei do with Tamekazu Michiko hours earlier at Zakoba-chō, and continued their eastward progress, with the injured and exhausted Setsuko no doubt staggering under the weight of her dying classmate.

As they followed a road skirting the southern foot of Hijiyama Hill, the girls encountered a soldier at an intersection attempting to direct evacuee pedestrian traffic.[2] The soldier—who also seemed to be conducting a cursory visual triage on the stream of human misery passing his checkpoint—took one look at the girls and pointed them toward the southeastern slope of Hijiyama.

Still carrying Michiko piggyback, Setsuko followed a line of walking wounded snaking its way up toward an air raid shelter dug into the hillside. When Setsuko reached this ad hoc aid station—a substantial concrete-reinforced affair originally constructed for personnel from the nearby Kasumi-chō Arsenal[3]—she found it swamped by such numbers of victims that she could not even make out its entranceway.[4] With no better plan at the moment, and no doubt beginning to feel the full weight of the day's mental and physical exhaustion as her adrenaline waned, Setsuko set Michiko down under a tree and sat beside her to rest. Several hours passed while they waited to see how the situation at the aid station would unfold.

From their perch, Setsuko could see down into her neighborhood of Danbara, only a few hundred meters away, and she wondered what had happened to her family and home. But she would put off checking in on them while she still had Michiko in her care.

Sometime after noon, there was a commotion when aircraft engines were heard overhead. A soldier shouted something about an approaching enemy plane and ordered everyone not yet safely inside the shelter to evacuate farther up the hill to get under deeper foliage cover.[5] After what had happened the last time a B-29 had flown over the city, no further encouragement would have been necessary to get everyone within earshot (and still capable of movement) to comply with the evacuation order posthaste.

Responding to the directive, Setsuko pulled Michiko back up piggyback to join the scramble of people running or crawling up into the tree groves and undergrowth on the hill slope. Picking a dense stand of bamboo for a hiding spot, she set Michiko down again and hunkered down to wait out the commotion, no doubt half expecting the imminent detonation of yet another world-shattering bomb. But the American plane—a reconnaissance aircraft taking after-action photos—passed over and continued on its way without incident.

As her adrenaline wound down again from this latest round of unwelcome excitement, Setsuko was overcome with profound exhaustion. This was accompanied by waves of nausea that caused her to vomit the meager late-wartime contents of her stomach until all that was coming up was a gooey yellow substance. She vomited some more before passing out, then fading in and out of consciousness for the next several hours.

Eventually, she was awakened by a youthful male voice from on high echoing down through the canopy of green bamboo overhead:

"Are there any injured people around here?"[6]

The voice belonged to a soldier—a member of a patrol combing the slopes of Hijiyama for victims hiding or otherwise immobilized in the undergrowth. Following Setsuko's called-out response, the soldier found and then escorted the girls back down the hill to the aid station they had tried to enter before. This time they did not have to wait in line, although the interior of the shelter was still crowded to overflowing with moaning and dying people.

———

Before she was destroyed by Little Boy, Kitakoji Michiko had been the class cutup of Hata-sensei's West Homeroom—a girl who, by all accounts, generated and was followed by laughter wherever she went.[7] In her homeroom group photo taken a year earlier, Michiko's jocular, distracted face is conspicuous among the neat rows of stern-looking classmates sitting or standing around her in their Navy-style white sailor blouses, baggy *monpe* work pants, and uniformly identical hairdos—a sort of Louise Brooks banged bob called a *kappa atama*. This hairdo made the girls—especially the ones with thicker hair—look like they were wearing black helmets with little squarish apertures exposing their faces from the upper eyelids down to the chin.[8] It was the de rigueur mandated hairstyle for schoolgirls in wartime Japan.[9]

While everyone else in the picture is looking directly at the camera, Michiko is looking slightly away from it, the expression crossing her face giving the impression that she is looking at something or someone behind and to the right of the cameraman. In the shot, the length of her conspicuously narrow, oblong, and slightly motion-blurred face is only accentuated and exaggerated by the curtainlike effect of the *kappa atama* helmet hair hiding her cheeks.

Michiko's classmates likely saw in this face—with its long lantern jaw and close-set narrow eyes—a mirror of the effervescent and comically inclined personality of its wearer, and it would not have looked out of place on a silent-film-era comedian. But someone with a modicum of knowledge of ancient Japanese history would have reacted with a knowing nod and perhaps even a slight bow of respect when they saw it and made the association with the Kitakoji name, for Michiko had a face of ancient Yamato court aristocratic pedigree that, to the well-informed Japanese observer, was as instantly recognizable as a Hapsburg lip would be to a European genealogist.

While Tominaga Chieko's cosmopolitan airs and comparatively sophisticated tastes, though genuine, were vestiges of the accumulated refinement of a couple of generations of Kyoto mercantile success, Kitakoji Michiko was a bona fide Japanese blue blood. Though she would have vehemently denied this within earshot of her salt-of-the-earth classmates, if she had availed herself of the services of a modestly competent genealogist, she could probably have traced her ancestors back to the dawn of recorded Japanese history in the seventh century.[10] As it was, and without cracking a book, she had known that her family had been in Hiroshima at least since the sixteenth century as retainers of the Mōri samurai clan when the place was little more than a guardhouse-cum-tollgate sitting atop an alluvial plain of reeds and sandbars.

In 1598—nine years after Hiroshima Castle was completed—Michiko's ancestor Kitakoji Gonmaru, assuming the monastic name of Gen'kiyo, became the head abbot of Seifukuji Temple in Niho, which, like its topographical neighbor Hijiyama, was still an islet in Hiroshima Bay at the time.[11] Nearly three and a half centuries later, with Niho (and Hijiyama before it) long since connected to the Honshu mainland by centuries of landfill and land-reclamation projects, the family was still in Seifukuji Temple, now administered by Michiko's father, Head Abbot Kitakoji Gen'ei. And although the temple—as with Japanese Buddhism in general—no longer enjoyed the prestige and influence it had enjoyed before the State Shintō ideological revolution of the Meiji Restoration, Seifukuji still enjoyed the fierce loyalty of its local parishioners and remained an important locus of community life in Niho.[12]

Although it is doubtful that Sakamoto Setsuko knew all the details of Michiko's illustrious ancestors, she would have been aware that, in Niho at least, the Kitakojis were still a very important family. Perhaps acting on a hunch that people from her neighborhood would be eager to help the daughter of such an important local family, Setsuko called out over the moans of the dying people crowding the air raid shelter.

"Is there anyone here from Niho?"[13]

An adult male voice answered back in the affirmative, and a lightly injured man, a Kasumi-chō Arsenal worker who introduced himself as Kajikawa, came over to see the girls. During the course of his short exchange with Setsuko, Kajikawa's tone and demeanor changed immediately to one of urgency and respect when he determined the identity of Setsuko's partner. Not only did Kajikawa know who the Kitakojis were, but he and his family were parishioners (*danka*, in Japanese) of Seifukuji, doubtless with generations of gravestones and *ihai* memorial tablets on the temple grounds to show for it.

Forgoing further discussion, Kajikawa declared that he would run the two kilometers back to Niho to tell Abbot Gen'ei about his daughter. Probably bowing to the girls—certainly to Michiko—he then turned on his heels and ran off into the smoky late-afternoon heat.

When Kajikawa arrived at Seifukuji Temple, he was told that soon after the explosion that morning, Abbot Gen'ei had headed off to the city to look for Michiko and he had not been heard from since. Upon receiving this report, Kajikawa quickly cobbled together a makeshift stretcher out of bamboo poles and a sheet of canvas tarp; then he set off for the Hijiyama aid station with it to bring Michiko home.

At the aid station, Kajikawa and Setsuko gingerly lifted Michiko onto the stretcher, then set off for Niho. Even though Setsuko's home was only a few hundred meters away in Danbara, she insisted on first accompanying Kajikawa all the way to Niho to make sure her classmate got home before she worried about checking in with her own family.

It was nightfall when Kajikawa and Setsuko arrived at the gate of Seifukuji Temple with Michiko's stretcher. Abbot Gen'ei had since returned home, so he was there to receive what was left of his daughter.

Nearly four decades later, when author/journalist Seki (née Tominaga) Chieko interviewed Gen'ei—then close to ninety but still abbot of Seifukuji—for her book on the fate of West Homeroom, the old abbot claimed that when Michiko had been carried through the gate and up into the family rectory,[14] she muttered, *"Tadaima"* ("I'm home"), in the traditional Japanese fashion.[15]

The Japanese are as prone to experiencing intense emotions as anyone else. However, at least in polite Japanese society—and at least as long as that institution has existed as such—there have been rules about how, where, and in front of whom such emotions can and cannot be openly indulged. Accordingly, to keep interlocutors within the boundaries of what was considered socially acceptable behavior, the Confucianist- and Zen Buddhist–influenced culture of aristocratic courtiers and samurai evolved highly formulaic protocols over long premodern centuries to mediate dialogue between non-intimates in such scenarios.

These protocols live on today in the rules of formal Japanese social intercourse that help people avoid the humiliation of "losing it," so to speak, in front of non-intimate others—a fate that, as in olden times, is considered one of the most excruciating faux pas in the Japanese social canon, particularly when the principals involved are adult males. The emotional alchemy works its embarrassment-avoiding magic when the principals closely follow the prescribed protocols. Operating on a sort of social autopilot, one person offers up stock lines from a script to an interlocutor who (as a fellow acculturated Japanese) knows them in advance; then the first person receives stock responses in return. Thus, a potentially humiliating situation is transformed—or defused—into an almost routine or even mundane exchange of platitudes, with the expression of intense emotions safely deferred until after the completion of this ritual and the dispersal of its participants.

Although the specifics of the exchange at Seifukuji on the night of August 6 do not survive, we can be fairly certain that Abbot Gen'ei—scion of ancient courtiers and samurai that he was—would have stuck to his expected formal script, especially considering that he was in the presence of one of his parishioners. After bringing Michiko up into the rectory and laying her out on the tatami-matted floor of the main parlor, Gen'ei, Kajikawa, and Setsuko would have sat around Michiko on their knees in the formal Japanese *seiza* sitting style.

Then Gen'ei would have thanked but also apologized to his daughter's would-be rescuers in formulaic utterances interspersed with multiple exchanges of *seiza* bowing—hands palm down on the tatami—between the dialogue participants.

Fulfilling their half of the customary script for such situations, Kajikawa and Setsuko would have responded by waving off these expressions of gratitude and apology by apologizing, in turn, for not having taken better care of Michiko. It is not hard to imagine that Setsuko's participation in the exchange involved an extra-emotional meta level of shame—and under the direct gaze of her dying classmate's father, no less—over the fact of her own survival.[16]

At the conclusion of this gratitude-apology exchange, there would have been another round of *seiza* bowing before Kajikawa and Setsuko took their leave to allow the Kitakojis to attend to their family grief work in private.

Gen'ei passed a sleepless night tending to his dying daughter, who continued to pass in and out of consciousness. When she moaned for water, he would go out to the temple well to bring some back and wet her mouth with it. But when she whimpered at the sound of aircraft engines passing overhead throughout the night and asked for her father to hold her, he could not, because there was no place he could place his hands on her body without her screaming in pain.[17]

Kitakoji Michiko took her final breath at 1130 the next morning. Her ashes are interred in Seifukuji's cemetery, which occupies the hillside behind the temple and the kindergarten that Gen'ei established after the war, perhaps, in part, to honor the memory of his daughter. Decades after Michiko's death, he still wistfully fantasized about what a wonderful teacher of small children she might have grown up to be.[18]

Sakamoto Setsuko finally made it back to her family late on the night of August 6. No members of the household had perished in the catastrophe—at least not immediately—but as Setsuko's quarter-century-long struggle with radiation poisoning was just beginning, so was her concurrent struggle with survivor guilt. She would outlive neither.

LEADING DANBARA

Ōiwa household
Danbara Naka-machi
2.1 kilometers east-southeast of Ground Zero

WHILE SAKAMOTO SETSUKO and Kitakoji Michiko were hunkered down in a bamboo stand on Hijiyama Hill, while Noguchi Ju'ichi was rescuing his daughter's ossuary jar from the flames consuming Minami Takeya-chō, while Yamazaki Masutarō was looking for his Ichijo student daughter in Zaimoku-chō, and while the Tominagas were passing a socially excruciating afternoon at their would-be evacuation destination on Tanna Hill in Ōkō, Ōiwa Kōhei was still stacking corpses in Danbara Naka-machi with his unnamed Akatsuki mentor/counterpart.

Around midafternoon, word began going around Danbara that the fires from the city were about to breach Hijiyama Hill and work their way into the neighborhood. The Akatsuki corporal released Kōhei from his ad hoc labor detail and told him to go home and get his family members to evacuate the area.

Kōhei did as he was told. Needing no further convincing, his mother immediately went into action getting the family ready to evacuate.

Seventy-year-old Grandmother Ōiwa, however, was having none of it, begging off on participation in the evacuation on the pretext that someone had to hold down the fort in Danbara in case other family members returned home. Although externally uninjured, she was already completely exhausted from the day's stress and possibly already experiencing the onset of ARS.

Kōhei, his mother, and the five-year-old Harada cousin from Kagoshima fled Danbara, heading east under the smoky false dusk of slate gray skies. They walked about two kilometers to the east before their progress was halted by the Enkō River in the agricultural district of Shinonome. As there were no bridges along this stretch of the river and the only other Enkō crossings led to an urban industrial neighborhood around Hiroshima Station and the *Kokutetsu* locomotive barns, which were still burning fiercely, they would have to see out the rest of the central-city conflagration here.

Although their journey had been short in terms of distance covered, it had been arduous in every other way. Everywhere they had gone, the air had been acrid with the stench of burned flesh and humming with the moans of the dying, occasionally pierced by the sudden wails of the trauma mad or the newly bereaved. All along the way, the Ōiwas had had to step over and around bodies stretched out or curled up on the roadway leading out of Danbara.

The worst part of navigating this ghoulish topography had been the ailing people on the ground, who, as the Ōiwas walked by, would grab hold of their ankles and inevitably beg for rescue and/or water, a constant occurrence that would have been annoying had it not been so traumatizing—particularly for the little Harada boy. Every time another hand had reached out and grabbed one of their legs, the family had had no choice but to kick it off or stomp on it and keep going. As the threesome had passed over and through this vale of human misery, Mrs. Ōiwa constantly reminded the boys not to look down or back, lest empathy tempt them to tarry. The next time someone grabbed them, they might not let go.

Eventually, the threesome came upon a vineyard where hundreds of other landlocked evacuees and victims were already encamped. Someone—perhaps the vineyard owners themselves—had passed around a stack of old newspapers to use as sitting mats. The

Ōiwas received some paper and staked out a spot with it; then they joined their new temporary neighbors watching the grim light show in the roiling orange and iron-colored sky to the west.

The vineyard, following standard Japanese viticultural practice, had its vines interlaced into overhead lattices for ease during the harvest—an arrangement that in this case provided Kōhei and his fellow refugees with plenty of low-hanging but not-quite-ripe fruit. The traditional Japanese social ethos against helping oneself to things that were not one's own notwithstanding, all present under the lattices seemed to have reached an unspoken understanding that current circumstances were extenuating enough for pilfering taboos to be temporarily suspended. In the case of the Ōiwas, who had brought no canteens or other containers for liquids on their evacuation, the grapes would be their only source of water. Luckily, none of the three had suffered any serious burn injuries, which mercilessly dehydrated those who suffered from them, so the sour grapes would be sufficient (albeit with effort) to carry them over what was going to be a long night passed in the rough.

UNANNOUNCED GUESTS

Tanna Hill

3.8 kilometers southeast of Ground Zero

BECAUSE OF GRANDMOTHER Tominaga's arthritic knees, a walk from Ujina to Tanna Hill that should have taken thirty or forty minutes ended up taking nearly two hours. And as an expectation-stomping coda to their frustration-dogged schlep, the Tominagas finally arrived at their would-be hilltop sanctuary—the farmhouse owned by Mr. Tominaga's subordinate—only to find that it was just as bomb damaged as their place back in Ujina.

Given that the whole point of the hike had been to secure a safe and comfortable place to ride out the next day or two, choosing to stay with this family—whom the Tominagas barely knew and who had a half-wrecked house to boot—did not seem to make much sense now. Moreover, if they did choose to impose on these people, this would entail the added complication of Mr. Tominaga being henceforth indebted to his subordinate—a face-risking scenario for the higher-ranked counterpart in a Japan that was still bound through and through, top to bottom, with rigid status consciousness, social rules, and protocols. Perhaps with such considerations in mind, the Tominagas called a quick huddle—before they even reached the front door of the farmhouse—to weigh the option of simply turning around now and heading back to Ujina to take their chances in their own home.

In the end, the debate was settled by Grandmother Tominaga's knees, Chieko's still iffy gastrointestinal tract, and the midday heat, which was now climbing above thirty degrees Celsius.[1] While the sun was still cloaked and filtered through smoke and haze in the ZTD, it was blazing at brutal early-August strength everywhere else in suburban Hiroshima (as burn victims evacuating from the city center were discovering to their extreme discomfort). Even for the uninjured, unarthritic, and regular, the prospect of walking around outside in this heat for longer than a few minutes at a stretch would have been daunting.

The new plan was to drop in at the subordinate's house, but instead of staying a night or two, as originally intended, the Tominagas would make the visit more something along the lines of a social call. After resting up for a few hours and waiting for the temperature to cool down a bit, they would make good their escape to head back to Ujina—assuming it was not aflame by then.

As telephone service in the city was down, the Tominagas had been forced to show up at the house unannounced—a major Japanese social faux pas. The circumstances were, of course, extenuating, and the original offer had been open and was presumably standing. Still, the unannounced aspect of the visit rendered it stilted and uncomfortable from the start, with things going from bad to worse when the Tominagas found the house already crowded with other people— presumably friends and/or relatives of the household evacuated from the city. Treading gingerly, the Tominagas made themselves small in an unoccupied corner of the living room, hunkering down for what had all the earmarks of an unbearably long afternoon.

A few hours later, when the Tominagas had just about worked up the nerve to thank their hosts and take their leave, there was a commotion at the front door. Several of the other people in the house jumped up to see to the disturbance, then came back into the living room cradling a shattered and horribly burned boy about Chieko's age; they then laid him down on the tatami floor.

It turned out to be the subordinate's son, who had been at one of the firebreak sites that morning. The Tominagas had not even known of his existence until he, thermal ray flayed and dying, was laid out in front of them.

The Tominagas tried to help out however they could—at the least, by staying out of the way—but it was soon obvious to everyone that they were fifth wheels. Now, because the Tominagas had a renewed motive to get out of there, another hushed family conference was convened to discuss a proposed return to Ujina posthaste. However, it was eventually determined that to leave now would be poor form, considering their hosts' current straits.

In the end, the Tominagas stayed on a respectable few more hours, during which their hosts attempted to keep up brave faces in front of the boss' family. In the resulting intolerable atmosphere of decorum-throttled grief, Chieko's perfectly unblemished presence only underscored the cringeworthy situation, with the unvoiced *Why isn't your child laid out on the floor, burned to a crisp, too?* lingering in the air like a stench.

The Tominagas at last took their leave well after dark, no doubt imagining hot eyes on their backs as they headed off down the footpath from the house. With their own intact, unburned child in tow, they slunk away into the orange-tinged, smoke-stinking night.

The trek back to Ujina was a nocturnal repeat of the morning's miserable march—albeit more somber and contemplative this go-round. Grandmother Tominaga continued to complain incessantly about her knees, which compelled the group to take frequent rest breaks. During these stops, Tanna Hill's elevation afforded the family a panorama of the destruction that had been visited upon their adopted city. Off to the north and northwest, nearly the entirety of the Ōta Delta looked like a glowing bed of charcoal. This orange expanse was striated by the black ribbons of the delta's waterways, and punctuated here and there by the fire-silhouetted hollow black skeletons of modern high-rise buildings like the Fukuya department store and the *Chūgoku Shimbun* headquarters in the central business district. Behind these, where Hiroshima Castle should have been standing like a proud sentinel over the skyline, there was nothing. Like almost everything else, the castle had simply disappeared, leaving nothing but an ember field surrounded by a moat.

———

The Tominagas arrived home to find that although the flames from the city had not reached this far south, the district had not escaped the cataclysm completely unscathed. This point was reiterated every time the anguished cry of some mother or wife in the neighborhood shattered the night's silence as yet another firebreak child or downtown worker was carried home for the last time.

Machiyo eventually came home, slightly injured and physically exhausted but, like everyone else in the house, too nerve jangled for sleep. With the family now reunited, its members attempted to process the shocks of the past sixteen or so hours by talking them out. And although the rest of the family had just spent what was probably the longest day of their respective lives, Machiyo's stories were by far the most harrowing.[2]

Her school day had begun mundanely enough. From 0800, she and some hundred eighty other lower-year students had assembled in the college auditorium—a lightly constructed, barnlike wooden building—to participate in what was known as a *kokumin girei* ("National Ritual").[3] This was a type of morning motivational ceremony that became popular in the country during the war, particularly in educational settings. It was similar in function to, but much more ostentatiously stage-managed than, the more common and pedestrian *chōrei* morning formations customarily convened at schools and workplaces.

After a call to assembly with a solemnly tolled bell, the *kokumin girei* script prescribed group singing of the Kimigayo imperial anthem; bowing in the direction of the Imperial Palace in Tokyo; a minute of silence for the war dead; and prayers for victory.[4] This would then typically be followed by a short speech—either topical or more abstractly exhortatory in content—from some authority figure, either institutional or, on a special commemorative occasion, invited.

In the case of the teachers college *kokumin girei* on the morning of August 6, the ceremony concluded with a speech by college president Tsuyama Saburō[5] on the subject of the girls' upcoming war labor. Later that week, these students were scheduled to be dispatched to join upper-grade schoolmates already working at the Mizushima Aircraft Manufacturing Company plant in neighboring Okayama Prefecture.[6] In his talk, President Tsuyama stressed the vital importance of aircraft manufacture in the nation's war effort, particularly in the context of the kamikaze tactics that were proving so effective against the enemy's warships. Ending with a reference to the supernatural "divine wind" (*kamikaze*) that had delivered Japan from the threat of foreign invasion in the thirteenth century, he assured the assemblage that, with their help, it was certain to blow once again to bring final Japanese victory. On this rousing note, the president stepped down from his speaker's dais and headed for the auditorium exit.[7]

Just then a flash filled the space, which sent all the students flat onto the floor as they had been trained to do since childhood. Lying facedown between the rows of auditorium benches, with their hands behind their heads and their thumbs in their ears, they waited perhaps ten seconds until a shock wave hit the building, causing its windows to blow in and its ceiling to collapse.[8] Miraculously, no one in the auditorium was killed. The girls had been saved: by their quick reflexes and years of air defense training; by the sturdy construction of the auditorium's benches; and, conversely and somewhat ironically, by the cheap construction of its ceiling/roof.

After extricating themselves from under the toppled structure, Machiyo and many other schoolmates sought first aid at the Army Mutual Hospital next door. But when they arrived, the facility was already filling up with far more seriously wounded victims. A few of the girls might have been lucky enough to receive a swab or two of Mercurochrome before they were swept, en masse, to help pull off-duty nurses out from under the wreckage of a collapsed dormitory on the hospital campus.[9]

Machiyo stayed on performing this rescue work until around noon, when she began to feel nauseated. Excusing herself, she headed back to the teachers college campus next door, where undamaged classrooms had since been converted into aid stations. As she was passing by the front entrance of the main campus building, out of the corner of her eye, she caught a glimpse of what she thought to be a large pile of gray and black rags someone had left out on the steps. Then the pile moved slightly. Machiyo stopped to look at it more closely and realized that the pile was alive; it was a young girl whose scalp had been scorched completely bald and who also appeared to be either partially or completely blind. All her clothes had been burned off except for the elastic band of her underwear, which was still around her waist. The gray and black "rags" Machiyo originally thought she had seen were actually the girl's skin hanging from her body like curtains, some long enough to be trailing on the ground.

When Machiyo's brain finally processed the full horror of what she was looking at, she screamed.

Hearing the scream in a familiar voice, the burned girl spoke.

"Aren't you Tominaga Chieko's older sister?"

"Yes," Machiyo managed. "Who are you?"

It was Hi'ura Ruriko, Chieko's class president, the first of four horrifically injured second-year Dai Ni Kenjo girls who somehow managed to straggle back to campus after a forced march of more than three kilometers from Zakoba-chō.[10] Machiyo's encounter with her was the moment that Dai Ni Kenjo got its first inkling as to the fate of Hata-sensei's homeroom.

Someone fetched a stretcher for Ruriko, and Machiyo and several other girls tried to lift her up onto it. But her body was so completely and deeply scorched—down to raw dermis—that there was no place to hold her that did not produce screaming pain when touched. Still, it had to be done. Fighting back tears of their own, the other girls called out encouragements to the screaming Ruriko as they lifted her up. When Machiyo grabbed hold of Ruriko's ankles to help in this task, she was left with fistfuls of charred skin that slid off into her hands. For the rest of her life, Machiyo would marvel at the sheer will it must have taken for Ruriko to walk as far as she did in such a condition—and blind, no less.[11]

At some point in the ordeal, Ruriko and her would-be rescuers were joined by their male PE teacher, Fukuzaki Hiroshi.[12] A rare yet-to-be-conscripted bachelor still in his twenties, Fukuzaki-sensei had been at his dormitory in Misasa-machi in the northwest end of the city, about two kilometers from Ground Zero, when the bomb went off. In the wake of the explosion, he had set off for the teachers college campus at once, but he had been forced to take a roundabout route via Hiroshima Station to avoid the burning ZTD—twice having to swim across body-choked waterways en route—before finally arriving in North Ujina nearly four hours later.

As the Akatsuki trucks from Ujina were already transporting people between the Miyuki Bridge and the harbor, and Army Mutual Aid Hospital was one of their stops along the way, it did not take long to flag one down to take away Ruriko's stretcher. Before being loaded onto the truck, Ruriko's last thoughts were of her classmates; she implored Fukuzaki-sensei to organize a search and rescue party to go up into the city to look for the rest of the West Homeroom members.

At this, Fukuzaki-sensei turned to the other girls, calling out to them and everyone else within earshot to follow him back to the city if they were willing to risk their own lives to try to save their schoolmates. In short order, he was at the head of a band of teachers college and Dai Ni Kenjo sisters resolutely marching up Rijō Street to face the smoke and unknown, on the way passing endless files of human misery heading in the opposite direction. However, by the time they reached the east foot of the Miyuki Bridge, the mixed cadre of soldiers, Keibōdan officers, and policemen attempting to officiate over the chaotic scene was not allowing anyone to attempt to get across to the opposite bank of the Kyōbashi, which was now burning furiously.

Fukuzaki-sensei's rescue team originally intended to wait out the fires until they were given clearance to cross, but after a while, when it became obvious that this was not going to happen anytime soon, he told the girls to go back to the campus and help out in the aid stations there. He would try to make it into the city on his own and get help for whomever he could find.

It would appear that Fukuzaki-sensei's eventual progress into the city roughly paralleled that of the Saitō Unit, in terms of both ground covered and the time it took to cover it. When he reached Senda-machi about 1330 hours, there were still at least ten blocks or so of impassable burning city between him and the Zakoba-chō firebreak site. He was, however, able to reach Red Cross Hospital on Rijō Street; Akatsuki trucks were already going up that far to relieve the hospital of its overflow of patients. As it was only some three hundred meters from the Zakoba-chō site, there was a possibility that some of the West Homeroom girls were there.

When Fukuzaki-sensei arrived at Red Cross Hospital, now some six hours or so since the explosion, it was filled to bursting with victims. So many had sought aid there that the hospital's front lawn and traffic roundabout were filled with the dead and dying, as well—up to and even beyond the front gate and spilling out into Rijō Street.

Fukuzaki-sensei did not even make it to the main building before he found people from Dai Ni Kenjo: Near the main entrance to the hospital campus, Hata-sensei, Sakai Tamie, and Tamekazu Michiko from West Homeroom were prostrate on the lawn. Lying on her side, Hata-sensei was still clutching Tamie in the same baby-cradling posture Sakamoto Setsuko had seen hours earlier at Zakoba-chō. Both were dead. Michiko, however, was alive, still holding on to her teacher and as horribly burned as her dead companions. Fukuzaki-sensei brought Michiko and Hata-sensei's body out onto Rijō Street and flagged down an Akatsuki truck, which carried them all the way to the teachers college campus. For some reason that has never been determined—but possibly on the orders of the crew of what would have been an already overloaded Akatsuki truck—Fukuzaki-sensei left Sakai Tamie's body behind on the Red Cross lawn.[13] Her remains were never recovered.

Back at the teachers college / Dai Ni Kenjo, just as at Ichijo and every other school that had sent students out to do firebreak work that morning, frantic parents were beginning to converge on the campus to inquire about their children. Around 2000 hours, a Dai Ni Kenjo teacher named Arita Chieko set up a reception desk in front of the entrance to field inquiries from these family members.

Arita-sensei stayed manning the desk even though she knew that her house in Senda-machi, where she lived with her sister, had burned down.[14]

Later in the night, a soldier with a truck came to the school and told Arita to come with him to an aid station set up at an Army barracks on Tanna Hill, because one of the school's students was calling for teachers from Dai Ni Kenjo. Arita-sensei got someone to replace her on the desk, and she got into the truck with the soldier.[15]

After a short ride to Tanna Hill, she was shown to a room in the big wooden barracks illuminated with lightbulbs powered by electricity from gasoline-operated Army field generators. The floor was strewn with wounded, dying, and dead lying on straw mats and covered with Army blankets.

The student who had been pleading to see a Dai Ni Kenjo teacher was Hi'ura Ruriko, who was somehow still alive—though fading in and out of consciousness and between lucidity and delirium—more than twelve hours after suffering her grievous burns.

Ruriko stirred when she heard someone kneel down next to her mat, and when she heard her teacher's familiar voice, she began apologizing profusely for neglecting her duties as class president by failing to take a final roll call before evacuating their firebreak site.

In the middle of this exchange, a small man in the khaki serge *kokuminfuku* civilian wartime uniform favored by managerial types showed up in the ward, escorted by a military orderly. Taking in the scene, the small but seemingly self-important man asked, in a loud voice, "Is this the place?" After being assured that it was and that his daughter was there, he was taken to stand before Ruriko's mat. It was her father, Hi'ura Yoshito.

Declining the opportunity to kneel next to his daughter, he instead took one look at her, then told Arita-sensei, "I'm sorry, miss, but I have to go home and see to my other family members." Then he turned around and left.

Shortly thereafter, Ruriko said something about feeling sleepy, then started mumbling half-coherent apologies again about the missed roll call. Then she drifted off to sleep and never woke up.

"THEY'RE ONLY SLEEPING . . ."

Grounds of Bunri University
Senda-machi
1.4 kilometers from Ground Zero
Morning of August 7

AS AUGUST 7 dawned over their temporary refugee camp at Bunri University, the Noguchis once again assessed their injuries. The burns on Mr. Noguchi's face and neck were painful, but they were not potentially life-threatening, nor were they worse than they had been the previous day. The deep laceration on Mrs. Noguchi's leg, however, was showing early signs of suppuration. The family consensus on the matter was that this wound was in urgent need of professional medical attention—at least something better than a jury-rigged tourniquet made from a piece of ripped cloth—and that finding this was going to require an off-campus foray.

Luckily for the Noguchis, the fires in the vicinity of the university appeared to have subsided enough for such an expedition to be considered. Leaving their heavier baggage behind with their evacuee neighbors, the family ventured off into the ashy silence of the city. Picking their way through wreckage and corpse-strewn streets in Minami Takeya-chō and Senda-machi, they eventually reached Rijō Street and Red Cross Hospital.

Now nearly a full day after the explosion, the front lawn and hallways of the hospital were still covered with the dead and dying. Next to the front gate, makeshift billboards were in the process of being erected by Akatsuki soldiers utterly exhausted after a brutal, sleepless night of rescue work and firefighting. These were the same Saitō Unit men, including Corporals Tsuchiya and Zhen, whose forward headquarters was in the Hiroden carbarn across Rijō Street.

The billboards next to the hospital gate carried manifests, penned at the Saitō Unit outpost, listing identified victims, both living and dead. They also served as message boards that bomb survivors could use to leave memos for family members, colleagues, etc., about their present whereabouts—relaying information, for example, about the location of a temporary evacuation site or aid station / Army hospital to which they might have been taken. These billboards—and others like them at various points in central Hiroshima—would become critical hubs of survivor activity over the coming days and weeks.

Although the Red Cross buildings themselves were still standing and functioning, they had suffered extensive bomb damage, with most of their windows blown in. Indoors, the situation was bedlam. The wards were overflowing with victims, and the air was putrid with the reek of their burned skin and the commingled stench of their blood, lymphatic fluid, and every variety of human effluvia. The latter substances—primarily but not exclusively liquid in composition—rendered slick and treacherous any patch of ground, floor, or staircase underfoot not occupied by a human body.

Complicating any attempts at navigating this space, those victims still among the living incessantly moaned and begged for water, and would grab at the shins and ankles of passersby to press their pitiful entreaties. In scorched and cracking voices, some would even croak out their own names and addresses, on the slim-to-zero chance that some passing Samaritan would take note of this information and get word to worried loved ones back home.

The Noguchis threaded their way through this grasping gauntlet of human suffering until they were able to flag down a harried orderly. During their brief interaction, Mr. Noguchi was able to get some oil applied to his burns, which would have to suffice for the time being.

But Mrs. Noguchi's leg wound—which was clearly in need of proper disinfection, draining, and stitches—received nothing more than the same stingy swipes of Mercurochrome that Kazuko got for her minor scratches and cuts.

Still, the Noguchis might have been lucky to have received even this much care; everywhere else, the walking (or limping) wounded were being turned away. Across the city, medical supplies were nearly completely depleted, and the Red Cross was no exception. Moreover, most doctors and other staff had already gone one or two nights without sleep, working at full throttle under horrific circumstances, and they were beginning to feel the full effects of the resultant fatigue. Given the situation, patients whose injuries were not immediately life-threatening could receive no more than cursory care, and Mr. Noguchi might have had to pull rank as a senior national bureaucrat to get even that for himself and his family.

Sent on their way after their rudimentary treatments, the Noguchis decided to take a roundabout route back to their evacuation site via Minami Takeya-chō to check on their house and neighborhood. As they had feared, there was nothing worth salvaging in the smoldering ruins of the house—and nothing at all left of their neighborhood except for ashes, wreckage, and corpses in various degrees of recognizability as having once been human.

Kazuko never manifested the semihypnotic, psychologically numbing trauma defense response reported by Ōiwa Kōhei and so many other hibakusha. This meant that, emotionally speaking, she had to take every horror that confronted her at full face value and right on the chin. To survive and function in such an environment, she was forced to resort to mind tricks; in this case, she constantly mumbled, "They're only sleeping . . . They're only sleeping . . . ," as she stepped gingerly over the bodies and/or carbonized black lumps on the ground all around her.

Incredibly, some of these prone bodies were still alive, albeit barely. Hearing the passing footfalls of potential rescuers—or at least of water-bearing angels of mercy—one of them would occasionally stir and a hand would go up, then grasp at a leg or just air. This movement was inevitably accompanied by a one-word, barely audible moaned entreaty for "Mizu . . ." Kazuko, as a well-trained schoolgirl of her era, knew the rule about not giving water to wounded people; thus, she would not have complied with these requests even if she had had any water at hand.

After returning to the university and sharing the bad news about Minami Takeya-chō with their neighbors, the Noguchis conducted another family conference as to what to do about Mrs. Noguchi's leg. As the Red Cross was now clearly out of the picture for the foreseeable future, and assuming the same held true for the Army Mutual Aid Hospital farther south, they were going to have to find proper medical care somewhere else—and quickly. The pain from Mrs. Noguchi's injury was increasing as steadily as its infection was advancing, and all of the adults in the group would have had enough basic first aid knowledge to know that gangrene, sepsis, and eventually death could follow if said care was not secured as soon as possible.

Throughout the ordeal of the past twenty-four hours, the Noguchis had been accompanied by two members of their neighborhood's other *erai hito* Establishment-figure household—the wife and adolescent son of an IJN captain named Sugita, who was some kind of VIP at Kure Naval Arsenal. During this time, Mrs. Sugita and her son had come to believe that the Noguchis—in particular, the quick executive instincts of Mr. Noguchi—were to thank for their survival so far. Perhaps toward partial repayment of this familial debt, they offered to help their putative rescuers carry their belongings—which included Reiko's ossuary jar—and get to wherever they had to go to find aid for the now critically ailing Mrs. Noguchi.

For the time being, because everything to the north and west had been destroyed and the way east was blocked by the Kyōbashi, there was only one cardinal direction in which to continue their first aid search. Taking their final leave of the Bunri University encampment, the fivesome retraced the Noguchis' earlier steps back to Rijō Street, then took this south, with the limping Mrs. Noguchi doing her best not to slow the group down too much.

Although Reiko's thick ceramic ossuary jar was not the bulkiest

item the group was carrying during their trek, it was certainly the un-
wieldiest. Due to a lack of more suitable conveyance, it had to be cra-
dled like an infant in the crook of one arm, with a free hand used to
hold down its unfastenable lid lest its contents be spilled by the jos-
tling movement of walking or, far worse, in the catastrophic event of a
stumble and fall on the roadway. Even with various members of the
group taking turns bearing this sacred cargo, it was becoming increasingly burdensome for the weakened and exhausted group. When they
reached the western foot of the Miyuki Bridge, they dropped in at the
police *kōban* patrol station there to inquire as to the possibility of temporarily leaving the jar in the care of the authorities. The request was
accepted, presumably involving some exchange of paperwork/receipts,
and the Noguchi/Sugita band continued across the Kyōbashi. Following Rijō Street as far as it went, they eventually reached Akatsuki
Command HQ at Ujina Wharf—their last hope for proper first aid for
Mrs. Noguchi after being rebuffed everywhere else along the way.

Unfortunately for them—and especially for Mrs. Noguchi—Ujina
Wharf and the Akatsuki hospital there were still swamped with thousands of dead, dying, and injured. Many of these victims—including
growing piles of corpses—were awaiting ferrying to Akatsuki medical/
quarantine facilities on Ninoshima or Kanawajima, where the triaged
living would receive intensive first aid and the dead would be cremated in industrial-grade incinerators originally installed to dispose
of diseased IJA pack animals returning from military campaigns on
the Asian continent.

In the cursory triage assessment that the Noguchis received upon
their arrival at Ujina, it was made clear that none of their injuries—
including Mrs. Noguchi's steadily worsening leg wound—was considered sufficiently dire to merit either attention from a doctor or the
expenditure of precious first aid resources. Now literally at the end of
the road—and their collective rope—the family had no choice but to
sit in place and contemplate their next move.

While these considerations were underway, Captain Sugita's adolescent son took it upon himself to try to reach his father (who still
had no knowledge of his family's condition or whereabouts) in Kure.

The precise details of his itinerary to the naval arsenal have been lost to history, but the risky and arduous trip bore fruit. Sometime in the late afternoon, a shiny IJN staff limo—with young Master Sugita in it—pulled up in front of the group and whisked Mrs. Sugita away, presumably to a more comfortable refuge and never to be seen again.

But these presumptions were incorrect. To the Noguchis' great surprise and immeasurable gratitude, the same staff car returned for them a few hours later, after nightfall. In the interim, Captain Sugita had heard all about the ordeal from his son and now considered himself indebted to the Noguchis for helping his family get out of Minami Takeya-chō and find refuge on the university campus. As a gesture of gratitude (and, one would assume, with strong encouragement from Mrs. Sugita), he had arranged to keep the car for a few more hours so that the Noguchis could join his family in their temporary refuge in Miyajima, on the western shore of Hiroshima Bay.

Although their *deus ex machina navalis* evacuation to Miyajima had succeeded in getting them away from the stench and horror of ruined Hiroshima and put a roof over their heads for the first time in some thirty-six hours, the move had been inconsequential in terms of access to better medical care. Mrs. Noguchi's leg was getting worse seemingly by the hour, and by the morning of the eighth, the situation was becoming dire. Unable to walk unassisted by this point, in addition to running a raging fever as her body attempted to fight off the infection, she was taken to the only medical facility within walking distance: the clinic of a neighborhood ophthalmologist who had neither anesthesia, antibiotics, nor proper surgical tools on hand.

Taking one look at Mrs. Noguchi's wound, however, he knew that time was of the essence if his new patient's leg—if not her life—was to be saved. Giving her a rolled-up rag to bite and ordering her husband and daughter to hold down her arms and ankles, the doctor went to work on the wound with what were probably not much better than kitchen utensils. Mrs. Noguchi screamed until she passed out, but the "operation" was eventually successful. The wound was drained, cleaned out, dusted with combat medic's sulfa powder, and stitched up. Mrs. Noguchi's leg and life had been saved.

RETURN TO DANBARA

Danbara Naka-machi
2.1 kilometers east-southeast of Ground Zero

BY THE END of their sleepless night of August 6–7, the Ōiwas had gone nearly a full day with no food other than the unripe grapes they had plucked from the trellises of the Shinonome vineyard. In addition to being exhausted and hungry, they were also dehydrated, filthy, and dew soaked. Their present circumstances did not offer much prospect of any of that changing anytime soon.

After the family gleaned snippets of evacuee conversation and noticed the appearance of the skies to the west, they believed that the conflagration had subsided. With this new information in hand, the Ōiwas decided to chance a trip home. Gathering up their meager belongings and rousing the little Harada cousin to his feet, the threesome set off to retrace their steps from Danbara Naka-machi the previous afternoon.

Many of the prone people they passed along the roadside would have been the same ones who had grabbed at the trio's ankles and moaned for water the day before. But now these figures lay motionless and twisted up with rigor mortis, and the only sounds hanging over the scene would have been the high grass and trees in the fields and orchards of Shinonome rustling in the morning breezes off the Enkō River, and the weary *geta* wearers—the Ōiwas and their fellow road stragglers—shuffling in syncopated clip-clops as they headed back to see what was left of their city.

When the three arrived home after their somber morning trek, Grandmother Ōiwa, their house, and most of Danbara Naka-machi were still standing. Contrary to the warnings they had received the previous afternoon, the fires had never made it over Hijiyama's crest or around its flanks to reach the neighborhood.

During the Ōiwas' absence, the Akatsuki soldiers on the scene had cleared most of the bodies from the streets, and these were now piled up on the athletic field of nearby Hiroshima Girls' Commercial School, awaiting permission from on high for outdoor cremations within city limits to commence.[1] As the odor that had begun to permeate the neighborhood by late afternoon suggested, this was a task that was already long overdue. Although the corpses there and throughout Hiroshima might not have yet reached full-blown putrefication, by the end of their first full day under a hot August sun, they were getting there in a hurry. They were emitting a smell that would linger in clothes, homes, and the air for weeks to come, and that was just beginning to attract the scouting parties for what would soon be a book of Exodus–worthy plague of blowflies.

Late that night, Mr. Ōiwa returned early from his business trip to the Sea of Japan side of Honshu. Due to the remoteness of his location, it had taken some hours after the event for the news of Hiroshima's destruction to reach him. But once it did, he dropped everything he was doing to get back to the city as quickly as possible.

Even with his *Kokutetsu* credentials smoothing every train connection he had to make along the way, it still took him until the evening of August 7—traveling straight through the previous night—to reach the outer suburbs of Hiroshima. From that point, Mr. Ōiwa and his fellow travelers were obliged to detrain and walk along the crossties the rest of the way into the city. As they did, they passed endless streams of horribly injured and disfigured people coming from the opposite direction.

Although Mr. Ōiwa, in his urgency, might have been initially loath to slow his pace, he was eventually compelled to stop and approach a random file of staggering survivors. "My son is a first-year student at Hiroshima Prefectural Junior High," he called out. "Does anyone know what happened to the school?"

"All of the first-year Itchū students are dead," someone replied. "Completely wiped out."

After the war, Ōiwa Senior never talked about what was going through his mind in the moment he heard those words. But in their wake, his footsteps could only have become heavier as each one brought him closer to the moment when, he assumed, he would have to face the unbearable.

But this moment never came. When Mr. Ōiwa finally arrived home, long after nightfall, he did so to find not only his house still standing, but his son alive in it.

"My father had been sure I was dead," Ōiwa Kōhei recalls, seventy-three years later, before adding somewhat redundantly, "He was so happy when he saw that I wasn't."

On a gray rainy-season morning in June 2018, I am sitting at the dining table in Ōiwa's comfortable western Tokyo suburban home. There is a large-scale US Army Air Forces map of prebombed Hiroshima laid out on the table between us. During our talk, Ōiwa has been using it to trace his movements of August 6–7, 1945.

"I only survived," Ōiwa adds, "because my father was away on that business trip."

The business trip saved his mother's life, as well. She had originally planned to run an errand in the city that Monday morning, and would have been downtown right around the time of Little Boy's detonation if she had not stayed home to look after Kōhei's malaise—something that had been possible only because Mr. Ōiwa had not been there to disapprove of what he undoubtedly would have regarded as malingering.

The third life saved by Mr. Ōiwa's trip was his own; if he had not been on the opposite side of Honshu on the morning of August 6, he would have been at his office in the heart of the central business district when Little Boy exploded three-quarters of a kilometer away. Being in his sturdy concrete office building might have let him live an hour or so longer than if he had been out on the street at the moment of detonation, but that likely would only have increased his suffering before his inevitable end. In that alternate universe where his business trip never happened, he might have ended up the "well-dressed gentleman who died in our entranceway begging for water" in the family lore of some other household.

FACING MONSTERS

Tominaga household
North Ujina
3.4 kilometers south of Ground Zero

IN HIROSHIMA AND Nagasaki memory narratives, hibakusha often frame their survival of an atomic bombing as a process of death and rebirth or, perhaps more literally, as a metamorphosis.[1] Such metaphors may be particularly apt for hibakusha who eventually recovered from horrific injuries to reemerge, after arduous rehabilitations, into postwar "second" lives. But it would also apply to hibakusha whose recovery is incomplete and whose long "second" lives, as a result, have been plagued with ongoing bomb-related ailments. These would include the thousands—perhaps tens of thousands—of hibakusha who have undergone repeated hospitalizations and surgeries for radiation-exposure-related cancers over long postwar lives—generally from middle age on—never knowing when the next relapse will occur. Moreover, these bomb-related-cancer sufferers are often also tormented by fears that—despite official assurances to the contrary—the atom bomb genetic damage that has caused their own illnesses has been transmitted to children and grandchildren.[2]

Many hibakusha also suffered non-life-threatening but nevertheless life-altering disfiguring injuries such as permanent epilation or thick, ropy keloid burn scars on their faces, necks, and limbs, which are difficult to hide from the view of others in a hot and humid climate like Japan's. As a result, hibakusha so afflicted have been forced to endure long decades of social anxiety and self-esteem issues, most intensely and agonizingly, perhaps, during what should have been their prime romantically and sexually active years from adolescence to early middle age. On account of their disfigurements and the suggestion of atomic contamination they entailed, thousands were ostracized and their lives were derailed; suicides were far from uncommon among young hibakusha in the first few decades after the bombing.

Although many card-carrying hibakusha (i.e., recognized—and recompensed/pensioned—as such by the Japanese government) escaped actual physical injury in August 1945, they have nevertheless wrestled with a raft of psychological injuries shared with all other hibakusha. Such injuries, which are lifelong and from which there is no permanent recovery, would include PTSD and vivid memories of horrors experienced and witnessed; survivor guilt; unresolved grief over lost loved ones; health-issue anxieties; or, as is typically the case, some combination of all of the foregoing. Moreover, and perhaps in the most abstract (but not necessarily less traumatic) manifestation of such psychological injuries, grief can even play out in what might be considered a philosophical dimension—in the hibakusha's perceived loss of belief in a stable and predictable world where things, both good or bad, are supposed to happen for reasons that make moral sense. The bombs, then—from this perspective—destroyed not only their respective targeted cities, but also the narratives within which hundreds of thousands of people in those cities framed and made sense of their lives and the world.

In her prebombing life, Tominaga Chieko was a privileged and high-spirited child who inhabited a predictable and stable world. Even with the onset of the war, her lived environment was one in which each day was a reassuring (if rather tiresome and spartan) repetition of the one before it, and in which even with all the chanting and bamboo spear drills and lousy food and brave talk of the necessity for brave sacrifice, the conflict—at least for her—was still something abstract happening to other people far away.

In Chieko's stable world, responsible adults were in charge. Smart, competent, important men like her father were protecting everyone from any real danger. Sirens were in place to warn of approaching enemy bombers. Radios and newspapers reassured everyone that the emperor's valiant forces had not been retreating since the fall of Saipan—they were luring the enemy closer to the Home Islands for a final decisive battle in which the divine wind would blow to save Japan and deliver victory. And even with her mother frequently muttering under her breath that these were all lies, the prevailing assumption in the Tominaga household—at least among the womenfolk—was that when all this war nonsense eventually blew over, they would all still be standing—perhaps a bit skinnier and sleep-deprived, but otherwise no worse for wear—and life would go on as usual.

Of course, all this control and stability suffered the occasional temporary wobble—for example, when nudged by the constant air raid warnings of the summer of 1945, or when some neighborhood household's son or husband returned from overseas in a tiny military-issue ossuary box. Still, these daily reminders of a dangerous and unpredictable outside world, in and of themselves, were never enough to flip Chieko's world on its ear.[3]

But the comforting certainties of that world began to unravel the moment she saw the mushroom cloud over downtown Hiroshima. And the shock did not end there; the ensuing visual and psychic slideshow of horror she was forced to witness on August 6 was a daylong assault against her once-firm belief that the world made sense and that the grown-ups in charge knew what they were doing. By nightfall, she was no longer the innocent girl who had awakened that morning, and of all the shocks and existential body blows she endured on that longest day, the news that her sister, Machiyo, brought home that night about Dai Ni Kenjo might have been the most damaging.

"It seems like something terrible happened to your homeroom," the dust- and blood-streaked Machiyo said when she arrived home from the teachers college campus that night. "Your class president came back to school looking like a monster."[4]

The first full day of Tomonaga Chieko's second life began in the comfort of her own futon, when she woke up—no doubt with Machi-yo's words still ringing in her ears—and realized that nothing was ever going to be the same again. At this point, she was not aware that five other girls had also been absent from Hata-sensei's homeroom. Therefore, for all she knew, she was the only surviving member of her class.

By the mores of her 1945 Japanese lifeworld, the fact of her own survival—when her classmates had presumably all died performing their patriotic duty—meant that she was already under a pall of shame and suspicion. Saddled with this perceived opprobrium, Chieko assumed that, at least as long as she lived in Hiroshima, she would have to go about her daily life with that personal legacy tattooed across her forehead.

Compounding this discomfort would be the jealousy she would have to endure, for not only was she a survivor of Hata-sensei's home-room, but she had weathered Hiroshima's catastrophe unscarred, un-injured, and unbereaved. In a city where thus unscathed survivors were relative rarities immediately after the bombing, Chieko, in her daily life from now on, would encounter people who would despise her on sight for the fact of that immaculate survival alone—and even more so, perhaps, once they learned about the freak luck behind it. If she were going to continue living in Hiroshima, she would have to learn how to look such people in the eye and not allow their knee-jerk scorn and disdain to define who she was.

Or she could simply run.

As a rich girl with an overprotective and indulgent mother—a mother who could not have given a damn what their Ujina neighbors thought of her or her family—Chieko would have had that option. If she wanted, she could have quit Dai Ni Kenjo and even left Hiroshima. The Tominagas could have afforded to send her back to Tokyo to go to some high-class girls' school—assuming there were any there still standing after all of the American incendiary raids. Or she could have gone away to stay with relatives in Kyoto—a city that had not been bombed, and where she would have had her pick among any number of respectable girls' schools, as well. But if she chose this option—now in full knowledge of what had happened to her classmates yesterday—that act of cowardice would incur a life sentence of dishonor from which there would be no escape, no matter how far away from Hiroshima she ran.

She did, however, have control, starting today, over the course her "second" life would take. And as she saw it, she had no choice but to go back to school—not only out of the altruistic, decent impulse to see what she could do to help, but just as important to be seen doing so. She would show up for duty, appropriately humbled by what everyone would no doubt consider her undeserved (and suspect to be her malingering-tainted) luck. Of course, she would never be so gauche as to crow about the good fortune of her survival, nor—and this was a distinction of critical importance—would she allow herself to appear ashamed of it.

Around noon on August 7, Chieko headed for the Dai Ni Kenjo campus.[5] Not long after she had left her house, however, she began to get cold feet about what she was attempting to do. Figuring things might go easier if she were not alone, she took a detour from her usual route to school to call at the house of Hayashi Toshiko, an Ujina girl from East Homeroom. Chieko knew, from the previous Sunday's fateful rock, paper, scissors round between Hi'ura Ruriko and her East Homeroom counterpart at Zakoba-chō, that Toshiko had been at the East Parade Ground on truck patch duty with the first-grade girls on August 6. As Chieko was soon told, Toshiko had been lucky enough to be under tree cover at the moment of Little Boy's detonation, so she avoided being burned by thermal rays. She had been knocked off her feet and tossed a few meters by the blast effect, but she had otherwise escaped with only minor scrapes and bruises.

Toshiko had also been dreading going back to school; like Chieko, the East Homeroom girls were all too aware that they were still alive only because of sheer luck—in their case, the blind fortune of their class president winning a silly playground game. So it was only natural that they, too, in the culturally inflected Japanese way of interpreting their situation, felt ashamed as well as guilty about their survival.

But after a quick, mutually encouraging tête-à-tête with Chieko, Toshiko agreed that they had to go back to school today. Thus emboldened, at least to an extent, by each other's company, the pair headed off to face whatever monsters—figurative or literal—awaited them at the teachers college / Dai Ni Kenjo.

When Chieko and Toshiko arrived at the campus, the first thing they noticed was that the main classroom building—a two-story wooden structure—had been buckled by the blast force of the previous day's explosion.[6] The building was not in imminent risk of collapse, but it was nevertheless perceptibly bent in a boomerang shape, concave in the direction of the central city, as if a southeast-facing giant standing on the athletic grounds had kicked it squarely at center mass.[7] All of the glass panes in the windows had been blown out.

Inside the building, the least damaged classrooms had been converted into aid stations. These were staffed not only by the teachers college faculty and girls trained in basic first aid, but also by a cadre of Akatsuki soldiers and other uniformed personnel, some of whom appeared to be trained medics.

In the classrooms, the still, sweltering air was filled with the smells of burned flesh, blood, and unmentionable substances. The floors were covered virtually wall to wall with victims—in turn moaning, motionless, or screaming—laid out on portable tatami mats or Army-issue blankets liberated by Akatsuki Command from the nearby Army Clothing Depot. Between the rows of these scorched, shattered bodies, narrow lanes had been left that were just barely wide enough for the orderlies to make their rounds, and also to provide *seiza* kneeling space for the large numbers of family members—many of whom had been there all night—who filled the rooms to overflowing.

Chieko and Toshiko moved along the corridor of the school building, peering into classrooms to look for familiar faces. They eventually came to the school's tatami-matted tea ceremony room, where several of their teachers and middle-aged mothers were clustered around a group of dimunitive prone bodies—Dai Ni Kenjo girls who had miraculously made it back to campus.[8] Some of these girls had been ferried there by Akatsuki trucks that had picked them up where they had collapsed along Rijō Street, but a handful of them—including the late Hi'ura Ruriko—had somehow walked all the way back from the firebreak worksite in Zakoba-chō under their own power.

Machiyo's account of the previous night did not come close to doing justice to the sheer physical devastation these West Homeroom girls had suffered, although her use of the descriptive word "monster" turned out to have been all too accurate. The girls laid out on the classroom floor had been, in a word, destroyed. What little was left of them, as Chieko recalled over seventy years later, could hardly have been called human. They had been so badly burned that they could be distinguished only by their raspy, barely audible voices. Because they had been looking up at the sky when they heard *Enola Gay* and the *Great Artiste* powering through their post-bomb-drop escape turns, and had begun cheering when they mistook the latter's radiosonde parachutes for bailing crew members, even their tongues and the insides of their mouths had been flash-burned by the fireball.[9] Their eyes—for the girls who still had any—were barely perceptible slits in swollen rust-brown faces pebbled with burn blisters and slashed with blast-effect debris lacerations. Several of the girls were already dead. After the first few seconds she spent in the room, Chieko could not look at them anymore. All she could do was weep.

In light of Chieko's complex emotions regarding her own pristine survival, it might have been even more painful for her to be in the presence of her classmates' mothers. Some, if not most, of the mothers bravely endured their agony, compelled by the rules of decorum and the mores of the time to act—at least in public—as if they were proud and grateful that they and their children had been given this opportunity to make so grand and grave a patriotic sacrifice for their emperor and the land of their ancestors.

But occasionally, a mother—particularly if she was seeing her child for the first time since the bombing—would react more like one would expect a parent to react, i.e., with openly and loudly expressed horror, rage, and hot, uncontrollable grief. Panicked disbelief—as per Kübler-Ross's classic stages-of-grief model—was also frequently in evidence among these new arrivals to the classroom aid station. In one particular case, which Tominaga still recalls with a trembling voice seventy-odd years on, the mother of one of the burned girls—West Homeroom student Honji Fumie—arrived in the room and started shouting, "This is not my child! This cannot be my child!"[10]

At some point, one of the Dai Ni Kenjo teachers noticed Chieko standing there and told her that her best friend, Tamekazu Michiko, was still alive—barely—and that her father had taken her home last night. As Chieko and Toshiko, preparing to head off for the Tamekazu home in Ujina, paid their parting respects—which would have included apologies for not having been of more use in the present circumstances—the teacher thrust paper *uchiwa* paddle fans into their hands.

"Here," the teacher said, before adding somewhat ominously, "You'll need these to shoo away the flies."

Just as they were about to leave the building, someone told them that Hata-sensei's body was in a nearby room. The girls went to the room, just next to the entranceway, where they found a solitary adult-sized body laid out on a tabletop, its head covered with a white cloth. Before they had a chance to think over their next action more prudently, the girls pulled back the cloth and, seeing the unrecognizable mass of gore underneath it, screamed simultaneously. Hearing this, Fukuzaki—the male gym teacher—darkened the doorway and, encountering the girls there, recruited them to help him with a task he had been putting off since yesterday: cremating Hata-sensei. They did this in the schoolyard, using wooden slats from the damaged outer walls of the campus building as fuel.

With this grim duty performed, the girls were finally free to head off for Michiko's house, where they arrived after a walk that probably felt longer than it actually took. They were greeted at the door by Mr. Tamekazu, who led them into a tatami-floored living room. Michiko was laid out on a futon next to her mother—also barely alive—who had been at the Zakoba-chō firebreak site with a neighborhood women's volunteer labor team. Her appearance was so horrific—even worse than her daughter's—that Chieko was unable to lay eyes on her again for the duration of the visit, even when speaking with her.

Although Michiko's face, neckline, lower arms, and legs were all horribly burned, the skin on her upper arms and torso appeared only slightly reddened. This was the area of her body that had been covered by her school blouse. Flash burn lines clearly demarcated where the skin that had been protected by her blouse ended and the skin that had been exposed to full-force thermal rays began.

The previous June, Dai Ni Kenjo had received a civil defense directive—likely from Hiroshima Military District—that the students' usual white blouses were too easy to spot from enemy aircraft, so they were ordered to be dyed *kokubōshoku* ("National Defense color"). This was supposed to be a dun brownish khaki, like an Army uniform, but the dye the girls had been issued with instead turned the blouses a dark grassy green. Chieko and Michiko both hated the color and always wore their usual white blouses, instead. Whenever anyone at the school would challenge them about their nonregulation clothing, the girls would claim their green ones were home being washed. This quietly waged, ongoing campaign of self-assertion against conformity and defiance of authority was an inside joke shared between the girls all summer.

In one of the countless anecdotes of ugly irony surrounding Hiroshima's firebreak tragedy, the dark green of their classmates' dyed blouses was apparently almost as effective at absorbing thermal radiation on the electromagnetic spectrum as black would have been. Conversely, by reflecting back Little Boy's thermal rays to the extent that it did, Michiko's white blouse likely gave her an extra day of life—just long enough for her best friend to watch her dying in agony before her eyes.

The air in the Tamekazus' living room was permeated with the same unspeakable stenches that filled the campus aid stations, and its oppressive stillness was only occasionally disturbed by a mumbled platitude from the guests and a rasped stock response from the hosts—the rote rituals of polite Japanese social discourse observed even in extremis—before the ambient soundscape of tortured breathing and the buzzing of hungry flies returned to fill the vacuum of excruciating silence.

It was not long before everyone in the room—living and dying alike—realized the obvious but unspoken truth hanging in the humming, reeking air: The visitors were late for the door. But the occasion had one last souvenir of traumatic memory baggage for Chieko to carry for the rest of her life.

As she was about to leave, Mrs. Tamekazu rasped, "How lucky you were to be absent yesterday."

Chieko had no idea how to reply to that either in that moment, or over the next seventy-five years.

After a final customary apology for having imposed on their hosts, Chieko and Toshiko made good their exit posthaste.

By the time Chieko gathered sufficient courage to return to the Tamekazu house some weeks later, Michiko and her mother were both long dead. On that occasion, she performed one last formal ritual for her friend when she accepted an invitation from Michiko's father to stand an incense stick on the *butsudan* memorial altar in the living room.

Chieko never managed to work up either the heart or the stomach to go back there again.

FALLOUT

WHILE KŌHEI MIGHT have survived Little Boy, he did not escape its wrath entirely unscathed. During the weeks following the bombing, he began exhibiting textbook radiation sickness symptoms: All his hair eventually fell out (taking months to grow back), and his gums began to bleed so badly that he could not brush his teeth. Moreover, the flying-glass cut on his shin refused to heal, and trying to keep the wound clear of the relentlessly fecund blowflies and their loathsome larvae was a constant struggle during the final weeks of that bleak summer. If Kōhei took his eyes off the wound and forgot about it even for an hour or so, the next time he looked, it would inevitably be tented over yet again with a wriggling off-white clump of fresh maggots dining on the flesh of their host with a faintly audible, crunchy chewing sound.

The flies and their squirming progeny were everywhere, all over everything and everyone, living and dead alike. And each one of the corpses still left out in the open on the streets, in parks, and in rubble was an olfactory homing beacon leading swarm after swarm of the ravenous insects straight into the city.

Once the citywide cremation orders came down on August 8, the Akatsuki soldiers and their civilian volunteer helpers in Danbara

Naka-machi could not burn the bodies quickly enough. Whenever they found a corpse, they would bring it to Hiroshima Girls' Commercial School and toss it onto burn piles awaiting diesel-fuel dousing and cremation of almost industrial efficiency. When Kōhei watched this operation underway, it seemed that the soldiers and civilian volunteers treated the corpses more like sacks of garbage than like people. Given the grisly nature of their task, we can assume that the emotional shutting down so often observed in survivors among the atomic ruins was also operant here on the part of the cremation workers. Because of the gruesome circumstances under which they toiled, no one except perhaps for a grieving parent could have faulted them for failing to stand on ceremony, as it were, and taking refuge in the psychological sanctuary of affectless numbness. Kōhei certainly would have understood how they felt. He had stark and recent personal memories not only about what it was like to handle hundreds of scorched and blast-flayed corpses at a stretch, but also about the emotional and psychological expediences required to keep from losing his mind while doing so.

Despite the grim nature of the work at hand, the operations had about them something of an informal atmosphere. People seemingly came and went as they pleased, occasionally taking a corpse with them when they left. Often, a family looking for a loved one would show up at the schoolyard cremation ground, find the body in question, then take possession of it after some cursory exchange of paperwork with the Akatsuki NCO or *Keibōdan* official in charge. Although some of these family groups would carry the body away and out of sight—presumably to take it home for more ceremonious funeral rites—most people would just build a makeshift pyre on some nearby corner of open space and cremate the body on the spot, with no one thinking the worse of them for it; then they would take the ashes away in a bucket, bag, or box.

Although finding a suitable empty spot for a single-body pyre was not particularly difficult, finding enough fuel was a challenge not only because regular civilians could not readily get their hands on diesel or any other petroleum-based fire accelerant, but also because there simply was not enough wood lying about, and the soldiers were not giving away any of the timber that was being hauled in on Akatsuki trucks because they needed this for their own large-scale crematory operations. Although this lack of wood everywhere else in central Hiroshima was the result of nearly every shred of organic matter having already been consumed by the explosion's thermal rays and subsequent conflagration, there was little to no wooden wreckage for potential pyre fuel use in Danbara because most of its houses and other wooden structures were still intact.

Due to this fuel shortage, it was a common sight in the neighborhood to see bereaved families scouring dry streambeds and scrounging around in junk piles for kindling and more substantial pieces and planks of wood. No one, after all, wanted to be caught short, fuel-wise, and end up being stuck in the nightmare scenario of having an incompletely cremated loved one on their hands.

While these scenes of grieving family were tragic to witness, Ōiwa posits that at least these dead were able to get heartfelt send-offs from loved ones. In this sense, one might even consider them fortunate, compared to the faceless tens of thousands who were cremated in anonymous burn piles, leaving behind families who would spend the rest of their lives bereft of the closure of being able to confirm the fate of the missing, leaving their front doors unlocked at night on the chance that the disappeared loved ones—ostensibly keyless—might miraculously return while their families were asleep.

But Kōhei and his family had more than mere psychological stressors to deal with; the simple animal-survival task of finding food and water was another daily challenge for the household, even with their *Kokutetsu* connections. Outside those rare occasions when they might come into a culinary windfall such as a meager pouch of rice or a can of mandarin oranges, they ate and drank pretty much whatever they could get their hands on. Family staples during this lean season included painstakingly apportioned scraps of vegetables from the truck patch in their yard, and pumpkins liberated from amateur-farmer-tended patches along the Ujina Line tracks in their neighborhood. To keep hydrated, they drank whatever water they could scrounge from cisterns, wells, and rain barrels.

Most people in Hiroshima were too preoccupied with their day-in-and-day-out struggle for bare survival subsistence to keep up with news. In Ōiwa's recollection, this state of de facto information blackout was so total—and likely compounded, in his case, by his father's reticence about such matters at home—that he heard that the war had ended only about a week after the fact. Any radios in the city that had survived the fires were mostly otherwise inoperable at the time because their cabinets had been wrecked by Little Boy's shock wave or their vacuum tube innards had been fried by its electromagnetic pulse. Likewise, newspapers were few and far between because the editing and printing facilities of the local daily, the *Chūgoku Shimbun*, had been destroyed, and the general logistical chaos in Hiroshima meant that very few newspapers were finding their way into the city from the outside. So unless one had direct access to someone who worked on one of the still functioning local civilian or military administrative organs, the days and even weeks following the bombing had a near-total news blackout aside from neighborhood gossip networks.

Of more immediate consequence, information blackout conditions meant that most otherwise "uninjured" people in the city (and in its outlying areas where "black rain" had fallen) had no idea, until it was too late, that almost anything they ate or drank that did not come out of a can was making them sick. Many hibakusha who believed that they had survived the bomb's wrath because they had escaped external, mechanical injuries would eventually die as a result of the substances they ingested during the immediate post-bombing period, when Hiroshima was still "hot" with residual radiation. Now, nearly eighty years since the bombing, hibakusha are still fighting and succumbing to various forms of cancer that are the direct result of this exposure.

The ionizing type of radiation produced by the fission of uranium or plutonium in a nuclear weapon destroys living tissue primarily in two ways: via initial and residual radiation. The physiological havoc that these two kinds of radiation cause progresses according to varying pathological schedules, depending on the type and dosage intensity (total amount plus speed of absorption) of the radiation in question.[1]

The quickest and most direct of these sorts of biological destruction results from exposure to the initial radiation produced by the shower of high-energy gamma rays, X-rays, and neutrons released in the instant of a nuclear explosion. Traveling in straight line-of-sight paths at light speed (gamma rays and X-rays) or near light speed (neutrons), this radiation impacts living tissue like nanoscopic high-velocity bullets. It causes most of its destruction of tissue by severing DNA chains in the chromosomes of living cells, thereby rendering them incapable of carrying out their evolved function of regulating mitosis—the constant process of cellular division and regeneration that replaces the cells in a human body as they naturally die off. The consequences of this cessation of mitosis are most quickly manifested in those parts or organs of the body where the normal cellular life span is the shortest and thus the turnover of this regeneration/reproduction is the most rapid and urgent.[2] Organs so affected include bone marrow, where blood cells are produced, and the lining of the gastrointestinal tract. When these individual cells reach the end of their natural life spans, and they cannot be replaced because DNA strands have been broken "faster and/or in higher volume than the body can repair this damage," the radiation victim literally begins to decompose from the inside out while still alive.[3] Among those thus fatally irradiated, the fortunate die quickly.

The second vector by which the radiation from a nuclear weapon (or any other nuclear catastrophe, such as a Chernobyl-type event) can kill is by either robbing electrons from, or adding electrons to, the atoms that make up living tissue. This chemical phenomenon, known as "ionization," can be caused by the gamma rays and neutrons of initial radiation, but it can also be caused—albeit perhaps with less subatomic violence—by residual radiation in the form of the alpha and, to a lesser extent, beta particles that are fragments of the nuclei of atoms produced as a by-product of fission.[4] However, unlike neutrons and gamma rays or X-rays, which impact an atom-bombed environment (and all of the living things in that environment) only in the instant of detonation before continuing to fly off near light speed in ballistic straight lines, alpha and beta particles can linger in the environment in the form of fallout for days and weeks. In the case of already radioactive U-235 or Pu-239—unfissioned remnants of the imperfect critical mass explosion in the cores of Little Boy and Fat Man, respectively—the residual radiation could theoretically remain in soil for centuries, slowly leaching alpha and beta particles during their glacially paced radioactive decay into atomically stable isotopes.

The biological consequence of this ionization is that life-sustaining matter in the body of an exposed organism is transformed into matter that is not supposed to be there—i.e., toxins. Even water itself—which makes up some 70 percent of the mass of a human body—can be turned against the organism when ionizing radiation breaks the bonds between hydrogen and oxygen atoms in a water molecule, sending these atoms careening around inside the body, where they can rebond to form compounds such as hydrogen peroxide[5]—a substance that is highly destructive to biological tissue. This effect alone can result in illness or death in a person exposed to a severe enough dose of ionizing radiation.

Of particular relevance to long-term hibakusha pathology, the ionization process can also affect DNA not only by destroying it outright—as in the case of an atomic bomb's burst of initial radiation—but also by causing mutations in limited areas on the double-helix molecule that allow it to continue functioning . . . just not as it has evolved to do. When DNA is no longer able to regulate mitosis properly, cell production goes haywire, proliferating out of control and resulting in the formation of cancer. Whether or not the organism so affected survives or succumbs to this cancer is determined by any number of factors, including the received radiation dosage and physiological characteristics such as genetic predisposition to cancer, malnutrition, and other factors. In other words, some organisms (e.g., cockroaches, famously) are simply more resistant to—more readily able to self-repair from—radiation exposure than others, and this disparity will manifest itself literally as the difference between life and death.[6] This disparity can also be observed between individual humans, and it had ramifications for the Ōiwa family.

"There seems to be quite a bit of variation between individuals as to how much exposure to radiation their bodies can resist," Ōiwa Kōhei says as we are discussing the topic of hibakusha and cancer. In August 1945, his grandmother was in her late sixties, but as Ōiwa puts it, being that age in those days was like being ninety years old now. She could move around and function in normal daily life, but she was not in robust health by any means—and that was *before* the bombing. Apparently, her resistance to radiation exposure was low, as was that of Kōhei's five-year-old cousin.

In September, Mr. Ōiwa recommended sending the little cousin back to Kagoshima "while he is still healthy"—evidently he already suspected that something was wrong and judged that the considerate course of action would be to reunite the child with his parents for the last weeks or months of his life. Mr. Ōiwa used his National Railways pull to secure passage to Kagoshima for himself and the boy; even for a National Railways executive, this was not easily accomplished in those days, when the nation's transportation grid was still in postwar chaos and jammed to the breaking point by the simultaneous return of millions of demobilized servicemen from overseas to their hometowns and families in Japan. Both the boy and Grandmother Ōiwa were dead by December. Due to the chaotic state of health care in early-postwar Japan—particularly in Hiroshima and Nagasaki, with their shattered infrastructures and tens of thousands of lingering dying—it was never determined by any medical professional that Grandmother Ōiwa's or the little cousin's cause of death was a direct consequence of radiation exposure during August 6–7. But there can be little doubt that their ingesting of radioactive air/dust, water, and food in the days and weeks after the bomb played a role in their demises, as was the case with thousands of other victims in the atom-bombed cities throughout the long autumn and winter of 1945–1946.

THE ZAKOBA-CHŌ STONES

Postwar Hiroshima

UNTIL THE MOMENT of Emperor Hirohito's surrender broadcast, few of His Majesty's loyal subjects seemed to have abandoned the Imperial Era belief system that narratively framed their wartime struggles and suffering as worthy and ennobling.[1] This is not to suggest that an overwhelming majority of Japanese adults believed in final victory anymore (though most would have carefully kept to themselves any doubts along such lines). Rather, it was more that the prospect of having to go on living after that belief system had been invalidated by defeat—especially after all the sacrifices that had been made for it so far—was something too terrible to contemplate.[2] It was this mindset—which was essentially religious in nature and function—that sustained Japan's war effort to the bitter end. Until the emperor said otherwise, Japan's holy struggle was ongoing and this belief system remained on life support, despite the Americans by this point having burned most of the country's urban areas to the ground and forced most of the populace into the early stages of slow starvation. This was true even in Hiroshima and Nagasaki after the total devastation that had been visited upon those communities.

While still hunkered down within the psychological ramparts of the Imperial Era belief system, even the bereaved parent of a Hiroshima firebreak child might yet have wrung a measure of grief-transcending meaning out of their family tragedy by clinging to the idea that the death of their son or daughter had been a patriotic sacrifice in the service of emperor and country. As long as these beliefs held true, their child's death had not been in vain.[3]

But when Dai Ni Kenjo second-year West Homeroom student Kaiho Kikuko died on August 20, five days after the surrender broadcast, the Imperial Era belief system was in free fall. In the resulting vacuum of meaning that now prevailed in Japanese cultural space— with, one would imagine, particularly jarring despair amid the ruins of Hiroshima and Nagasaki—Imperial Era god terms like "immortal cause" and "brave sacrifice" had been rendered at least temporarily meaningless, if not absurd.[4] Thus invalidated, they could no longer function as designed—that is, to transform at least some of the bitterness and despair of the bereaved into something closer to solemn, ennobled pride. In the absence of this magic, Kikuko's family was left with nothing but a home city in ruins, a half-destroyed house, and a daughter, dead at fourteen, who in a better world should have lived into her nineties.

Kikuko's death had an additional consequence: It left Sakamoto Setsuko as the lone survivor of the original thirty-eight-member-strong Dai Ni Kenjo firebreak crew. Setsuko's very Japanese interpretation of this distinction would end up altering the trajectory of her life. For the next quarter century, she accepted her sole-survivor status—with the occasional nudge from adults in her environment— as a weighty, destiny-bequeathed mantle of obligation to the memory of the girls of West Homeroom and their bereaved family members. She would never escape the demands of this role.

Her public debut in this capacity came in March 1946, when she attended a memorial ceremony for the teachers college / Dai Ni Kenjo casualties held at Sengyōji Temple in Ujina to mark the seventh month after the bombing.[5] Although Setsuko had by this time weathered the worst of her ARS, the event still would have physically taxed her. Her half-year-long struggle to recover from her injuries had weakened her considerably, and her radiation-compromised immune system left her hypersensitive to temperature extremes, prone to fatigue and malaise, and with little resistance to colds and other infections.[6]

The ARS had also affected Setsuko's physical appearance, leaving her, in her own words, "a sorry sight to see."[7] Like many female hibakusha, she was particularly self-conscious about the loss of her hair. In March 1946, her scalp had only partially recovered from the complete epilation that she—like Ōiwa Kōhei and thousands of other hibakusha—had experienced in the first weeks and months after the bombing.[8] In Japanese culture, the beauty afforded by the blessing of abundant, lustrous black hair has traditionally been regarded as being as important to a woman as life itself. But Little Boy had robbed Setsuko and thousands of other girls like her of this Japanese birthright of feminine pride and dignity—for some, permanently. In recognition of the particular agony of this disfigurement—and perhaps out of consideration as much for the comfort of the gazer as for the shame of the gazed upon—it was customary in Hiroshima and Nagasaki schools in the first few years after the bombing for female students suffering from radiation epilation to be given special permission to wear hats, headscarves, or cotton *bōsaizukin* hoods in class.

In a misery-loving-company sense, feeling like a "sorry sight" might have been a little more tolerable, psychologically, in the immediate aftermath of the bombing, when so many others in Setsuko's daily environment also bore visible physical manifestations of their traumatic experience. But the dynamic of this tenuously balanced self-consciousness would have been thrown out of kilter once the occupation and full-scale reconstruction of Hiroshima began, and the city quickly filled up with non-hibakusha newcomers who made little or no effort to hide their flashed glances (or open stares) of pity and disgust when they caught sight of a maimed or disfigured hibakusha.

When Setsuko had first been approached by school officials about performing the honor of reading the eulogy for her fallen classmates at the Sengyōji ceremony, she must have been appalled at the prospect of standing bareheaded under the gaze of hundreds of people. Moreover, many among the assemblage would be bereaved family members of her classmates—which could have only compounded her trepidation about participating in the event, particularly in such a conspicuous role. She would have already met many of the bereaved families one household at a time when, in the first weeks after the bombing, she dutifully made the rounds to stand incense sticks for her classmates on their family *butsudan* altars. But she had yet to be in a situation where so many of these families would be gathered together in one place, and where the local press would likely be in attendance, and where the ever-dreaded *"Why are you still alive, while my daughter is dead?"* (self-)recrimination—even if left unuttered and if only imagined by Setsuko—would surely be hanging in the air over the venue like a black cloud.

But Setsuko's sense of obligation eventually won out over her fears. To honor and uphold the memory of her classmates—as well as, perhaps, to excise from her life narrative the part where she was eternally obliged to be ashamed of her survival—she would face down her guilt and shame demons. She accepted the eulogy request.

On the day of the Sengyōji ceremony, Tominaga Chieko, who had not been invited to offer any remarks before the assemblage, watched the proceedings from the back of the venue. She felt a mixture of pity and admiration as she watched the once vigorous tomboy Setsuko—in her now conspicuously weakened physical condition, and with the pink of her scalp still visible through her thin hair—assume her position at the front of the venue and bow to the assembled mourners.

Turning about to face the flower-bedecked altar at the appointed time, Setsuko began to deliver the eulogy in a quavering voice, pausing frequently to swallow back tears. While she endured this ordeal, there must have been palpable tension among all in attendance as to whether or not she would be able to make it through to the end. But Setsuko soldiered on. As the last syllable of her speech trailed away in the incense-smoky air, most of the assemblage was in tears.

At the close of the Sengyōji ceremony, the mourners made a pilgrimage to the Zakoba-chō site, which at the time was not much more than a desolate patch of brownfield with a few squatters' shacks poking out of the rubble here and there. Joining the Sengyōji group were the combined student body and faculty of Dai Ni Kenjo and the teachers college. Front and center for the proceedings was a simple wooden memorial plank with hand-brushed lettering, which Hi'ura Ruriko's father, Yoshito, had taken upon himself to have built and erected on the site at his own expense.

After 1946, memorial ceremonies were held at the site every August 6, with Sakamoto (later Hirata) Setsuko in attendance as a featured speaker every year until 1969. On these occasions, her comments would have included not only prayers offered up for the repose of the departed, but of more immediate social and symbolic urgency, the customary apologia-cum-apologies to the assemblage for her own undeserved survival, which were expected of a Japanese rhetor in such circumstances.[9] Tominaga Chieko would be there for nearly all of the ceremonies, always watching from the back row—ever a fellow mourner, but also, and inevitably, the same permanent outsider she had been since she first moved to the city in 1944.

Hi'ura Yoshito was another faithful annual-ceremony participant. His regular attendance—which continued well into the 1970s, when it was finally curtailed by physical frailty—far outlived his simple wooden plank memorial, which was replaced in time for the August 6, 1952, ceremony by twin stone pillars similar to a certain austere style of Japanese gravestone. Set to the side of this arrangement was a smaller stone inscribed with a brief explanation of what and who was being commemorated on this site.

The timing of this new memorial unveiling was significant not only as it marked the religiously auspicious seventh anniversary of the bombing, but also because it happened mere months after the official end of the Allied occupation, with Japan's signing of the Treaty of San Francisco. The 1952 bomb memorial ceremonies in Hiroshima (and Nagasaki), then, were the first to be held free of the rhetoric-inhibiting gaze of Allied occupiers.

The newly fluid dynamics of Japanese war-interpretation discourse resulting from this "freedom"—with the field now open to participation by conservative/revanchist voices that SCAP had muzzled from 1945 to 1952—are reflected in the language used in the inscriptions on the Zakoba-chō pillars. Making an appearance here are numerous Imperial Era belief system god terms, such as *junkoku* ("martyrdom for the national cause"), *aikoku* ("patriotism"), and *eirei* ("heroic souls"). Moreover, predefeat martial values are conspicuously evoked with use of the hoary idiom *sange* ("falling like cherry blossoms in the wind")—a euphemism for death in battle that was often used in wartime news reports of kamikaze suicide-attack missions. The new discursive leeway also opened the way for the Zakoba-chō girls to be described not only as having been killed by the atomic bomb but—and with verily stunning rhetorical boldness for 1952 Hiroshima, where such language would have bordered on sacrilege—in the context of aiding the war effort, which was framed in the narrative of the inscription as a worthy venue of patriotic, heroic, and thus meaningful sacrifice.

On the fronts of both stones, *Memorial to the Martyred Students* is inscribed in large, highly stylized lettering evoking the sophisticated brushwork of a master calligrapher. In smaller, simpler lettering below this are inscribed the names of the schools whose students are being commemorated. One totem pillar is for the students of Hiroshima Women's Teachers College and Yamanaka Girls' School. The other is for Dai Ni Kenjo. An explanatory stone on the site features the following text:

> *The martyred students at rest here*[10] *endured much hardship while performing various defense-related labor tasks during the Pacific War.*[11] *But on August 6, 1945, while they toiled at munitions plants or on firebreak sites, their precious young lives were lost, like cherry blossoms in the wind, when the atomic bomb was dropped. We, who cannot but feel heartbreak when considering the purity and passion of their patriotism and the agony they must have suffered, have erected this Martyred Students Memorial on the spot where most of them met their end so that we may console their heroic spirits for eternity.*

Also noteworthy in this passage is the conspicuous absence of the postwar Hiroshima god term *heiwa* ("peace"). As has been previously discussed, its inclusion was and continues to be virtually de rigueur in

Hiroshima bomb memorialization. But its absence here—which in 1952 Hiroshima could only have been by design—is a not-so-subtle challenge to the approved "Hiroshima was sacrificed for peace" narrative that was already supposed to have occupied pride of place in local historical consciousness by this time.

The rhetoric of the Zakoba-chō stones suggests that while the Imperial Era belief system might have been on the outs in August 1945, it was well on its way toward a partial rehabilitation seven years later—at least among a certain demographic of war bereaved. Although it is possible that the wording, tone, and imagery used in the memorial might have been the brainchild of a single individual in the community of Zakoba-chō bereaved possessing sufficiently forceful influence and ardor—Hi'ura Yoshito, in this context, comes to mind as a possible candidate—it is difficult to imagine that such a blatant challenge to the approved Hiroshima narrative (and postwar Japanese pacifism as a whole) could have been erected without a decisive majority of the families signing off on it.

It is possible that the bereaved families (parents) simply missed the memo on the approved Hiroshima narrative, and they fell back on obsolete Imperial Era forms of hagiography in their memorial as a consequence of lifelong rhetorical habits; they had had ceremonial language like that drilled into their heads their whole lives, making it as natural and fitting for them as Bible verse for a Christian, and when it came to crafting ceremonial language on their own, they used what they already had at hand in their linguistic toolbox. Another possible explanation—and I believe the more likely—is that the families were more comfortable with the idea that their children had died heroically for their emperor and the eternal land of the ancestors than with the idea that they had been sacrificed for some emotionally neutered (not to mention defeat-imposed) abstraction like Peace.

In either case, the evidence is clear, literally carved in stone, that a substantial number of these bereaved family members still insisted on the continuing validity of the Imperial Era symbolic universe belief system—surrender broadcast, Treaty of San Francisco, postwar pacifism, and approved Hiroshima narrative be damned. As Tominaga

Chieko would discover during fieldwork research a quarter century later, many of the firebreak parents never progressed beyond this stage of half-defiant, half-desperate resistance to the approved Hiroshima narrative, with their grief-work process as a result truncated, stagnant, and unfinished for the remainder of their days.[12]

In sharp contrast to this mindset, there was not much love lost for the derailed Imperial Era belief system in the early-postwar period among younger Japanese of Sakamoto Setsuko and Tominaga Chieko's generation. This was true not only in Hiroshima and Nagasaki but across the country. With fewer years of their lives invested in that now ostensibly defeat-debunked ideology, and being too young to have lost children in the war (with all the symbolically and psychologically complicated grief / meaning-making work, as per the firebreak parents, that would have entailed), younger Japanese were comparatively free in the postwar period to turn their backs on wartime martial-valorizing values as vestiges of a bygone world that they now regarded not only as shameful and guilt tainted but, perhaps most damning of all, pathetic. In the future they envisioned for themselves and their country, the New Japan they had been promised during the long years of foreign occupation would belong to them and not to the older, war-complicit generations. And there would be no place in that future for flowery rhetoric glorifying war as a venue for ennobling and meaningful sacrifice.

Or so they thought.

———

Setsuko and Chieko were not close during their time at Dai Ni Kenjo. Chieko regarded her local counterpart as yet another of the provincial, uninquisitive, patriotic-jargon-regurgitating rustics she had come to loathe at Dai Ni Kenjo and in Hiroshima in general. In return, Setsuko no doubt regarded Chieko as a stuck-up, city-slicker softy with suspect loyalties and insufficient ardor for the war effort—an assessment apparently shared among most of their classmates.

There was little change in the temperature of their relationship when the girls returned to school in November 1945—along with the other five August 6 absentees from Hata-sensei's class—as new members of the sole remaining second-year homeroom. Although everyone by this time knew at least the rough outline of Setsuko's white-knuckled Little Boy survival story via word of mouth, Chieko and the other firebreak absentees never shared with their heroic classmate the reasons for their own lifesaving absences on that fateful day. In fact, during the remaining two and a half years that they would all spend together as classmates, the survivors never even discussed among themselves why each had been absent on August 6. No one outside the Tominaga family, for example, would know about Chieko's grape episode until some forty years later, with the 1985 publication of her best-selling memoir about her Hiroshima experiences.

In 1948, Dai Ni Kenjo and other prewar-era public girls' schools in Hiroshima were closed as part of a round of SCAP-directed nation-wide educational reforms. In Hiroshima, girls' school students of Chieko's age cohort—sixteen at the time—were given the option of ending their formal schooling then and there, with a junior high diploma, or being parceled out (pending successful entrance exams) to new coed public high schools in their local school districts. As Chieko and Setsuko both had plans for college, which was still a relative rarity for Japanese girls at the time, they chose the latter option, with Chieko attending Kokutaiji High School—which had been built over the ruins of the old Itchū campus in Zakoba-chō—and Setsuko attending Minami High School in Danbara.[13]

After parting ways for high school, the girls would see each other every August 6 at Zakoba-chō, with Setsuko always up front and center and Chieko always lurking in the back, out of the line of sight of the bereaved parents. The two eventually became closer in their twenties, but by this time, their lives were already on widely divergent trajectories.

HIBAKUSHA OMERTÀ

Postwar Hiroshima

AS WITH SO many other boys in Ōiwa Kōhei's age cohort, Japan's defeat slammed the door on his boyhood dreams of a military career, leaving in its wake a sense of lost identity that would only be papered over with pale postwar substitutes. But life went on, and while recovering from his radiation sickness from late 1945 to early 1946, he resumed his studies in November 1945 as one of only nineteen surviving boys from the Itchū class of 1951, which was now not even big enough to fill a single classroom.[1]

During the first year or so after the bombing, Kōhei was tormented by feelings of shame and unworthiness over his own survival. He experienced this with particular acuteness under the gaze of bereaved family members—especially of age peers from the neighborhood who had perished on, or as an eventual result of, August 6 firebreak duty. In some ways, this shame might even have been more traumatic for him than the bombing itself and its immediate aftermath. While he can recall the latter set of experiences in near-photographic detail nearly eighty years later, he has almost no memory whatsoever of the year or two of his life after returning to school—an environment in which he had to rub shoulders daily with August 6 Itchū campus survivors, whose numbers were gradually whittled away by bomb-related ailments over the long autumn and winter of 1945–1946. Moreover, almost all of his surviving classmates and every other person he encountered in his daily life outside his home had lost at least one immediate family member.

"Living in Hiroshima in those days," Ōiwa tells me in 2018, "it was incredibly difficult to tell other people that you had not lost anyone in your family."

One of the last episodes Ōiwa recalls before his memories of late 1945 to 1947 go blank was of a visit to the house of his best friend from childhood—a Danbara boy whose family never saw him again after he set out for firebreak duty on the morning of August 6. After a few months, the boy's mother had come to accept that her son was never coming home, and, accordingly, she had begun praying for (and *to*, as per Japanese custom) his soul every morning before the family *butsudan* altar. Coming into this information via the neighborhood gossip network, Mrs. Ōiwa told Kōhei that he should visit his late friend's house and light a memorial incense stick for him. Given that Kōhei was at this time still nearly paralyzed with shame—even to the point of avoiding going outside the house at all unless absolutely necessary—he was naturally loath to come literally face-to-face with his survivor guilt and August 6 trauma in the incarnation of his dead friend's mother. To make the expected ordeal more endurable, Kōhei asked his mother to accompany him. But Mrs. Ōiwa stood firm. Her son would have to do this on his own.

When the day for his unannounced visit came, Kōhei steeled up his nerves and set off for his friend's house. As soon as the bereaved mother opened her door to see Kōhei standing there, she grabbed him up into a long hug—a gesture of unusual physical intimacy in the Japan of that era—while her body was racked with sobs. Kōhei followed suit, in short order, with his own tears—a reaction he experienced as cathartic, at least for the moment. But he still had a long road of psychological and emotional recovery ahead of him. Three-quarters of a century later, that recovery is still a work in progress.

In early 1948, Kōhei secured admission to High School #6 in Okayama. These so-called "number high schools" were directly

administered by the national Ministry of Education and had been established during the Meiji Era as academies for the cultivation of future generations of elite civilian leadership. Winning a spot at one of
them virtually guaranteed a student later admission to one of the old
imperial national university campuses, with the University of Tokyo
being at the acme of this academic pyramid in terms of prestige and
future prospects. However, the national educational reforms of 1948
eliminated the number school system and, with it, what should have
been Kōhei's certain path to future membership in the country's elite.
Instead, he ended up at the new coed Minami High, built for his
school district, which encompassed Danbara, Minami Takeya-chō,
Senda, and other neighborhoods in east-central Hiroshima.

Despite these setbacks, Kōhei's father—still an executive at the
Hiroshima branch office of the National Railways—continued taking
a passionate interest in his son's academic career. When Kōhei matriculated at Minami High, Mr. Ōiwa became active in the school's
PTA. There he made the acquaintance of another member who soon
assumed a leadership role—a career Ministry of Agriculture and Forestry bureaucrat named Noguchi Ju'ichi, the proud and extremely
protective father of a bright-eyed, well-mannered daughter named
Kazuko.

The fathers were delighted when they found out that Kōhei and
Kazuko had entered into a relationship that was gradually developing
into something more substantial than friendship. The youngsters
were an excellent match in terms of temperamental compatibility and
upbringing. They were also both hibakusha—circumstances that would
entail challenges to come, of course, but that also came with one significant advantage: There would be no ugly inquiries from non-
hibakusha potential in-laws regarding the possibility of genetic damage
and other health concerns. The young bomb survivors could not
know what—if anything—their childhood exposure to Little Boy's radiation had already done to their chromosomes or was going to do to
their bodies in the future, but at least they knew they would be facing
that future together, and without having to worry about one set of
parents crowing, *I told you so*, if anything did eventually go wrong.

The couple married not long after Kōhei graduated from Okayama University and began his employment with the stock brokerage firm Nikkō Securities, Ltd. Although Kōhei's job took the family around to various postings in Japan, they eventually settled in the Tokyo-Yokohama metropolis, where they live today.

Kōhei—Ōiwa-san—did not start talking to people about his bomb experiences until middle age, and then only to close friends and colleagues at work, once he was a securely established "salaryman" on his way up the managerial ranks at his company. Part of the reason for his long reticence on the subject was the obvious factor of being averse to revisiting memories whose capacity for pain and horror had hardly diminished with the passage of time. A perhaps even more compelling reason for him was that in his eyes—and in a very Japanese way of looking at things—he had not suffered enough, compared with what most other atomic bomb survivors had endured. As such, he felt he was unqualified as a legitimate vessel of bomb memories and interpreter of the hibakusha experience. There was also a socially and professionally pragmatic reason for his silence: fear of hibakusha discrimination and/or ostracism, both for himself and Kazuko. The young couple had made a clean break from Hiroshima to move on with the rest of their lives. All things said and done, it made sense to keep mum about their Hiroshima past with anyone outside the family. And for long decades, this is exactly what they did.

But the Ōiwas were certainly not outliers in this respect. Even today, there are many hibakusha—perhaps even the majority of them—who not only do not want to talk about their experiences, but who go to great measures to hide this identity from others. Some have hidden it even from their own children, wanting to shield them not only from shame, but also from having to live with constant trepidation regarding congenitally transmitted chromosomal damage from radiation. Some have been so averse to revealing this aspect of their identity to others that they never even applied for the *hibakusha techō* (again, the "Atom Bomb Survivor's Card"—ID for qualification for a national government support program initiated in 1957), which would have given them monthly cash stipends and free medical coverage for bomb-related ailments, regardless of their individual financial situation, for the rest of their lives. And while this need for privacy may not now be quite as intensely felt as it was in their youth, when job or marriage prospects potentially hung in the balance, the perceived need to hide this identity that has channeled and overshadowed their lives for nearly eighty years is nevertheless still a daily reality for many.

For Ōiwa, the pressure to maintain his reticence about his hibakusha identity began to ease after his retirement from Nikkō. He had spent the entirety of his life up to that point as a diligent overachiever—first as a scholastically gifted and ambitious student, then as a hardworking corporate warrior during Japan's postwar-economic-boom decades. Now, bereft of this once identity-defining role and thus presented with days no longer crammed morning to night with company obligations, he may have temporarily found himself somewhat rudderless—a common postretirement predicament, of course, for former hard-charging executive types in any culture. Still, he was not ready to hang it all up and—as his culture expected of a man of his status and age—devote his remaining days to hobbies and puttering around the house. He still had his health, a decent amount of gas left in the stamina tank, and a working lifetime's worth of executive skills. He was ready to apply these personal qualifications to new challenges and toward making new contributions. He just had to find a worthy outlet.

Ōiwa had long known of the existence of the local branch of the Hidankyō (the Japan Confederation of A- and H-Bomb Sufferers Organizations) in his western Tokyo suburb. Over the years, he quietly introduced himself to a few individual members, though it was not until his retirement—and after prompting and encouragement from his small circle of hibakusha acquaintances—that he felt comfortable about "going public" with his own hibakusha status. Once he did and formally joined the group, though, Ōiwa's daily schedule quickly returned to a level of busyness that felt more natural for him. Soon, he was talking about his hibakusha experiences in peace education lectures at local schools and community halls—an activity Kazuko also started when she felt confident and comfortable enough to do so.

It was not long before Ōiwa's executive skills found an outlet at higher levels in the Hidankyō organization. In 2015, he became the president of Tōyūkai—the umbrella group for all of the Hidankyō branches in the Tokyo metropolitan area. In this capacity, his biggest public exposure to date was probably when he provided commentary for NHK's live coverage of President Obama's visit to Hiroshima Peace Park in May 2016.

Hiroshima and Nagasaki are rapidly fading from living memory, and this is a concern that is constantly on Ōiwa's mind. In 2019, with the death of classmate Kodama Mitsuo, he became the last survivor of what should have been the Itchū class of 1951. He will also likely be the last Tōyūkai president with authoritative and accessible narrative memories of surviving an atomic bombing. There are still more than four thousand hibakusha living in Tokyo, and there will be someone to take his place to head Tōyūkai.[2] But this next president will probably have only flashbulb memories—if they have any memories at all—of someone who experienced an atomic bombing as a small child or toddler. In this sense, the eventual end of Ōiwa's tenure will also entail the end of an era for the organization.

A WAR MEMORIAL IN A PEACE PARK

Postwar Hiroshima

AFTER THE WAR, Mitsubishi let go of its Ujina warehouse management subsidiary, Hiroshima Kai'un. This was the direct result of SCAP's policy of breaking up large corporate *zaibatsu* conglomerates deemed complicit in facilitating the Imperial Era war machine. This particular divestment also had the benefit, for the parent corporation, of putting a layer of legal and financial separation between itself and any postwar reckoning regarding recompense and/or restitution for the Korean and other colonial laborers who had toiled in its wartime Ujina operations.[1]

The postwar corporate-level shake-up also resulted in Tominaga Chieko's father losing his executive status with Mitsubishi, compelling him to stay on at Hiroshima Kai'un permanently. This was a bitter irony for Mrs. Tominaga, trapping her in a place that she loathed and that she would have had to tolerate for only another year or two had her husband still been an elite Mitsubishi man. But while the couple was now mired in the anticlimactic denouement of Mr. Tominaga's once glittering career, they nevertheless maintained both the will and the financial wherewithal to ensure that their daughters eventually escaped their provincial purgatory and made it safely back to civilization in the Tokyo–Osaka urban corridor.

Their older daughter, Machiyo, was the first to make good her getaway when she left Hiroshima to attend Hōsei University in Tokyo. In happier times, she would have been able to reside in the family's Tokyo pied-à-terre in Sugamo—and likely with a domestic servant or two—but all that was gone with the wind and up in smoke. Virtually no one outside the imperial household and the out-of-sight megarich had domestic servants anymore—the war had put paid to that aspect of genteel Japanese upper-middle-class culture, never to be seen again— and the Tominagas' Tokyo house had burned down in one of the Twentieth Air Force's mass incendiary raids on the capital.[2]

As a result, Machiyo was compelled to search for lodging near her campus—only to be turned away time and time again by prospective landlords as soon as they heard that she had come from Hiroshima. From the perspective of the average Japanese, the atomic bombings and the hibakusha were still subjects of mystery and trepidation at this point because of postwar media censorship (both occupation-imposed and voluntary/domestic) strictly limiting what could be publicly discussed about these topics. That Hiroshima and Nagasaki had both been destroyed by horrendously powerful American bombs employing some kind of new technology was known, as was the fact that the bombs had done horrific things to human bodies, but medical details were missing, and moreover, heartstring-tugging human-interest-type stories would have to wait until the end of the occupation to become canonical tropes of popular Japanese media content. In the meantime, the resultant Occupation Era vacuum of reliable bomb-related information constituted optimal conditions for ugly rumors and unfounded fears about the hibakusha to sprout up like mushrooms on wet logs—with the most pernicious and tenacious being that their bomb-related injuries, ailments, and even bodily scarring were pathogenic and contagious.

Although Machiyo was eventually able to secure a place to stay in Tokyo, her encounters with hibakusha discrimination continued. As most Japanese urban residences at the time did not have their own bathing facilities, most city dwellers had to use commercial bathhouses for their daily ablutions. However, the first time Machiyo went to her neighborhood bathhouse and revealed her scarred back (from the auditorium ceiling collapse on August 6) in the changing room, the bathhouse's proprietress barred her from returning on the grounds that her appearance would frighten/disgust the other customers.[3] Such treatment dogged the lives of hibakusha for long decades throughout the postwar period.

Upon Chieko's 1950 graduation from Kokutaiji High School, she joined Machiyo in the capital, matriculating at the department of French literature at prestigious Waseda University. Apparently, her own Hiroshima connection did not seem to affect her new life negatively in any significant way—perhaps because of her lack of bodily scarring, and also because Machiyo might have taught her the ropes on how to avoid the subject of Hiroshima with Tokyo interlocutors.

After Waseda, she went on to a career in journalism, starting off as a spunky cub reporter for the *Mainichi Shimbun*—one of Japan's major daily national newspapers—before settling into a journalistic niche in homemaking- and consumer-related issues that was less threatening to the egos of male colleagues. Over the next quarter of a century, balancing her writing career with marriage and motherhood, Seki (née Tominaga) Chieko continued to make annual pilgrimages most years to meet up with Sakamoto Setsuko at the August 6 Peace Park and Zakoba-chō ceremonies. But for the other 364 days of every year, she did everything she could to forget about Hiroshima.

Sakamoto Setsuko went on to lead a very different life. Bound to home ground by obligations and sentiment (including not a little survivor guilt), she never left Hiroshima, reliving the scene at the firebreak—in one way or another—on a continuous time loop for the rest of her life. This was true not only in the sense of her lifelong dedication to memorial activities, hibakusha rights activism, and peace education, but also in her choice of career.

After Minami High School, she followed in the footsteps of her childhood hero, Hata-sensei, matriculating at her old teacher's alma mater to major in Japanese. Following graduation, she was employed by the Hiroshima Board of Education as a junior high teacher.[4] Ironically, her last workplace was Kokutaiji Junior High, which was constructed adjacent to the high school of the same name a few years after the war. In 1970, Sakamoto died of stomach cancer, leaving behind a husband and two sons, three and eight years old.[5] Her death was likely caused by her exposure to radiation a quarter of a century earlier, mere meters from the Kokutaiji classrooms where she spent her last teaching years. She was thirty-seven.

Seki's more involved reengagement with her own Hiroshima past came in middle age, after her own children had grown up and she gradually began to sense that writing for housewives' weeklies was a younger woman's game. The direct impetus for the "Hiroshima turn" in her life and craft occurred in the mid-1970s, when she was approached by Machiyo with the idea of helping compile and annotate a photo album cataloguing the hundred-fifty-odd atomic-bomb-related memorials and public artworks in Hiroshima.[6] Eager for a change and the opportunity to take up a new project that was not related to child-rearing and smart shopping tips, Seki accepted the offer.

While investigating the origins of the Memorial Tower for Mobilized Students ("the Tower") in Peace Park, Seki encountered a story that made her realize, with something of a start, how estranged she had become from the pulse of the hibakusha community during her decades away from Hiroshima. Because she had been sequestered away in Tokyo all those years, the cultural space of her daily life had been inhabited almost exclusively by like-minded intellectuals who shared her scorn and resentment of what most saw as the "bad old days" of Japanese militarism, which had come so close to killing them all. Over time, Seki gradually assumed that the rest of Japan—with the exception of the occasional right-wing crackpot—had long since shared the broad strokes of that historical viewpoint. For her, the idea that there were still people—and in Hiroshima, no less—clinging to the Imperial Era belief system was something that, for her, seemed incomprehensible.

The Tower of Seki's interest is a sort of white-tiled pagoda-style stupa built in 1967 by the Hiroshima branch of the Association of Mobilized Student Labor War Victims ("the Association"). Its construction cost of some eighteen million yen (about seventy million in 2021 Japanese currency)[7] was primarily funded through donations collected from bereaved families in Association branches around the country.[8]

Located along a heavily trafficked park path leading to the world-famous Atomic ("Genbaku") Dome, the Tower's plaza takes up a sizable chunk of public real estate—a reflection of the powerful local patronage and political backing the project enjoyed in 1960s Hiroshima. Next to the Cenotaph, it receives the second-longest line of park visitors—both Japanese and foreign—waiting to offer incense, flowers, and prayers every August 6.[9]

Standing at the foot of the Tower—where the abovementioned offerings are made—is a bronze statue of Kan'non-sama, the Buddhist goddess of mercy. Arranged on either side of Kan'non-sama are stuccoed-wall sections on which are hung three bronze bas-reliefs depicting young people busily engaged in war-production work on machine shop floors, in sewing factories, and in farm fields. However, and as a perceptive visitor with a modicum of Hiroshima knowledge may notice—and find odd—there is no plaque depicting firebreak-clearing work. But most visitors, apparently, do not notice this.

Most Japanese are familiar with the story of the Hiroshima firebreak children, at least in broad strokes, before they ever visit Peace Park, and as has already been explained, the city abounds in individual monuments to their sacrifices. Therefore, if a typical Japanese visitor overlooks the explanation of the Tower's raison d'être inscribed on a fourth bronze panel—which is rather easy to do, especially in unfavorable light and/or with a line of other tourists waiting behind them—it would be extremely easy to walk away from a pilgrimage to the Tower with the mistaken assumption that it exists here in Peace Park because it is dedicated exclusively to the memory of Hiroshima's firebreak children. While this is not an unreasonable assumption to make, given its name and its prominence in the nation's most prestigious atomic bomb memorial space, it is not, in fact, the case, as is revealed in both the narrative content and wording choices ("peace," for example, is conspicuously absent) of the mission statement inscribed on the Tower's explanatory plaque:

> *During the Second World War, over three million students from*
> *around the country were mobilized as volunteer laborers to help*

boost production and other aspects of the war effort, sacrificing
years of their youth and scholarly careers to perform this service.
Among these students, over ten thousand lost their lives, including
over six thousand killed by the atomic bomb in Hiroshima. This
tower was built by sympathetic parties to comfort the souls/spirits
of these students, whose bright-eyed futures, ambitions, and
dreams were cut short when they became martyrs for the land of
our ancestors.

As the passage clearly suggests, the Tower was not constructed to convey the usual local Hiroshima pacifist narrative about pitiable, passive Little Boy victims sacrificed for world peace. Rather, the protagonists of the Tower's national scale narrative were martyrs whose deaths, while depicted as regrettable, are also depicted as the result of patriotic motives. The implication is that the "victims" commemorated on this particular Peace Park memorial were not really "victims" at all—they were heroes who exercised a degree of personal agency in meeting their fates. Accepting this message at face value, the implication is that the imperial state did not put these children in harm's way to suffer meaningless deaths so much as it provided them with a venue for meaningful sacrifice in the service of a grateful nation.

Although the Tower is located in Peace Park, it is not a peace memorial. It is a war memorial. The distinction is significant and, improbably, has historical roots in the earliest days of hibakusha rights activism.

If any one person could be said to be responsible for the eventual construction of the Mobilized Students Tower, it was a pioneering hibakusha rights activist named Nakamae Taeko. Similar to Sakamoto Setsuko, Nakamae had by the 1950s already published accounts of her experiences (albeit, unlike Sakamoto, using a pseudonym) and achieved a degree of local notoriety as one of the "miraculous" mobilized student laborer survivors of the atomic bomb—in her case, while working as an operator at the Hiroshima Telephone Exchange a mere six hundred meters from Ground Zero. Her injuries from this ordeal were grievous. In addition to nearly succumbing to a particularly

grueling case of ARS, she lost an eye in the explosion and suffered facial disfigurement that required numerous plastic surgery procedures
to repair.[10] Compounding her own and her family's grief, her younger
sister, Emiko—a first-year student at First Hiroshima Girls' School
(Kenjo)—died from injuries incurred while working on the 100-Meter
Firebreak (present-day Peace Boulevard).

With her dual Hiroshima identity as both wounded hibakusha
and bomb-bereaved family member, Nakamae had a foot firmly planted
in both of these "survivor" communities. These credentials, combined
with her natural communication skills and dogged determination,
ideally positioned her to do extraordinary things in Hiroshima memory activism, even at her still relatively tender age. She did not waste
that opportunity.

In Hiroshima in August 1955, Nakamae received major public exposure at the first World Conference Against Atomic and Hydrogen
Bombs, where she was handed the microphone to talk about her hibakusha experiences.[11] Her decision to "come out" as a hibakusha in this
manner was not only personally courageous, but also historically significant. Although there was already a burgeoning catalogue of widely
read Japanese atomic bomb literature at the time, including compila-
tions of testimonies by hibakusha (often using pseudonyms), it was
almost unheard of for a "common citizen" (that is, not a professional
intellectual or literary type) hibakusha to self-identify as such in a
public venue. At this stage in the postwar era, most hibakusha—as we
have seen with Ōiwa Kōhei's testimony—were still ashamed of that
identity, fearing lost employment or marriage opportunities, social
ostracism, and other forms of discrimination. And during the early
postwar era, these fears were well founded—not only as we have seen
with Tominaga Machiyo's experiences in late-1940s Tokyo, but even
in Hiroshima and Nagasaki.

After sharing her atomic-bombing experiences with the conference assemblage, and no doubt with the rapt attention of the room,
Nakamae went in for her big pitch. She talked about the plight of
bomb-invalided former Hiroshima firebreak children and other mobilized student laborers, and of the suffering of the bereaved families

of those who had been killed by the bomb. As Nakamae was wont to say, the student laborers who had been maimed or killed on August 6 had incurred these misfortunes while in the service of their country as "industrial warriors" putting life and limb on the line just like any other soldier in combat; by this logic, it was only reasonable that these former laborers and/or their bereaved families should receive compensation and/or reparations for their sacrifices—a subject the Japanese government had been avoiding up to this point primarily out of fiscal concerns.[12]

Nakamae's entreaty was timely in light of the recent resumption of government pensions and subsidies for invalided war veterans and military war-bereaved families. The military pension system had been abolished after the war as an undesirable vestige of Imperial Era militarism, but it was revived once Japanese conservatives returned to political power in Tokyo with the end of the occupation.[13] While the decision to resume military pensions had been welcomed by the millions of Japanese citizens who now benefited from them, the policy enjoyed far less than universal popular approval at the time, as it completely ignored the needs and suffering of the millions of civilian Japanese lives that had been ruined—or ended—by the war.

Nakamae's call for government compensation for civilian bomb victims was also a none-too-subtle swipe at the bilateral US-Japan accommodation that had been reached in the wake of the so-called *Lucky Dragon* Incident, when the crew of a Japanese long-range tuna boat had been exposed to radiation from an American H-bomb test in the Southwest Pacific the previous year. The incident—with its traumatic optics of American nuclear weapons once again victimizing Japanese bodies—caused a domestic political crisis of panic and indignation in Japan, a diplomatic row between the two countries, and a potential destabilization of American Cold War interests in a part of the world where superpower confrontation was consistently at its hottest.[14]

Popular Japanese indignation over the affair soon put domestic leadership in its sights when the news broke that, as a result of negotiations between the two governments, the Americans had agreed to pay a solatium of some two hundred thousand dollars (nearly two million in 2022 dollars) to each crewman of the irradiated tuna boat for emotional suffering (and not, as the Americans emphatically insisted, as more legally formal compensation). For the eighty million Japanese citizens who had been directly and traumatically impacted, in one way or another, by the war, the obvious and not unreasonable question that came to mind in light of this news was *So where is* my *reimbursement for emotional suffering?* It was a question neither Washington (for strategic reasons) nor Tokyo (for financial reasons) wanted asked.

This official anxiety was also something that could be leveraged to the benefit of the nascent ex–mobilized student laborer and hibakusha rights movements. To wit, if the Japanese government could make a highly visible, PR-friendly gesture of bestowing benefits only to special, very limited categories of war victims (i.e., mobilized students, hibakusha, former Manchuria colonists, among others)—and let it be known, in as face-saving a manner as possible, that this was all the additional war aid the still recovering nation could afford at the moment—the public at large might be convinced to shelve their own demands for reparations. This is precisely what ended up happening, with the temporary fix of this "good faith" moratorium—still regularly enforced in the twenty-first century by court rulings when necessary—now extending into its eighth decade.[15]

THE GADFLY

Hiroshima
Late 1950s

AFTER NAKAMAE'S SPECTACULAR debut in the public eye, things began to develop quickly for her chosen cause. Among the more significant of these developments was her making the acquaintance, in 1956, of a fellow invalided former student laborer, Hiroshima City Hall employee Matsumoto Kazuko.[1] In the summer of 1945, Matsumoto had been dispatched to a naval facility in Hikari, Yamaguchi Prefecture, where she lost a leg in one of the last air raids of the war.[2] By the mid-1950s, she had already set up a lobbying group in Yamaguchi Prefecture—roughly paralleling Nakamae's earliest efforts—that petitioned for government relief and pensions for invalided mobilized student laborers and bereaved families. Realizing their common cause, Nakamae and Matsumoto joined forces and proceeded to work tirelessly and rapidly to establish a Hiroshima branch of the Association of Mobilized Student Labor War Victims. The new lobbying group held its first meeting at Hiroshima Prefectural Auditorium in February 1957 with numerous local and national-level politicians and bureaucrats in attendance.[3]

The Association might have had some of its thunder stolen by the much larger and far more visible hibakusha rights movement, whose first major achievement was the passage of the Atomic Bomb Medical

Assistance Law in that year. But Nakamae and Matsumoto kept plugging away, working both PR and political/bureaucratic angles. They
scored their first triumph in 1958 when the Ministry of Health and
Welfare agreed to a temporary five-year pension allocation for student
labor war victims.[4] The Association's ultimate goal was then fulfilled
in 1967 when the mobilized student laborers were officially recognized by the ministry as having died or been invalided in military-
related wartime service to the nation, thus qualifying them and/or
their survivors for lifetime military pension benefits.[5]

When Seki first learned all of this—decades after the fact—she
was troubled by the implied symbolism of the state's institutional
"militarization" of her dead Dai Ni Kenjo classmates. To her, it was
almost as if the state were killing them a second time. Still, she could
not entirely fault their families for taking advantage of these government pension funds. Many of the families had already been leading
hardscrabble existences when their daughters were still alive. Thirty
years later, when Seki began interviewing them, many were still im-
poverished, having missed out on the rocket sled of miraculous economic growth that had lifted most of their countrymen up into a
comfortably consumerist, middle-class standard of living by the beginning of the 1960s. The bereaved Dai Ni Kenjo parents—now in old
age—had suffered grievous loss in 1945, and they had been suffering
ever since. As Seki saw it, they deserved some degree of restitution,
even if critics might point out that the bereaved families of the half-
million-odd civilians killed—or the many millions more rendered
homeless and financially destitute—by conventional American bombs
had never received formal restitution for their sacrifices.

Seki was incensed, however, when she discovered in the early
stages of her book research that the Ministry of Health and Welfare,
following standard operating practice at the time, had unilaterally
shared (without permission of the bereaved families) its new "military"
casualty lists of student laborers killed in the war with Yasukuni Shrine
in Tokyo. As a result, these students—including Seki's classmates—
were being officially venerated there as "nation-protecting deities,"
alongside the souls of the nation's uniformed war dead.[6] In 1969, as the

crowning gesture of this official apotheosis, the students enshrined in Yasukuni were also awarded, via their families, official certificates of commendation from Prime Minister Satō Eisaku and the Order of the Sacred Treasure, 8th Class,[7] a medal for service to the nation.[8]

Seki saw all of this political theater as a cynically sentimental ploy not only to win votes for the conservative Liberal Democratic Party then in power, but more ominously as part of a long-game strategy on the part of archconservatives in the upper echelons of the Japanese state to step over the bodies of her dead classmates and redeem the legacy of Japan's war in the national consciousness. Seki channeled her anger over this into generative energy for a new creative project: She would write a book about the circumstances of each one of her classmates' deaths and the present-day circumstances of their bereaved families. Readers could then judge for themselves whether the girls of Dai Ni Kenjo second-year West Homeroom were apotheosis-worthy war heroes nobly fallen for emperor and nation or, more aptly, pitiable victims of pigheaded policymakers who never should have let the war go on as long as they did.

When Seki began interviewing bereaved family members, she expected that her subjects would share her anger over what she saw as the blatant symbolic exploitation of their daughters in the Yasukuni enshrinement. What she found was quite the opposite: Almost all of her interviewees expressed enthusiastic pride and gratitude about the enshrinement and the official commendations, and they were in fundamental agreement that their daughters had died as the equivalent of soldiers, heroically contributing to Japan's war effort. Some of these parents might have assumed this posture as a countermeasure to the cognitive dissonance that they experienced because they were taking money for their daughters' deaths from the very same state that had sent the girls to those deaths. Perhaps some were still clinging to the old Imperial Era belief system as a way of imbuing those otherwise soul-crushingly horrific deaths with some transcendent, heroic meaning. Still others might have simply been afraid to raise an opinion that might earn them the enmity of the community of the Dai Ni Kenjo bereaved.

Seki's book is titled *Hiroshima Dai Ni Kenjo Ni-nen Nishi-gumi: Genbaku de Shinda Kyūyūtachi* (*Second Hiroshima Prefectural Girls' School, Second-Year West Class: My Classmates Who Died from the Atomic Bomb*). It is a heart-wrenching record of tragedy and trauma, on both collective and individual levels. It achieved great critical acclaim and quickly reached bestseller status, and was still in print thirty years later when I first encountered it at the beginning of my own hibakusha research.

The book, however, also saw its share of controversy—first of all, for what many readers saw as Seki's excessively frank and at times even irreverent expression and tone, considering the extreme sensitivity of her subject. Her portraits of her dead classmates and family members are generally respectful, but they do not follow the de rigueur Hiroshima narrative rules that call for hagiographies that confer sainthood on the bomb victims and the bomb bereaved. Rather, they are honest depictions of real people with human flaws. For example, Seki makes frequent note in the book of the ignorance and pettiness of many of the Hiroshima natives she encountered after moving to the city, and details the ostracism to which her classmates subjected her at school.

Seki also pulls no punches in taking aim at the usual low-hanging fruit that has become a standard target of ire in Hiroshima literature: the wartime Japanese state; people and institutions—like conservative Japanese politicians and Yasukuni Shrine—still clinging to the Imperial Era belief system and tirelessly and guilefully attempting to exonerate the war it made possible; and, of course, Little Boy itself and the decision to drop it. Seki breaks no new ground in raking these over critical coals. Where she does do so, however, is in the criticism that she levels at subjects that would normally be off-limits in Hiroshima literature: for example, in her drolly sarcastic descriptions of her Dai Ni Kenjo classmates' bereaved families' reverent gratitude for the Yasukuni enshrinement of their daughters. She also violates the ultimate taboo by criticizing the approved Hiroshima narrative itself, calling out what she sees as its excessive sentimentalism and exclusive focus on Japanese victimhood, which in the 1980s still ignored the thousands of Korean victims of the bombing. As Seki points out, the approved narrative in the last years of the Shōwa Era still conveniently glossed over the inconvenient historical context of Hiroshima's pre-bombing identity as a center of Japanese military activity and war production. In Seki's estimation, the best way to honor her dead class-mates was not with flowery hagiography—of either the Imperial Era or postwar narrative varieties—but rather through brutal honesty re-garding the causes and circumstances of their deaths.

This was not an opinion that was widely shared in Hiroshima in the 1980s. Needless to say, the book did not win Seki many friends in the Hiroshima memory community, nor among the hibakusha com-munity as a whole, many of whose members refused to talk to her anymore after its publication. But this newest round of ostracism did not deflect her from her new chosen path as a hard-bitten truth teller. She would follow it unwaveringly for the next thirty-five years.

Seki's last big moment in the public eye came in 2013 when she sued then prime minister Abe Shinzō, charging that his official prayer visit to Yasukuni Shrine the previous year was a violation of the religion-state separation clause of Article 20 of the Japanese Constitu-tion. The suit did not demand damages—just a court order to the ef-fect that the prime minister and other government officials had to refrain from further prayer visits to Yasukuni in an official capacity. Lower courts avoided ruling on this case until the Tokyo District Court finally ruled in favor of the defendant on April 28, 2017.

In an *Asahi Shimbun* article covering the verdict, Seki had some pointed comments to offer:

> *I could never have imagined that someday my classmates would be enshrined at Yasukuni Shrine as "little soldiers," and be worshipped there by the Prime Minister. It is truly regrettable that the court does not recognize that this practice is so clearly unconstitutional. . . . My blood runs cold to think that, if I hadn't been sick that day, I would have suffered an "honorable death" from the atomic bomb and would now be worshipped as a "heroic spirit." . . . I cannot allow the Prime Minister to be given special*

*treatment in being allowed to visit Yasukuni and pray to the war
dead as "heroic spirits"—a practice that is directly tied to prewar/
wartime militarism. I plan to continue fighting this.*[9]

During their lifelong journeys of post-bomb reckoning and recovery, every Hiroshima survivor—lest they succumb to crushing and
potentially life-ending nihilism—has had to find a way of making
meaning out of what they endured—and lost—in August 1945.

Ōiwa Kōhei and Noguchi Kazuko followed life path scripts that
were fairly standard for a young upper-middle-class married couple
during Japan's economic boom years, burying themselves in work and
homemaking before the downtime and breathing room of senescence
presented them with the opportunity, and perhaps the imperative, to
face their Hiroshima demons in a meaningful and visible way—in
their case, through hibakusha rights activism and public bomb experience testimony.

Sakamoto Setsuko dedicated her radiation-truncated post-bomb
life to testimony and education and, perhaps more than anything, to
picking up and pushing on with the life Hata-sensei—cheated out of
a longer and more fulfilling career of her own—left behind on the
front lawn of Red Cross Hospital on August 6.

Nakamae Taeko, staring into a personal early-postwar abyss,
overcame a broken body and mind by gaming both fiscal and sym-
bolic/ideological conservative agendas to achieve her own agenda of
easing suffering in Hiroshima. To accomplish this, of course, her public persona and the pitch of her messaging had to be fine-tuned so as
not to offend—if not to actually flatter—the sensitivities of powerful
1950s and 1960s politicians and bureaucrats who had themselves been
active and influential in the Imperial Era regime (and thus complicit
in war responsibility).

In February 2019, I had the wildly coincidental good fortune to
meet and speak one on one for about half an hour with Nakamae Taeko
as she was waiting to make a presentation at a symposium at the Hiroshima Peace Memorial Museum. At the time, I knew Nakamae's
name primarily from her well-nigh-canonical miraculous-survivor-

of-August-6 personal history, and I can remember being shocked as our conversation hit its stride and she began dropping old wartime propaganda terms like "heroic spirits" and "land of our ancestors"—it was the first time I had ever heard a hibakusha use this kind of language unironically or outside of a strictly historical context.

Later, at the symposium, I felt the audience (whom I judged by age and appearance to be seasoned Hiroshima memory community participants) stiffen up and even audibly gasp at several points when she used this same language in her presentation. But nobody raised any objections in the Q and A afterward. Perhaps Nakamae's hibakusha street cred is too hallowed to be challenged. To what extent her comparatively ancient régime–friendly rhetorical style is sincere and not merely pragmatic and calculated is something that will probably never be known. In any case, her tireless messaging and lobbying accomplished its original mission of securing government compensation for the war-victimized mobilized student laborer community. There is a highly visible memorial in Peace Park that stands as a physical testament to that success, and that will probably still be standing centuries after Seki's book has gone out of print.

Of the five hibakusha life paths we have examined in this section, the one Seki Chieko crafted for herself—as a gadfly speaker of inconvenient truths to the approved Hiroshima narrative—is by far the loneliest. During the intensive fieldwork phase of the research for my own book, I attended dozens of hibakusha memorial ceremonies, symposia, and other events. On these occasions, I almost always ran into Seki Chieko, and she would invariably be alone, wearing her hibakusha event game face—a mixture of inquisitive interest, pride, mild irritation, and defensiveness—and sitting in the back row of the venue with the press people, student volunteers, and other outsiders. I often wonder whose influence on the Hiroshima narrative will end up being more enduring—hers or Nakamae Taeko's. Spoken words disappear into the air the instant they are uttered. Newspaper interviews end up lining garbage cans or dissipate into the ever-expanding ether of the Internet. Book paper eventually turns to dust. But bronze and stone endure.

"ATOMS FOR PEACE"

Western Tokyo suburbs
Present day

AMONG THE DOZENS of hibakusha I have interviewed over the years, Ōiwa Kōhei impresses me as one of the most poised and dispassionate. When he is recounting his Hiroshima experiences, his facial expression is always neutral and composed, his words crisply enunciated, the tone and timbre of his voice deep, calm, and unwavering, even when he is describing details of shuddering horror and crushing sadness. This portfolio of communication skills—no doubt honed and polished over long decades in corporate management—is something I imagine has also served him well in his years of hibakusha activism, whether giving testimony at peace education lectures for schoolchildren, chairing occasionally boisterous Hidankyō meetings, or negotiating with stubborn Ministry of Health and Welfare bureaucrats for expanded government assistance for his fellow atomic bomb survivors. Even so, and in a trait he probably shares with most hibakusha, he is not immune to sudden attacks of bomb-related PTSD.

Anyone who has spent more than a year or two in Japan is no stranger to earthquakes. During my thirty-five years here, I have experienced dozens of temblors strong enough to get my heart racing and the flatware clinking in my cupboards for a few seconds, and a couple that have sent me diving under the dining room table, chest tight and hands shaking with bad adrenaline. Living in an environment this seismically active entails living with the fact that eventually—in the next few decades... next year... next month... tonight—the Big One is going to hit. Even if you are lucky enough to survive it, your home probably will not, and you will be living on a school gymnasium floor for a few weeks or months until you figure out your next move. As such, it is prudent, from time to time, to review your preparedness for such a contingency. You go over neighborhood evacuation routes in your mind. You try to keep your bugout bag up-to-date and a stock of drinking water on hand. The rest of the time, for your sanity's sake, you try not to dwell on it too much.

For Ōiwa-san, who has lived in Japan more than twice as long as I have, the number of perceptible earthquakes he has experienced would probably be up into triple digits. But the Tohoku Earthquake that rocked northern and central Japan on March 11, 2011, was something else entirely, even for him.

The shaking began at 1446 and lasted for some six minutes. Even in Tokyo, some three hundred kilometers from the epicenter, it was difficult for people to stay on their feet without grabbing onto something for support. High-rise office buildings and condos swayed like palm trees in a hurricane. There were injuries and a few fatalities from falling building materials. The subway- and train-based transportation network was thrown into chaos for days afterward.

This lengthy and powerful temblor was stressful enough, but it was not until Ōiwa began seeing the devastation closer to the epicenter on the TV news that he felt true fear. This triggered a days-long rolling anxiety attack that was one of the worst episodes of bomb-related PTSD he had suffered in decades.[1] Long-suppressed old feelings of dread, vulnerability, and helplessness began to well up in him as live-news helicopter shots from the Tohoku coastal region showed the earthquake's tsunami—a speeding sheet of water stretching to the horizon, black with topsoil—swallowing up towns, cars, fields, and tens of thousands of people.

As the evening wore on, the news began devoting more airtime to the fires—another Hiroshima memory trigger—that were sprouting up in devastated areas. That night, the long incendiary arm of the quake even reached as far as an oil refinery on the eastern shore of Tokyo Bay, with live video feeds from the site showing gantries toppling and gas tanks going up like something from a Godzilla movie.

In ensuing days, after the waters had receded and the fires had gone out, ground-based news camera crews were able to venture into the hardest-hit areas—coastal sites like Kesennuma, Rikuzentakata, and Ishinomaki. Ōiwa physically shook while watching footage of these sites. The lush green mountain-ringed seaside towns and fishing harbors wiped out by the March 2011 tsunami had once been bustling communities full of hardworking adults and happy children. Now they were gray wastelands with barely one cinder block left on top of another. These tsunami-scoured zones of total destruction reminded Ōiwa of the rubble field that had been central Hiroshima for over a year after the bombing, during which time he could stand in front of the main station and see all the way to Koi—a view that should have been blocked by nearly 4.5 kilometers of buildings, houses, and trees, but they had been blasted and burned as flat as a drumhead in the wake of Little Boy's fury and fire.

When Ōiwa returned to his Tōyūkai activities in later weeks, he heard that many other hibakusha had had the same response to the news that he'd had. Triggered by the visuals of the destroyed Tohoku towns, they had been shaken to the core by visceral memories of Hiroshima and Nagasaki. But for Ōiwa and probably most hibakusha still alive in 2011, the most insidious and unsettling consequence of the Tohoku disaster was the return of radiation anxiety to their daily lives—something most had not experienced since the nationwide panic in the wake of the *Lucky Dragon* Incident in 1954, when tons of irradiated fish entered Japan's food supply. Most had assumed that they would never again have to deal with fears like those that had terrorized them in their youth. But those old monsters were back. And this time, what had spawned them was not American-designed bombs, but American-designed nuclear reactors.

The boiling-water reactors installed at Tokyo Electric Power Company's Fukushima Dai'ichi Nuclear Power Plant in the late 1960s were designed by the GE Corporation.[2] Like most commercial reactors (and the original Hanford, Washington, reactors that had produced plutonium for the bomb that destroyed Nagasaki), these had been designed to employ water from natural sources to cool their cores and prevent nuclear meltdowns. In most places where such reactors operate, the water for this use is supplied by nearby rivers. In the case of Fukushima, however, the reactors were placed directly on the coastline to use ocean water for their core cooling systems.

Although GE designers had built a degree of earthquake resistance into the reactors, they never anticipated them being swamped by tidal waves. But on March 11, 2011, this is exactly what happened when the ten-meter-high tsunami generated by the Tohoku Earthquake inundated the Fukushima facility, causing three of its reactors to fail. With their coolant systems rendered inoperable by the seawater damage, the now unregulated slow-critical reactions of uranium fuel in these reactors soon reached temperatures high enough to melt through their steel-and-concrete core containers. The resulting radiation leak necessitated the evacuation of hundreds of thousands of regional residents from their homes. Ten years on, many of these radiation refugees are still living in temporary housing camps. Cleanup work at the Fukushima facility itself is expected to last well into the second half of the twenty-first century, if not longer.[3]

The first domino in the causational chain that eventually resulted in GE-designed reactors spewing radiation across the Tohoku region was tipped over nearly sixty years before the disaster. In December 1953, then US president Dwight David Eisenhower delivered what has come to be known as his "Atoms for Peace" speech in New York City, before some thirty-five hundred delegates of the UN General Assembly. In the speech—considered "one of the most significant . . . of the postwar era, a statement in the 'grand design' tradition of the Marshall Plan"—Eisenhower sought to rehabilitate the image of nuclear technology in the eyes of the world.[4] Downplaying its association with destruction and touting its purportedly peaceful uses, he pledged that the United States would dedicate "its entire heart and mind to find the way by which the miraculous inventiveness of man shall not be dedicated to his death, but consecrated to his life."[5] Toward these ends, he pledged to share American nuclear know-how with the world as a new source of clean and nearly limitless energy, and called for the formation of a new UN agency to regulate the global community of peaceful atom users he envisioned. Carried live by the globe-spanning Voice of America propaganda radio network, Eisenhower's declaration was a triumph of American soft power. It would also turn out to be a boon for America's nuclear industry.[6]

Despite its traumatic national experience at the hands of American nuclear power less than a decade earlier, certain parties in the Japanese political elite showed an early interest in hopping aboard the "Atoms for Peace" bandwagon. There were several reasons for this. The first was cultural/ideological. In the early 1950s, before the US-Soviet space race temporarily seized the world's imagination, atomic/nuclear energy symbolized the cutting edge of science and technology. It was the very face of "modernization."

Ever since the blunt-force-trauma culture shock of its engagement with the outside world in the mid-nineteenth century, after two and a half centuries of self-imposed isolation, Japan has assumed a headlong rush toward economic and technological modernization, almost at any cost, in its eagerness to match and even surpass the power and accomplishments of its regional (China) and civilizational (the West) rivals. This sort of "Damn the cultural disruption and social upheaval, full speed ahead" fervor for modernization has functioned almost as a second civic religion, paralleling and complementing whatever ideological framework has been dominant in the country at the time.[7] This was true during the wholesale adoption of Western ways in the Meiji and Taishō Eras, as well as during the disastrous experiment with ultranationalist militarism in the early Shōwa Era. It continues to fuel individual motivations and collective/national agendas even today, albeit in considerably less passionately competitive form than in eras past.

This historical context is critical for understanding the official narratives of national experience that were politically possible in early-postwar Japan, which was still rebuilding from the ashes of its collapsed Imperial Era ideology. The god-term status of "modernization" in the Japanese worldview even proved useful for certain early-postwar Hiroshima and Nagasaki narratives, with the bombs and the technology behind them, as we have previously considered, being framed as a kind of Promethean gift of fire for twentieth-century humanity. Although the official "atom-bombed cities were sacrificed for the peace and prosperity we now enjoy" narrative pushed by both local and national Japanese authorities from the early postwar on (with SCAP approval) can appear outrageous to a twenty-first-century reader, it was not something that had been simply spun out of thin air and foisted upon the Japanese public as a cynical political and diplomatic expedient. The groundwork had long since been laid in the psyches of that public to accept the idea that modernization was next to godliness, and therefore a noble and even sacred national goal occasionally requiring weighty sacrifice. As the Japanese public was already primed to accept such narratives, this gave a running start to PR initiatives to convince the Japanese people of the early 1950s that it was imperative that "modernization" now involved—and required—a national embrace of nuclear energy.

Another reason for enthusiasm regarding "Atoms for Peace" was more pragmatic. Japan's experience of the Allied naval and air blockades from 1943 to 1945 had emphatically demonstrated that the nation's reliance for its energy needs on imported fossil fuels, transported by a vulnerable oceangoing tanker fleet, was a critical national Achilles' heel. And in the early 1950s, simmering contemporary East Asian Cold War tensions only emphasized this point. Nuclear power, in contrast, held forth the promise of eliminating such concerns at a stroke; if this technology were to be adopted, and a suitably sizable stockpile of enriched uranium fuel were to be secured in peacetime, it would provide the nation with a nearly inexhaustible energy source. Moreover, the threat posed to national security by vulnerable shipping lanes would be minimized, if not eliminated altogether, if and when full-scale war returned to the region.

A secure, domestic source of plutonium—a waste product of nuclear power generators—would be an additional potential strategic "benefit" for Japan in this scenario. The technological back door this left open for the eventual domestic production of nuclear weapons was a topic that was avoided by politicians and scientists within earshot of the Japanese public, who had an understandably severe aversion to the thought of their country ever having anything to do again with nuclear weapons. But the prospect of Japanese nukes was experienced rather differently in the backrooms of national political power.

The push for a resurrected Japanese nuclear research program (the first incarnation, centered on Tokyo Imperial University—the modern-day University of Tokyo—had been interrupted by both Curtis LeMay and the occupation) and eventual commitment to nuclear power generation was initially set in motion in March 1954 when an energetic young conservative politician, former Imperial Japanese Navy officer, and future prime minister, Nakasone Yasuhiro, submitted a bill to the Diet toward these ends.[8] The bill passed a month later—incredibly, a month after the *Lucky Dragon* Incident—and as a result of the new law, the Japanese Atomic Energy Commission was established on January 1, 1956. One of its inaugural commissioners was Yukawa Hideki, the Nobel laureate in physics who had helped to discover the strong nuclear force.[9]

As part of President Eisenhower's global "Atoms for Peace" campaign, American policy and money were also behind Japan's move toward atomic power generation. In short, American geostrategic aims would be served if Japan could be kept close to hand and comfortably nestled within the West's Cold War camp as a reliable client for US reactor technology and uranium supplies. But before all of this could happen, the Japanese public—whose collective "nuclear allergy" had returned with a vengeance in the wake of *Lucky Dragon*—would need a bit more convincing. A nationwide PR blitz for "Atoms for Peace" was forthcoming—with both Japanese political and US State Department backing—and the solemn, symbolic weight of atom-bombed Hiroshima itself would be flipped and utilized as one of the most symbolically significant early vectors of this effort.

As we have noted above, the Japanese public by this point had already been primed, to an extent, to make a mental association between "prosperity" and "modernity" and, as a 1950s corollary of that, between "modernity" and "nuclear technology." Therefore, it was not as much of a leap of logic as a twenty-first-century reader might expect for someone in 1950s Hiroshima to be open to the idea of prosperity—a very sought-after commodity in a recently ruined city—being borne on the semi-magical wings of a barely understood and awesomely powerful new technology. As historian Ran Zwigenberg has noted, "For many [in still rebuilding Hiroshima], peace was equated with capitalist prosperity, which meant the building of a modern city." He goes on:

> Urging Hiroshima to look forward and not backward . . .
> promoters [of the "Atoms for Peace" message] sought to silence or
> co-opt opposition and push for an optimistic interpretation of
> Hiroshima's postwar history. Amazingly, atomic energy stood at
> the center of this effort to rationalize and convert Hiroshima into
> a modern, consumerist and capitalist city. . . . That Hiroshima
> could be presented as a center for atomic energy was the result of
> the commitment to modernity shared by all political sides in
> Japan.[10]

The most notable manifestation of these early Hiroshima-centered PR efforts was the opening of an exhibit—appropriately titled "Atoms for Peace"—at the Peace Park museum in 1956. Cosponsored by Hiroshima Prefecture; Hiroshima City Hall; Hiroshima University; the local daily newspaper, *Chūgoku Shimbun*; and the local American cultural center, the exhibition met with some initial local pushback, the most significant coming from the recently opened museum itself.[11] When first approached with the proposal for the exhibit, founding curator Nagaoka Shōgo replied, "This is a place to show the history of Hiroshima's suffering . . . [not] to sing the praises of . . . nuclear power."[12] But one middle-aged and otherwise mild-mannered academic was no match for the governmental forces arrayed against him (which included probably decisive pressure from city hall, which paid his salary and funded his museum). Succumbing to the same,

Nagaoka was compelled to vacate a substantial portion of the muse-um's permanent displays of atomic-bombing artifacts—many hand-collected by Nagaoka himself shortly after the war—to make way for the new joint US-Japan exhibit.[13]

"Atoms for Peace" ended up being a huge visitor draw for the mu-seum. The displays in the show included models of reactors, nuclear-powered trains and planes, and a full-sized mock-up of the type of "Magic Hand" apparatus used by nuclear workers to manipulate lumps of plutonium behind protective glass.[14] All things considered, the exhibit was a smashing success.

———

After nearly twenty years of surveying war (and peace) monuments in Japan and Europe, I have come to believe that very little in or about the layout or design of memorial space is accidental. For it to be otherwise would entail the risk of visitors coming away with mistaken interpre-tations of the narrative being mediated (at great expense) by the sculpted bronze, carved stone, and carefully plotted layouts at hand.

Taking this truism at face value, it is difficult for me to believe that it was a matter of sheer coincidence when the Ichijo Memorial—with its iconic schoolgirls-meet–$E = MC^2$ motif—was moved from its original location on the Ichijo schoolgrounds to a new location on Peace Boulevard on August 6, 1957, only a year after the opening of "Atoms for Peace" in the Hiroshima Peace Memorial Museum directly across the street. I have never been able to determine whether the source of the original proposal was internal—that is, from the school community (inclusive of its bereaved family association) itself—or im-posed by an external agency. In either case, the memorial has occupied a sizable plot of prime public real estate on Peace Boulevard ever since.

In conjunction with the memorial's movement to its present loca-tion, someone involved in the process determined it prudent to add a smaller, supplementary "explanatory" stone to the installation, set off to one side. On the front (i.e., facing the pedestrian and vehicular traf-fic on Peace Boulevard) surface of the new stone, the words "atomic bomb" (*genbaku*) and "soul consoling" (*irei*) are at last up front and center, unselfconsciously and in full public view. But it is on its rear surface where the stone's messaging performs what is clearly its intended main function—including an unusual meta explanation for the memorial's movement from its original site. As such, it is particularly interesting as an artifact of Hiroshima discursive history. It reads:

> This memorial was erected on August 6, 1948, on our school grounds, by the Association of Bereaved Families in honor of the 679 teachers and students of Hiroshima Municipal Girls' School who met with their ends as a result of their encounter with the atomic bomb while engaged in firebreak-clearing near this spot as volunteer laborers in service of our country. In 1957, on the occasion of the thirteenth anniversary of their deaths, the memorial was moved to its present spot.[15]
>
> The sculpted relief on the front of the memorial is the work of Kōchiyama Kensuke, and it depicts our precious students who came to our nation's aid in its hour of peril being comforted by the message "You were the world's first victims of atomic power ($E = MC^2$), and your noble sacrifice has contributed to the cultural advancement of humanity."

While the explicit mention in this text of the atomic bomb as the agent of the tragedy being commemorated here is not particularly noteworthy in a post-occupation Hiroshima memorial, it is interesting to note how the author(s) still seem to take Cold War diplomatic sensitivities into careful consideration. This is particularly evidenced by the girls' deaths being explained "as a result of their encounter" with the bomb instead of more directly attributing those deaths to Americans killing them. The occupation might have been over by this point, but even a bereaved-parents association had to respect the reality of Japan's new semicolonial dependency on America—including protection under the "nuclear umbrella" of American H-bombs for its defense in an East Asian region that was a simmering hot spot in the

US–Soviet confrontation then dividing the globe. And even if such matters were not of any particular concern to the bereaved Ichijo parents, they most certainly would have been for the city hall officials who would have to sign off on (or who requested in the first place) relocating the memorial to such a prominent spot on Peace Boulevard.

The appearance of multiple references, in the supplementary stone's text, to the Ichijo girls having died while performing war-related public duties also speaks to a newly emerging vector in Hiroshima's political mood in 1957—nascent stirrings of which we observed in the early-post-occupation conservative-rhetorical toe dips of the 1952 Zakoba-chō memorial, and in the Mobilized Students Memorial Tower, which went up in 1967 in Peace Park. It should be noted here that the year of the Ichijo Memorial relocation was also the year in which Nakamae Taeko and Matsumoto Kazuko formed the Hiroshima branch of the Association of Mobilized Student Labor War Victims—newly recruited members of which would have undoubtedly been counted among the five-hundred-plus bereaved Ichijo families.

Finally, there is the matter of the line "You were the world's first victims of atomic power ($E = MC^2$), and your noble sacrifice has contributed to the cultural advancement of humanity." The sentiment contained in the first half of this line is reasonable (with the pulled rhetorical punch of substituting the more neutral "power" for the more explicitly violent and potentially resentment-stoking "bomb"). However, the part about the girls' deaths having been a "noble sacrifice" for peace and progress—serving as harbingers for the introduction of nuclear energy toward the betterment of humankind—rings tragically hollow after Chernobyl and Fukushima. Still, people writing memorial rhetoric in the 1950s cannot be faulted for having been unable to see into the future; the overall tone of desperate optimism is of a piece with the sacrificed-for-peace story long since firmly established, by that point, as the official narrative of Hiroshima's bomb experience.

From 2016 to 2019, I attended each of the official memorial ceremonies held at Peace Park every August 6; they were scheduled to coincide with the 0815 hour when Little Boy exploded over the city in

1945. After these events, 1 always stopped to observe a smaller ceremony that takes place every year in front of the nearby Ichijo Memorial. The gathering was convened under tents that shielded participants
from either rain or shine, as the case might have been, and that were
emblazoned with the name of the event's sponsors, Funairi High
School. This is the coed school that, upon its establishment in 1948,
took in Ichijo's surviving students, and that is now—and presumably
in perpetuity—the custodian of the memory of its dead.

The event was always well attended—typically by a few hundred
people sitting on folded metal chairs. As per the normal protocol for
such Hiroshima (and Nagasaki) affairs, participants with living memories of 1945 were given pride of place, seated in the first few rows
closest to the rostrum. Providing background music—a mixture of
contemporary easy listening, school anthems, and instrumental arrangements of nostalgic (for the old folks) popular period songs—was
Funairi's competent brass band. These performances were interspersed
with the expected speeches by superannuated Ichijo alumni, bereaved
family members (only siblings are left now), and, of course, local politicians. Unlike the bigger municipal ceremonial venue, where 1 never
got as much as a side glance from my Japanese fellow participants, 1
got occasional stabbing "Avast, interloper" glares at the Ichijo ceremonies. Recognizing the perception of my presence as an intrusion, 1 always stood near the rear, where there were large cardboard-backed
displays of Ichijo-related photos facing the Peace Boulevard sidewalk.
For these displays, an attempt was made to find copies of photos of
each of the girls who died on or as a result of August 6, 1945. Almost
all of the photos appeared to have been taken after the girls had become Ichijo students. But one photo stood out in this respect. It was
of a pretty, full-cheeked little girl dressed up in traditional finery for
her seventh-birthday *shichigosan* ceremony—a coming-of-age recognition celebrated with Shintō rites (surviving early childhood having
been an accomplishment bordering on the miraculous in Japanese
days of yore). The girl in the photo was Yoshimura Mieko—the daughter of the Akatsuki Command general who found her body in a burn
pile probably only meters from where the Ichijo Memorial stands

today. As I looked at the photo, it struck me that this might have been the only photograph of his daughter that Lieutenant General Yoshimura had left after the war.

In the annals of Hiroshima memory, there are anecdotes of bereaved parents—fathers, in particular—so overcome by grief over the horrific and sudden loss of their children that they destroyed every physical vestige of the child's existence in their possession: photos, report cards, clothes, drawings—everything. In her Dai Ni Kenjo book, Seki Chieko wrote of one such harrowing account with the bereaved father of one of her classmates still forbidding her name to be uttered in his presence more than thirty years after her death. As someone who has witnessed firsthand what the sudden death of a child can do to a parent, I find such accounts particularly harrowing, but I can also understand—viscerally—how they can happen.

When Seki Chieko was still mobile enough to do volunteer work and show school groups of junior high school students around Hiroshima every August, she would always stop her charges in front of the Ichijo Memorial and ask the children if they knew where they were standing. A few hands would inevitably go up, followed by an answer of "Peace Boulevard." This response would perfectly set up Seki's stock takeaway lesson for the moment.

"On August 6, 1945," she would say, "six thousand children your age were killed right here. Bits and pieces of them are still here, under your feet. People may call this 'Peace Boulevard' now, but what you are actually standing on top of is the world's biggest graveyard."

PART FOUR

THE SURVIVOR

THE BRIGHT LIFE

Higashi Yamato City
Greater Tokyo
Present day

IT IS A sunny Saint Patrick's Day, and I am on my way to interview Hiroshima hibakusha Yamaguchi Sayoko. To reach her house, I am riding the Chūō Line out to Tachikawa, on the northwestern edge of the Kanto Plain, which is the widest expanse of flat land in the Japanese archipelago and home to some thirty-seven million residents of the Greater Tokyo metropolitan area.[1] To get some idea of the general layout and feel of the place—at least outside its shiny skyscraper center—imagine putting the entire population of Canada up in mostly low-rise housing on a patch of land marginally larger than Connecticut, then squeezing them in cheek by jowl between sprawling factories, farms, military bases, shopping malls, public hospital complexes, parks, and hundreds of school and college campuses.

The total combined land area of the Japanese Home Islands of Honshu, Kyushu, Shikoku, and Hokkaido is smaller than the American state of Montana. Over three-quarters of that area is occupied by densely wooded peaks and ridges that are too steep and landslide-prone for large-scale settlement or agriculture, and that could, in a production pinch, be used as shooting locations for a Japanese remake of *Grizzly Adams*. As a result of this topographical fate, almost the entirety of Japan's population (some seventy-five million people during World War Two, and one hundred twenty million now), the farms to feed it, and the institutions to keep it literate, orderly, productive, protected, and entertained are squeezed into what's left: a total area about the size of Indiana.[2]

For the past millenium or so, most of the population of the archipelago has been concentrated along a narrow Pacific coastal corridor stretching from Tokyo in the east to Fukuoka in the west. The oldest significant urban centers along this strip of land tend to be clustered around the mouths of rivers flowing down from catchment areas and headwaters in the country's mountainous interior to empty into the Pacific Ocean. This pattern of settlement did not evolve so much because these waterways served as transportation conduits to and from that interior—as in the case of most river-based civilizations—but rather, because they tended to create large, pool-table-flat alluvial plains perfectly terraformed for rice paddy agriculture and living space for the people producing and consuming that rice.

This classic template of Japanese land use has undergone significant variation only from the late nineteenth century on as rapid industrialization has introduced revolutionary transportation advances into the environment. The first of these was the advent of a national railroad system, followed in the mid-twentieth century by highway construction and mass automobile ownership. These quantum leaps in infrastructure squeezed new possibilities for urban (and suburban) development out of the Japanese landscape, mostly in valleys and inland plains deep in the interior, off the beaten coastal corridor path, that had been bypassed in earlier eras as barely habitable boondocks.[3]

Tokyo has been transforming boondocks into commuter suburbs, of a sort, since the first railroad connecting the city with neighboring Yokohama was laid in the late nineteenth century. But the metropolitan area's exurban sprawl began assuming its present gargantuan scale only when commuter train lines started pushing out into the deep Kanto hinterlands from the early twentieth century—a process interrupted by military buildup and war before resuming anew from the mid-1950s, accelerating apace with Japan's miraculous postwar economic recovery. During this latter burst of growth, suburbs sprang up on top of reclaimed agricultural land and the brownfield of bombed-out wartime factories.

Collectively, these train-commuter bedroom towns were the dazzling "city upon a hill" of a New Japan, which had beaten its swords of imperialist expansion into plowshares of export-driven economic growth. In the process, tens of millions of Japanese were pulled up and out of grinding poverty and into a nascent mass-consumerist middle class of white-collar workers and decently paid factory workers enjoying what contemporary pundits referred to as the *akarui seikatsu*—"the bright life."[4] For these diligent and committed stakeholders in the grand postwar social project, having two kids, a car, and a cozy little vinyl-sided chipboard place in a Kanto-megalopolis bedroom town was the very manifestation of the New Japanese Dream.

Younger World War Two veterans and older baby boomers formed the demographic backbone of this new middle class of postwar strivers, and their materialistic values, priorities, aspirations, and consumer tastes shaped Japanese popular culture and mores throughout the second half of the twentieth century. Signing up for thirty-five years of mortgage payments and forty years of multihour daily commutes on packed trains to get their families out of the noise, crowds, and air-polluted crush of the inner city, these new homeowners believed that they were giving their children better lives without the war and privation they had known during their own childhoods and adolescence. By most measures they would have been right—certainly in terms of diet, sanitary conditions, and access to a public education system that was no longer dedicated to transforming their children into emperor-worshipping suicide soldiers.

But for subsequent generations of middle- and upper-middle-class Japanese—the pampered and more cosmopolitan offspring of those selfless mid-twentieth-century suburban sodbusters—"the bright life" seems to have lost much of its sheen. The Generation X kids who grew up in Tokyo bedroom towns in the 1980s and 1990s are now members of the Tokyo-centric corporate, professional, and cultural elite, and they have largely rejected their fathers' vision of what

constitutes "the good life." They eschew enduring hours a day schlep-
ping to and from work on packed trains and never getting to know
their children. After migrating to the big city for college, these second-
generation suburbanites voted with their feet. Opting for typically
tiny and exorbitantly expensive central Tokyo apartments, they have
left their now superannuated parents to live alone in the old home-
steads, on suburban side streets and cul-de-sacs that once shimmered
with the frisson of social mobility on steroids and echoed with children's laughter and piano lessons, but are now as quiet as tombs.

Higashi Yamato City, where Yamaguchi lives, is part of the conge-
ries of such bedroom towns forming a roughly forty-kilometer-deep
belt of exurban sprawl pressing in on the three sides of central Tokyo
that are not fronted by the western shore of Tokyo Bay. To get there,
I change trains at Tachikawa Station, where I board a nearly de-
serted midmorning monorail—all Bubble Era retro-futuristic shiny
aluminum—that clears the dimly lit brutalist cocoon of its terminal
with a transition to bright daylight that is swift and sudden. Blinking
through the glare, I watch as we pass a massive IKEA mall on the former site of what was once the IJA's Tachikawa Air Base. After this, the
landscape stream quickly emulsifies into more recognizably Japanese
scenery and infrastructure—tight clusters of houses and low- to mid-
rise apartment blocks randomly interspersed with industrial plants,
convenience stores, car dealerships, more big-box stores, and fleeting
glimpses of Old Japan in the occasional rice paddy and tree-ringed
Shintō shrine. This panorama of muted earth tones, asphalt gray, and
abrupt splashes of primary-colored store signage stretches away to
blurry, brownish, smog-smudged horizons in all directions, the vast
flatness of this Kanto landscape—again, a topographical anomaly in
this country—relieved only by the random vertical accents of (mostly)
dormant smokestacks, multistory concrete school buildings, and
strings of power-line utility towers.

Even though Google Maps reminds me I am still in Tokyo, the
scenery clickety-clacking past the monorail windows bears no resemblance whatsoever to the imagery of the metropolis we usually see in
the media, with its dark-suited corporate warriors and androgynous

blue-haired cosplayers frolicking amid twenty-story-high LED billboards and glittering skyscrapers invariably shown in exotic counter-
point to narrow, red-lantern-festooned wooden alleyways and Buddhist
temples. All of these places do, of course, actually exist, but most nominal Tokyoites do not live in them (or, for that matter, have blue hair). It
is rare to meet someone from "Tokyo" who does not endure a daily
commute of at least thirty or forty minutes between the bland burbs
where they actually live and the eminently more Instagram-worthy,
Blade Runner–meets–*Shōgun* central downtown area where they work
or study. When someone tells you they "live in Tokyo," it usually means
someplace that looks like Tachikawa, and Tachikawa looks more or
less like any other flat area in the Japanese archipelago.

A recorded announcement interrupts my midmorning monorail
pensées and tells me we have reached my stop. Toting my customary
Interview Day travel kit of a notebook, maps, recording equipment,
and an overpackaged box of souvenir confectionary, I wend my way
through silent, winding, sidewalk-less side streets, relying on my
iPhone for navigation. The houses close behind the cinder block walls
and high hedges that hem in the narrow roadways are looking a bit
creaky and soot streaked, and I place them at about forty or maybe
even fifty years old, meaning they have outlived by a factor of at least
two the planned obsolescence built into them by their real estate de-
velopers. About every fourth or so house that I pass has shuttered
windows, a yard with severely overgrown weeds, and no bicycles or
car out front; this would be a fairly standard long-term-unoccupied/
abandoned-house ratio for an average Japanese suburb anywhere outside of the Kanto Plain, but I am nevertheless a bit surprised to see
this in a neighborhood that is, at least on paper, part of Greater Tokyo.

Yamaguchi Sayoko greets me with a smile at the front door of her
two-story house, which she and her husband, Yoshito, bought after
his retirement from Mitsubishi Heavy Industries. She has been its
sole occupant since Yoshito's recent passing.

Although this is the second time we have met, the diminutive,
effervescent Yamaguchi expresses renewed surprise at our relative
height difference and the size of my shoes as I step out of them and up

into the house. How much of this reaction is sincere and how much is performance I cannot know, but I play along, making a comically resigned facial expression I accompany with a New York shrug. We share a little laugh. Although this call-and-response schtick has gotten a tad stale for me after about the ten thousandth time in my long decades here, the laughter is a welcome release of tension, considering Yamaguchi's recent loss, for one thing, and also considering what we are going to be talking about for the next few hours. I sense that my sentiments are shared.

My hostess accepts my proffered souvenir with gracious enthusiasm and shows me to the living room, where there are still some ceremonial items—Japanese Roman Catholic, in this case—from Yoshito's wake held here several weeks previously. I offer my condolences again (the first time was over the phone), then bow to her husband's formal funereal photo while bringing my hands together in a Japanese prayer gesture.

Yamaguchi has cleared the living room table for our talk, and after a few more rounds of conversational conventionalities—the weather, ailments, garden-variety Trumpy angst—I use the tabletop to spread out what is, along with my digital sound recorder, the most important tool for my atomic-bomb-survivor research interviews: one of my poster-sized high-resolution maps of the atom-bombed cities created by United States Strategic Bombing Survey (USSBS) cartographers in 1945–1946. Although the maps were drawn postwar—with overlay representation of the scope and ferocity of the atomic bomb damage— the institutions, installations, infrastructure, street and neighborhood names, etc., of the cities are represented exactly as they were at the instant before their atomic destruction, or at least as close as wartime American intel could determine from aerial reconnaissance and postwar USSBS personnel could confirm from captured data, interrogations of Japanese officials, and boots-on-the-ground man-in-the-street surveys.

For most of the hibakusha I have interviewed while researching this book, these are the first detailed, navigation-grade maps they have ever seen depicting their childhood hometowns as they existed

immediately before the bombs.[5] As such, these cartographic time capsules are always objects of interest and nostalgia for the hibakusha,
resuscitating long-dormant memories of old neighborhoods, parks,
movie theaters, schools, and shopping arcades and other snapshots of
daily life in a midsized regional city in early-twentieth-century western Japan before all of these things were wiped off the face of the
earth.

Leaning over my map, Yamaguchi and I are looking at an expanse
of land that for almost the entirety of its geological history was not
much more than a seven-kilometer-wide cove with a wall of mountains close in at its back. Had the vagaries of its geological history
been different, it would have stayed that way and ended up just another typical Seto Inland Sea waterfront settlement—perhaps an oyster-
farming village along the coastal Kure Line with a few skinny citrus
orchards hacked into the hillsides.

But this cove was exceptional: It had a slow-flowing, silty river
emptying into it, and the story of that river—and an alluvial anomaly
it experienced about seven hundred years ago—is the story of how a
craggy backwater in the samurai fiefdom of Aki eventually became
one of the most important harbors and transportation hubs in western Japan and, in August 1945, the target of the first American atomic
bomb dropped in anger.

By 1945, the accumulated effects of seven centuries of alluvial sed-
imentation, four centuries of increasingly ambitious land-reclamation
projects, Japan's nineteenth-century latecomer industrial revolution,
and the nation's early-twentieth-century rise to world-class military
power had caused Hiroshima to grow up, around, and out from the
original marshy site of Hiroshima Castle into a modern city of some
quarter of a million people.[6]

Viewed on a map, the coastline of Hiroshima Bay looks like a side
view of the roof of a cavern, from which the Ōta Delta's tightly
grouped islets hang like a crooked cluster of stalactites. I ask Yamaguchi where she was living in August 1945, and she points at the northern
tip of one of the stalactites close to the middle of the map. Under her
finger, letters—in a staid Army Air Forces typeface—read "TAKAJO

MACHI" (old Japanese for "Falconers' District").[7] The eponymous neighborhood—absorbed into Honkawa-chō in the 1960s—is directly across the Honkawa from Lord Mōri Terumoto's castle grounds and, east of that, the economic-administrative core of downtown Hiroshima. It is also across the river and a short walk upstream from what was known in 1945 as Hiroshima Prefectural Exhibition Hall, which today is the haunting ruin of toppled masonry and twisted steel girders registered with UNESCO as the Hiroshima Peace Memorial—also known as the Genbaku or Atomic Dome.

While Takajō-machi might once have housed the Mōri clan's master falconers, and later occupied what should have been prime real estate close to the heart of the modern city, this history belies the fact that in 1945, the neighborhood—for a variety of demographic and economic factors—was decidedly low-rent.

"It was a real skid row," my hostess recalls.

Yamaguchi Sayoko was born on October 23, 1930—as the fourth of what would eventually be five children of Yamaguchi Shōkichi (b. 1876) and his wife, Mume (b. 1891)—in Kujima-mura, a remote hamlet deep in the mountains of western Hiroshima Prefecture. The nearest train station, Hatsukaichi, was ten kilometers away—down the mountains and a sociocultural world away on the Hiroshima Bay shoreline. The route between the station and Kujima was serviced by a bus that made one round trip per day, but not many of the villagers were inconvenienced by this lack of transportation infrastructure. Most of them eked out a living within walking distance of their corrugated tin- or thatch-roofed huts, doing something forestry-related or else working the stingy slopes of the mountains that ringed the community for whatever meager agricultural products (mushrooms, bamboo shoots, and the like) they would yield.

Along with many other residents of the Chūgoku region's mountainous hinterland, Sayoko's father took a shot at bettering his station in life by emigrating to America in the early twentieth century. For some reason that has long since been lost to Yamaguchi family lore, the five years he spent in the orange groves of California did not work out for him, and he returned to Hiroshima in his mid-thirties, a few years after the Russo-Japanese War. At the time of Sayoko's birth, Shōkichi, then in his mid-fifties, had started a second family and was earning his keep as a charcoal maker—an arduous and unhealthy occupation that was very common at the time for economically disadvantaged people in regions of Japan where there was not much else in the way of economic activity or employment opportunities.

In the traditional arrangement, charcoal makers would enter into a sharecropper-like partnership under which they would clear otherwise essentially worthless mountain slopes of unwanted trees and undergrowth, burn this scrap wood down to charcoal in earthen kilns (called *yanagama*) purpose-built (then dismantled) right on the spot, then split the profits on the sale of the charcoal with the landowner. It was a tough racket with plenty of competition, so to help out with overhead, Sayoko's mother was in charge of packaging the finished charcoal sticks in straw *tawara* bales to bring to market.

Decades of breathing charcoal smoke and dust and a lifetime of manual labor and poverty gradually took a physical toll on Shōkichi. Although fifteen years younger, Mume was also ground down into poor health by the physical and mental strain of this lifestyle. In 1936, forced by these circumstances to leave their hardscrabble mountain existence in Kujima-mura behind, the couple and their four younger children moved in with their eldest daughter, Michie (b. 1920), and her husband in Uchikoshi-chō, near Yokogawa Station in the northern reaches of Hiroshima City. After the move, their son, Shizuo (b. 1923), gave up on any further education for himself and instead began working as an adult to put food on the table for his infirm, aging parents and his three younger sisters—Yoshimi (b. 1929), Sayoko, and Shizue (b. 1934). In 1937, six months before her seventh birthday, Sayoko began her own formal education when she entered nearby Misasa Elementary School.

The next year, Shōkichi died at the age of sixty-two. Adjusting to these new circumstances, Mume moved her family once again, this time to Takajō-machi, where they lived on the second floor of a distant

Yamaguchi relative's house before moving again, a few months later, into an apartment of their own in the poorest alleyway in the neighborhood. The family's financial straits were so dire by this point that they could not even afford to give Sayoko streetcar fare to continue commuting to Misasa Elementary, forcing her to walk the five-kilometer round trip every day from the age of eight to fourteen.

HARMONICA HOUSES

Takajō-machi
Six hundred seventy meters northwest of Ground Zero

FAMILY DWELLINGS IN prewar Japan—whether urban, suburban, or rural—were not built to last. Their lightness and fragility—compared to their contemporary Western counterparts—were design specs that facilitated and made more affordable complete top-to-bottom reconstruction (though roof tiles were often reused; see below). In general, this would happen once every generation or so—the span of time after which it was assumed these structures would otherwise fall victim to earth(quake), wind, fire, water, and/or termites unless the natural course of this inexorable demise was preempted by human intervention.

The light construction of Japanese houses also prioritized natural ventilation and the use of sunlight, where available, for illumination and warming. This latter design consideration was particularly important as the houses' overall composition of wood, paper, and tatami matting provided virtually no heat insulation, making attempts at space heating resource- and effort-wasting exercises in futility and conspicuous consumption.

With a few pushes of sliding wooden or rice paper doors, entire walls—usually south facing—could open up to a garden or backyard (e.g., Ōiwa Kōhei's living room). In a fully opened configuration, the result was a sort of beachside-cabana effect that nearly eliminated the distinction between "indoors" and "outdoors," creating a very "Japanese" aesthetic space suitable for green tea sipping, haiku composition, meditation, and the like.

The illumination and warming considerations of these design features, however, were often mutually contradictory—for example, in houses in which yawning apertures also left the house interiors (and thus the physical comfort of their inhabitants) very much at the mercy of seasonal climate. Winter posed particularly daunting challenges, when these can't-decide-if-they're-inside-or-outside spaces would be transformed into virtual refrigerators (even with the doors shut). Summer brought its own challenges, as well, when flies, mosquitoes, roaches, stinging centipedes, and other multilegged creatures would run (or fly) amok in Japanese interiors, coming and going at will in the absence of window/door screens. In general, though, these visitations were more accepted than abhorred, it being considered a mark of maturity and character to be able to tolerate these intrusions of Mother Nature in one's personal space with bemused panache, if not Buddha-like admiration of the life force in these undaunted, doggedly determined, and often seemingly ingenious bugs. Still, whether one was a would-be bodhisattva or not, mosquito netting around one's futon was de rigueur for anyone desiring a decent night's sleep anytime between May and November.

The sole exception to the overall light construction of typical contemporary Japanese dwellings was their immensely heavy roofs, which, because of the thick ceramic tiles they employed, could easily weigh several tons, even for an average-sized family house. One important function of this heavy roofing material was as top-down ballast to prevent wooden house frames from being blown away by the typhoons that regularly lashed the archipelago during summer months. Due to the considerable energy expended in their production and transportation, tiles were (and still are) quite expensive. As such, they were a high-priority recycling target for the prewar housing-construction industry (e.g., the roadside recycling piles of the Hiroshima firebreak teams). They also accounted for the lion's share of the weight that trapped victims under the wreckage of homes or other buildings when these structures collapsed in the wake of either natural or, as the case might have been, man-made catastrophes.

Another aspect of traditional Japanese residences deserving of note is what might be called their "architectural egalitarianism." In most other cultures, it is usually not difficult—given enough visual data—to make a fairly accurate spot assessment of the socioeconomic status of a given household based upon the physical appearance of its dwelling. However, this has never been as straightforward a matter in Japan. In 1945, outside of the imperial family and, perhaps, a figurative handful of nouveau riche entrepreneurs in Tokyo and Osaka, almost everyone else in the archipelago lived in an unpainted wooden house roofed with gunmetal gray ceramic tiles, and this was so whether the breadwinner of a given house was a doctor, a sharecropper, or anything in between.

The tatami-matted interior of an average Japanese dwelling of the era was also spartan and uniform; this space could be altered, adjusted, and channeled according to need or occasion, again, by opening or closing sliding wooden or translucent rice paper doors. These doors could also be easily removed altogether to create a single large space, as might be temporarily required to host a special event like a wake, wedding party, or neighborhood meeting. In design considerations for such houses, privacy was prioritized relative only to the potentially probing eyes of neighbors and outsider passersby. Inside the houses themselves, privacy between/among household members was practically nonexistent.[1] In this interior arrangement—which a modern and typically fiercely individualist Westerner accustomed to the luxury of personal space would probably quickly experience as socially claustrophobic—one was essentially "onstage" in one's expected familial role 24/7. If one wanted "alone" or "me" time—to recharge one's introvert batteries, say, or to seek refuge after a family spat or the like—there was little recourse other than to try to find it somewhere outside the home, say, in a nearby park, on a river embankment, or even in an empty schoolyard.

Although it was an important cultural norm, this "architectural egalitarianism" was by no means absolute. Socioeconomic class markers were present in traditional Japanese interiors, for example, but these tended to be subtler than their Western equivalents, primarily limited to the quality of craftsmanship and the type of wood used in construction; the presence or absence of *tokoma* room alcoves specially designated for the display of flower-arrangement vases and/or artwork; and perhaps the frequency with which the tatami matting was changed out. More conspicuous markers for a household's socioeconomic status would have been the size of the plot of land that the house occupied; whether there was any spare real estate not covered by the house and, if so, whether this was used for a pristinely pruned garden or, alternately, as an outdoor storage space / junk pile; and, last, whether the entire household plot was enclosed by a gated wall. Consequently, and in general, the more walled-in household compounds with well-tended gardens there were in a given inner-city residential district, the higher its overall socioeconomic level. And in this context, few displays of family wealth in prewar Japan were more ostentatious than owning a house with a giant walled-in garden in the middle of a densely populated downtown district.

In Yamaguchi Sayoko's downtown Hiroshima neighborhood of Takajō-machi, dwellings with walled-in, gated compounds were few and far between compared with, say, Ōiwa Kōhei's Danbara neighborhood. In most cases, Takajō-machi dwellings were directly abutted by other dwellings; their entrances opened directly onto the streets or alleyways they fronted; and they were, again, relatively uniform in terms of basic layout and their standard wood/paper/tatami construction materials. The lifestyle and lived daily environment of the neighborhood's working-class and working-poor residents should be considered fairly representative of the various Hiroshima neighborhoods we have encountered so far, albeit perhaps with an added patina of wear and tear and a relative lack of amenities.

Yamaguchi's family lived in the last of a row of wooden two-story apartments lining a narrow dirt-paved alley. Each unit was identical in appearance and design, and shared a common roof and thin wall partitions with its adjoining neighbors. From the air, the property would have looked like long rows of parallel barracks in a dusty Army camp.[2]

The alley frontage of each unit was no wider than what was required to allow its sliding front door to open fully—probably not much more than the span of a grown man's outstretched arms. Yamaguchi informs me, with a wan smile, that Hiroshima residents used to call these dwellings "harmonica houses" because the tight alignment of their identical front doors made the rows resemble the comb of a harmonica. The visual analogy would have been especially apt during the hotter months, when residents customarily left these doors open for ventilation.

In addition to being firetraps, the row apartments left much to be desired in the way of creature comforts. They were not furnished with plumbing. Toilets were closeted holes off the living room floor and tucked out of sight under staircases to second-floor lofts. These apertures led directly to wooden septic buckets called *koeoke* under the floorboards. The contents of these buckets would be carted away once a week or so, free of charge, by tradesmen who sold this night soil to farmers as fertilizer.

Cooking in the row apartments was done in hard-clay, slurry-floored kitchens—shoe- or at least sandal-wearing areas (as opposed to the no-shoe-zone tatami-floored interiors) set at ground level in the backs of the apartments. Cooking was done there on a double-eye wood-fire stove called a *kamado*—a loaf-shaped mound of slurry-covered earth built around twin firepits, each with its own aperture on top where the pots, pans, or kettles in use would be placed. Water for household use and for drinking (after thorough kettle boiling on the *kamado*) was drawn from a communal hand-pumped well in the alleyway.

The communal water pump doubled in function as an important locus of female social life. To wash dishes or do laundry, the row apartments' womenfolk would pull big copper-belted wooden tubs called *tarai* out to the pump and perform the task on the spot, usually while engaged in lively banter with peers engaged in identical drudgery. A wash cycle required first working the laundry load into a soapy lather either by squatting over the *tarai* to knead the dirty clothes by hand or, for old-school types who favored efficiency over decorum, stepping barefoot into the *tarai* and stomping the clothes clean. Each item would then be scrubbed out and rinsed on a slatted wooden washboard.³ For drying, clotheslines were strung behind the units, which faced the backs of mirror-identical row apartments on the next alley over.

Bathing also posed challenges, both physical and financial. When residents wanted something more substantial than a sponge bath after a long, sweaty day, they would have to go to a commercial neighborhood *sentō* bathhouse. The entrance fee for such facilities was generally ten sen—about two hundred yen or two American dollars in today's currency. Large poor families would have had difficulty indulging in such luxury every night, so most made going to the bathhouse a once-a-week event. For Japanese with living memories of this more spartan era, the postwar lifestyle novelty of being able to take baths or showers in their own houses or apartments whenever and as often as they wanted must have initially seemed to border on the miraculous, if not downright decadent.

At the front entrance of each rowhouse apartment unit was a slurry-floored foyer called a *doma*—a more literally down-to-earth version of the wood- or tile-floored *genkan* entranceways in more upscale housing—where residents and visitors would take off or put on shoes depending on whether they were coming or going. For the Takajō-machi apartments, this space was about the size of two conjoined old-fashioned public phone booths. In addition to its function as a shoe-changing zone, it also served, as in any traditional Japanese home, as a sort of frontier post between the cleanliness and order of the unshod inner living space—elevated off the foundation of the house by about thirty centimeters—and the unclean chaos of the ground-level, shoe-requiring outside world. This symbolic borderline function would have been especially critical in a lower-status home that directly opened up onto the street (i.e., that did not have a front yard and/or a household-compound-enclosing gate and wall). The *doma/genkan* was a liminal zone not only demarcating inside and outside, but also up and down, high and low, sublime and vulgar; it was the place where, no matter how ostensibly humble the abode, visitors were compelled to leave their shoes behind and literally elevate themselves to a higher plane to be granted the privilege of passage and entrance. Once within this inner sanctum, they were expected to comport themselves with appropriate respect for the space and its full-time occupants.[4]

Socially, the *doma/genkan* served as an informal anteroom where the outside world could be dealt with at arm's length, with all of the operant shoeless-interior / shod-exterior border-station protocols respected. The lady of the house, for example, kneeling on the edge of the elevated wood- and tatami-floored living area, might have used the *doma/genkan* to interact with a tradesman or salesman standing in the doorway (keeping a respectful distance from—and by tacit understanding uninvited into—the inner sanctum of the home), or with neighbors dropping by for a quick casual chat who were either too busy or too lazy to step up into the living room for a longer visit (which would have also compelled the hostess to prepare green tea, at a minimum, for the guests).[5] Alternately, having a visitor sit on the step-up ledge of the interior while keeping their shod feet down on the clay floor was a perfectly acceptable *doma/genkan* protocol compromise, perhaps particularly so in a community like Takajō-machi, where residents, in general, would have tended to be pretty comfortable with informality.[6]

When the Yamaguchis moved into the neighborhood, the unpretentious quality of the local social dynamic would have helped to ease the family's transition to their new life in the row apartments, where everyone else was just as poor as they were. By the time they took up residence, the eldest daughter, Michie, had already married and left home, and the only son, Shizuo, had secured employment through extended family connections in a Tokyo iron foundry. Both of these older children sent money home to their mother when they could.

Sayoko and her older sister Yoshimi also chipped in to help make ends meet, doing after-school work as domestics for a local well-to-do rice merchant. Mume made a small contribution to the family finances by doing piecework at home. This consisted mostly of folding and gluing strips of onionskin paper into envelopes used as packaging material for colored origami paper or small packets of the sewing needles for which prewar Hiroshima was famous.

"All these years later, I can still remember the smell of the glue my mother used," Yamaguchi recalls. "And whenever I smell something like it now, it takes me right back to our place in Takajō-machi."

Despite the Yamaguchis' best efforts to improve their situation, poverty constantly tugged at the family's sleeves. Nevertheless, Mume still clung to an optimistic parental hope of eventual socioeconomic advancement for her children, and regarded this goal as meriting sacrifice in the present and investment for the future, even if that meant tightening a familial budget already on its last belt hole. Accordingly, in spring 1943, she decided that Sayoko should stay on for the two-year higher-education course at Misasa Elementary. This would have given her daughter at least a small leg up in life relative to other poor kids, who rarely went beyond the legal end of compulsory education in grade six. But the continued and now also increased tuition to make Sayoko's extra schooling possible was another drain on the family's coffers.

Things got even tougher in 1944, when Shizuo joined the Navy (in lieu of inevitable eventual conscription into—and presumably a more likely muddy and miserable demise in—the Army). As his new military pay was a mere pittance compared with his decent iron-foundry salary, this development involved the loss of an important revenue source for the Yamaguchi household.

As their financial hardships compounded, the Yamaguchis eventually had no choice but to go on public assistance to continue putting food on the table. One of Sayoko's regular after-school chores during this lean season was to go down to city hall to collect the family's monthly welfare allowance of forty yen (about eighty thousand yen or eight hundred US dollars in 2022 currency). This stipend would have provided the family members—assuming there was food available for the Takajō-machi neighborhood cooperative that week—with a subsistence diet probably only slightly below the average 1944 Japanese per capita daily consumption of two thousand calories (compared to thirty-four hundred for their American contemporaries).[7]

A typical evening meal for the Yamaguchis at the time would have been rice (increasingly unhulled or "whole grain" as the war progressed) or rice stretched by mixing it with cheaper barley. Depending on the vagaries of the neighborhood's food-rationing situation, this might have been accompanied with a block of tofu or some skinny strips of grilled fish for protein, maybe with some pickled cabbage or radish on the side for sodium and a little extra flavor. This would have been a pitiably modest repast in prewar Japan, but by March 1945, when the tightening noose of the American naval blockade and aerial mine-laying campaign had seen per capita Japanese daily consumption drop to fifteen hundred[8] calories a day, such a meal would have bordered on the luxurious. Plain white rice—the staple of the peacetime Japanese diet—was by this point beyond most people's wildest dreams. The only Japanese eating it in with any regularity in 1945 were those who had cash to spare for the black market or who were in the military and stationed on the home front, where almost all of the domestically produced rice crop was going to feed the armed services and into storage in closely guarded defense-supply stockpiles for the anticipated imminent American invasion of the Japanese Home Islands.[9]

The spring of 1945 also saw Mume facing a big decision regarding the family—specifically, about what fourteen-year-old Sayoko should do now that she was about to graduate from her higher-education course at Misasa Elementary School. In the public education policy of the era, all Japanese children were legally obligated to graduate from elementary school. At the life juncture of elementary-school graduation, it was a perfectly honorable and not at all unusual career choice for a child from humble origins to forgo further education (as Sayoko's older siblings, Michie, Shizuo, and Yoshimi, had done) and enter full-time employment. But even for the 46.9 percent of Japanese boys and 43.6 percent of girls who went on to higher education in 1945,[10] the decision to do so was now basically meaningless, from the perspective of actual education, as all of these children were being conscripted into war work anyway, whether "voluntary" or, for the luckier, recompensed.

As there were no elderly or invalided family members in the Yamaguchi household, Sayoko did not have the draft-deferral option of staying at home on the pretext of helping her mother with housework. War work was going to get her, one way or another, so the choice she faced was whether to go on to girls' school—again, the female equivalent of junior high—and get a paid munitions plant *teishintai* job; to get one of these *teishintai* jobs without the pretense (and expense) of going to a school (where she would not have been learning anything in any case); or to stay home and wait for the *tonarigumi* neighborhood association to eventually rope her into unpaid volunteer labor; doing farmwork; clearing firebreaks with other unemployed "adults" in the central business district; or, most arduous of all, excavating defensive earthworks and underground bunkers for the Army.

In the end, Mume held on to her optimism about her children's future, and it was determined that Sayoko should go on to girls' school. The constant financial strain of feeding her children would ease up some once Sayoko's *teishintai* salary began coming in, and it would lighten up once again later that summer when her youngest daughter, Shizue, was evacuated—as an air raid precaution—to live with an aunt in the mountains of western Hiroshima Prefecture.

GREEN SAND

Midori-machi

3.2 kilometers south-southeast of Ground Zero

IN MARCH 1945, Sayoko graduated from her two-year elementary-school higher-education course at Misasa and passed the entrance examination for Number Two Municipal Girls' School (Dai Ni Ichijo). With her completion of an elementary-school higher course, she had already attained the highest level of schooling in the history of her family. This qualification also meant that she was able to matriculate at Dai Ni Ichijo as a third-year transfer student. If all went according to schedule, she would finish her "studies" (primarily on some munitions plant floor) in April 1947 with scholastic credentials equivalent to a male junior high graduate—at the time the highest to which any Japanese student could aspire if they did not go on to university, teachers college, or technical/engineering vocational "high" school.

Compared with Ichijo, its more academically rigorous (at least before the mass student mobilization of 1944) municipal sister institution, Dai Ni Ichijo was more of a secretarial school. In August 1945, it had an enrollment of 417 girls under the tutelage of eleven full-time faculty members. In terms of curriculum and institutional mission, it actually had more in common with Tominaga Chieko's Dai Ni Kenjo—another war-era expansion school established with the aim of training female office workers to free up young men for military service. Like its prefectural counterpart, it was apparently considered too small— and the war situation now too dire—to merit a new dedicated campus to be built for it. For the brief duration of its institutional existence, Dai Ni Ichijo had to borrow classroom space from Municipal Number Three Elementary School in Midori-machi, north of Ujina.

Sayoko's first day on this campus was one of the few she and her classmates actually spent together inside a classroom. The day after their entrance ceremony and orientation briefings, the members of the Dai Ni Ichijo class of 1947 joined the ranks of some three million other students mobilized for full-time war labor across the country. For Sayoko's homeroom, this would mean working at the massive Japan Steel complex in Mukainada. Although Sayoko had performed earlier part-time mobilized labor service at a government-run cigarette factory in Hiroshima when she was still a Misasa student, the Mukainada job, as a *teishintai* position, would be her first experience of an arduous full-time job that, in peacetime, would have been performed by adult male professionals.

At Japan Steel, Sayoko and her classmates were assigned to the day shift on a foundry floor. The work there involved casting aluminum aircraft parts using the green sand process. The girls' employment followed the seat-of-the-pants on-the-job-training format that was standard for students thrust into hazardous war plant work. As the crucible handling and pouring during the casting process were considered too dangerous (and important) to be left to anyone but the few experienced craftsmen left at the plant, the Dai Ni Ichijo students were instead assigned to the job of packing the sand in wooden mold boxes in preparation for accepting molten aluminum.

Though it occupied the lowest rung on the foundry floor in terms of expertise, the girls' sand-packing task still required a certain degree of care and precision. If an errant drop of their sweat or other superfluous moisture fell into the mold, it would pop like a firecracker when molten aluminum made contact with it during the pouring stage. This would destroy the mold and send up a shrapnel geyser of superheated sand and molten metal that could have caused serious burn injuries, in addition to inevitably ruining the part being cast. Sayoko and her coworkers were constantly warned—not with undue hyperbole—that if they were not exacting and mindful in their work, precious military aircraft and their dashing young pilots would be lost to crashes as a result.

Although conditions were arduous and inherently grubby, Sayoko and her classmates approached their war work with undaunted devotion, wearing wide white headbands emblazoned with oversized red *hinomaru* sun circles as an expression of their enthusiasm and faith in final victory. This faith was something they held on to with fierce intensity even as the food began running out and the air raids started. And if they ever occasionally felt their own enthusiasm flag in their personal heart of hearts, there were always trustworthy, knowledgeable adults to buck them back up. For example, what should have been the otherwise jarring and cognitively dissonant reality of American planes now flying overhead at all hours of the day or night was attributed by teachers and the news media to a strategic masterstroke on the part of Japanese war planners to draw the enemy closer to the Home Islands, where they would be vanquished in a final decisive battle in which every Japanese who could hold a gun or a bamboo spear would take part. That explanation made perfect sense when no one had access to alternative and more objective sources of information. Sayoko never entertained the possibility that Japan might be eventually defeated.

The routines and rituals that circumscribed the tone and rhythm of most mobilized students' daily lives underscored the military (or at least militaristic) atmosphere in which they had been immersed since childhood, and there were constant reinforcements and reminders of the proud and weighty obligations expected of each of them in this hour of national destiny. She and her coworker classmates considered themselves to be soldiers—participants on active duty in a national total-war effort that they fervently believed would eventually end in victory. In this context, they often lamented their regret to one another—and even to family members—that they had not been born as boys, who could enjoy the supreme honor of donning the emperor's uniform to fall in battle and be immortalized in Yasukuni Shrine someday.

In Hiroshima, younger students performing volunteer (i.e., not *teishintai*) labor usually formed up in ranks on their school grounds every morning for pep talks and instructions, after which they would march to their daily workplaces, in formation, with school banners flying and the latest popular propaganda songs on their lips. Although these marched commutes were important for maintaining stalwart fighting spirit, they were also the consequence of a somewhat more (and literal) pedestrian factor: Students, at least officially, were banned from using public transporation in order to give riding priority to commuters engaged in more vital war work at offices in the central business district or, going in the other direction, factories on the city's outskirts.

In contrast to the footsore lot of younger volunteer workers, Sayoko's *teishintai* status as a nominal employee of Japan Steel came with the perk of free use of public transportation, outside certain strictly proscribed travel zones, as she was officially considered to be doing vital war work. For a typical workday commute, she would leave home a little before eight in the morning and hop a streetcar at Sakan-chō at the western foot of the Aioi Bridge. This would take her east through Kamiya-chō and Hatchōbori in the heart of the central business district, eventually arriving at Hiroshima Station around 0815. There, she would meet up with her student coworkers and they would ride the Kure Line train together out to the Japan Steel complex in Mukainada.

Sunday, August 5, 1945, was the last day Sayoko made this trip.

The following day saw August's scheduled electrical brownout across various industrial districts in Hiroshima, including Mukainada. As the crucibles at Japan Steel could not melt aluminum without electrical power, there would be no green sand casting on August 6 and thus no need for the Dai Ni Ichijo girls to be at the plant. Accordingly, the school's administrators decided to use the day for homeroom sessions at the Midori-machi campus (3.2 kilometers south-southeast of Ground Zero). If they had instead opted to give the girls a day off—as was often the case for *teishintai* workers at factories affected by scheduled brownouts—Sayoko would have been at home in Takajō-machi with her mother (seven hundred meters west-northwest of Ground Zero) when Little Boy detonated.

August 6 would be the girls' first time to see the inside of a classroom in weeks, and Sayoko, for one, was happy for the break from the usual foundry-floor routine, even though the schedule change meant she would have to leave home a little earlier than usual. Disrupted routine notwithstanding, the day's schedule had little effect on the quality or amount of her sleep; the constant air raid sirens the night before ensured that she had not gotten any.

Like most residents of Japanese cities after March 1945, the Yama-guchis were obedient to civil defense guidelines in their daily (and nightly) routine. They scrupulously observed light discipline after dark, using blackout curtains as directed. They left the radio on when they went to bed, keeping one ear open throughout the night to receive and, if necessary, respond to air raid updates from NHK. They had a "bomb shelter," of sorts, in their apartment—again, as per civil defense instructions; a workman neighbor had been kind enough to dig this for them under the living room tatami-floor pallets (and at eye level with the *koeoke* night soil bucket). Against the likelihood that this "shelter" would prove insufficient in a full-blown incendiary raid, the members of the Yamaguchi household also slept in their daytime clothes, so they could make a quick escape outside and down to the relative sanctuary of the banks of the Ōta Honkawa if and when everything went up in flames in the middle of the night.

Around the time *Straight Flush* was first detected by the air defense HQ bunker at Hiroshima Castle, Sayoko rolled off her futon to eat a quick breakfast of radish broth with her mother and older sister Yoshimi, who would be going to *teishintai* work at a post office in nearby Sumiyoshi-chō later that morning. The only morning ablutions to be attended to involved not much more than a splash of water on the face. Nor was there much in the way of dressing ritual, because, as usual, the three had slept in their clothes: Sayoko and Yoshimi in their work outfits of cotton blouse and baggy *monpe* work pants, and

Mume in her favorite blue-and-yellow-ochre-patterned day kimono. As per their usual morning routine, the threesome sat on the tatami around their small folding dining table, eating and chatting until it was time for the girls to head off to work or school.

Sayoko headed for the Sakan-chō streetcar stop a little after the *Straight Flush* all clear at 0731. As usual, she took the streetcar headed east, but this morning, instead of continuing on to Hiroshima Station, she transferred to a southbound Ujina Line streetcar on Rijō Street. This dropped her at Takanohashi—the farthest south she was allowed to ride the Ujina Line streetcar (as she was not going to *teishintai* work on this day) and still only half of the way to her campus. She had to cover the remaining 1.5 kilometers on foot. Luckily for her, the girls in her school were issued rubber-soled canvas sneakers, called *zukku*, so she would not have to make the morning's quick march to school in the wooden *geta* sandals many other mobilized students—e.g., Tominaga Chieko and her Dai Ni Kenjo classmates—had to wear.

When Sayoko arrived at her classroom, a student was writing the day's schedule on the blackboard while the rest of the class waited for the teacher to arrive from the faculty room. Sayoko thought it would be a good idea to take notes of what was being written on the blackboard, and she bent over in her chair to retrieve a notebook from her book bag. At that instant, the brightest, whitest light she had ever seen flashed through the classroom's north-facing windows. Instinctively, she turned away from the flash and dove the rest of the way under her desk, face toward the floor. Once in this position, she opened her mouth, plugging her ears with her thumbs and using the rest of her fingers to protect her eyes and face—just as she and her classmates (and everyone else in the country) had been trained to do—and waited for an explosion.

Only one of Sayoko's classmates—her friend Tanaka—had also hit the floor in response to the flash. All the other girls were still sitting up at their desks and facing the wood-framed windows—likely wondering about the strange light—when the glass panes imploded in a storm of shards some nine or ten seconds later. Simultaneously, the wooden school building wobbled under a violent shock accompanied by a tremendous roar. This was quickly followed by the sounds of screams, cracking support beams, clattering roof tiles, and falling ceiling panels.

For long moments, Sayoko stayed crouched under her desk, too terrified to budge. But eventually, the moaning and crying of her classmates—steadily increasing in volume as the pain-numbing effect of their initial shock wore off—compelled her to raise her head and look around.

The classroom was completely wrecked, and only Sayoko and Tanaka were uninjured. The rest of the girls, now honeycombed by glass shrapnel, were still on the floor or trying to pull themselves up to their feet, moaning in pain, crying for help, and bleeding profusely. Sayoko and Tanaka ran to the faculty room to find their teacher, but no one was there. Returning to the classroom to see what they could do to help, they found that almost everyone had somehow roused themselves up off the floor to make good their escape. There was only one girl still there—whose name Yamaguchi remembers only as Ueno; she had been pinned between a wall and the floor when the lintel of the classroom's doorway collapsed and broke her leg.

Moving quickly to evacuate the shuddering, groaning building, Sayoko and Tanaka pried Ueno out from under the doorframe, then, picking her up under her shoulders, hustled their charge (and them-selves) to safety. Once outside, the girls saw that the roof tiles of all the houses in the neighborhood had been blown off. These and galax-ies of twinkling glass fragments were now scattered about on the roadways of the narrow streets.

Despite the widespread damage before their eyes, the girls could not see any bomb crater. Nothing was on fire or even emitting smoke. Sayoko wondered how it was that something that had flashed that brightly, made that much noise, and shaken the school building and neighborhood that violently had not left a big smoking hole and a bunch of collapsed houses nearby.

The discussion ended inconclusively, and in any case the girls had more important things to attend to, the most urgent of which was to find help for Ueno. Army Mutual Aid Hospital was the major medical facility closest to the school, about half a kilometer away, so the trio decided to go there. Nearing the hospital, they began to encounter injured people in steadily increasing numbers. As was quickly becoming clear, whatever had exploded earlier this morning had not just scattered roof tiles and broken glass in Midori-machi. Judging from the numbers of people they were seeing, snippets of conversations they were overhearing, and the ugly dark sky to the north, they realized that the explosion had affected all of Lower Hiroshima—if not the entire city.

When they reached the hospital, the wards and corridors were already rapidly filling up with explosion victims, among whom the burn cases got priority attention from the medical staff. It took several hours until the girls were finally able to wave down a doctor willing to take the time to bother with a mere bone fracture case. He gave Ueno a quick field-dressed splint for her leg and sent the three on their way.

The girls then headed for the Ueno home, which, luckily for them, was also nearby. When they arrived, Ueno's mother took her daughter off her rescuers' hands with profuse gratitude and apologies. Sayoko never saw either of them again.

With the morning's rescue obligation now behind them, Sayoko and Tanaka were free to begin their long respective journeys home. As they proceeded northwestward up Rijō Street, the fact that the streetcars were no longer running provided another ominous inkling of the scale of the catastrophe, as did their encounters with swelling numbers of victims, whose injuries resembled the ones they had seen in the hospital. Up to this point, sometime between 1100 and noon, Sayoko had been so cranked up on adrenaline by the fear and stress of the explosion aftermath, then so busy taking care of Ueno, that she had completely forgotten about her own family members. It was only as she and Tanaka walked up Rijō Street, gazing at the hazy dark gray shroud of orange-underlit smoke hanging over the city center, that she began to feel her first flutters of panic thinking about her mother and Yoshimi.

Despite the heat, the girls put on their padded cotton *bōsaizukin* hoods—as they had been trained to do in a disaster situation—and pressed on toward the city. On the way, Sayoko came close to becoming immobilized by the first few corpses and hideously burned people she saw—victims either staggering in the opposite direction toward Army Mutual or Ujina or else lying motionless along the sides of the roadway. But Sayoko's experience was similar to those of many other hibakusha, and a survival instinct response to this tsunami of traumatic sensory overload saw her initial panic and revulsion begin to fade away into sanity-protecting—and forward-motion-facilitating— emotional numbness.

As with everyone else in the area trying to follow Rijō Street up into the city, the girls found their progress temporarily blocked at the Miyuki Bridge by the fires furiously burning on the opposite bank of the Kyōbashi River. A cooler-headed adult might have realized that the girls could have made it home by making an end run around the fiercely burning city center. They could have done this by going up the east bank of the Kyōbashi past Hijiyama, then hooking a left at Hiroshima Station to head west—essentially running the same route, in reverse, that the PE teacher Fukuzaki-sensei was then in the process of taking from Misasa to reach Dai Ni Kenjo. But Sayoko and Tanaka were not cooler-headed adults, and their panic azimuth for "home" was the streetcar route they already knew. As far as they were concerned, the only way back to their homes was across the Miyuki Bridge, up Rijō Street, then left/west at Kamiya-chō to the Aioi Bridge. Once they had crossed that, Sayoko's Takajō-machi home would be a stone's throw away to the right, while Tanaka would have to walk another two kilometers or so to the north and cross one more bridge at Yokogawa to reach her family's home in Ōshiba.

Locked into this planned course of action, they had no choice but to sit on the bridge and wait for Rijō Street to open up. In the meantime, they watched in dazed silence with hundreds of other people as soldiers, police, and *Keibōdan* tried to fight the walls of roaring red flame on the west bank. After at least two and possibly even three hours, the flames there subsided to a degree at which the authority figures at the western foot of the bridge could begin waving people through to continue up Rijō Street.

An unseen male voice somewhere near the head of the crowd shouted out, "We can go home now!" Everyone who could still stand rose to their feet and began squaring away their baggage in preparation to resume their trek. Then, as the crowd began to lurch forward, another anonymous male voice called out, suggesting that everyone wet a handkerchief and tie it around their face because the air in the city was otherwise certain to be too hot to breathe.

When Sayoko and Tanaka reached the west bank, they followed people down the embankment stairs to the water's edge to wet their handkerchiefs in the irradiated river water. They then tied these over their noses and mouths, pulled their *bōsaizukin* hoods back on, and pushed on into the city. Some stretches of Rijō Street were still burning; occasionally, columns of flame on opposite sides of the street would briefly shoot up—like earthbound solar flares—to join up and form short-lived archways of fire over the middle of the roadway. The girls passed under several of these on their way north.

Once the girls reached Takanohashi—the neighborhood near city hall and Bunri University where Sayoko had alighted from her street-car some six or so hours before—the fire hazards were largely behind them. This, however, was not due to any miraculous firefighting accomplishment. Rather, it was only because there was nothing there left to burn. In the northerly direction of their homes, everything in the girls' field of vision had been completely incinerated.

Faced with this bleak vista, the girls stood in place trying to figure out their next move. As they did so, they began to hear doleful, pleading moans all around them. Overwhelmingly, these pleas consisted of one word—"Water . . ."—and they were uttered by people who seemed about to die at any moment. Occasionally, someone might manage a more ambitious entreaty like "Please take me to Red Cross Hospital. . . ." But the girls had no water, so they could not help anyone with that. Moreover, they had already walked far past scenes of hellish bedlam at Red Cross, and they were not about to run the fire gauntlets on Rijō Street again to take people all the way back there.

The girls picked up their pace toward Kamiya-chō to get away from this miserable scene. While making good their escape, Sayoko avoided eye contact with the pleading people and repeatedly called out to everyone and no one in particular, "I'm sorry! I have no water! I can't help you! I just want to go home!"

As Yamaguchi recounts this scene, I can see that she is still (and quite understandably) rattled by these memories. I decide not to press this particular line of questioning, but she continues on her own.

Even now, she tells me, she occasionally dreams about the burn victims along the roadside in Takanohashi, particularly in times of stress. But in her younger decades, she was plagued by these dreams nightly.

In the usual version of the nightmare, she is pursued by legions of charred black figures chanting, *"Water! . . . Water!"* over and over while she tries to run away and suddenly finds that her legs do not work.

"I'm sure that no one came to save those people I passed," she says. "Every one of them must have died where they lay. . . . Even now, every time I think of those people, I silently pray to them for forgiveness."

THE BOY

AS SAYOKO AND Tanaka pushed into the ZTD, Rijō Street became increasingly clogged with rubble and bodies. By the time they reached "Bankers' Row," near the major streetcar crossing intersection with Kamiya-chō, their pace slowed to a crawl as each step they took required a laborious process of finding secure footing.

At the Kamiya-chō intersection, the way east, toward Hatchōbori and Hiroshima Station, showed some signs of having already been partially cleared. Unfortunately for the girls, they were headed in the opposite direction, toward the Aioi Bridge, and this way was covered in high piles of twisted sheet metal, concrete wreckage, and countless charred and torn-apart bodies. The roadway there was distinguishable from its surroundings only because the piles of wreckage that covered it were slightly lower and more level than the lumpier piles where buildings and storefronts once stood. Any of the scattered, shattered shells of recognizable structures that were still standing were too few and far apart to provide a sense of bearings.

Sayoko suspected that no one else had passed through this stretch of Aioi Street since the bombing, and at the moment there was not another living person in sight. Picking their way over the rubble during their treacherous trek to the bridge, the girls found it nearly impossible to take a step without stepping on a body, a body part, or some other patch of gore, and stepping too far or abruptly to avoid the same was to risk taking a spill on jagged wreckage. At one point, a nail from a piece of sheet metal popped through the sole of Sayoko's *zukku*. As she stopped to check her foot for injury, she came face-to-face with a human head with its eyeballs dangling out of their sockets. She was momentarily stunned, but a second wind of emotional numbing immediately kicked in to squelch this reaction. Without giving another thought to the head underfoot, she slipped her *zukku* back on and resumed climbing over the wreckage piles.

Recalling this scene, Yamaguchi falls quiet for a moment before trying to describe how she was able to keep going.

"In a situation like that, the human heart disappears," she says. "When I try to explain that in my lectures to schoolchildren, it's impossible. . . . It's a shocking tragedy when a single person dies before your eyes, but when many do all at once? Soon you're like 'Oh, here's one. . . . There's another . . . and another. . . .' It almost frightened me, how easily I was able to turn off my emotions like that. But I had to. I had to step on and over dead people to get home. If I'd been unable to do that, I wouldn't have been able to go on."

There is another pause before she repeats sotto voce, her voice halfway between clinical observation and confession, *"Sonna toki ni, ningen no kokoro ga kieru.* (The human heart disappears at a time like that.)"

It took the girls over an hour to traverse the five hundred meters from the Kamiya-chō intersection to the foot of the Aioi Bridge, where the volume of rubble finally began to taper off. From this vantage point, Hiroshima appeared utterly flat in every direction. To the west, north, and east, Sayoko could see all the way to the mountains ringing the delta.

On the opposite bank of the Ōta Honkawa, where Takajō-machi was supposed to be, there was nothing but a smoking rubble field. When Sayoko was faced with this scene and what it implied about her mother's fate, the tiny but stubborn hope that had kept her going to this point was snuffed out in an instant. Utterly defeated, she sat down on the ground, spent, done, ready to give up and die on the spot.

For the first time since the explosion, she began to weep.

Tanaka joined her, and the girls' mutually reinforcing wails rose into a single screamed crescendo of disappointment, exhausted frustration, and rage. With no one around to see or hear them, they were free to cry themselves hoarse, and did so.

Once they were all cried out, the girls sat in silence for long meditative minutes, looking at the hazy red sun beginning to go low. On the far bank of the river, there were no people, no barking dogs, no birds, no signs of life whatsoever. The only things moving in this Hades on earth laid out before their eyes were darting tongues of flame, plumes of smoke, and an unending sluggish stream of flotsam and bodies drifting by in the river current.

Tanaka finally broke the silence—speaking, in a sense, from a position of advantage. Her home was two kilometers farther to the north. It might have been true that everyone in Sayoko's family was dead, but the possibility that the explosion and the fires had not touched Ōshiba still allowed Tanaka the luxury of hope.

"Hey," she said to Sayoko. "*Ganbatte miyō.* (Let's go for it.)"

The spark of hope Sayoko got from Tanaka's remark spurred her to remember that Takajō-machi had a designated evacuation area in the rural district of Kawachi, about ten kilometers away in the northern approaches to the city. This was where residents were supposed to set up an encampment in the event that the neighborhood met with some calamity (like a flood or an earthquake—or an incendiary raid). Perhaps by some miracle, she thought, her mother and Yoshimi might have survived and they could now be waiting for her in Kawachi. That possibility, though paper-thin, was enough to get her up and going again.

The girls rose to their feet and ventured out onto the bridge. Although it was still standing, its roadway was buckled and twisted, and its handrailings had toppled northward. The footing there was not nearly as treacherous as it had been atop the rubble mountains of Aioi

Street, but the girls still proceeded slowly and carefully. Neither wanted to end up in the body-clogged Ōta Honkawa.

Once safely across, they continued west on Aioi Street. This was— or had been—a semi-suburban part of the city, so there was far less rubble on the roadway there than in the central business district. This made for much easier going as they headed toward their next waypoint— the streetcar intersection in Tōka'ichi-machi—where they would wheel right and head north toward the Yokogawa Bridge and, eventually, their respective destinations.

At least, that was the plan.

Along the way, Sayoko did not even bother to take a second look in the direction of Takajō-machi. There was nothing there now except roof tiles, ashes, and death. It was meaningless to give the place another thought, and she did not want to start crying again—certainly not with another ten kilometers of walking ahead of her.

The area around Sayoko's usual tram stop at Sakan-chō was strewn with the burned remains of people who had probably been caught in the open at 0815 while waiting for the streetcar. There were also numerous horses that had fallen by the roadsides—perhaps where they were being pulled by farmers and tradesmen headed to or from the bridge at the moment of the explosion. Now the heat-swollen bellies of these poor beasts were burst like water balloons, spilling tangled ropes of pink intestines out onto the ground. This was another traumatic visual Sayoko would have to carry around for the rest of her life, but at the moment, as with everything else in the day's nonstop stream of horrors passing under her gaze, she did not let the horse corpses rattle her nerves or slow her flow.

In the midst of this grim scene, the girls caught sight of a concrete box cistern—the type deployed in urban neighborhoods around the country for air defense firefighting. When they walked over to it to rewet their handkerchiefs and maybe splash a little water on their faces, they saw that it was bone-dry and packed wall to wall with charred black corpses. The people these pillars of charcoal had once been had probably jumped into the tank to escape from the fires, only to be boiled and, finally, incinerated in their would-be sanctuary.

"They were stacked like pencils in a pencil holder," Yamaguchi recalls.

When the girls reached the Tōka'ichi-machi streetcar crossing, a young man hobbled out of the dusky gloom to approach them. He was a few years older than they were—possibly even a university student— and did not seem to be burned. He was, however, limping and apparently in terrible pain. Sayoko looked down at his bad leg and saw that the jagged end of a foot bone was poking right through the canvas of his *zukku*.

According to the young man, whose name Sayoko never learned, he had been working at the Seiyōkan—a fancy restaurant on the seventh floor of a Bankers' Row office building—when the explosion occurred.[1] When he came to, he was lying on Rijō Street. He was not sure how he had ended up there, and he did not explain how he had gotten all the way from there to Tōka'ichi-machi with that foot—a journey that had just taken Sayoko and Tanaka probably the better part of two hours with the advantage of fully functioning legs.

The young man explained that he wanted to get back to his family home in the Gion District, about five kilometers to the north, and that—for self-evident reasons—he needed help getting there. The girls unhesitatingly assented to his request, but Tanaka inserted the proviso—with apologies—that she would be of help only as far as Yokogawa Station. From there, she would be heading off on her own to try to find her family in Ōshiba.

Using the same shoulder-propping technique they had used with Ueno that morning, the girls walked northward while the young man hobbled along between them on his good foot. Every few hundred meters or so, they would stop so the girls could switch load-bearing shoulders. These shoulder-change stops, especially, had to be done with extreme care, because whenever the young man's bad foot made any kind of contact with the ground, he experienced excruciating pain.

After hobbling a very long kilometer and a half, the trio reached Yokogawa Station. There they found an aid station set up in the Misasa Credit Union. All the windows had been blown out of the

two-story concrete bank building, but otherwise it was still structurally sound. In the wake of the fires that had completely consumed
everything else in the vicinity of the station, it was the only substantial structure still standing, and now it was filled with injured victims
being attended to by Navy medics.[2]

The girls carried the young man in and managed to flag down a
doctor to look at the shattered foot. The doctor took one look at the
protruding bone and, without even taking off the *zukku*, sprinkled a
little Mercurochrome on it, told his patient that he would just have to
make do with that, and sent the trio on their way.

Outside the aid station, Tanaka took her leave. As with Ueno and
everyone else from Dai Ni Ichijo, Sayoko never saw her again.

Progress slowed considerably now that Sayoko had to carry the
young man by herself. After walking another kilometer and a half, the
pair reached the Shinjō Bridge. This was one of the crossings connecting the tip of the northernmost Ōta Delta islet with mainland Honshu, and the last bridge before the young man's home in the Gion
District, which was still about a kilometer away up the Ōta valley.
Sayoko and the young man crossed the span in near-total darkness as
the moans of suffering people lining both banks of the Yamate River
below wafted up on the humid night air.[3]

It was late at night when the pair finally reached their destination—
a big house on a large plot with its own cow stall. There was a joyous
and tearful reunion with the young man's parents when their son
showed up at the front gate with his diminutive rescuer. Through
tears, the mother explained that the father had spent the better part
of the day looking for their son in the city, and had just returned,
empty-handed and despairing, not long before.

At this point, Sayoko was ready to soldier on to make the final five
kilometers of the forced march to Kawachi that night, but after the
Gion parents were given some of the details of the half day she had
just spent saving their son, they insisted that they be allowed to express their gratitude by giving her a bath and dinner and having her
spend the night at their house. Sayoko modestly declined these offers,
perhaps initially suspecting that they might have been made out of a

sense of obligation, in which case she would not want to be seen as taking advantage of the situation. But the parents were insistent and, ultimately, convincing. As they pointed out, it was late, there were no trains running, Kawachi was still a far way off, and Sayoko was clearly exhausted. She could get a fresh start to Kawachi early the next morning.

Once the parents had sequestered their broken boy away in a back room, the mother prepared a meal for their guest. It was the most sumptuous feast Sayoko had seen in years, and she felt grateful and flattered by the gesture and effort, but her guts were so knotted that she was barely able to get anything down. She forced down a few bites, out of politeness, and felt a pang of guilt later when the mother came to take away the barely touched dishes of precious food.

Sayoko was next given a clean towel and *yukata* bathrobe, then shown to the bathroom, where a steaming *gyūnyūburo* milk bath awaited, ostensibly with the cooperation of the family's dairy cow. Sayoko wished she could have indulged in this rare luxury and kindness with the enjoyment it deserved, but after the day she had just experienced, this was impossible. Her body might have been comforted by the warmth of the milk bath, but her mind was still in torment, trapped as the day's horrors—and imagined visuals of her mother under the wreckage of their apartment—flashed before her eyes in an endless loop. Weighed down by these thoughts and visions, she sank deeper into exhausted depression.

After the milk bath, the mother showed Sayoko to an upstairs guest room, where a fresh futon had been laid out for the honored guest. When Sayoko was confronted with this newest round of kindness and generosity, her thoughts returned to her own mother, and she felt her eyes well up with tears.

Sayoko spent a long while staring out the guest room window, which faced in the direction of downtown Hiroshima. From there, she watched underlit red clouds slowly drift over the still burning city. Imagining her mother and Yoshimi somewhere underneath that sky and almost certainly dead, she felt tears begin streaming down her face. She was still crying when she finally decided to turn in.

Despite the most bone-deep exhaustion she had ever experienced, sleep was elusive while the day's traumatic images—again, both real and imagined—continued to flash past her mind's eye. There might have been a point, in the wee hours of the morning, when she was finally about to nod off, but this slipped away when the young man of the house began screaming in pain downstairs as his desperate parents tried to comfort him. Imagining the pathos playing out beneath her futon and the tatami floor, Sayoko found herself grieving for someone other than herself for the first time since the explosion.

Some hours later, she was dozing in a half-awake fugue state when the mother of the house poked her head in the guest room doorway to deliver probably the cheeriest "Good morning" she could have managed under the circumstances.

Sayoko had now been awake for nearly forty-eight hours straight.

Outside, August 7 was turning out to be just as sunny and beautiful as August 6 had been—at least up until 0815. Sayoko found it difficult to believe that the horrors of the previous day and night had actually transpired between two such beautiful mornings. For the briefest merciful moment, it almost seemed possible that it all might have been just a bad dream. But then all the images began rushing back. The previous day's catastrophe had happened. It was real.

The mother prepared breakfast, but as with the previous night's meal, Sayoko could barely manage a bite, and once again the young man of the house—who was now ominously silent—was nowhere to be seen. Sayoko wondered if he had survived the night.

After a round of profusely expressed mutual gratitude with the mother, Sayoko took her leave. The visual memory of the young man's parents waving farewell, standing under a front gate framed in bright red crepe myrtle, is one Yamaguchi can still recall as clearly as if it happened yesterday.

One day about a year after the war, Sayoko was passing through the Gion District. Taking advantage of the occasion, she decided to drop by the young man's house to pay her respects and, if this proved necessary, stand a stick of incense for him at the family *butsudan*.

The lady of the house greeted Sayoko at the front gate—which still had its happy archway of bright red crepe myrtle—and related the news that their son had passed away on the last day of the war. Unlike the traumatic experiences so many hibakusha reported having had when they encountered the parents of dead peers in the period immediately after the bombing—encounters Sayoko also experienced—there was none of that tense atmosphere of accusation and surviving-child envy (for lack of a better term) on this occasion. The bereaved mother was gracious and seemed genuinely happy to see that Sayoko had survived. Moreover, as the mother related, if her son had not had the good fortune of meeting Sayoko at that intersection in Tōka'ichi-machi, her husband and she would never have seen him again. They were eternally grateful to Sayoko for giving them one last week with their boy.

THE MOTHERS

Kawachi-mura

Ten kilometers northwest of Ground Zero

SAYOKO ARRIVED AT Kawachi sometime around midmorning on August 7. After asking around as to the whereabouts of evacuees from Takajō-machi, she was directed to a large farmhouse. There, in a big tatami-floored living room, she found some fellow harmonica house residents and other neighbors, who—considering that they were still alive—had ostensibly been far away from Takajō-machi when the explosion occurred.

But her mother and Yoshimi were nowhere to be found. As the implications of their absence began to register, Sayoko sat down on the elevated floor ledge where the tatami room opened out onto the farmhouse yard. Swamped by a new wave of grief and disappointment, and feeling every bit of the accumulated effects of consecutive days of crushing exhaustion, she stared out at the sun-drenched yard in a daze.

In the midst of this mental fugue, she was suddenly and rudely yanked back into the here and now by a harsh, familiar female voice calling from across the room.

"Hey! Aren't you Sayo-chan?"

Sayoko turned to face her interlocutor. It was the mother of a girl named Sumiko, who had been a neighborhood friend in Sayoko's earlier childhood.

"Our Sumiko hasn't come back," Sumiko's mother snapped while swiftly closing the distance to get in Sayoko's face. Then her voice ratcheted up into an accusatory shriek. "What are *you* doing here?!"

She punctuated the latter remark by grabbing and shaking Sayoko's shoulders, her face twisted up in a combination of indignation, despair, and rage. Then, just as suddenly as her outburst had boiled over, she broke down in racking sobs.

But the woman was far from defeated. In fact, she had not yet begun to fight. While still weeping, she latched onto Sayoko's hand with a death grip that suggested both frantic desperation and the likelihood that she had no intention of letting go anytime soon.

"That moment was the guiltiest I have ever felt about my own survival," Yamaguchi recalls, possibly adding another motive—to the more obvious pity and intimidation—for why she remained in this excruciating situation instead of trying to escape: She might have believed, even subconsciously, that she deserved to be dragged over the coals a bit.

"It was not until marrying and having my own children," she says, "that I was able to understand how Sumiko's mother must have felt."

Around this time, an announcement made the rounds that an Army truck was ready to ferry people to Takajō-machi if they wanted to look for loved ones. The panicked mother's ears perked up at this, and she lurched back into action mode. Bolting upright, she pulled Sayoko out to the roadway and manhandled her onto the truck bed with other evacuees. Captor and captive rode in tense silence during the thirty-minute drive into the city.

The truck's passengers dismounted to find what Sayoko already knew: There was nothing left of Takajō-machi but scattered mounds of roof tiles and ash. Here and there, the mauve gray monotony was broken up by the odd concrete air defense cistern or cast-iron pump spigot poking up out of the rubble. As the other residents filed off into this bleak landscape to begin their own hopeless searches, Sumiko's mother pulled Sayoko along by the hand until coming to a stop on a pile of roof tiles.

"I think our house was around here," she pronounced to her captive. "We are going to sit here and wait for Sumiko to come back."

The pair sat in this spot for the rest of the day, under a blazing sun, with no shade or cover and no water or food. As the hours progressed, bodies underneath the rubble began to stink in the heat. But Sumiko's mother made no attempts at conversation. Instead, she shouted, "Sumiko! Sumiko!" at the mute ruins of Takajō-machi over and over until she went hoarse, all the while clutching Sayoko's hand tightly. Bolstered by a flimsy but—for the time being—still functioning psychological scaffolding of angry desperation and unreasonable hope, she had not cried since the farmhouse, and she showed no signs of giving in to despair now.

During this interminable interlude, Sayoko passed the time—perhaps as a means of holding on to her own sanity—by looking out over the rubble and trying to mentally picture what had been standing there the day before. At one point, she was fairly certain she had determined the location of her family's place, which had been about fifty meters away from Sumiko's. But the moment she tried to get up and go over to take a look, she was yanked right back down by her captor's death grip.

Around sundown, the Army truck returned to take everyone back to Kawachi. Nothing changed in the captor-captive dynamic once they arrived at the encampment; Sumiko's mother still refused to let go of Sayoko's hand, and she was still holding on tight when the pair went to sleep on the farmhouse floor tatami that night. Sayoko still made no attempt to escape the situation.

August 8 was a miserable repeat of August 7. The Army truck once again took them to Takajō-machi, and another day was spent on the same patch of rubble under the same blazing sun while Sumiko's mother incessantly and almost mechanically called out for her daughter and Sayoko stared off into space. At the end of the day, the two rode the truck back to the camp, again in silence, with Sumiko's mother still holding on to Sayoko's hand.

Yamaguchi has no recollection of eating or drinking anything throughout this entire two-day ordeal, nor how or even if either captor or captive ever went to the bathroom in the interim.

Sayoko's day of liberation finally dawned on August 9. Her unlikely rescuer was Sumiko's father, who had shown up at the Kawachi encampment that morning. He was likely just beginning to process the implications of his daughter's absence from the camp when he caught sight of his wife clutching on to the Yamaguchi girl. Like a patient father addressing a hysterical child, he carefully and firmly explained to his wife that the girl she was holding was not Sumiko and that she had to let her go. Now.

With his words, all the frantic energy that had sustained his wife's angry denial and fight over the past two days seemed to melt away in a moment. She released her involuntary daughter replacement and promptly burst into tears.

Sayoko's last image of the scene was of a sad man trying in vain to console a sobbing woman. She never saw either of them again.

Not long after this, Sayoko experienced her first joy since the explosion when Yoshimi showed up at Kawachi. Upon catching sight of each other, the sisters ran into each other's arms and wept.

That morning, Sayoko took her fifth and final ride on the Takajō-machi Army truck shuttle. But this time she was accompanied by her sister. During the ten-kilometer ride into the dead city, sixteen-year-old Yoshimi recounted her August 6 experiences. When the explosion occurred, she had been at work in the post office near the Sumiyoshi Bridge (about 1.5 kilometers southwest from Ground Zero). She dove under a desk in the four to five seconds between the flash and the arrival of the shock wave. Miraculously, she had not received as much as a scratch during the collapse of the post office, but she had, however, been trapped under her desk by the wreckage. While she struggled to find a way out of her predicament, she traded encouragement with another female employee—the postmaster's sister—who had sought shelter and was now also trapped under another desk in the office.

The two had just managed to crawl to freedom when a strange black rain began to fall.[1] When Yoshimi made it to Kawachi three days later, she was still wearing the same white blouse, stained gray and dirty brown with the stuff, she had been wearing on the day of the explosion.[2]

After escaping from the ruins of the post office, the women had taken a boat across the Ōta and made their way to the Yoshida-chō house of the postmaster's relatives. Yoshimi had stayed with them until she left for Kawachi on the morning of the ninth.

When the Army truck from Kawachi arrived at Takajō-machi, the sisters got out and started digging around in the rubble near the spot that Sayoko had determined, during her long hours there with Sumiko's mother, was the location of their apartment. Amid the ashes, they found the blackened skull of the three-year-old son of their next-door neighbors, the Tomitas. Reorienting from this grisly find, the sisters shifted their excavation efforts a few meters over and soon began unearthing fragments and shards of familiar-looking cups and bowls. Realizing that they were standing over what had been their kitchen, they began digging with renewed vigor, expecting to find their mother under the rubble at any moment. But they came up empty.

Wrapping up the fruitless Takajō-machi excavations, Yoshimi suggested that they move the search down to the Ōta Honkawa, where the Army was lining up bodies along the embankments for identification while they waited to be cremated. The sisters started from the Honkawa Bridge, a few hundred meters downstream from Aioi Street. In addition to the corpses lined up on the embankment, there were still many the soldiers had yet to retrieve, eddying in place in low-tide shallows. Yoshimi and Sayoko took the embankment stairs down to the water's edge and waded out into the midst of the bodies. They looked closely at every one that they could grab hold of and that still had some semblance of a face. The sisters were able to identify the remains of numerous neighbors and acquaintances during this water search, but at least as far as they could ascertain, their mother's body was not there.

Next, they worked the opposite bank of the Ōta, and then both banks of the Motoyasu—still finding nothing—before returning to street level on the east bank of the Motoyasu. There they ventured inside the half-collapsed domed ruins of the Hiroshima Prefecture

Exhibition Hall. Its once grand exhibition galleries were filled with hundreds of bodies, with many, as Yamaguchi recalls, for some reason sitting upright. The only audible sounds in this eerie space were of blowflies swarming over the corpses and, in the distance, the echoed commands of soldiers and police officers manning field crematoria. There was no sign of their mother.

As they were about to close up their exhibition hall search, they noticed that the sun was getting low. Unless they wanted to walk ten kilometers, they were going to have to hurry to catch the Army truck to Kawachi. But when the girls arrived back in what had been their old neighborhood, the other evacuees who should have been sifting through the rubble there were nowhere to be seen. Realizing that the Army truck had left without them, Sayoko started to cry.

"What use is crying going to do?" Yoshimi snapped before grabbing Sayoko's hand and pulling her away in the direction of Tōka'ichi-machi to begin the long haul to Kawachi. They would be retracing the same route Sayoko and her classmate Tanaka had taken almost exactly seventy-two hours earlier.

When they got to Tōka'ichi-machi, they saw an Army aid station that had been put up along the main north–south street leading to Yokogawa Station. The structure was not much more substantial than a lean-to, with a "roof" of corrugated metal sheets propped up on a light frame of wooden beams. Woven reed mats, hung from the eaves like curtains, served as the structure's "walls." The girls decided to go in and look for their mother, bowing as they entered and apologizing for the intrusion to everyone within earshot.

There were about twenty patients here. Each was laid out on the ground on top of a tatami mat—the wood-framed type used in house flooring. The girls made a quick round of the space and confirmed what they had expected going in: no mother. With another apology delivered to the lean-to's occupants, they left and continued north.

When they reached the Yokogawa Bridge, they encountered another of the curtain-walled Army aid stations, essentially identical to the one they had just left in Tōka'ichi-machi. Anticipating yet another disappointment, and with nightfall imminent, the sisters briefly considered bypassing it and pushing on to Kawachi. After some discussion, they agreed that it would be better to check anyway rather than to regret it later. Muttering, "What's the use?" and "She's not going to be here either . . . ," they made their way toward the lean-to.

While they were still outside, the girls caught a glimpse, through the opening between two of the reed curtains, of familiar-looking blue-and-yellow-ochre kimono fabric. Uttering quick apologies to whoever was lying behind it, they pulled back the curtain and could not believe their eyes. It was their mother—Mume—stretched out on a tatami mat.

While her daughters bawled with joy and relief, Mume—in a faint, cracking voice—said, "Thank goodness you are alive." Reaching up to stroke her daughters' cheeks, she began weeping, too.

Once her tears subsided, she began telling them about her August 6.

She had been in the kitchen when she saw the flash, which she barely had time to register before everything went black. When she came to, she found herself buried under the wreckage of the apartment. The air—filled with dust and, ominously, smoke—was difficult to breathe. Somewhere over her head, she could make out a small patch of daylight. With her free right hand, she began moving bits of wreckage out of the way, piece by piece, to try to open a path toward the light. Eventually, she was able to crawl free.

Noticing that fires were closing in on Takajō-machi, she determined that the best escape route out of the area was to the west. She set off, barefoot, for her sister-in-law's place in Nakahiro-machi, on the west bank of the Tenma River. Normally, she would have taken the Hirose Bridge to cross the river, but this wooden span had been destroyed by the explosion. Meanwhile, there were fires coming up behind her, and the air was becoming superheated and increasingly difficult to breathe. She had no choice but to try to wade across the river. But in her injured (and catastrophically irradiated) condition, she did not make it far before she felt her strength drop off steeply. Whatever adrenaline had carried her this far was now tapped out. Just as she began to feel herself slip under the surface of the river, she was pulled out of the water by a soldier who watched over her for several hours until they eventually came to the Yokogawa Bridge aid station.

As she listened to her mother's miraculous evacuation story, Sayoko shuddered when she realized how close she and Yoshimi had come— twice—to possibly never finding their mother: first, when they had missed the Army truck back to Kawachi; and second, when they had come so close to giving this lean-to a pass as they made their way north.

THE FISHING VILLAGE

Yokogawa, Hiroshima
1.3 kilometers north-northwest of Ground Zero

AFTER THE INITIAL elation of their reunion, Yoshimi and Sayoko were faced with the hard reality of their mother's condition. She was burning up with fever and in the grip of a lethargy that made every physical movement—even just speaking—an effort that seemed to tax her to the limits of her endurance. She had not been able to eat or keep any food down since breakfast with her daughters on August 6, three and a half days ago. This might have explained some of her lack of energy, but it was clear there was more to it than that. Mume was seriously ailing from something, but her daughters had no idea what it was.

The only visible injury Mume had from the bombing was a small burn on one of her elbows. But now, three and a half days later, it showed no signs of the beginnings of any normal healing process. In addition to the burn, Mume also had large circular discolorations around her eyes. These were not painful to the touch and thus did not seem to be bruises or contusions of any kind, but they were conspicuous and unsettling.

"They were like the patches around a panda's eyes," Yamaguchi recalls, "but purple . . . not black."

Still, neither the burn nor the unusual skin discoloration seemed sufficiently dire to explain the severity of Mume's condition. And while Yoshimi and Sayoko would have been correct in dismissing the elbow burn from consideration as something potentially life-threatening, they could not have known that the purple circles around their mother's eyes, the high fever, the lethargy, and the complete loss of appetite were all of a set of symptoms of grave portent: The August 6 new-type bomb had emitted something that had destroyed the natural regenerative capacity of more cells in Mume's body than her still functioning cells could replace or repair. Too much damage had happened too quickly, and as a result, she was dying from the inside out.

Nor were there any explanations forthcoming from the two orderlies who seemed to be the only staff manning the aid station— soldiers who were barely older than the Yamaguchi girls and clearly in over their heads. As there were no medicines or salves on hand to administer to the fifteen or so patients in their charge, actionable care on the part of the soldiers was limited to not much more than attending to body-soiling issues and placing wet towels on the foreheads of the feverish.

Beyond their heartfelt but completely ineffective towel therapy, any other treatment the soldiers could provide was limited to palliative care. The no-water-for-the-injured combat-medicine rule of thumb had apparently been waived at this particular aid station, and the soldiers gave the patients water when they were thirsty—which was constantly, especially for the burn victims. When their patients' pain was especially bad, the soldiers—lacking any supply of analgesics—could not offer much more than softly voiced encouragements and the laying on of sympathetic hands.

Adding to the overall atmosphere of filth and misery, the blowfly-and-maggot plague that had descended upon the city in earnest from the morning of August 8 did not overlook the aid station. The pain and maddening itching caused by the maggots immeasurably compounded the misery of patients already in agony from injuries and rapidly worsening ARS. Although any scrape, laceration, or bodily orifice was fair game for the egg-laying flies, they reserved particular enthusiasm for the oozing wounds of burn victims, which seemed to draw the flies like homing beacons, and in which the insects' larval offspring positively thrived.

The soldiers did what they could to try to pull the maggots off their patients, but it was a losing battle. They were no match for the fecundity of the swarming insects rioting in this target-rich environment. Luckily for Mume, she was not severely burned or lacerated, so she was not particularly tormented by the flies, which in any case had plenty to occupy their attention and appetite elsewhere.

The girls passed their first night in the aid station sleeping directly on the ground, flanking their mother's tatami mat and holding tightly to its cherished occupant. As the lean-to was not substantial enough to merit its own field generator, the interior went pitch-black with nightfall. Making their rounds in the dark, the soldier-orderlies must have done so relying primarily on their sense of sound and touch. But despite the total darkness, stomach-turning smells, and bloodcurdling sounds of her current environs, Sayoko lay next to her mother that night and experienced a sense of reassuring peace and calm happiness that she would never forget.

This comforting interlude was short-lived. In the middle of the night, a man on a nearby tatami mat began repeatedly calling out for his mother, and woke up everyone in the lean-to. In time, the man's initially desperate voice steadily weakened, then eventually faded out for good.

Even after all the death Sayoko had seen over the past three days, there was still something terrifying and oppressively intimate about being in that pitch-black space with a stranger taking his last breath. While the soldiers rustled around in the dark to take the dead man away—most likely to the nearest field crematory—Sayoko tightened her hold on her mother and tried to go back to sleep.

When Sayoko and Yoshimi woke up on the morning of the tenth, Mume's fever had still not broken. Following the soldiers' example, the girls took turns going down to the river to wet towels for her forehead—a ritual that by this point might have been a gesture of filial devotion as much as it was a well-meant but futile attempt at actual therapy. But at least it gave the girls a confidence-boosting and

anxiety-reducing locus of control regarding their circumstances, and
Mume was fortunate to have loved ones by her side to offer such emotional support. The other patients in the lean-to were not so lucky:
Alone and dying, they spent their remaining time moaning and writh-
ing on their tatami mats or staring into space as they waited for the
end. When that end arrived for one patient after another, other dying
people were immediately brought in to take their places on the va-
cated and effluvia-soiled tatami mats.

Later that morning, Yoshimi announced that she was going to try
to make her way to the Yamaguchi relatives' place in Nakahiro-machi,
which Mume had been attempting to reach when she was rescued
from the Tenma River. No good deed going unpunished, Yoshimi's
recon mission caused her to miss out on the *onigiri* rice balls the soldiers distributed around the lean-to shortly after she left. These had
been made with pure white rice—a luxury most likely courtesy of the
Army Food Depot in Ujina—and Sayoko, with her appetite now recovered, was able to enjoy this rare delicacy thoroughly. It had been so
long since she had last eaten real white rice—probably since before the
war—that she had almost forgotten what it tasted like. Mume, however, had no appetite at all. After taking one bite of her own rice ball,
she gave the rest of it to Sayoko.[1]

In the afternoon, Yoshimi came back from Nakahiro-machi bearing mixed news: The Yamaguchi relatives were all right and their
house was still standing, but there was no room at the inn. They had
maintained, with regrets, that they simply did not have the space or
wherewithal at the moment to take in three more people.

Yoshimi had also returned from her expedition bearing gifts: As a
parting gesture, the Nakahiro-machi Yamaguchis had given her five
or six ripe tomatoes from their truck patch wrapped up in a *furōshiki*
cloth to take back to the aid station. These were promptly cut up with
a knife borrowed from one of the soldier-orderlies, and everyone in
the lean-to received a slice. The afternoon treat provided a brief respite from the prevailing gloom hanging over the hot, humid, and
death-reeking space.

With the Nakahiro-machi house now out as a potential refuge, the girls decided that they would try Mume's family—the Ōshimos— at the home of her brother Kōichi in Miya'uchi, a suburb on the western shore of Hiroshima Bay. As they had no access to telephones in their current situation, they would just have to show up at the doorstep and hope for the best. But they would cross that bridge when they came to it. First, they had to figure out how they were going to travel the fourteen kilometers to get there.

On the morning of the eleventh, they were presented with a solution when they heard that westbound San'yō Line service from Yokogawa Station had resumed. The news that the trains were temporarily fare-free to handle evacuee and relief traffic from and to the city was also welcome, as the Yamaguchis, at the moment, had nary a thin sen among them.[2]

Eager to escape their current situation as soon as possible, and aware that, in the miserable aid station, Mume was getting nothing in the way of care that they could not provide themselves in more comfortable surroundings, the sisters hurriedly made preparations to get moving. After offering thanks to the soldiers and farewells and apologies to the other patients for the presumptuous cheek of daring to leave the aid station ahead of everyone else, the Yamaguchi women headed off for Yokogawa Station. Mume was too weak to walk, so Yoshimi, the older and larger daughter, had to carry her piggyback the half kilometer to the depot. Once there, she had to continue carrying Mume through pushing, impatient crowds to board a train that was already hopelessly mobbed. None of the passengers was willing to give up a seat for the obviously ailing Mume. But things went easier for the obviously struggling Yoshimi when a cluster of passengers shuffled out of the way to make room for her to set her dying mother down on the floor.

When the Yamaguchis arrived in Miya'uchi, they were taken aback at how lovely it was—certainly in comparison with what they had just escaped. There were no visible effects whatsoever from the bomb here other than, perhaps, a temporary increase in foot traffic on the roads. As they walked through the village, it was hard to tell there was even a war on; everything was as green and tranquil as the Yamaguchis remembered it from peacetime visits.

The Ōshimos' house was not spacious by any measure, but Uncle Kōichi and his family were happy to take in his sister and nieces when they arrived, and they promptly joined in the caregiving rotation for the rapidly declining Mume. Uncle Kōichi even prepared a poultice of crushed raw land crab—a local folk remedy, apparently—to apply to his sister's burn. It was completely ineffective, but the Yamaguchis were touched by the gesture nevertheless.

The Ōshimos were also generous enough to share their meager rice rations, although the feverish Mume was unable to partake of any. In place of solid food, and despite the sweltering weather, she constantly asked instead for hot green tea and would complain about it being tepid when it was brought to her, even when the beverage was still only seconds out of the kettle. Seeing this, Sayoko began to process the reality that her mother's ailing was not a temporary condition and that various functions of her body—and perhaps also of her mind—were beginning to shut down. Nevertheless, she did what she could to help her mother be as comfortable as possible in whatever little time she had left.

On August 13, Miya'uchi's sole air raid siren sounded moments before American Hellcat fighters came in for strafing runs—probably attacking the fishing port and train station as targets of opportunity on their way back to their aircraft carriers from their primary missions. The Ōshimos had evacuated to the shelter trench in their yard when the siren started, but as Mume could not be moved, Yoshimi and Sayoko stayed to huddle with her on the living room tatami as the low-flying planes roared over, rattling the roof tiles and the windows of the house with their screaming engines. If she had to die, Sayoko thought, at least it would be at her mother's side.

Miya'uchi raised no antiaircraft fire of any kind. Nor were there any Japanese defenders in the air—a typical situation in the final months of the war, when most of the country's planes had been sequestered away in camouflaged revetments and caves, where they were being held in reserve for higher-priority kamikaze missions in the fall. Thus unopposed, the American attack was long and unhurried—almost leisurely. The planes would come in low, zooming hither and thither over the rooftops to shoot up the village with machine-gun fire before climbing to altitude, turning around, and coming in for more.

Eventually, Sayoko's irritation and curiosity got the better of her fear and she ran to the *genkan* to take a look outside. As soon as she slid open the front door, an American pilot must have caught sight of the movement, because a plane immediately banked in for a strafing run on the house. Bullets kicked up dust in the front yard—scant meters from Sayoko's feet—before the plane roared over, low enough for her to catch a brief glimpse of a begoggled and broadly grinning American pilot. At this, she bolted back to the living room and got under the futon covers with her mother.

The atmosphere in the Ōshimo household quickly returned to normal after the nevertheless not unprecedented drama of the air raid, and in the meantime, Mume's decline continued. Perhaps knowing that her time was limited, she began asking to see Shizue, her youngest daughter, who had evacuated Hiroshima to live with Mume's older sister, Ozaki Hama, in the mountain hamlet of Yūwa-mura, where the Ōshimo siblings had been born and raised. Uncle Kōichi was able to get a telegram through to Yūwa-mura that afternoon, and a response finalized plans for Shizue and Aunt Hama to visit. They arrived around noon on the fourteenth, after walking nearly eight kilometers down from the deep mountains to reach seaside Miyauchi.

Around two that afternoon, Mume called everyone to her futon.

"Yoshimi, Sayoko, Shizue . . . ," she said in a weak voice, "Mother doesn't have much longer, so listen to me. . . . Promise to take care of each other, and to never become the kind of person who causes trouble for others. If your brother comes home, I want you to take care of him, too."

Then Mume turned to her brother and sister-in-law.

"Please look after my children . . . ," she managed through labored breathing and tears. "*Onegai . . . onegai . . .* (Please . . . Please . . .)"

A few seconds later, she took her last breath. In that moment, Sayoko wanted nothing more than to die with her mother, and her screamed declaration to that effect was met with a quick surge of sobs from the assembled before a shroud of somber silence descended upon the space.

=====

After passing the night in a bedside wake for Mume, the Yamaguchi-Ōshimo funeral party walked down to the bay. Uncle Kōichi led the way, pulling his sister's blanket-wrapped body in a wheelbarrow while the womenfolk of the two families brought up the rear of the procession. At the water's edge, a temporary cremation spot had been designated to handle overflow from the atomic bombing—the returned remains of Hiroshima commuters from the village or of refugees, like Mume, who had made it all the way to Miya'uchi only to die there. Corpses were cremated in the order that they were brought in, and while the bereaved families waited for their turn, they combed the beach for pyre fuel.

Mume was burned at noon, just as Emperor Hirohito was addressing the nation—speaking to his subjects directly for the first time to tell them that the war had "not necessarily developed in Japan's favor." In his speech, His Majesty added that the Americans had begun to employ a "cruel new weapon" to bring about this unfortunate turn of events, and that if not only the Japanese race and its culture but human civilization itself were to survive this menace, Japan had no choice but to "endure the unendurable," accept what had happened, and take on the task of rebuilding toward a better future.

The funeral party found out that the war was over only after they had made their way back up to the village. In the instant that Sayoko heard this news, she felt relief at the idea that this meant there would be no more air raids. But she entertained this comforting thought for only a moment before silently scolding herself for the selfish indulgence of daring to experience joy upon hearing of Japan's defeat. The news hit Sayoko hard, as she had always considered herself an exemplary and to-the-bone *gunkokushōjo* ("devoted little soldier girl"), and having this happen on top of the loss of her mother immeasurably compounded her dejection. Thinking of all that the war and the bomb had taken from her, she felt that she had nothing left to live for. Her life and her world were in shambles, and her sole aspiration at the moment was what she had loudly professed in the Ōshimos' living room the day before: to follow her mother into death as soon as possible.[3]

This was Sayoko's mindset for the next two months as she lived with Yoshimi at the Ōshimo house (Shizue had returned to Yūwamura with Aunt Hama shortly after the funeral). But things finally took a turn for the better on October 27—four days after Sayoko turned fifteen—when, much to the tearful joy and relief of his sisters, Shizuo showed up at the Ōshimos' *genkan*, still in his Navy uniform.

Shizuo had been working in machine shops at Yokosuka Naval Arsenal when the war ended, and he had been stuck there assisting the American-supervised dismantling of the base until his demobilization a few days earlier. He had known all this time that Hiroshima had been completely destroyed by something people were calling an atomic bomb, but with no way of contacting a home that no longer existed, the fate of his loved ones had been left to his imagination. He had made the multiday-long, seven-hundred-kilometer trip from Yokohama expecting the worst, and these trepidations about the fate of his family members seemed confirmed beyond doubt when he saw what was left of Takajō-machi. During this grim sojourn, he suddenly remembered his uncle Kōichi in Miya'uchi and headed back to the train station. He hoped against hope to find his family with the Ōshimos, even as he prepared for the worst.

He was overjoyed to find his trepidations disconfirmed this time around—at least partially—and kept up a brave face when he was handed his mother's ossuary jar to embrace.

He let his sisters do his crying for him.

BLACK-MARKET YAMS

Kōya'ura, Aki District
Ten kilometers south-southeast of central Hiroshima

AS THE NEW head of the Yamaguchi household, twenty-two-year-old Shizuo now had mouths to feed. For the time being, this familial need was being covered by the generosity of the Ōshimos. But with his sisters' Miya'uchi sojourn now stretching into its third month, the proud ex-Navy man must have found it intolerable to depend on Uncle Kōichi's largesse one day longer or one meal more than absolutely necessary—particularly in this season of nationwide near starvation. In their rural location, amid barely interrupted fishing and agricultural activity, the Ōshimos might have been relatively well situated for food compared to most of their compatriots, but they were by no means completely impervious to the privations of the time. Outside the mess halls and PXs of the nation's new American military bases, life in early-postwar Japan was not putting meat on anyone's bones.

Eager to escape the accruing shame debt of his present circumstances, Shizuo did not have time to dwell upon his mother's death, nor upon the post-defeat loss of identity and purpose that accompanied the loss of his uniform—a condition that he shared with millions of other young men in the desolate Japanese autumn of 1945. He banished these affairs of the heart to the basement of his psyche, filling his days instead with the effort to find work and then, in time-honored

Japanese fashion, burying himself in it. With commendable alacrity, he found a full-time position putting lathe operator skills he had picked up in the Navy to use in the locomotive shed of the Hiroshima Railway depot.

By the end of November, he applied for and secured public housing for himself and his sisters in Kōya'ura—a hardscrabble hamlet on the coastal road between Hiroshima and Kure. But before the siblings could make the move and set up their new household, a decision had to be made about custody of eleven-year-old Shizue. Uncle Kōichi and Aunt Hama expressed concern about the ability of Shizue's siblings to care for a child under the difficult circumstances then prevailing in Hiroshima. Considered but left unvoiced among these objections/reservations might have been concern over what would come to pass in the young household when one or both of the girl's bomb-exposed older sisters succumbed to some yet-latent radiation ailment. Nevertheless, Shizue was adamant about wanting to go to Kōya'ura, and in the end, her wishes were respected. With thanks and apologies to Uncle Kōichi and the rest of the Ōshimos for an unforgivably long imposition of three months, the siblings headed off to Kōya'ura to begin their new life together as a family.

The public housing project they moved into had originally been put up as barracks for wartime civilian workers at Kure Naval Arsenal, and durability and comfort had evidently not been prioritized during the facility's design and construction. The units offered little in the way of interior privacy, and the apportionment of utilities was typical for contemporary Japanese working-class housing: In the Yamaguchis' two-story apartment, there was a sink with a faucet and a wood-fire *kamado* stove for cooking in the upstairs kitchen, an electrical socket on each floor, and no bath. Having running water—at least in the kitchen—was a major improvement over their old lifestyle, but other than that, the new place was basically more of the same quality of life that the family had known in the old Takajō-machi harmonica house—only much less conveniently located this time around. Still, the siblings were proud of their new independence, and they did what they could to turn the place into a home.

In the distribution of family duties, the two eldest siblings worked days, with Shizuo at the train depot and Yoshimi returning to her old job at the Sumiyoshi post office, which had been hastily rebuilt after the bombing and was now up and running again. Shizue resumed her studies to finish compulsory education (under the prewar education system) at Kōya'ura Elementary School. As for Sayoko, the responsibility for keeping everything running smoothly on the home front fell on her narrow but sturdy shoulders. In this homemaker role, she spent most of her days outside scrounging for food for the household.

The end of hostilities had brought no improvement in the late-war food-supply crisis in Japan, and the situation was considerably exacerbated as more than 5.5 million servicemen and civilian colonists began to make their way home from the far-flung reaches of Japan's former overseas empire.[1] Near-starvation conditions were the norm for most Japanese for at least the first year or so of the postwar period, especially in urban areas, and a nationwide humanitarian catastrophe was averted—only narrowly—by a massive infusion of emergency food aid via the Licensed Agencies for Relief in Asia (LARA), a program for the distribution of American charity aid that was regulated and logistically assisted by the occupation forces.[2] But the LARA aid could go only so far; more often than not, there simply was not enough food to go around, and having cash on hand was not always enough to surmount the problem, either by legal means or by alternatives. Even for the Yamaguchi household, with its two gainfully employed, full-time breadwinners, feeding four mouths was a constant—and frequently frustrating—challenge. During some lean stretches, the family was forced to subsist for weeks on end on nothing but flavorless sweet potatoes that Sayoko was able to score from the black marketers who plied their trade behind Kōya'ura Station. On days when the police and MPs disrupted this trade, as they were wont to do on occasion, the Yamaguchis would go to bed hungry.

The family's situation enjoyed a vast improvement in 1948 when Yoshimi's postmaster boss, Mr. Matsuoka, introduced them to better housing in the Gion District. After the move, Shizuo got a higher-paying lathe operator's job at the nearby Mitsubishi Heavy Industries

plant, where Sayoko—now eighteen—also found part-time employment. She worked the day shift and, with classmates consisting almost entirely of other Mitsubishi workers, took night courses toward
her GED (under the post-1948 national education reform) at the new
Kabe Prefectural High School. Being able to return to school was a
tremendous boost to her self-esteem, as the interruption of her studies first by war labor mobilization and then by grinding postwar
poverty had long been a source of regret and shame for her.

Shizue also thrived in the new environment, enrolling as a student at Gion Junior High School.[3] Quite out of the blue, for all concerned, the Gion move also led the now fourteen-year-old girl to Jesus.

CHRISTIANIZING JAPAN

DURING HIS 1945–1951 tenure as supreme commander for the Allied powers (SCAP), General Douglas MacArthur ruled as a virtual modern-day *shōgun*, wielding powers of dictatorial fiat with flair and charisma undergirded by a lifetime's worth of unshakable faith in the divinely ordained nature of his own infallibility. Never a man to let policy set by mere mortals impede the fulfillment of his destiny, the general saw his mission in vanquished Japan as much more than the mere application of efficient military governance; he sought nothing less than to transform country, culture, and people—lock, stock, and barrel—into something more amenable to the requirements of American empire and Western civilization.[1] This mission required him "to be . . . a theologian of sorts . . . ,"[2] MacArthur later said while reminiscing about the period, during which he took it upon himself to provide the "spiritual guidance" that he believed Japan needed in the wake of its defeat.[3]

The centerpiece of MacArthur's grand vision for the future of the country was his passionately held conviction that everyone in it— from the emperor on down—should accept Jesus Christ as their personal savior. And he was not discreet about expressing his views publicly, once proclaiming his hope "that Japan will become Christianized," assuring his audience that "every possible effort to that end is being made."⁴ When reminded by his own administrative staff that such a policy went against the very same separation of religion and state concept that the occupation forces were using to dismantle State Shintō, MacArthur responded that "[as long as] no religion or belief [was] *oppressed*, the Occupation [had] every right to propagate Christianity" to save Japan from what he was convinced was its spiritually rudderless condition.⁵

Approaching their mission, the general and his fellow crusaders seem to have started off with bad directions and on multiple wrong feet. First, they were unrealistically optimistic regarding the gratitude with which they assumed the Japanese people would embrace an alien belief system imposed by (or via) an army of foreign occupation. Still heady with victory, MacArthur and the missionaries were deeply steeped and supremely confident in the superiority and centrality in human history and affairs of their own Judeo-Christian worldview. This gave them a certain air of cultural arrogance to which the still freshly humiliated Japanese were stingingly sensitive and, as such, naturally but by no means uniformly resentful.

On a philosophical/theological level, this same arrogance also seems to have rendered MacArthur and his inner circle of SCAP yesmen unable to conceive of a culture being able to function without a faith-based revealed religion as its foundational keystone—a function that, they assumed, had been previously fulfilled by the State Shintō that had recently been catastrophically delegitimized by Emperor Hirohito's surrender.⁶ This misconstruing of State Shintō as a "religion" in the Western sense led, in turn, to another crucial misinterpretation: that its demise had discredited Japanese culture in toto, thus rendering eighty million Japanese hearts and minds—now presumably bereft of a functioning belief system—into so much clay for their new Christian masters' hands. This erroneous reading of the lay of the land of Japan's postwar cultural landscape led to an almost palpably giddy expectation on the part of the country's occupiers that the Japanese man in the street would, as if grasping at straws, accept the first replacement belief system that came along after the collapse of State Shintō and its emperor cult. Taking this assumption to its logical conclusion, the Americans believed that if enough missionaries could show up as johnnies-on-the-spot before representatives of a rival ideology could do the same, Japan would be Christianity's for the taking—a goal that, admittedly, made a certain realpolitik sense against the backdrop of the opening rounds of the Cold War as American strategists fretted over the possible spread of Socialist thought in Japan via post-defeat disillusionment among the general populace and, more specifically, the enchroachment of Soviet influence via Communism.[7]

Missionary zeal and optimism in the high fever of this early-postwar moment was embraced not only by SCAP, but also by Washington policymakers and numerous influential figures in American Christianity whose organizations provided a large share of funding for LARA aid. Dr. Louie D. Newton, president of the Southern Baptist Convention, declared that the occupation presented "an opportunity without counterpart since the birth of Christ for the spread of Christianity among the peoples of the Far East."[8] In 1947, a Protestant missionary returning to America from a tour of duty in Occupied Japan reported that "the Christian gospel now finds an open door" in the country.[9] Seeing the opportunity to use a gospel hammer to strike geostrategic iron while hot, Washington shared in the enthusiasm and lent a hand; with the encouragement and active assistance of SCAP and the blessing of the Truman White House, Japanese-language-trained missionaries—and Japanese-language Bibles—were dispatched along with church-funded LARA aid to the occupied country by the shipload.[10] But in the end, not even the flooding of the supposed spiritual vacuum of postwar Japan with Bibles and bright-eyed missionaries could change the reality that the native culture was more resilient than the occupation forces had anticipated, and that its contituents were in no hurry to toss their cultural baby away with the bathwater of the now debunked State Shintō.[11]

In their respective attempts to fathom and penetrate Japan, the shoals upon which Francis Xavier in the sixteenth century, MacArthur in the twentieth, and all the other ultimately disappointed Christian missionaries in between inevitably foundered were their fundamental respective failures to grasp one critical point: Over its long centuries of evolution, Japanese culture has imbued its human constituents with an innate immunity to exactly the kind of existential exigence—the hunger for answers to impossible "why" questions about the "meaning of life," etc.—that has primed Westerners to crave the spirtual comfort offered by Christianity. A person does not harbor fears about the fate of their immortal soul if they do not believe in— or cannot even really conceive of—such a thing in the first place.

In the Japanese solution to the human condition, people could lead meaningful lives through the diligent performance of social roles and duties in the immediate here and now. Moreover, none of this socially constructed Japanese reality required any kind of theological validation—only an innate shared awareness that this worldview was held by an overwhelming majority of the people who inhabited the country, where they were sufficiently shielded from alternatives by the formidable culture-protecting ramparts of geographical distance/ isolation, a notoriously difficult native language, and, last but not least, a natural proclivity for xenophobia. Thus safely guarded and blissfully immersed in the framework of their own culture—which conditioned them from birth to be satisfied with their lot and to keep their noses to their assigned grindstones—the Japanese were entirely capable of leading perfectly satisfying and meaningful lives without the imprimatur of a divine Creator, the belief in an immortal soul, or the expectation that someone "up there" was actually listening to the prayers they offered (mostly for good luck) at shrines or temples.

For people securely ensconced in an existentially well-shielded cultural space like Japan's, the idea of whiling away one's life yearning for transcendent meaning and musing about eternity would seem patently pretentious and ridiculous—if not downright decadent, morally suspect, and malingering—when there was always honest work waiting for idle hands. While Japanese culture appeared to the outside observer to be abundantly festooned with all manner of brocade-robed trappings and incense-wreathed rituals of religion, these visible artifacts of spirituality were, at least for the Japanese layman, less in the nature of liturgical expressions of faith and yearnings for the divine of the kinds familiar to Westerners and more along the lines of reminders of obligations and reassurances of stability and continuity expressed through the faithful preservation of tradition—existential guardrails for the smooth governance of society. The bottom-line message of all these traditions and rituals that ordered and provided rhythm to Japanese daily life was a simple one: Because they promoted the common good, the virtues of duty, selflessness, frugality, and tradition were sacred ends in and of themselves; therefore, to be a good person, valued by others, required nothing more than their faithful observance.

Schools and workplaces were more important than temples or shrines in the maintenance of this fundamentally Confucianist belief system, which required no scripture, no supernatural embellishment, no personal relationship with divine beings, and no guarantee of personal immortality beyond a humble assurance that a lifetime of selfless hard work would be its own reward, contributing in some way—be that great or small—to the eternal continuance of family, community, and way of life. From the perspective of people thus protected and existentially grounded, the appeal of Christianity's selling points was meager, particularly in light of the sacrifices that conversion to the faith would demand and the risk of social ostracism it would entail by smacking of cultural betrayal and disloyalty to one's ancestors.

As with all fundamentally insular cultures, the traditional Japanese meaning-making system functioned optimally in an echo chamber; as such, its minders and guardians were ever wary of its potential disruption by outside influence. Although the first Portuguese barques that began showing up off the coast of Kyushu in the mid-sixteenth century were initially welcomed as curiosities and harbingers of potential mercantile opportunity, the wielders of Japanese political power soon began to fear the Christian proselytization that came as part of the intercultural exchange as just such a destabilizing force—as something that, left unchecked, could bring cultural chaos and possible regime collapse in its wake. When one considers what Portugal and Spain were already doing in other parts of the world at the time— exploiting colonial beachheads in Central and South America and Oceania secured beforehand by landing parties of missionaries and mercantile carpetbaggers—this suspicion was not unreasonable. In response to this perceived threat, the shogunate that ruled Japan from the early seventeenth century to the mid-nineteenth century closed the archipelago to foreign intercourse and waged a campaign of merciless extermination against Christianity during its entire time in power.[12] Even with the subsequent so-called opening of the archipelago to Westerners and Western know-how, the new Meiji regime busily using this know-how to turn Japan into a major modern world power nevertheless saw it prudent to maintain bulwarks against the unchecked spread of Christianity; unable to resort to the torture, forced apostasies, and outright slaughter available to their political forebears toward such ends, they created State Shintō instead.[13]

A loss of political legitimacy along the lines that the shogunate and the modern, nation-building Meiji Era government feared was exactly what happened to Japan in 1945—at least temporarily. And in the classic modus operandi of would-be Western colonizers since the days of Hernán Cortés, it was a lapse the Allied occupation—spearheaded, in part, by missionary opportunists—moved quickly to exploit.

These efforts enjoyed a degree of early success. There were undoubtedly significant numbers of Japanese for whom their native belief system was functioning at less than optimal capacity—with obvious psychological consequences—during the period of instability and chaos in the immediate aftermath of the war. Under such circumstances, some Japanese might have converted to Christianity because it appeared to offer a quick fix for their temporary existential confusion. Hiroshima and Nagasaki—essentially sociocultural tabulae rasae in the aftermath of the bombings—could be considered textbook examples of this phenomenon, and as such, the cities saw considerable missionary activity immediately after the war. But postwar converts—whatever their motives—never materialized in numbers sufficient to bring about a critical mass of fundamental change in Japanese culture itself. Not even in the atom-bombed cities.

What MacArthur had accurately perceived in early-postwar Japan as a rudderless condition was not indicative of some mass crisis of spirituality or cultural collapse. Rather, what he was actually observing was Japanese culture and the Japanese state in the midst of a reset, wobbly while the former processed the psychological shock of defeat and the latter adjusted to the collapse of its legitimizing ideology. Full cultural and political recovery would begin with the return of a convincing native framework of meaning making to Japanese life—one in which the Japanese could immerse themselves with the same intense sense of duty fulfillment and belonging as the belief system that had given their lives meaning prior to the 1945 surrender. Once that replacement ideological apparatus was up and running—and based this time not on militarism, but on neo-mercantilist capitalism—Christianity's great moment of opportunity in Japan had passed, probably never to return.

After three years of energetic Christian proselytization efforts with the full blessing and active (if not always flagrant) political and even logistical support of SCAP, the number of Japanese Christians had barely budged since the beginning of the occupation; it still stood at the same 0.6 percent of the national population.[14] Eventually, even MacArthur knew he was licked—at least on this front. By 1949, with presidential aspirations now in the rearview mirror of his life (greatly reducing the return on investment for continued soldier-of-Christ grandstanding on his part) and more important geostrategic fish to fry in the wake of the "loss" of China to Mao Zedong's Communists, the general found himself having to admit that "pride of race . . . would prevent most Japanese from becoming Christian."[15]

A NODE OF CHRISTIAN ACTIVITY

Catholic Diocese of Hiroshima

WHILE THE BIG-PICTURE assessment of the faith's future in Japan might have been bleak, there were a handful of nodes of Christian activity in the archipelago that flourished in the postwar period. This was not, for the most part, a result of SCAP-backed Occupation Era missionary work. Rather, it was because vibrant Christian communities had already existed in these places before the war. One such region included the capital and neighboring Yokohama, where Christianity had made inroads through the sheer volume and degree of Western cultural influence and intercourse that Central Honshu had experienced since the mid-nineteenth century.[1]

Christianity enjoyed greater success, both traditionally and in the modern era, in the western part of the country—particularly in Kyushu, where Francis Xavier and the Jesuits first made landfall in Japan in the mid-sixteenth century.[2] A key center of the faith's influence in the region was the four-hundred-year-old Catholic community in Nagasaki, where an essentially direct atomic bomb hit killed nearly half of the city's twenty thousand faithful. Nevertheless, that community was able to claw its way back from the brink of extinction under the stewardship of the politically savvy Bishop (later Archbishop) Paul Aijirō Yamaguchi and the charismatic leadership of Nagasaki Medical

College professor Nagai Takashi.[3] By the late 1940s, with considerable support and encouragement from the commander of local occupation forces, US Army lieutenant colonel (and observant Catholic) Victor Delnore, Nagasaki's Catholic community had made amazing strides toward recovery and had also achieved worldwide name recognition as a sentimentally appealing symbol of a peaceful "new" Japan's rebirth from atomic ashes.[4]

Hiroshima was another node of Christian activity in western Japan, albeit on a far more modest scale. The establishment in the city of a small but vigorous Catholic community had been accomplished largely through determined (though far from spectacularly successful) missionary efforts beginning in 1882.[5] Over subsequent decades, a handful of sparsely but loyally attended parishes had been established across the city proper, and a Jesuit novitiate—prominent in the national Catholic community—had been built on a hilltop in the suburban Gion District neighborhood of Nagatsuka.

In 1923, the Chūgoku region was elevated to an apostolic vicariate of the Diocese of Osaka.[6] Its seat was established at the Church of Our Lady's Assumption in the central Hiroshima neighborhood of Noborichō.[7] Leadership of the new Vicariate of Hiroshima was entrusted to a cadre of scholarly German Jesuits affiliated with Sophia (Jōchi) University in Tokyo.[8] With a few exceptions, these Germans were not, as a group, particularly blessed with charisma or gripped with missionary zeal, and a case could be made that many of them were more interested in studying esoteric aspects of their host culture than in preaching the merits of their own.[9] For this and myriad other reasons—including local cultural obstacles—long decades of proselytization on the Jesuits' part had produced only perennially small numbers of regular Catholic parishioners—hundreds compared with Nagasaki's thousands—and, with the exception of a significant but relatively brief uptick in the wake of the atomic bombing, downright abysmal numbers of new converts. Still, despite its relatively small size, the Hiroshima vicariate punched above its weight in terms of local prestige. This was due in large part to what was widely perceived (and appreciated) as the sincerity, perseverance, and erudition of its Jesuits—almost all of whom were fluent and literate in Japanese—and because of the order's long and respected contributions to education and tireless charity work in the city.

The outbreak of war with America and its allies presented challenges to the vicariate, but these were not insurmountable. While the white faces and culturally alien clerical garb of the Jesuits drew increased and occasionally hostile attention from local authorities and self-appointed civilian superpatriots,[10] the Germans were able to carry on business as usual, as they were not subject to detention in wartime internment camps. Nor were Spanish and Irish clergy, as they were considered neutral nationals. Three French nuns at the small Misasa Convent (2.3 kilometers from Ground Zero) were also treated as neutral nationals—even after their homeland rejoined the Allies upon its liberation from Nazi occupation in 1944—and they were similarly allowed to go about their business unmolested for the entirety of the war.[11] Others in the vicariate, however, were not so lucky: Belgian Jesuit Ernest Goossens, along with eleven American nuns—teachers at Seishin Girls' School (present-day Notre Dame Seishin Women's University)—were rounded up and sent off to spend nearly two years in Miyoshi Internment Camp, deep in the mountainous interior of Hiroshima Prefecture, before their repatriation in September 1943.[12]

The Jesuits also received a tremendous boost in prestige with their courageous and selfless actions in the aftermath of the atomic bombing.[13] Although the Nobori-chō rectory was only 1.2 kilometers east of Ground Zero, its sturdy construction saved the lives of its residents. After the blast, the walking wounded there bandaged up themselves and their colleagues and, in a highly visible and courageous act of charity that the Japanese residents of the city would never forget, rushed out into the burning streets of their neighborhood to help other victims, ignoring their own injuries and the very real danger that—as visibly conspicuous Caucasians—they might be set upon by enraged mobs at any moment.[14] Similarly, care for bomb victims tendered by the Nagatsuka novitiate—4.7 kilometers northwest of

Ground Zero—also garnered considerable goodwill from the people of the city, regardless of religious affiliation, particularly in the local Gion District.[15]

The master of the Nagatsuka facility—responsible for the spiritual guidance and professional training of thirty-five young Jesuit novices (both Japanese and foreign)—was a small, wiry, prematurely balding, and dazzlingly intellectual thirty-seven-year-old Basque named Pedro Arrupe. Before entering the Jesuit order in 1927 to begin his formal training for the priesthood, Arrupe was a medical student at the Complutense University of Madrid, where his outstanding intellect, scholarly discipline, and maturity beyond his years had won him admission at the tender age of fifteen. After the dismantling of the Jesuit organization in his homeland at the hands of the new Spanish Republican government in 1932, Arrupe continued his studies toward ordination in Belgium, the Netherlands, and the United States before receiving his first missionary posting—to the Jesuit vice province of Japan—in 1938.[16]

What would eventually stretch into a twenty-seven-year-long sojourn in the country began with a two-year program of intensive Japanese-language study at the Nagatsuka novitiate. After this, Arrupe was dispatched to the Jōchi Catholic Settlement in Tokyo to continue his language development and familiarize himself with the folkways of the Japanese working poor—a traditionally key target demographic for Christian missionaries in the country. He was then assigned to missionary duties in Yamaguchi Prefecture, Hiroshima's neighbor to the west. This was the old stomping ground where Xavier, another Basque Jesuit, had once similarly toiled to spread the gospel among a largely unappreciative and eventually hostile native populace some four centuries earlier.[17] As with his sixteenth-century Jesuit predecessors, Arrupe also eventually had a brush with local authorities because of his religious activities: During his Yamaguchi mission, he was arrested by the local Special Higher Police on a trumped-up suspicion of espionage immediately after the Pearl Harbor attack, and he was detained for over a month.[18] Despite his legal status as a Spaniard and thus a diplomatically protected neutral national, he was subjected to rigorous interrogation and other hardships during his detention.[19]

After his release, he was posted back to the Hiroshima vicariate, where he became master of the Nagatsuka novitiate. He was serving in this capacity on the morning of August 6, 1945, when shattered survivors from the city began staggering up the slope to Nagatsuka in search of help. Putting his old medical school training to good use, he quickly organized his novices to help him convert the novitiate building into a field hospital. Over ensuing days, weeks, and months, he and his "medical team"—augmented in short order by local volunteers—cared for hundreds of in- and outpatient bomb victims. Even though the novitiate initially had almost nothing at hand in the way of medical supplies, it boasted a survival and recovery rate that would have been the envy of the professional staff of an established hospital.[20]

Riding on a wave of gratitude and goodwill in Gion throughout the early years of the postwar period, the Nagatsuka novitiate could count among its accomplishments highly successful proselytization efforts at the local Mitsubishi Heavy Industries plant. These were conducted with the full support and blessing of corporate management (who likely found this eminently preferable to their workers falling under the sway of Socialist/Communist rabble-rousers).

Another early high point for the burgeoning local Catholic community was reached when the young German Jesuits at Nagatsuka built a church and kindergarten compound directly adjacent to the Mitsubishi plant in 1949.[21] This effort was led by the energetic Father Lorenz Laures (1915–1993), the strapping young nephew of Father Johannes Laures, SJ, a Sophia University professor who had achieved academic renown before the war as an economist and a historian of the early Catholic experience in Japan.[22] To what—if any—extent the elder Father Laures used his influence to get the Jesuits to send his nephew to Japan is information that has been lost to the ages, but the posting kept the young German cleric in Sophia University and Nagatsuka and not in a Wehrmacht chaplain's uniform on the Russian front during the war years. Ever since arriving at Arrupe's novitiate, the younger Laures—a rare exuberant extrovert among the company he kept—tended to be at the center of the action whenever physically arduous work had to be done, and he was always enthusiastic about interacting with Japanese civilians in Gion.[23]

Late in the afternoon of August 6, 1945, word had reached the novitiate that four of their Jesuit brethren in the Nobori-chō rectory—including Father Hugo Lassalle, the vicar of Hiroshima and the senior Jesuit in Japan at the time—had been badly injured in the explosion that had apparently destroyed the city that morning.[24] The church and rectory had both burned down in the fires following the blast, and the four clerics were now awaiting rescue about five hundred fifty meters north of Nobori-chō in Izumi-tei Park (modern-day Shukkei-en Garden) on the west bank of the Kyōbashi River, where hundreds—perhaps thousands—of other survivors were seeking shelter from the fires.

Upon receiving this report, Arrupe organized a rescue party—including himself, Laures and five other German priests, and two Korean novices—to go into Hiroshima to find their colleagues and bring them back to Nagatsuka.[25] The party immediately began making preparations for the expedition, including crafting a makeshift stretcher from scrap lumber and canvas strips. Just before they set out, Arrupe made the observation that the workaday, Roman-collared clerical uniforms they were wearing at the moment might make them conspicuous foreign targets for the vengeful rage of survivors in the city (the faces of the Westerners in the search party would already be conspicuous enough).[26] Accordingly, he directed the rescue party to change into rough mufti. Ironically, as the change of clothes obfuscated their easy identification as clerics—particularly in the dark and smoke-shrouded environment they were about to enter in downtown Hiroshima—Arrupe's decision came close to getting them all killed.

After a trek of several hours, the rescue party reached Izumi-tei Park long after nightfall. There they found Lassalle and the three other Nobori-chō rectory Jesuits—Hubert Cieslik, Wilhelm Kleinsorge, and Hubert Schiffer—alive but in varying degrees of injury. Bandaging the wounded up with the meager supplies at hand (including newspapers) and bundling the more seriously injured Lassalle and Schiffer up on their makeshift stretcher, the party was getting ready to set off on the long walk back to Nagatsuka when their attention was drawn to an approaching commotion. A senior Japanese officer at the head of a patrol of soldiers had overheard the rescue party speaking in a foreign language (German) and was now charging the Jesuits, yelling loudly and brandishing an unsheathed katana sword. Assuming that those in the incongruous party of foreigners were American soldiers or spies, the apoplectic officer seemed determined to behead them on the spot.[27]

While Father Arrupe and the rest of his colleagues were apparently frozen in place by the sudden development of this life-threatening situation, the quick-thinking Laures was able to keep his wits about him. Miraculously not getting shot while doing so, he charged the approaching officer and grabbed his sword arm. Then, while the officer was probably registering his own shock, Laures managed to communicate, in the best Japanese he could muster in the heat of the moment, that he and his party were not Americans but Germans.[28] After a few moments of dicey back-and-forth, the situation was defused when the officer was eventually convinced of his error. Sheathing his sword, he mumbled some excuses about the need to be vigilant about enemy parachutists, and he and his patrol went on their way.[29]

CONVERSION

Nagatsuka Jesuit novitiate
Gion District, Hiroshima
4.8 kilometers north-northwest of Ground Zero

IN YAMAGUCHI SAYOKO's memories of late-1940s Gion, Father Laures "was a ball of energy." Never really one for the kind of daily schedule favored by most of his colleagues—with time carefully set aside for long hours of scholarly solitude, prayer, and quiet reflection—the young German priest was constantly on the move. When not building churches or blowing his gospel horn to save souls at Mitsubishi Heavy Industries, he was making the rounds at night on his noisy motorcycle—a gift from his wealthy sister in Germany and an attention-grabbing rarity in postwar Japan—to proselytize at the homes of the Nagatsuka novitiate's Gion neighbors. He was also an enthusiastic and much-beloved Sunday school instructor for local children and Bible-class teacher for local adolescents and adults—team-teaching after morning Mass with the equally beloved but temperamentally very different Father Arrupe, who, with his ever-present beatific smile and invariably mellow demeanor, was a smooth natural at what might be called the soft sell. At the end of every Sunday Mass, Arrupe used to stand outside the door of the novitiate and greet each parishioner by name, always adding, "*Mata raishū ne* (See you next week)," to make sure they understood that they were expected to return.

In stark contrast with the mellow Arrupe, Laures was something of a firebrand. Once, while making a particularly emphatic point during a sermon, he brought his hand down on the pulpit with such force that he broke his wristwatch. Despite his dramatic rhetorical style—which from the perspective of a Japanese audience would have seemed quite alien, coming from a religious authority figure—Sayoko believes Laures was able to bring in a sizable number of converts in Gion through sheer charisma and enthusiasm alone. And at least for a while, the number of worshippers who came to Mass each Sunday seemed to increase weekly.

Although he was generally liberal and almost playful in his approach to most other things, Laures' old-school Jesuit side came out during Mass, when he was hypervigilant and uptight about decorum and protocol—often to the amusement of the cheekier local children. When another priest had the pulpit, or when the congregation was singing or praying, he would stalk around the tatami-matted floor of the church and scold parishioners—usually elementary-school-aged boys—for behavioral infractions or perceived lack of sincerity, which he was known to punish by witholding communion occasionally. He also held parishioners of all ages to a very strict dress code for Mass, prohibiting the showing of bare arms, legs, and feet, even in the unairconditioned, hellish heat of a Hiroshima summer.

These weekly flashes of his inner martinet aside, the well-being of his parishioners was always on the young priest's mind. Acutely conscious, in particular, of the grinding poverty most of them had to endure in their daily lives, he did what he could to make their lives easier. The Nagatsuka novitiate seems to have been one of the institutions entrusted by local authorities with LARA aid supply distribution in the Gion District, and whenever a new shipment came in, Laures would make sure that everyone got their share. On one such occasion, he gave Sayoko a bolt of navy-blue corduroy cloth from which she made her first Western-style single-piece dress to wear to work (she had been wearing her school uniform—the only real clothes she owned—for everyday dress up until then). She wore the navy-blue dress for years.

Shizue had been the first of the Yamaguchi siblings to begin attending Bible classes at the novitiate after being invited to do so by a
junior high school classmate. It was not long before Sayoko and Yoshimi noticed the glow of inner peace and purpose their youngest sibling seemed to have about her when she came home from her studies
with Laures and Arrupe every Sunday. The foreigners' enthusiasm for
proselytization seems to have rubbed off on her, as well, as she soon
began pestering her older sisters to start attending the novitiate sessions with her. Sayoko and Yoshimi were initially loath to give up
their only day off from work for this purpose—especially when nice
young men became part of their lives—but in the end they were no
match for the persuasive power of Shizue's earnest enthusiasm. After
a while, the sense of community provided by the goings-on at the novitiate began to grow on the Yamaguchi sisters and rapidly draw them
into the faith.

In the meantime, to ensure that the new sheep in his flock did not
lapse during the week, Father Laures made sure to keep the Yamaguchis' flat at the Mitsubishi family dormitory in his regular nighttime
proselytization rounds. In a soul-saving hat trick that most certainly
would have gotten the young German in the good graces of Father
Arrupe, Laures eventually managed to convert all three of the Yamaguchi sisters; Shizue was the first to be baptized, in 1948, after which
she started doing part-time work at the Gion Church kindergarten
with nuns from the Congregation of the Sisters of the Immaculate
Heart of Mary (Junshin Sisters)—trained preschool-education specialists who had been dispatched to Gion by their Nagasaki mother
superior, Sister Ezumi Yasu. Sayoko and Yoshimi followed her into the
faith the following year when they were both baptized by Laures on
Easter Sunday 1949.

Although not for Laures' lack of trying, there was yet one holdout
in the Yamaguchi family—Shizuo. Long after the Yamaguchi sisters
had all undergone their baptisms, Laures continued to come around
to the Mitsubishi dorm for his weekly visits as he battered away at the
spiritual ramparts of this stubborn would-be convert. But it was of no
use; as Shizuo put it when he finally convinced the headstrong young

German to lift his siege, he was all in favor of his sisters exercising the new postwar freedoms and their right to follow any religion they chose. But as the surviving head of the Yamaguchi household, he did not have that luxury. He had greatly enjoyed their years of Bible study together. He appreciated the wisdom and human decency of the teachings of Jesus. For all he knew, the God and heaven stuff might even all have been true. But family duty was family duty, and as such, he was less concerned about his own soul than he was about his obligation to attend to the graves of his Pure Land Buddhist parents and offer up prayers for his Yamaguchi ancestors. He would do this for the rest of his days, until his death in 2007.

As for Sayoko's sisters, their Catholicism remained a central part of their lives—also to the end of their days.

After winning her fiancé over to the faith, Yoshimi was married at Gion Church in 1953 in a ceremony officiated by Father Laures. She started a family with her husband and stayed in Hiroshima until her death in 2006 from leukemia—a common later-life bane of hibakusha.[1] Her attending physician at Hiroshima Red Cross Hospital and Atomic-Bomb Survivors Hospital attributed her development of the blood disorder to her exposure to radiation in 1945, probably most critically from the black rain that had soaked the clothing she wore for days after the bombing.

Upon her graduation from Gion Junior High, Shizue attended Funairi High School before matriculating at Junshin Junior College in Nagasaki, where she majored in preschool education. In 1955—at the age of twenty-one, and seven years after her conversion to Catholicism—she took her vows to enter the Junshin Sisters. Like most nuns in the order, she went on to a career focusing on kindergarten teaching. She stayed on the job until forced to retire due to poor health in her early seventies. The cause of her physical decline was soon diagnosed as leukemia, for which she began receiving inpatient treatment at the Archdiocese of Nagasaki–administered Saint Francis Hospital. Although she had not been directly exposed to Little Boy's burst of initial radiation, Yūwa-mura—where she had been living with her aunt at the time of the bombing—had been in one of the wide-ranging precipitation zones of the black rain that fell over the Greater Hiroshima area on August 6, 1945. Her physician at Saint Francis attributed her leukemia to her childhood exposure there.

During the year or so in which Shizue was hospitalized, Sayoko would fly down to Nagasaki once a month to spend a weekend with her. On the occasion of her August 2007 visit, however, Shizue's physician quietly suggested to Sayoko that she try to extend her stay for a week, as her sister did not have much time left. When Shizue heard about Sayoko's plans to extend her visit, she expressed her displeasure about being responsible for making her sister stay away so long from her husband back in Tokyo. Refusing to be persuaded otherwise, she held her ground until Sayoko agreed to go home. When the doctor asked Shizue if she would not feel better with a family member around, Shizue replied, "The sisters of the order are my family. I'll be fine." As Sayoko was heading out the door of the hospital room, Shizue said, "Well, I guess the next time we meet will be at my wake."

Six days later, she was dead.

"Shizue was a saint all of her life, to the end of her days," Sayoko recalls. "She was always a peerless example of how to live. . . . I've never seen someone die so beautifully and peacefully. . . . She was truly a person blessed by God."

BREAKING THE SILENCE

Higashi Yamato City
Greater Tokyo
Present day

SHORTLY AFTER BEGINNING her part-time work at Mitsubishi Heavy Industries in 1948, Sayoko met a tall, handsome, and almost comically taciturn full-time employee named Tado Yoshito. Six years her senior, Yoshito had been lucky enough to avoid conscription for most of the war because of his work at Mitsubishi. But the IJA had eventually caught up with him, and he had passed the entirety of his miserable but mercifully short time in uniform stationed in Shikoku, preparing defenses against the Allied invasion. In Matsuyama, some sixty kilometers across the Seto Inland Sea from Hiroshima, he heard Little Boy's explosion and watched with his stunned squad mates as the mushroom cloud poked up over the horizon.

The couple's relationship deepened through their mutual attendance first at Bible classes at the Nagatsuka novitiate, then at Gion Church—where they were married in 1954 in a ceremony once again officiated by the ubiquitous Father Lorenz Laures. Over the next three decades, Sayoko followed Yoshito around to various Mitsubishi postings, raising a prodigiously large family in company housing. During this period they spent most of their time in the Kanto area, and it was where the couple decided to stay after Yoshito's retirement.

When Yoshito left Mitsubishi in 1985, the Tados bought their house in Higashi Yamato City near Yoshito's last place of full-time employment. Sayoko continues to live there today. One of her first memories of the moving day was of walking through the front gate of the house and into its preplanted garden, where there was a big bush of bright red crepe myrtle. As soon as she laid eyes on it, she flashed back to the front gate of the Gion farmhouse where she had passed the night of August 6–7, 1945. In her mind's eye, she could see the grateful but melancholy faces of the parents of the broken boy she had brought all the way home to Gion; she remembered them waving goodbye as she set off for the Kawachi-mura evacuation site and her encounter with Sumiko's mother. All of this came back to her in an instant, casting a sad little cloud—which she kept to herself, as usual— over what should have been an otherwise happy first day of the beginning of the rest of her life with the man she would love through thick and thin.

———

Until the political earthquake of the *Lucky Dragon* Incident threw open the floodgates of hibakusha discourse from the mid-1950s on, Sayoko remembers there being a strong but unspoken understanding among bomb survivors never to talk about their experiences—not only in public, but even with one another. And being interrogated about the bombing by curious non-hibakusha at school or in the workplace—even when the questions were genuine expressions of concern and sympathy—was something most hibakusha dreaded and loathed. In Sayoko's experience, this moratorium on "war stories" about the bomb had little to do with fear of being revealed to others as a hibakusha—a waste of mental and emotional energy, in any case, when almost everyone else in her daily environment, even down to the foreign priests in her church parish, was a hibakusha, as well. What was really behind the hibakusha omertà of the first ten years or so after the bombing was a perfectly natural but—as most hibakusha eventually realized—ultimately hopeless attempt to forget that worst

day in their lives. With survivor guilt of the type experienced by hibakusha like Sayoko—who were ashamed at how little they had suffered
relative to others—the code of silence became even more restrictive.

Sayoko kept quiet about the bombing and avoided any kind of memorialization sites or activities related to it for well over a quarter of a
century, even during the long postwar years she spent in Hiroshima.
Her troubled relationship with her bomb memories, though, began to
loosen up after the Tados moved to Higashi Yamato City in the early
1970s on the occasion of Yoshito's last Mitsubishi posting. The move
also coincided with the approach to adulthood of her oldest children—
a life milestone that, along with her own entry into middle age,
marked on her part a period of reflection on and reassessment of the
road she had traveled so far.

In the midst of these momentous life changes, Sayoko began
sharing in the fellowship of other atom bomb survivors one evening a
month after joining the Yamato-kai—the Higashi Yamato City branch
of the Hidankyō hibakusha organization. Following the practice of
most Hidankyō branches around the country, the Yamato-kai would
select one member to attend the official memorial ceremony at Hiroshima Peace Park every August 6 as a representative of the group. In
1975, Sayoko was picked as the year's representative to make the Hiroshima trip. Although she had never attended one of the Peace Park
ceremonies nor even watched one on television, and had, in fact, never
even entered the park or visited its museum because of her bone-deep
fear of experiencing traumatic flashbacks, she was not prepared to risk
the enmity of her newly found support group by refusing to perform
her appointed task. She made the trip, and, just as she had feared, in
the middle of the ceremony while she was sitting with the assemblage
in sight of her old Takajō-machi neighborhood, she had an anxiety attack that was so bad, she came close to passing out. Upon her return
to Tokyo and her attendance at the next Yamato-kai meeting, she dutifully reported the details of her trip, ending with a recounting of
what she had experienced at the ceremony and a polite request that
she not be asked to go through it again. To this day, she has never
watched a Peace Park ceremony on television, and she has never been

to any kind of exhibition of atom-bomb-related materials or artifacts, either in Hiroshima or anywhere else.

One morning at home in 1989, Sayoko was working in the kitchen when her peripheral vision suddenly went dark. A moment later, she passed out and collapsed on the floor. Luckily, Yoshito was on hand to call an ambulance. At the hospital, Sayoko underwent various tests, after which the attending physician informed her that she had very high blood pressure. She has managed this just fine with medication over the ensuing decades, but still, the fainting spell was a coming-attractions trailer of approaching senescent frailty—the kind many of us, including the author, first experience at the tail end of middle age.

Moreover, as is inevitably the case when an atomic bomb survivor experiences a sudden health issue out of the blue, the occasion also evoked fears about 1945 radiation-exposure damage finally rousing from long dormancy—a scenario the inveterately optimistic Sayoko had largely successfully managed to banish from daily consciousness for decades. Reassuringly, her doctor did not believe the problem to be bomb related—adding that the high blood pressure was more likely a combination of advancing age, genetic predisposition, and, probably more than any other factor, working too selflessly and hard for her family—something Sayoko had been doing her entire life. Immersed in her old-school Japanese-female-duty ethos and, since late adolescence, sustained by her Catholic faith, she had always selflessly and consistently put the interests and needs of others ahead of her own—until her body pumped the brakes at the gates of old age.

After the fainting episode and the hypertension diagnosis, Sayoko called Yoshimi in Hiroshima for advice, as she usually did when something was on her mind with which she did not want to burden her husband and children. The gist of the conversation was that while fate might have given Sayoko a pass this go-round, she might not necessarily be so lucky the next time. If the worst ended up happening, and the ailment turned out to be something bomb related, she could at least avoid becoming a ruinous financial burden on her family if she would finally get around to getting a *hibakusha techō* card.

Getting the card was something Sayoko had been resisting doing ever since the enactment of the national Atomic Bomb Medical Assistance Law in 1957, even though she was more than qualified for the benefit. The most important reason for her resistance was that, quite simply, she did not feel that she deserved it. As far as she knew, she had not received as much as a scratch from Little Boy, whereas there were tens of thousands of other hibakusha she was certain had suffered so much more than she had. But the brief brush with mortality she had had with the fainting episode—and her talk with Yoshimi (like Shizue, a hibakusha-card holder for decades by that point)—helped her to realize that, as a wife and mother, her health was not just her own concern alone. The Tados still had one more daughter's college tuition to help pay off; it was daunting to imagine what would happen to her schooling if the family's savings got sucked up by medical expenses during a lengthy hospital stay, perhaps involving expensive treatments and surgeries. Moreover, Yoshito might still have decades more to live (as turned out to be the case); the thought of him having to do that alone, and trying to make ends meet on nothing but his Mitsubishi pension, was equally sobering to contemplate.

After mulling over various equally dismal scenarios involving the consequences of some future long-term hospitalization bereft of government hibakusha benefits, Sayoko finally broke down, swallowed her survivor guilt, and decided to apply for a card. After asking some of her fellow Higashi Yamato City hibakusha association members about the application procedure, Sayoko took the Chūō Line into the city to visit the agency responsible for processing hibakusha affairs in the Greater Tokyo area—the Bureau of Social Welfare and Public Health at the Metropolitan Government Office Building in Yurakuchō.

The impromptu interview at the health office started off on the wrong foot when the clerk at the first window Sayoko approached got testy with her because she had not called in beforehand to make an appointment. Then, after she was begrudgingly sent on up the line to the next bureaucrat, she was flat-out accused of lying when she gave her initial broad strokes accounting of her activities and movements on and after August 6, 1945. Pulling a large, thick medical tome of some kind down from the bookshelf behind him, the bureaucrat flipped back and forth between well-thumbed pages, pointing to various pie charts and data tables in his attempt to convince Sayoko that her story was impossible—that if she really had been in all of those places on August 6, and for as many hours as she claimed, she had no business being alive right now.

According to the bureaucrat's figures, Sayoko had received two sieverts of radiation just from being within a three-kilometer radius of the explosion. This was more than enough to cause nonfatal (but still excruciating) ARS in any person so exposed, and it did not jibe with Sayoko's account of having not experienced so much as a tummy rumble or a moment of cold sweat in the days and weeks after the event. Five sieverts is the so-called LD_{50} number—enough to kill half the people so exposed within a month, and to plague for the rest of their lives the health of those who survived. After some more data-table crunching and map referencing, the bureaucrat calculated that Sayoko had received six sieverts just by the time she had reached the intersection of Rijō and Aioi Streets. Factoring in the subsequent residual radiation her body would have absorbed sitting for two days on a pile of rubble only seven hundred meters from Ground Zero, her exposure would have been practically off the charts.

Several months later, when a formal medical interview was held for the second stage of the application, Sayoko was handed a Hiroshima map and asked to give a step-by-step rundown of her hibakusha experience. Once again, the investigating officials—including physicians this time—accused her of lying. Still, she insisted that she was telling the truth, and she persisted through the red-tape runaround of the application. The debate finally became moot when administrators at Midori-machi Junior High School in Hiroshima—the wartime site of Sayoko's alma mater, Dai Ni Ichijo—confirmed her presence on campus at the time of Little Boy's explosion. This by itself was sufficient for her to qualify for a card, which Sayoko finally received about half a year later. Nevertheless, she still harbored lingering qualms and guilt over her newly won qualification.

Around this time, she was presented with an opportunity to put at least some of this self-doubt and guilt to rest when one of her daughter's old junior high school teachers was transferred to Higashi Yamato City. Sayoko's daughter had, for some reason or another, told her class many years earlier that her mother was a Hiroshima survivor, and this information had remained in the teacher's memory ever since. When he found out that the Tados were now living near his new junior high school posting, he contacted Sayoko and asked her if she would be willing to come talk to his students about her hibakusha experiences. Although she initially balked at the request—having never talked about the bomb with anyone outside of her immediate family and, since the 1970s, her Yamato-kai colleagues—it dawned on her that perhaps sharing her bomb story with young people, in the interest of peace education, was a way of working for the hibakusha card she otherwise felt she did not deserve. While still harboring some trepidation, she called the teacher back and accepted the request.

The school where she was to give her talk had a reputation for being rough; many of the students lived in nearby housing projects for families on public assistance, and delinquency was rampant. The teacher warned Sayoko beforehand not to expect much in the way of the students' attention spans, attitude, or behavior during the lecture. These concerns, as it turned out, were unfounded.

On the day of the lecture, Sayoko opened her talk in the school gymnasium with a rhetorical masterstroke. Staring down her potentially hostile (or at least rudely inattentive) audience, she said, "I don't care about your posture while you're sitting there listening to me, but I want you to make sure to listen to what I have to tell you." From that point, she had her audience in the palm of her hand.

After her talk, during which many of the students and several of the teachers in attendance openly wept, there was a question-and-answer session. Because the students were Japanese teenagers, conducting this by having them raise their hands and ask their questions verbally was, of course, impossible, so instead, the teacher had them write their questions down. The teacher then collected these and handed them to Sayoko.

One of the comments still stays with her after all these years, and in retrospect, it changed the way she has thought about the bombing, what led to it, and what happened in its wake. In a young Japanese tough's rough lettering and coarse words, the commenter had written:

> What in the hell was the government thinking back in those days,
>   starting a war like that?
> What did the adults do about it?
> What did the government do for all the people who were killed?

"That student's comments really opened my eyes," Sayoko recalls. "They got me thinking about questions like that for the first time.... I realized what a naive fool I had been all along."

For the entirety of her post-bomb life up to that point, Sayoko had never thought about why the war had happened or why it had gone on as long as it had. She had never harbored any resentment against the Americans for dropping Little Boy, nor any against the Japanese government for starting a war they had no chance of winning. She had regarded all of these things—the tribulations and chaos of the war years and August 6—more along the lines of a string of natural disasters rather than as consequences of human agency that should be (and should have been) questioned, and for which people or at least institutions should be held to account. In subsequent decades, she has rethought a lot about her interpretation of the bombing and what it did to her life, her family, her country, and the world. She has also tried to catch up on her history education to redress previous gaps in her knowledge, and to be able to answer more authoritatively audience member questions after her talks. And while she might let slip a little anger over the bombing here and there in private conversation, she still steadfastly refuses to let any hint of indignation filter into her public messaging, other than a kind of abstract, philosophical, and ostensibly politically safe ire against the phenomenon of war itself. She does not see the advantage in victimized people passing the torch of rage to successor generations either as catharsis or as a toxic personal stab at symbolic immortality. And it is certainly not what Jesus would have done.

Since a string of successive hard-right conservative administrations took office in the governorship of Tokyo beginning in the late 1990s, "peace education" emphasizing the suffering of the Japanese people during the war has been discouraged in Tokyo public schools. This is because it is believed to be a primary obstacle for the nearly eighty-year-old Japanese reactionary dream of throwing out the SCAP-coauthored 1947 constitution—which commits Japan to a national policy of renouncing military force as a means of resolving international disputes—and introducing in its place a new, entirely "home-grown" constitution that would return the national polity to an incarnation closer in character and spirit to the one that was delegitimized and dismantled by its 1945 defeat. As a result, Sayoko's opportunities to address student groups have been sharply curtailed in the Greater Tokyo area. Still, she has continued to share her story with audiences in other venues, largely through the good offices of Tōyūkai, and she has been interviewed by NHK and several newspaper reporters in recent years.

In the years I have known Tado (née Yamaguchi) Sayoko, I have often marveled at how she has apparently remained so free of bitterness all this time, whereas I am quite certain that in her shoes—having endured what she endured and lost what she lost—I would have spent the rest of my days since August 6, 1945, stewing in traumatic memories and resentment. Some of her own children have found this baffling—even annoying—as well. At several junctures in his life, her second son, Yoshihiko, has asked his mother, "How can you not hate America—even just a little bit?" To this, Tado—with Gandhian wisdom—has always given the same answer: "If I were to hate America over what happened in the war, then I would have to hate my own country, too. And where would that leave me?"

Tado Sayoko—ninety-two years old as I write these words—has two superpowers that have allowed her not only to live, but to thrive as long as she has. One of these is her officially documented capacity for surviving radiation in dosages that would kill a team of Hazmat-suited Clydesdales—an ability that no specialist has ever been able to explain. Her second and, I believe, far more potent superpower is whatever combination of strength and flexibility of character she possesses that has allowed her to sublimate her traumatic memories and resentment through religious faith and love. She survived an experience that, by all rights, should have killed her—if not instantly, then at least decades ago by now, from leukemia or some other form of radiation-induced cancer. And whereas so many female hibakusha of her age cohort forwent having children because of fears of genetic mutation and birth defects, Tado and her husband took to heart their Lord's command to be fruitful and multiply, raising three sons and four daughters to productive and healthy adulthood. As of late 2022, thirteen grandchildren and six great-grandchildren are also counted among the Tados' descendants.

By any measure, Tado Sayoko has had an amazing run. Her long life has been filled with hardships—both before and after an atomic bomb tried but failed to kill her—but there has not been one second during those ninety-two years when she has not been surrounded by people who love and need her.

We should all be so lucky.

EPILOGUE

North Field, Tinian

August 6, 1945

2,560 kilometers southeast of the scheduled aiming point

for the second atomic bomb

NEWS OF *ENOLA GAY*'S success over Hiroshima reached the sleep-deprived generals and admirals in the North Field communications center first.[1] From there, the scuttlebutt that something really big had just happened—and that the end of the war was imminent—swept across Tinian and down through the rank and file in short order, accelerated by the hope that the old GI saw "Home Alive in '45" might just turn out to be true, after all. Inside the barbed-wire-enclosed compound of the 509th Composite Group—most of whose members had a somewhat more concrete but by no means complete idea of what that big "something" entailed—the news gave rise to spontaneous celebrations.

"We felt sure that Japan would surrender," recalled Paul Metro, a radar technician with the unit. "There was a double ration of free beer, Coke, and a flatbed truck with a band [parked on the 509th's baseball field]. . . . There were pie eating and egg tossing contests. Another contest was a three-man race in which the legs of the center man facing backwards were tied to the legs of the outside men."[2]

"Thousands of sandwiches, salads, and hot dogs were prepared and ready to be served," another 509th member remembered. "The mood was jubilant. The talk was that the war was over, we'd all be going home soon. The party would go on all day and well into the night."[3]

Outside the 509th's wire, the rest of North Field was still a working incendiary bomber base dedicated to the nightly incineration of Japanese cities. Curtis LeMay's XXI Bomber Command had accomplished this objective with such ruthless efficiency over the previous five months that it was running out of targets; its firebombs now mostly rained down on medium-sized towns in the fifty thousand population range. Everything else that had not been earmarked as a potential atomic bomb target or that had not been given a special stay of incendiary execution—like Kyoto—had already been burned to the ground.

On a normal morning, the base would have been humming with trucks as the 313th Bomb Wing's two-hundred-odd B-29s were readied for their next mission: their wings pumped full of aviation fuel and their hardstands piled high with crates of clustered incendiaries. But on the morning of August 6, the maintenance vehicles and bomb trolleys of XXI Bomber Command sat idle and its fuel pipes were dry; Japan's leaders were being given a breather to wrap their heads around what had just happened to Hiroshima before the incendiary raids— and the atomic bombings—would resume.

Some two thousand kilometers away to the northwest, *Enola Gay* was winging its way home. On board, the nerves and tension of the ingress and bomb run had been replaced by about an hour of immediate post-explosion excitement. This, in turn, was eventually replaced with a sense of fatigued relief; as the sleep debt collectively accrued over the previous few nights suddenly asserted itself, many of the crew members succumbed to its demands and dozed at their stations.[4]

Although he could now indulge his crew members' need for rest, Colonel Tibbets had to maintain at least some measure of alertness at *Enola Gay*'s flight controls. Switching back and forth between manual control and autopilot, he puffed on his pipe, alone with his thoughts.

"I reflected on the wonders of science," Tibbets recalled of these moments, over half a century later, "and rejoiced that the new weapon had surely made future war unthinkable."[5]

One plane back in the formation, the *Great Artiste*'s navigator, Captain James Van Pelt, was wide awake at his plot table station and in a somewhat different frame of mind. Turning to Sergeant Abe Spitzer—the radioman at the workstation next to his—he said, "You know, Abe, I've spent most of my life trying to learn how to keep people alive, and if I ever get to be a doctor, and I work day and night, year in and year out, bringing babies into the world and saving all the lives I can, I'll never even make a dent compared with the number of lives we took back there . . . not even a dent. . . . It's not a very pleasant thought, is it?"[6]

While Colonel Tibbets mulled over the first broad strokes of his Hiroshima apologia, and Captain Van Pelt pondered the balance of his soul in the moral ledger book of providence, preparations were underway on Tinian for the next atomic strike—assuming one would prove necessary. In one of three special air-conditioned assembly buildings in the 509th Compound, finished by Navy Seabee engineers just a month previously, Project Alberta technicians worked around and against the clock to prepare Fat Man for an August 9 mission.[7]

Some six hours after the first spontaneous celebrations had broken out on the island, a more formal ceremony to mark the historic day was about to take place a few hundred meters from where work on Fat Man continued unabated. As the Hiroshima strike force approached Tinian, the *Great Artiste* and photo plane with the call sign Dimples 91 slowed down so that *Enola Gay* could land first at North Field to bask in the accolades and undivided attention of what Tibbets called the "reception committee."[8] This consisted of essentially the same personnel who had seen the strike force off some twelve hours and fifteen minutes earlier: the usual Signal Corps cameramen and "over 200 officers and enlisted men, including practically all the ranking military brass that could be mustered in the Marianas at the time."[9]

After landing on runway Able of North Field, Tibbets taxied *Enola Gay* to a stop in front of the brass and cameras, and cut the engines.

After popping the forward crew hatch under the flight deck, the colonel was the first of the crew to emerge from the gleaming silver plane
and make his way down an access ladder to the tarmac.[10] There he
shook hands with General Carl Spaatz and the other VIP members of
Enola Gay's "reception committee" as the Signal Corps cameras clicked
and whirred. Behind him, the rest of the crew filed down from the plane
one by one to form a loose rank behind their aircraft commander. Once
crew and commander had assumed something resembling a present-
able position of attention, the medal ceremony began.

With another flurry of camera shutters, Spaatz pinned a Distinguished Service Cross onto the breast pocket of Tibbets' rumpled
flight suit before the men shook hands and exchanged a salute. Then
the general stepped out of the viewfinders to let the Pacific Theater's
new star enjoy his moment in the spotlight. Wearing the clenched
smile of a man not entirely comfortable with emotional displays, Tibbets turned stiffly in response to cameramen's requests, facing this
way and that, his arms and hands hanging straight down as if he did
not know what to do with them. With his rough workingman's face,
flight suit, and crookedly worn ballcap, he looked more like a stage-
struck rural garage mechanic than a man who had just changed the
course of human history.

Two and a half days later, no peace feelers were forthcoming from the
Japanese government—at least none that the Allies had found acceptable. At North Field, the elation of August 6 and the hangovers of August 7 were mere memories, and XXl Bomber Command had returned
to the industrialized efficiency of its nightly incendiary routine.

The 509th Composite Group was also back in the business of
atomic bombing; on the night of August 8, a hydraulically operated
platform in 509th's second atomic bomb loading pit hoisted the Fat
Man device up into the belly of a B-29 called *Bockscar*. Although the
bomber was normally piloted by its namesake, Captain Frederick

Bock, it would be flown for the second atomic strike mission—against the Kyushu arsenal city of Kokura—by Tibbets' second-in-command, 509th executive officer Major Charles Sweeney.

Bumped from their usual ride, Bock and his *Bockscar* crew would be flying the *Great Artiste*, which still had all its specialized gear in place from the Hiroshima mission, and thus was once again assigned duty as the strike force's instrument plane. Today, in addition to its complement of Project Alberta technicians and parachute-dropped radiosonde telemetry devices, the *Great Artiste* would also be carrying *New York Times* reporter William Laurence along as history's first journalistic observer of an atomic combat mission.

Three days before, in the final hours before the Hiroshima mission, an understandably preoccupied Tibbets had gently shooed the persistently inquisitive Atomic Bill out of his office and foisted responsibility for keeping him occupied and out of trouble on Lieutenant Jacob Beser, who was assured that he and his heavily Yiddish-accented charge would "have lots in common."[11] As it turned out, the normally low-key lieutenant did not share much in common at all with the pedantic journalist, outside of their religion of birth, and Beser had been obliged to fend off the man's prying questions about top secret aspects of the mission and special equipment ever since.

In the wee hours of August 9, after their final briefings, premission meal, and equipment issue, Beser, Laurence, and Commander Frederick Ashworth—the Project Alberta man in charge of Fat Man—rode out to the flight line in Tibbets' personal jeep.[12]

After a brief interlude of drama when it appeared that the mission might be canceled because of weather concerns and *Bockscar*'s faulty reserve fuel tank, Tibbets finally gave the go-ahead, and the aircrews and their various passengers headed off with their respective strike force planes—Beser and Ashworth to *Bockscar*, and Laurence to the *Great Artiste*. In contrast with August 6, there were no Hollywood klieg lights, VIPs, or milling throngs on hand for the scene, which was only desultorily recorded by a 509th unit photographer (the Signal Corps media people presumably having left days earlier, with the generals and admirals). It would appear that atomic bombing had already become routine—although Atomic Bill Laurence would not have described his own mindset as such at the time.

After boarding the *Great Artiste*, the Manhattan Project's embedded PR man was offered a front seat in the superfluous bombardier's station by Captain Charles Levy, who would take a series of iconic photographs of the morning's mushroom cloud some seven and a half hours later.[13] From his privileged perch on the flight deck, Laurence watched in awe and admiration as Captain Bock and the other crewmen went through their final checks and preparations for takeoff. "Man and machine had become one, a modern centaur," he recalled of the moment in his unmistakably Laurencian prose.[14] "All the nine members of the crew were miraculously synthesized before me into a new entity, of which the machine, with its maze of instruments and mechanical brains, was part of a whole . . . a chariot drawn by the power of eight thousand horses—eight thousand horses with wings."[15]

At 0350 Tinian time, the *Great Artiste* was wheels up.[16]

In a Pulitzer-winning (his second) *New York Times* piece published a month later, Laurence electrified the American newspaper-reading public with his firsthand account of flying on history's second atomic-bombing mission. He also used the piece to establish an early version of a key moral argument employed ever since in American conservative rhetoric: that the Japanese got what they deserved.

"Does one feel any pity or compassion for the poor devils about to die?" he wrote. "Not when one thinks of Pearl Harbor and of the Death March on Bataan."[17]

───

Twenty-five hundred kilometers away to the northwest, as the *New York Times* correspondent was being borne through night skies on his winged chariot toward the scoop of a lifetime, most of the hundred thirty thousand residents of Kokura were still hours away from waking up.[18] When they finally did, it would be under gray skies. The previous day, a substantial air raid had hit the nearby steel works at

Yahata and started fires in the surrounding residential areas that had killed some twenty-five hundred people.[19] A day later, lingering fires from the raid were still wafting smoke over Kokura, adding haze to the humidity and cloud cover already shrouding the town.[20]

Some hundred twenty kilometers to the southwest, in the small harbor city of Nagasaki, forty thousand people would soon be waking up to the last morning of their lives.

ACKNOWLEDGMENTS

ONE MORNING IN May 2016, my wife informed me that President Obama was going to visit Hiroshima later that month. As I had already been studying the Japanese experience of World War Two for many years by that point, I was naturally eager to witness firsthand this event, which I felt sure was going to be of historic significance (and in fact already was, simply for having been proposed, planned, and announced). Although all I ended up seeing of the president was a fleeting glimpse of a familiar silhouette through a window of his armored limo, the trip ended up having the life-changing follow-on effect of inspiring me to begin researching the atomic bombings of Hiroshima and Nagasaki.

As part of this research, I enjoyed the great honor and privilege of being able to interview dozens of hibakusha ("atomic bomb survivors"), primarily in Japan but also in Taiwan and Korea. Entrusted with this invaluable oral history testimony, I was determined to take as long as necessary to write it up right, with utmost respect, and in the high fidelity and rich detail it deserves. Toward this end, I would describe not only the bombings themselves—something countless authors have done quite effectively before me—but also the world those survivors had known before the bombs, and the New Japan they helped to rebuild from the rubble and ashes of the old. I hope that I have done these survivors (and their testimonies) justice, and that my efforts will make some contribution toward spreading the precious lessons they have for all of us for future generations.

I began the project in the late spring of 2016 under the assumption that, much like the book I wrote about former kamikaze pilots in the early aughts, writing this one would be a fairly straightforward affair of interviewing survivors and researching the historical context of their experiences. I had been there, done that, so to speak, and was confident the work this time around would proceed as smoothly. Eight years later, I rue that naivete, though in hindsight, I should probably be thankful for the overconfidence that naivete made possible, because if I had known beforehand what I was getting myself into, I might have abandoned the idea on the spot. By the time I finished this book, in the summer of 2023, I had put untold thousands of hours into learning (and in some cases relearning) about nuclear and electromagnetic radiation; particle physics; nuclear medicine; oncology and DNA; the thermodynamics and chemistry of explosions; the psychology of disaster survivors; the biographies of Curtis LeMay and Paul Tibbets; the social and gender history of the Japanese class system; the organization of the Twentieth Air Force; the architectural history of Japanese residential structures; the history of Japanese urban development; the geology of western Japan; the development of the B-29 bomber; the invention of napalm; moral and political perspectives on the indiscriminate bombing of civilians; the political and artistic history of war memorial construction in postwar Japan; metallurgy; the history of the Catholic Church in Japan; and many, many other subjects.

In the way of acknowledgments, I would like to recognize the individuals who have been indispensable in bringing this book (and its companion volume to follow in 2025) to fruition: my original acquiring editor for the project, Brent Howard; my editor at Penguin Random House/Dutton, Cassidy Sachs; and my agent (and dear friend of nearly half a century), Doug Grad of Doug Grad Literary Agency.

I would also like to acknowledge the contributions of my colleagues and students at Shizuoka University, the institution where I have spent nearly the entirety of my academic career, for their patience and understanding, and for providing me with a research environment that allowed me to immerse myself in this project at this level of detail—something I could never have done if I were a journalist writing against a deadline or a working author writing to put food on the table.

In addition to Shizuoka University, the following institutions have also been indispensable in supporting my research and, ultimately, bringing this book to fruition: the Japan Society for the Promotion of Science (JSPS); the Radiation Effects Research Foundation (RERF) at Nagasaki University School of Medicine; Nagasaki City Hall; Nagasaki Prefectural Office; Nagasaki Atomic Bomb Museum; the Catholic Archdiocese of Nagasaki; Hiroshima City Hall; Hiroshima Peace Memorial Museum; alumni of the former Hiroshima Prefectural Girls School; the Tokyo and Yokohama/Kanagawa Prefectural branches and national headquarters of Hidankyō (Japan Confederation of A- and H-Bomb Sufferers Organizations); the National Diet Library; Chūgoku Shimbun; the Korean Red Cross; the Tri-Service General Hospital (Defense Ministry of the Republic of China); the Red Cross Society of the Republic of China; Junshin Joshi Gakuen (Girls School); Pearl Harbor Aviation Museum; Battleship *Missouri* Museum; and the library at Shizuoka University.

My project would have long ago been stopped dead in the water without the kind help of the following native Japanese speakers who volunteered their time and effort to help me transcribe the hundreds of hours of recorded survivor testimony I collected during this project: Araki Paul Daisuke, Naomi Ellis, Itō Ryōko, Kawada Kō'ichi, Kusano Haruna, Kuwabara Moe, Murakoshi Masahiko, Nukaya Keiko, Onodera Shuko, Satō Shingo, Sawamura Midori, Sonoyama Akari, Sugaya Naomi, Suzuki Mayo, Suzuki Setsuko, Takechi Yuka, Tōyama Sayaka, Toyohara Chie, Tsuda Kotomi, Yamahana Alice, Yokoi Yuko, Yamao Minamo, Kiyofuji Suzune, and particularly Sayaka Jess Kankolongo Watanabe, who used her extensive personal contact network to recruit at least half of the volunteers listed here.

I would also like to thank the following friends and colleagues in academia, the fourth estate, and the professional English-Japanese translation community who have helped me with their guidance, expertise, and encouragement throughout this project: Tomonaga Masao, MD, Mine Mariko, Seki Chieko, Mordecai-Mark Mac Low, Takeuchi Yoshio, Shijō Chie, the library staff at Shizuoka University, Tagawa Mari, Tado Yoshihiko, Tom Pyszcznski, James Orr, Mark R. Mullins, Jim Bowman, Debito Arudou, Arakawa Shōji, Nishihara Jun, Sasahara Megumi, Kim Myungmi, Miyazaki Yoshinori, Sven Saaler, Roger Brown, Scott North, Nakano Ko'ichi, Watanave Hidenori, John Krinsky, Lee Dugatkin, Robert Hand, Eric Johnston, Jeff Kingston, Ran Zwigenberg, Robert "Bo" Jacobs, Lee Arnold, Mark Hudson, Steve McClure, Carl Freire, Jamie Findlay, M. Thomas Apple, Eugene Robinson, Perry Constantine, John Frederick Ashburne, Robert and Christina Hoover Moorehead, Todd Jay Leonard, Marc Helgesen, Jake Adelstein, Nevin Thompson, Eric M. Skier, Joel Sassone, Jeff Bryant, Burl Burlingame, North Compton, Hugh Graham-Marr, Mark Schilling, Katalin Ferber, Stafford Gregoire, Jacob Margolies, Noam Freedman, Garrett DeOrio, Walter Hatch, Alex Wellerstein, Barrett Tillman, Andy Bienstock, Fred Uleman, Aaron Gerow, Jud Eri Magy, Michael Penn, David McNeill, Bill Snyder, Dwight Swift, Mark David Sheftall, Abram Hall, Gerry Mullany, Tom Gill, Mike Boyce, John Munroe, Michael Pinto, Justin McCurry, Alex Kerr, Ginny Tapley Takemori, C. A. Edington, Theodore F. Cook, James House, Mark Schreiber, Earl Hartman, Andre Hertrich, Marc Ward, Jon Bauer, Hank Shelton, Brian Prager, Simon Alexander Collier, Hugh Ashton, Richard Lloyd Parry, Philip Seaton, Daryl Bockett, Jerry Piven, Laura Kawaguchi, Rod Lange, Brant Vogel, Ria Coyne, Tom Yulsman, and special thanks to Lisa Kadonaga and the late (and daily mourned, missed, and occasionally dreamed about) Phil Troy.

I would also like to thank loved ones who have provided generous support throughout my long years of (too often obsessively self-centered) immersion in this project, when I could have—and probably should have—been paying more attention to matters closer to home. In this latter category, I would include my wife, Nukaya Keiko, and sons, Levi Riku and Benjamin Dan Sheftall; my parents, George and Louise Sheftall; and my sister, Amelia Sheftall.

Finally, I would like to express my most heartfelt gratitude to the hibakusha who have entrusted me with interpreting their stories: first and foremost the late Seki Chieko, a Hiroshima hibakusha who provided indispensable help not only by sharing her own story with me but also by using her extensive personal contact network to secure me an "in" with the hibakusha community that allowed me to eventually interview dozens of other survivors. Her generous support and enthusiasm for my project were really the sine qua non factor behind all of it—particularly when I was just starting out.

I would also like to express my undying gratitude for the following hibakusha, many of whom are now no longer with us, who generously shared their precious time to sit for interviews and respond to follow-up information requests over the years: Chai Tsong Chin, Gunge Norio, Mayor Hiraoka Takashi Ikeda Masaho, Sister Itonaga Yoshi, Kano Michiko, Katayama Noboru, Kawada Kazuko, Lee Mi Cha,* Sister Kunihiro Setsuya, Edwin D. Lawson, Lee Jongkeun, Sister Matsushita Miya, Minematsu Ieko, Misaki Susumu, Mori Shige'aki, Murata Michiko (Tokyo Hidankyō), Nakamura Yūko, Ogura Keiko, Okuda Hagiko, Ōishi Matashichi, Ōiwa Kazuko, Ōiwa Kōhei, Pak Nam Ju, Sakamoto Toyoko, Sano Hirotoshi, Seki Chieko, Shimohira Sakue, Tado Sayoko, Archbishop Joseph Mitsuaki Takami, Tanaka Terumi, Tateno Sueko, Tomonaga Masao, Toyonaga Keisaburō, Tsuchiya Keiji, Yamamoto Hidenori, Yamamoto Mutsuko, Yanagawa Masako, and Zhen Su Bing.

---

*   Pseudonym.

NOTES ON NAMING CONVENTIONS, LANGUAGE USAGE, AND MEASUREMENTS

This book follows the Japanese convention for personal names—i.e., surname followed by given name(s)—unless the individual in question is already well known to readers by a Western name-order convention (e.g., Yoko Ono or Shohei Ohtani).

Female characters appear under their birth surnames unless they were already married at the time of their earliest appearance in the narrative timeline (or as otherwise noted).

For the transliteration of Japanese vocabulary items and proper nouns in the Roman alphabet, I have followed the Hepburn system that is standard in English-language Japanese studies, including the use of macrons for elongated vowels (e.g., ō, ū, etc.). Both macrons and *italic* font are used throughout the book for direct transliteration of Japanese speech, text, and vocabulary. Japanese terms (e.g., *hibakusha*) that are important in the context of the book but probably unfamiliar to most non-Japanese readers make their first appearance in *italic* font, then in regular typeface in subsequent appearances. For Japanese loan words like "kamikaze" or "kimono" and place-names such as Tokyo or Kyoto, with which readers are probably already familiar, regular typeface and English spelling is used throughout.

The insertion of an apostrophe in certain words or names (e.g., Kōno'ura or *tai'atari*) is used to indicate the glottal stop that can sometimes appear between vowels in spoken Japanese (similar to the pronunciation of "uh-oh" in English usage).

Metric system measurements are used in this book, with the exception of direct quotations from American material (in which case metric equivalents are added in parentheses).

GRANTS AND RESEARCH FUNDING

This research was made possible in part through regular research funding by my employer, Shizuoka University, and by the following JSPS grants: (C)24520726 "Postwar Memorialization Discourses in Defeated Communities: An International Comparative Study" (2012–2017); and (C)18K00908 "Hibakusha Lives and Collective Memory Communities in the 21st Century" (2018–present).

M. G. Sheftall
Shizuoka University
Summer 2004

REFERENCES

Akikitaso. (No date). *"Akikitaso no otera no go shōkai: Kōjimazan Seifukuji"* ("An Introduction to Aki North Group Temples: Kōjimazan Seifuku Temple"). Retrieved June 5, 2023, from Akikitaso website, http://www.akikitaso.net/temple/temple15.html.

Akimasa, H. (2019, September 27). *"Shirō ya! Hiroshima Jō, No. 61: Chūgoku Gunkanku Shireibu Bōkū Sakusenshitsu no nazo!"* ("Let's Find Out About Hiroshima Castle (No. 61): The Mystery of the Chūgoku CMD HQ Air Defense Bunker!"). Retrieved June 2, 2023, from *Hiroshima Shi Bunka Zaidan Hiroshimajō* (Hiroshima City Cultural Foundation [for] Hiroshima Castle) website, https://www.rijo-castle.jp/rijo/wp-content/themes/rijo-castle/assets/pdf/magazine/shirouya61.pdf.

Akita, M. (Ed.). (2010). *Hoshi wa miteiru: Zenmetsu shita Hiroshima Itchū Ichinensei Fubo no shuki shū* (*The Stars Are Watching: Collected Letters from the Parents of First-Year Students at the Completely Destroyed First Hiroshima Prefectural Junior High School*). Tokyo: Nihon Bukku Ēsu.

Akizuki, T. (2010). *Shi no dōshin'en* (*The Radius of Death*). Nagasaki, Japan: Nagasaki Bunkensha.

Alper, T. (1948). "Hydrogen Peroxide and the Indirect Effect of Ionizing Radiations." *Nature 162*, 615–616.

Alvarez, L. M. (1987). *Alvarez: Adventures of a Physicist*. New York: Basic Books.

AniMech Channel. (2019). *Green Sand Mould, Dry Sand Mould, and Skin Dried Mould (3D Animation)* [Video]. Retrieved September 14, 2022, from AniMech YouTube channel, https://www.youtube.com/watch?v=10Znx Zj6-lg.

Arayama, K. (2020, September 20). *"Hiroshima no Kūhaku, Hibaku 75-nen: Machinami saigen; Shashin ga kizamu hibakumae no Jisenji"* ("Hiroshima's Vanished [Past], Seventy-Five Years After the Atomic Bombing: Reconstructing Images of the Former City Through a Photo of Prebombing Jisenji Temple"). *Chūgoku Shimbun.*

Arthur W. Page Society. (No date). "About Page." Retrieved June 3, 2023, from Arthur W. Page Society website, https://page.org/site/about.

Arupe-shinpu no Reppuku wo Inoru Kai (Eds.). (2010). *Arupe-shinpu kaisōki Dai-ni han* (*Memories of Father Arrupe*, vol. 2). Hiroshima: Private printing.

Arrupe, P. (1970/2004a). "Recognizing the 'Hand of the Lord' at Eucharist." In K. F. Burke (Ed.), *Pedro Arrupe: Essential Writings* (pp. 51–63). Maryknoll, NY: Orbis Books.

Arrupe, P. (1970/2004b). "Surviving the Atomic Bomb." In K. F. Burke (Ed.), *Pedro Arrupe: Essential Writings* (pp. 39–51). Maryknoll, NY: Orbis Books.

Atomic Archive. (No date). "The Atomic Bombings of Hiroshima and Nagasaki: Propaganda." Retrieved June 3, 2023, from Atomic Archive website, https://www.atomicarchive.com/resources/documents/med/med_chp.2.html (dead link).

Atomic Bomb Casualty Commission. (Eds.). (1947). *General Report.* Washington, DC.: National Research Council.

Atomic Heritage Foundation. (No date). "The Franck Report." Retrieved June 2, 2023, from Atomic Heritage Foundation website, https://ahf.nuclearmuseum.org/ahf/key-documents/franck-report/.

Atomic Heritage Foundation. (No date). "Hiroshima and Nagasaki Bombing Timeline." Retrieved November 14, 2023, from Atomic Heritage Foundation website, https://www.atomicheritage.org/history/hiroshima-and-nagasaki-bombing-timeline.

Atomic Heritage Foundation. (No date). "Warning Leaflets." Retrieved June 2, 2023, from Atomic Heritage Foundation website, https://www.atomicheritage.org/key-documents/warning-leaflets/.

Atomic Photographers. (No date). "Charles Levy." Retrieved November 14, 2022, from Atomic Photographers website, https://atomicphotographers.com/photographers/charles-levy/.

Baeumler, D. (No date). "Jesuit Education in Japan: Prewar History of Sophia University." Retrieved June 6, 2023, from Sophia University, Digital Japanese History website, https://dh.japanese-history.org/2020-spring-japanese-history/jesuit-education-in-japan-pre-war-history-of-sophia-university/.

Bank of Japan. (No date). *"Shōwa 40nen no 1-man-en no okane ni kansan suru to dono kurai ni narimasuka?"* ("How Much Would Ten Thousand 1965 Yen Be Worth in Today's Money?"). Retrieved June 5, 2023, from Bank of Japan website, https://www.boj.or.jp/announcements/education/oshiete/history/j12.htm/.

Ba'ue, T. (2008). *"Heiwa Kōen: Hibakumae kara aru mono?"* ("Is There Anything Still in Peace Memorial Park Remaining from Before the Atomic Bombing?"). *Chūgoku Shimbun.* Retrieved November 13, 2023, from *Chūgoku Shimbun,* Hiroshima Peace Media website, https://www.hiroshimapeacemedia.jp/hiroshima-koku/exploration/index_20080323.html.

BCcampus. (No date). "Evolution of the Early Universe." https://opentextbc.ca/universityphysicsv3openstax/chapter/evolution-of-the-early-universe/ (link restricted as of June 3, 2023).

Becker, E. (1973). *The Denial of Death.* New York: Free Press.

Berger, P. L., and Luckmann, T. (1966). *The Social Construction of Reality: A Treatise in the Sociology of Knowledge.* Garden City, NY: Anchor Books.

Beser, J. (1988). *Hiroshima and Nagasaki Revisited.* Memphis, TN: Global Press.

Block, M. A., and Tsuzuki, M. (1948, March). "Observations of Burn Scars Sustained by Atomic Bomb Survivors: A Preliminary Study." *American Journal of Surgery 75*(3), 417–434.

Blume, L. M. M. (2020). *Fallout: The Hiroshima Cover-up and the Reporter Who Revealed It to the World.* New York: Simon & Schuster.

Boister, N., and Cryer, R. (Eds.). (2008). *Documents on the Tokyo International Military Tribunal: Charter, Indictments, and Judgments.* Oxford: Oxford University Press.

Boyer, P. (1985). *By the Bomb's Early Light.* New York: Pantheon Books.

Braw, M. (1991). *The Atomic Bomb Suppressed: American Censorship in Occupied Japan.* Armonk, NY: M. E. Sharpe.

Broad, W. J. (2021, August 9). "How a Star *Times* Reporter Got Paid by the Government Agencies He Covered." *New York Times.*

Brode, H. L. (1963). "Thermal Radiation from Nuclear Explosions." Santa Monica: RAND Corporation.

Brookings Institution. (2002). "The Costs of the Manhattan Project." Retrieved June 1, 2023, from Brookings Institution website, https://www.brookings.edu/the-costs-of-the-manhattan-project/.

Buchheim, R. W. (1958/2007). *Space Handbook: Astronautics and Its Applications.* Washington, DC: RAND Corporation.

Bunce, W. K. (1955). *Religions in Japan: Buddhism, Shinto, Christianity.* Rutland, VT: Charles E. Tuttle Company.

Burke, K. (1969). *A Grammar of Motives.* Berkeley: University of California Press.

Burke, K. F. (Ed.). (2004). *Pedro Arrupe: Essential Writings.* Maryknoll, NY: Orbis Books.

Burnie, S. (2021, March). "Fukushima Daiichi Decommissioning: Time for a New Long-Term Strategic Plan." Retrieved September 6, 2022, from Greenpeace website, https://www.greenpeace.org/static/planet4-japan-stateless/2021/03/8323f3ca-gpsummary_decommissioning_eng.pdf.

Butler, C. P. (1962, October 26). "The Light of the Atom Bomb." *Science 138*(3539), 483–489.

Butow, R. J. C. (1954). *Japan's Decision to Surrender.* Stanford, CA: Stanford University Press.

Catholic Bishops' Conference of Japan. (No date). "Diocese of Hiroshima. (Hiroshima, Okayama, Tottori, Yamaguchi, Shimane)." Retrieved October 13, 2022, from Catholic Bishops' Conference of Japan website, https://www.cbcj.catholic.jp/english/japan/diocese/hiroshima/.

Center for Action and Contemplation. (2020). "Contemplative Activists: Defender of Liberation Theology [Pedro Arrupe]." Retrieved March 1, 2023, from Center for Action and Contemplation website, https://cac.org/daily-meditations/defender-of-liberation-theology-2020-07-15/.

Chen, Y. (2001). "Imperial Army Betrayed." In T. Fujitani et al. (Eds.), *Perilous Memories: The Asia-Pacific War(s)* (pp. 181–198). Durham, NC: Duke University Press.

Chūgoku Shimbunsha. (1966). *Hiroshima no kiroku: Nenpyō / shiryō hen* (*Hiroshima Records: Timeline / documents compilation*). Tokyo: Miraisha.

Chūgoku Shimbunsha. (1974). *Genbaku no kiroku: Hiroshima* (*Atomic Bomb Documents—Hiroshima*). Hiroshima: Chūgoku Shimbunsha.

Cialdini, R. B., Borden, R. J., Thorne, A., Walker, M. R., Freeman, S., and Sloan, L. R. (1976). "Basking in Reflected Glory: Three (Football) Field Studies." *Journal of Personality and Social Psychology, 34*(3), 366–375.

Cieslik, H. (1983). *"Hakai no hi"* ("Day of Destruction"). In *Katorikku Seigi to Heiwa Hiroshima Kyōgikai* (Hiroshima Catholic Conference of Justice and Peace) (Eds.), *Hakai no hi: Gaijin shinputachi no hibaku taiken* (*Day of Destruction: The Atomic Bomb Experiences of the Foreign Priests*) (pp.18–38). Hiroshima: *Katorikku Seigi to Heiwa Hiroshima Kyōgikai*.

Cooling, B. F. (Ed.). (1994). *Case Studies in the Achievement of Air Superiority.* Washington, DC: United States Air Force Center for Air Force History.

Coox, A. (1994). "Air War Against Japan." In B. F. Cooling (Ed.), *Case Studies in the Achievement of Air Superiority* (pp. 383–452). Washington, DC: United States Air Force Center for Air Force History.

Correll, J. T. (2010, October 10). "Atomic Mission." *Air Force Magazine,* 73–76.

Correll, J. T. (2011, July) "Near Failure at Nagasaki." *Air Force Magazine.* https://www.airforcemag.com/article/0711nagasaki/

Craven, W. F., and Cate, J. L. (Eds.) (1953). *The Army Air Forces in World War II*, vol. 5, *The Pacific—Matterhorn to Nagasaki, June 1944 to August 1945.* Chicago: University of Chicago Press.

Creemers, W. H. M. (1968). *Shrine Shinto After World War II.* Leiden, Netherlands: E. J. Brill.

Crowl, P. A. (1960). *Campaign in the Marianas.* Washington, DC: Center for Military History.

De Bary, W. T., Tsunoda, R., and Keene, D. (1958). *Sources of Japanese Tradition,* vol. 2. New York: Columbia University Press.

Diehl, C. (2018). *Resurrecting Nagasaki: Reconstruction and the Formation of Atomic Narratives.* Ithaca, NY: Cornell University Press.

"Dō'in gakuto no tamashii yo yasukare" ("Rest in Peace, O Souls of the Mobilized Students"). (1967, July 16). *Asahi Shimbun.*

Dower, J. W. (2000). *Embracing Defeat: Japan in the Wake of World War II.* New York: W. W. Norton & Co.

Dower, J. W. (2010). *Cultures of War: Pearl Harbor / Hiroshima / 9-11 / Iraq.* New York: W. W. Norton & Co.

Drea, E. J. (1998). *In the Service of the Emperor: Essays on the Imperial Japanese Army.* Lincoln: University of Nebraska Press.

Eden, L. (2006). *Whole World on Fire.* Ithaca, NY: Cornell University Press.

Enomiya-Lassalle, H. M. (1992). *The Practice of Zen Meditation*. London: Thorsons.

Farrell, D. A. (2019). *Atomic Bomb Island: Tinian, the Last Stage of the Manhattan Project, and the Dropping of the Atomic Bombs on Japan in World War II*. Lanham, MD: Stackpole Books.

Federal Civil Defense Administration. (1953). *Impact of Air Attack in World War II: Selected Data for Civil Defense Planning; Division II: Effects on the General Economy*, vol. 2, *Economic Effects—Japan*. Washington DC: Federal Civil Defense Administration.

Fedman, D., and Karacas, C. (2012). "A Cartographic Fade to Black: Mapping the Destruction of Urban Japan During World War II." *Journal of Historical Geography, 38*(3), 306–328.

Feis, H. (1966). *The Atomic Bomb and the End of World War II*. Princeton, NJ: Princeton University Press.

509th Composite Group. (Eds.). (1945, August 31). *History of 509th Composite Group, 313th Bombardment Wing, Twentieth Air Force, Activation to 15 August 1945*. Tinian: 509th Composite Group.

"Foreign Jesuits Who Experienced the Atomic Bomb at Hiroshima on August 6, 1945." (2019, November 28). *Chūgoku Shimbun*. Retrieved June 4, 2023, from *Chūgoku Shimbun*, Hiroshima Peace Media website, https://www.hiroshima peacemedia.jp/blog/wp-content/uploads/2019/11/28725c6901e71031a6809 dofd1a4d19a.pdf.

Frankl, V. E. (1984). *Man's Search for Meaning*. New York: Washington Square Press.

Fujitani, T., et al. (Eds.). (2001). *Perilous Memories: The Asia-Pacific War(s)*. Durham, NC: Duke University Press.

Fujiwara, K. (2020). "Hiroshima, Nanjing, and Yasukuni: Contending Discourses on the Second World War in Japan." In M. D. Gordin and G. J. Ikenberry (Eds.), *The Age of Hiroshima* (pp. 201–218). Princeton, NJ: Princeton University Press.

Genbaku Higaisha no Shuki Hensan I'inkai. (Eds.). (1953). *Genbaku ni ikite* (*Living the Atomic Bomb*). Hiroshima: San'ichi Shobo.

"Genbaku Shiryōkan: Sono ayumi (Chū): Katararezaru Tenji" ("Evolution of the Hiroshima Peace Memorial Museum, Part 2: Exhibition on Atomic Energy"). (2019, April 21). *Chūgoku Shimbun*. Retrieved June 5, 2023, from *Chūgoku Shimbun*, Hiroshima Peace Media website, https://www.hiroshimapeacemedia .jp/?p=92003.

Gion Catholic Church. (No date). *"Gion katorikku kyōkai"* ("Gion Catholic Church"). Retrieved June 6, 2023, from Gion Catholic Church website, http://www.gionkyokai.jp/.

Gluck, C. (1985). *Japan's Modern Myths: Ideology in the Late Meiji Period*. Princeton, NJ: Princeton University Press.

Goodsell, D. S. (2005, May). "Fundamentals of Cancer Medicine—'The Molecular Perspective: Double-Stranded DNA Breaks.'" *The Oncologist, 10*(5), 361–362.

Grogan, B. (2019). *Pedro Arrupe SJ: Mystic with Open Eyes.* Dublin: Messenger Publications.

Groves, L. R. (1962). *Now It Can Be Told.* New York: Harper & Row.

Hachiya, M. (1955). *Hiroshima Diary.* Chapel Hill: University of North Carolina Press.

Hamai, S. (2011). *Genbaku shichō: Yomigaetta toshi: Fukkō e no kiseki (Atomic Bomb Mayor—A City Returned: The Path to Recovery).* Hiroshima: Committee for the Republication of Genbaku Shichō.

Hanley, F. (2016). *Accused American War Criminal.* Brattleboro, VT: Echo Point Books & Media.

Hansell, H. (1980). *Strategic Air War Against Japan.* Maxwell Air Force Base, AL: Airpower Research Institute, Air War College.

Harry S. Truman Presidential Library and Museum. (No date). "Press Release by the White House, August 6, 1945." Retrieved June 2, 2023, from Harry S. Truman Presidential Library and Museum website, https://www.truman library.gov/library/research-files/press-release-white-house.

Hasegawa, T. (2005). *Racing the Enemy: Stalin, Truman, and the Surrender of Japan.* Cambridge, MA: Belknap Press.

Hattori, E. (2010). *"Ichiya dake no kangō"* ("I Could Only Care for Him for One Night"). In M. Akita (Ed.), *Hoshi wa miteiru: Zenmetsu shita Hiroshima Itchū Ichinensei Fubo no shuki shū (The Stars Are Watching: Collected Letters from the Parents of First-Year Students at the Completely Destroyed First Hiroshima Prefectural Junior High School)* (pp. 103–108). Tokyo: Nihon Bukku Ēsu.

Havens, T. R. H. (1978). *Valley of Darkness: The Japanese People and World War Two.* Lanham, MD: University Press of America.

Hersey, J. (1946). *Hiroshima.* New York: Alfred A. Knopf.

Hewlett, R. G., and Holl, J. M. (1989). *Atoms for Peace and War, 1953–1961: Eisenhower and the Atomic Energy Commission.* Berkeley: University of California Press.

Hiroshima City. (1971). *Hiroshima genbaku sensaishi (Record of the Atomic Bombing of Hiroshima)* (*"Sensai"* in the endnotes), vols. 1–5. Hiroshima: Hiroshima City.

Hiroshima City. (1985). *Hiroshima hibaku 40 nenshi: Toshi no fukkō (Forty Years Since the Bombing of Hiroshima: The City's Recovery).* Hiroshima: Hiroshima City.

Hiroshima City. (No date.) *"Genbaku kankei no ireihi nado no gaiyō"* ("An Overview of Atomic-Bomb-Related Memorials/Monuments"). Retrieved June 4, 2023, from Hiroshima City website, https://www.city.hiroshima.lg.jp/site/atomic bomb-peace/9947.html.

Hiroshima City. (No date). "The Hiroshima Peace Memorial City Construction Law and Commentary." Retrieved June 4, 2023, from Hiroshima City website, https://www.city.hiroshima.lg.jp/uploaded/attachment/23440.pdf.

Hiroshima City. (No date). "Tour Site #42: Memorial Tower for Mobilized Students." Retrieved January 15, 2022. http://www.pcf.city.hiroshima.jp

/virtual/VirtualMuseum_j/tour/ireihi/tour_42.html (dead link as of June 6, 2023).

Hiroshima for Global Peace. (No date). "Medical Care in Hiroshima, a Military City." Retrieved June 3, 2023, from Hiroshima for Global Peace website, https://hiroshimaforpeace.com/en/fukkoheiwakenkyu/vol2/2-10/.

Hiroshima Gakuin High School Alumni Association. (2021). *"Genbaku to Iezusukai shinpu 2021"* ("The Atomic Bomb and the Jesuit Priests 2021"). Retrieved June 6, 2023, from Hiroshima Gakuin High School Alumni Association website, https://suiyukai.com/?p=2269.

"Hiroshima genbaku: Taiwanjin hibakusha ga shōgen" ("The Hiroshima Atom Bomb: A Taiwanese Hibakusha Testifies"). (2011, September 10). *Mainichi Shimbun* (Hiroshima edition).

Hiroshima Jō. (Eds.). (2015). *Hiroshima Jō to Rikugun (Hiroshima Castle and the Imperial Army)*. Hiroshima: Hiroshima Jō (noncommercial printing).

Hiroshima Ken Dōin Gakuto Giseisha no Kai (Association for Hiroshima Prefecture Victims of Student War Mobilization). (Eds.). (1995). *Dōin Gakuto: Dōkoku no Shōgen (War-Mobilized Students: Wailed Testimonies)*. Hiroshima: *Hiroshima Ken Dōin Gakuto Giseisha no Kai*.

Hiroshima Kenritsu Itchū Hibaku Seito no Kai (Association for the Atom-Bombed Students of First Prefectural Hiroshima Junior High School). (Eds.). (1974). *Yūkari no Tomo (Friends of the Eucalyptus)*. Hiroshima: *Hiroshima Kenritsu Itchū Hibaku Seito no Kai* (noncommercial printing).

Hiroshima/Nagasaki Editorial Committee for the Record of Atomic Bomb Damage. (Eds.). (1979). *Hiroshima/Nagasaki no genbaku saigai (Hiroshima/Nagasaki Atomic Bomb Damage)*. Tokyo: Iwanami Shoten.

"Hiroshima no kiroku: I'ei wa kataru, Ichijo ichinen gokumi" ("Record of Hiroshima: A Final Photograph Tells the Tale of Municipal Girls' School First Grade Class 5") (2000, June 23). *Chūgoku Shimbun*. Retrieved November 12, 2021, from *Chūgoku Shimbun*, Hiroshima Peace Media website, http://www.hiroshima peacemedia.jp/mediacenter_d/jp/abomb/00abomb/kiroku/ichijyo1/i5.html.

"Hiroshima no kiroku: I'ei wa kataru, Tenjin machi minami gumi" ("Record of Hiroshima: Tenjin-machi South Group"). (1998, December 15). *Chūgoku Shimbun*. Retrieved June 5, 2023, from *Chūgoku Shimbun*, Hiroshima Peace Media website, https://www.hiroshimapeacemedia.jp/abom/98abom/kiroku/981215_b.html.

"Hiroshima no koe: Imada Kōji-san" ("Memories of Hiroshima and Nagasaki: Messages from Hibakusha, Mr. Imada Kōji"). (2010). *Asahi Shimbun*. Retrieved June 4, 2023, from *Asahi Shimbun* website, https://www.asahi.com/hibakusha/hiroshima/h01-00286j.html.

Hiroshima Peace Institute. (Eds.). (2018). *Sengoshori wo meguru shomondai (Issues in Postwar Recovery)*, vol. 5. Hiroshima: Hiroshima Peace Institute.

Hiroshima Peace Memorial Museum. (2019). "Hiroshima Peace Memorial Museum Special Exhibition: Hiroshima Atomic Bomb Damage and

Restoration as Shown in Collections from Overseas." Retrieved June 5, 2023, from Hiroshima Peace Memorial Museum website, https://hpmmuseum.jp /modules/xelfinder/index.php/view/1856/2019kikaku_p_en.pdf.

Hiroshima Prefectural Government. (1976). *Hiroshima Kencho Genbaku Hisaishi* (*Hiroshima Prefectural Government Record of Atomic Bomb Damage*). Hiroshima: Hiroshima Prefecture.

Hiroshima Prefectural Government. (2011). "Shōwa 20-nen 9-gatsu [Makurazaki taifū]" ("The Makurazaki Typhoon of September 1945"). Retrieved June 6, 2023, from Hiroshima Prefectural Government website, https://www.pref.hiroshima .lg.jp/soshiki/100/makurazaki.html.

Hiroshima Shi Bunka Zaidan Hiroshimajō (Hiroshima City Cultural Foundation [for] Hiroshima Castle). (2015). *"Hiroshimajō to rikugun: Shiryō kaisetsusho"* ("Hiroshima Castle and the Imperial Army: Exhibition Companion Volume"). Hiroshima: Hiroshima City Cultural Foundation (for) Hiroshima Castle.

"Hiroshima wo shōbaku" (*"Incendiary attack on Hiroshima"*). (1945, August 7). Asahi Shimbun.

Hofmann, P. (1982, February 14). "The Jesuits." *New York Times.*

Horikawa, K. (2020). *Akatsuki no Ujina: Rikugun Senpaku Shireikantachi no Hiroshima* (*Akatsuki's Ujina: The Hiroshima of the Commanders of the Army Maritime Transport Command*). Tokyo: Kodansha.

Horikawa, K. (2015) *Genbaku kuyōtō* (*The Atomic Bomb Stupa*). Tokyo: Bungei Shunju.

Huang, C. (2016). *The Formation Process of Agricultural Policy in Modern Japan: The Establishment of the Food Control System* [Unpublished doctoral thesis]. Tokyo University of Foreign Studies.

Hyland, G. O. (2014). *War in the Pacific: A Chronology—January 1, 1941, Through September 30, 1945* (digital ed.). Retrieved March 22, 2021, from University of North Texas Libraries website, https://digital.library.unt.edu/ark:/67531/meta dc283775/m1/2/.

Imanaka, T. (2011). "Radiation Survey Activities in the Early Stages After the Atomic Bombing in Hiroshima." In M. Aoyama and Y. Ōchi (Eds.), *Revisit the Hiroshima A-bomb with A Database* (pp. 69–81). Hiroshima: Hiroshima City.

Ishimaru, N. (1988). *Sekai Heiwa Kinen Seidō* (*The Memorial Cathedral of World Peace*). Tokyo: Sagami Shobo.

Iwanami Shoten Editorial Staff. (2013). *Tachiagaru Hiroshima, 1952* (*Hiroshima Arises, 1952*). Tokyo: Iwanami Shoten.

Jacquet, B. (2010, March 7–8). "Compromising Modernity: Japanese Monumentality During World War II" (symposium presentation). "Front to Rear: Architecture and Planning During WWII." New York University, New York, NY.

Janoff-Bulman, R. (1992). *Shattered Assumptions: Towards a New Psychology of Trauma.* New York: Free Press.

Japan Broadcasting Corporation (NHK). (Ed.) (1981). *Unforgettable Fire: Pictures Drawn by Atomic Bomb Survivors.* New York: Pantheon Books.

Japanese Self-Defense Agency Defense Research Center. (1972). *Hondo Kessen Junbi* (*Preparations for the Decisive Defensive Battle for the Home Islands*), vols. 1–2. Tokyo: Asagumo Shimbunsha.

Jésuites de la Province de L'Afrique Occidentale. (No date)."Chronology of Father Pedro Arrupe Gondra, SJ (1907–1991)." Retrieved November 10, 2022, from Jésuites de la Province de L'Afrique Occidentale website, https://espao.com/wp-content/uploads/2019/02/Cronologa-del-P.-Pedro-Arrupe-ENG.pdf (dead link, last accessed January 20, 2023).

Jōhōji, A. (1981). *Nihon Bōkūshi* (*A History of Japanese Air Defenses*). Tokyo: Hara Shobo.

Junod, M. (1982, December). "The Hiroshima Disaster (II)." *International Review of the Red Cross Archive, 22*(231), 329–344.

Kadowaki, K. (1990). "Father Hugo Lassalle (1898–1990)." *The Eastern Buddhist* (*New Series*), *23*(2), 136–138.

Kaikōsha. (Eds). (2021). *Nankin Sen Shiryōshū I* (*Battle of Nanking Documents Collection*), vol. 1. Tokyo: Private printing.

Kamada, N. (2019, February). "Special Lecture on Medical Consequences of Little Boy Radiation Exposure" (joint lecture with Teramae Taeko). Hiroshima Peace Museum, Hiroshima.

Katorikku Seigi to Heiwa Hiroshima Kyōgikai (Hiroshima Catholic Conference of Justice and Peace). (Eds.). (1983). *Hakai no hi: Gaijin shinputachi no hibaku taiken* (*Day of Destruction: The Atomic Bomb Experiences of the Foreign Priests*). Hiroshima: *Katorikku Seigi to Heiwa Hiroshima Kyōgikai.*

Keever, B. D. (2004). *News Zero: "The New York Times" and the Bomb.* Monroe, ME: Common Courage Press.

"'*Kioku wo uketsugu': Miyakawa Hiroyuki-san—Joseito gisei chichi to tsutaeru*" ("'An Inherited Memory': Mr. Miyakawa Hiroyuki—Giving the News to the Father of a Girls' School Victim"). (2018, August 6). *Chūgoku Shimbun.* Retrieved June 4, 2023, from *Chūgoku Shimbun*, Hiroshima Peace Media website, https://www.hiroshimapeacemedia.jp/?p=85465.

Kirstein, P. N. (2009). "Hiroshima and Spinning the Atom: America, Britain, and Canada Proclaim the Nuclear Age, 6 August 1945." *The Historian, 71*(4), 805–827.

Kita, H. (1997). *Gunritsu hōtei: Senjika no shirarezaru "saiban"* (*Courts of Military Justice: The Unknown "Trials" of Wartime*). Tokyo: Asahi Shimbunsha.

Kitagome, S. (1955, October 20). *"Kokura no kawari ni Nagasaki; Tsugi wa Niigata wo yotei (Torūman kaikoroku)"* ("Nagasaki Was Bombed in Place of Kokura; Niigata Was Next [on the List] [Truman Memoirs]"). *Asahi Shimbun.*

Kitahara, M. (1984). "Japanese Responses to the Defeat in World War II." *International Journal of Social Psychiatry, 30*(3), 178–187.

Kitayama, S., Markus, H., and Kurokawa, M. (2000). "Culture, Emotion, and Well-Being: Good Feelings in Japan and the United States." *Cognition & Emotion, 14*(1), 93–124.

Knebel, F., and Bailey, C. W. (1961). *No High Ground: The Complete Eye-Opening True Story of the First Atomic Bomb.* New York: Bantam Books.

Kodama, M. (2005). *"Ikinokotta tomo wo osotta gan"* ("The Cancer That Afflicted My Surviving Friends"). Retrieved June 4, 2023, from Web Archive website, https://web.archive.org/web/20190314135734/http://www.geocities.jp/mk32924/page006.html.

Krauss, R., and Krauss, A. (Eds.). (2005). *The 509th Remembered: A History of the 509th Composite Group as Told by the Veterans Themselves.* Buchanan, MI: 509th Press.

Kristof, N. (1995, August 7). "Kokura, Japan: Bypassed by A-Bomb." *New York Times*, p. 7.

Kurokawa, M. (1976). *Genbaku no ishibumi: Hiroshima no kokoro* (*Atom Bomb Memorials: The Heart of Hiroshima*). Tokyo: Private printing.

Kurokawa, M. (1986). "Fragile Lives." In Sekimori , G., and Marshall, G. (Trans./Eds.). *Hibakusha: Survivors of Hiroshima and Nagasaki* (pp. 93–96). Tokyo: Kōsei Publishing.

Kushner, B. (2007). *The Thought War: Japanese Imperial Propaganda.* Honolulu: University of Hawai'i Press.

Kyōdō Tsūshin. (2021, October 25). *"Genbaku shibotsusha hitori no mimoto tokutei: Hiroshima shi ga mago ni ikotsu henkan"* ("Identity of an Atomic Bomb Victim Is Confirmed: Hiroshima City Returns Remains to Grandson"). Retrieved June 4, 2023, from Yahoo News website, https://news.yahoo.co.jp/articles/23c808ff887d51f729e4949b0ecfbfad250ccf05.

Laurence, W. L. (1940, May 5). "Vast Power Source in Atomic Energy Opened by Science." *New York Times.*

Laurence, W. L. (1945, September 9). "Atomic Bombing of Nagasaki Told by Flight Member." *New York Times.*

Laurence, W. L. (1946). *Dawn over Zero.* New York: Alfred A. Knopf.

Laurence, W. L. (1959). *Men and Atoms: The Discovery, the Uses and the Future of Atomic Energy.* New York: Simon & Schuster.

Laures, J. (1954). *The Catholic Church in Japan: A Short History.* Rutland, VT: Charles E. Tuttle Company.

Lifton, R. J. (1963). "Psychological Effects of the Atomic Bomb in Hiroshima: The Theme of Death." *Daedalus* 92(3), 462–497.

Lifton, R. J. (1968). *Death in Life: Survivors of Hiroshima.* New York: Random House.

Lifton, R. J. (1993). *The Protean Self: Human Resilience in an Age of Fragmentation.* New York: Basic Books.

Lifton, R. J., and Mitchell, G. (1995). *Hiroshima in America: Fifty Years of Denial.* New York: G. P. Putnam's Sons.

Little, J. B. (2003). "Principal Cellular and Tissue Effects of Radiation." In D. W. Kufe et al. (Eds), *Holland-Frei Cancer Medicine* (6th ed.). Hamilton, Ontario: B. C. Decker. Retrieved November 10, 2021, from NCBI website, https://www.ncbi.nlm.nih.gov/books/NBK12344/.

Logan, C. R. (1996)."*Something So Dim It Must Be Holy*": *Civil War Commemorative Sculpture in Arkansas, 1886–1934*. Little Rock: Arkansas Historic Preservation Program.

Luhmer, K. (1945). "Diary of Father Klaus Luhmer" (excerpt). Retrieved October 11, 2022, from Hiroshima National Peace Memorial Hall website, https://www .global-peace.go.jp/en/taikenki/en_taikenki_syousai.php?gbID=1648&dt=2106 01132155.

Machleidt, R. (2014, September 14). "Nuclear Forces." Retrieved June 3, 2023, from Scholarpedia website, http://www.scholarpedia.org/article/Nuclear_Forces #Historical_perspective.

Malloy, S. L. (2008). *Atomic Tragedy: Henry L. Stimson and the Decision to Use the Bomb Against Japan*. Ithaca, NY: Cornell University Press.

Mann, R. A. (2009). *The B-29 Superfortress Chronology, 1934–1960* (Kindle ed.). Jefferson, NC: McFarland & Company, Inc.

Markus, H., and Kitayama, S. (1991). "Culture and the Self: Implications for Cognition, Emotion, and Motivation." *Psychological Review, 98*(2), 224–253.

Marshall Foundation. (No date). "Tentative Draft of Radio Address by President Truman to Be Delivered After the Successful Use of the Atomic Bomb over Japan. Prepared by W. L. Laurence, Consultant to General Groves." Retrieved November 10, 2021, from Marshall Foundation National Archives Project website, https://www.marshallfoundation.org/library/wp-content /uploads/sites/16/2015/05/xerox1482-21C.pdf (dead link as of November 14, 2023).

Martindale, R. R. (1998). *The 13th Mission: Prisoner of the Notorious Omori Prison in Tokyo*. Austin, TX: Eakin Press.

Marx, J. L. (1967). *Seven Hours to Zero*. New York: G. P. Putnam's Sons.

Meditationhaus St. Franziskus. (No date). "Welcome Page." Retrieved June 6, 2023, from Meditationhaus St. Franziskus website, https://www.meditations haus-dietfurt.de/.

"Memories of Hiroshima and Nagasaki: Messages from Hibakusha. What Happened on This Date: 'It's Hot! Help! Water Please!'—Hiroshima 8/6 Re-created." (2005, August 6). *Asahi Shimbun*. Retrieved June 2, 2023, from *Asahi Shimbun* website, https://www.asahi.com/hibakusha/english/shimen /happened/happened-01.html.

Midori-machi Junior High School Students Association Report Editorial Board. (Eds.). (1980). *Kūhaku no gakusekibo: Dai-san kokumin gakkō no hibaku jittai wo tazunete (Blank Student Roll Book: An Inquiry into Number Three People's [Elementary] School in the Atomic Bombing)*. Hiroshima: Private printing.

Miller, M., and Spitzer, A. (1946). *We Dropped the A-Bomb*. (Republished as *We Dropped the Atom Bomb*. Uncommon Valor Series Edition.) Verdun Press.

Ministry of Education, Culture, Sports, Science, and Technology. (1962), *"Nihon no Seichō to Kyōiku [Shōwa 37nendo]"* ("Japan's National Growth and Education

[Ministry of Education Survey Bureau Report]"). Retrieved January 13, 2020, from Ministry of Education, Culture, Sports, Science, and Technology website, https://www.mext.go.jp/b_menu/hakusho/html/hpad196201/hpad196201_2_011.html (dead link).

Ministry of Health, Labor, and Welfare. (1969). *"Senbotsusha no izoku, senshōbyōsha nado no engo"* ("Support for War-Bereaved Families, War Invalided, and Others"). Retrieved June 6, 2023, from Ministry of Health, Labor, and Welfare website, https://www.mhlw.go.jp/toukei_hakusho/hakusho/kousei/1969/dl/16.pdf.

Ministry of Land, Infrastructure, Transport, and Tourism, Chūgoku Region Management Bureau, Ōta River Office. (2018). *"Ōtagawa hōsuiro no ayumi: Mizu to midori no heiwa toshi: Hiroshima no ishizue"* ("A History of the Ōta River Spillway: The Foundation of Hiroshima, Peace City of Water and Green Nature"). Retrieved March 8, 2023, from Chūgoku Region Management Bureau website, https://www.cgr.mlit.go.jp/ootagawa/ootagawahousuiro/pdf/20180207ootagawahousuironoayumi.pdf.

Ministry of the Environment. (No date). *"Hibaku nisei ni okeru senshokutai ijō"* ("Chromosomal Abnormality in Second-Generation Hibakusha"). Retrieved June 5, 2023, from Ministry of the Environment website, https://www.env.go.jp/chemi/rhm/h29kisoshiryo/h29kiso-03-06-02.html.

Misono, K. (Ed). (1945). *Medical Report of the Atomic Bombing in Hiroshima.* Tokyo: *Rikugun Gun'i Gakkō, Tōkyō Dai 1 Rikugun Byōin.*

Mitaka City Genbaku Taiken. "Noguchi Kazuko Testimony." Retrieved February 10, 2023, from Mitaka City Genbaku Taiken website, https://www.city.mitaka.lg.jp/heiwa/douga/hiroshima-nagasaki.html.

Miyamoto, Y. (2005). "Rebirth in the Pure Land or God's Sacrificial Lambs? Religious Interpretations of the Atomic Bombings in Hiroshima and Nagasaki." *Japanese Journal of Religious Studies, 32*(1), 131–159.

Mizukawa, K. (2019, November 29). "Striving to Fill Voids in Hiroshima, Part 1: Names Fall into Oblivion." *Chūgoku Shimbun.* Retrieved November 14, 2023, from *Chūgoku Shimbun,* Hirohima Peace Media website, https://www.hiroshimapeacemedia.jp/?p=95148.

Mizukawa, K. (2020, October 29). *"Kodama Mitsuo-san shikyaku: Hiroshima Itchū de hibaku, shōgen katsudō, 88sai"* ("Kodama Mitsuo, Exposed to Atom Bomb at Hiroshima Itchū, Survivor Testimony Activist, Dead at Eighty-Eight"). *Chūgoku Shimbun.*

Moore, R. A. (2011). *Soldier of God: MacArthur's Attempt to Christianize Japan.* Haworth, NJ: Merwin Asia.

Mori, S. (2016). *Genbaku de shinda beihei hishi (The Untold Story of the American Servicemen Killed by the Atomic Bomb).* Tokyo: Kojinsha.

Mori, S., et al. (No date). "Dutch POWs." Retrieved June 6, 2023, from Under the Atomic Bomb: American POWs in Hiroshima website, https://hiroshima-pows.org/chapter-5-page.

Morita, Y. (2018, September 27). *"Ron: Ichijo hi no hyōzō joseishi kara mieru no ha"* ("Looking at the Ichijo Memorial from the Perspective of Women's History"). *Chūgoku Shimbun.*

Morris-Suzuki, T. (1998). *Re-Inventing Japan: Time, Space, Nation.* Armonk, NY: M. E. Sharpe.

Mullins, M. R. (2022). *Yasukuni Fundamentalism: Japanese Religions and the Politics of Restoration.* Honolulu: University of Hawai'i.

Muranaka, K. (Ed). (1995). *Dōin gakuto shi: Hibaku 50-shū nen kinen* (*A History of Students Mobilized for War Labor: Commemorating the Fiftieth Anniversary*). Hiroshima: Hiroshima Prefectural War-Mobilized Student Victims Association.

Murphy, C. J. V. (1945, September). "The Air War on Japan." *Fortune, 32*(3), 117–123.

Murphy, C. J. V. (1945, October). "The Air War on Japan." *Fortune, 32*(4), 132–137.

Myfordboy Channel. (2009). *Metal Casting at Home, Part 10: Another Day in My Home Foundry* [Video]. Retrieved September 14, 2022, from YouTube, https://www.youtube.com/watch?v=M95bhPrDwAo.

Nagai, T. (Kuo, A. F. [Trans.]). (1945). *Atomic Bomb Rescue and Relife [sic] Report.* Nagasaki, Japan: Nagasaki Medical College.

Nagasaki City. (1977). *Nagasaki Genbaku Sensaishi* (*Record of the Atomic Bombing of Nagasaki*), vol. 1. Nagasaki: Nagasaki City.

Nagata, S. (Ed.). (1951/1969) *Genbaku no Ko* (*Children of the Bomb*). Tokyo: Iwatani Shoten.

Nakamae, T. (writing as Maki Kayoko). (1953). *"Sumire no you ni"* ("Like a Lily"). In *Genbaku Higaisha no Shuki Hensan I'inkai* (Eds.), *Genbaku ni ikite* (*Living the Atomic Bomb*) (pp. 254–257). Hiroshima: San'ichi Shobo.

Nakayama, S., et al. (Eds.). (2005). *A Social History of Science and Technology in Contemporary Japan*, vol. 2, *Road to Self-Reliance, 1952–1959.* Melbourne, Australia: Trans-Pacific Press.

Naono, A. (2018). *"Sensō higai juninron to sengo hoshō seido"* ("The Theory of 'Accepted Suffering' and the Postwar Compensation System"). In Hiroshima Peace Institute (Eds.), *Sengoshori wo meguru shomondai* (*Issues in Postwar Recovery*), vol. 5 (pp. 189–212). Hiroshima: Hiroshima Peace Institute.

National Defense Research Committee. (1946). *Fire Warfare: Incendiaries and Flame Throwers* (*Summary Technical Report of Division 11, NDRC*, vol. 3). Washington, DC: Joint Research and Development Board.

Neel, J. V. (1998). "Genetic Studies at the Atomic Bomb Casualty Commission— Radiation Effects Research Foundation: 1946–1997. *Proceedings of the National Academy of Sciences USA, 95*(10), 5432–5436.

NHK. (2011). *Ishibumi No Kanata Ni* (*Beyond the Memorial Stones*). Originally broadcast August 2011.

NHK. (No date). *Genbaku no Kioku: Hajimete uchiakeru kono omoi* (*Atomic Bomb Memories: My Feelings on Revealing This for the First Time*). Retrieved June 4, 2023, from NHK website, https://www.nhk.or.jp/archives/shogenarchives/no-more-hibakusha/library/shogen/ja/109/.

NHK. (No date). *NHK Web Tokushū: Ikinokotte, sumimasen* (*NHK Web Special: Pardon Me for Having Survived*). Retrieved June 10, 2022, from NHK website, https://www3.nhk.or.jp/news/html/20201127k10012733431000.html (dead link as of June 5, 2023).

Nihon Chishi Kenkyūjō. (1978). *Nihon chishi: Dai 17-kan Okayama-ken; Hiroshima-ken; Yamaguchi-ken.* Tokyo: Nihon Chishi Kenkyūjō.

Nishimoto, M. (2019, November 12). "A-bomb Memoirs Reveal August 6 Experiences of 16 Catholic Priests from Overseas." *Chūgoku Shimbun.* Retrieved June 6, 2023, from *Chūgoku Shimbun*, Hiroshima Peace Media website, https://www.hiroshimapeacemedia.jp/?p=96885.

Normile, D. (2020). "How Atomic Bomb Survivors Have Transformed Our Understanding of Radiation's Effects." Retrieved November 10, 2021, from Science.org, https://www.science.org/content/article/how-atomic-bomb-survivors-have-transformed-our-understanding-radiation-s-impacts.

Office of Assistant Chief of Air Staff Intelligence. (1944). "Air Objective Folder—Kure Area, no. 90.30." Washington, DC: United States Army Air Forces.

Okamoto, G. (2017, May 3). *"Hibakushi no kyūyū wa 'eirei' ka; Shushō no Yasukuni sanpai, yurusenu josei"* ("Are Her Classmates Killed by the Atomic Bomb 'Heroic Spirits'? A Woman Who Cannot Accept the Prime Minister's Visits to Yasukuni Shrine"). *Asahi Shimbun.* Retrieved December 15, 2021, from *Asahi Shimbun* website, https://www.asahi.com/articles/photo/AS20170502003367.html (dead link as of June 6, 2023).

Okayama Prefecture. (No date). *"Senshōbyosha senbotsusha izoku nado engo hō (Engohō) no shikumi"* ("An Explanation of the Functioning of the War Wounded / Sick Soldiers and War-Bereaved Families Aid Law [Aid Law]"). Retrieved November 14, 2023, from Okayama Prefecture website, https://www.pref.okayama.jp/uploaded/life/699391_6241035_misc.pdf (dead link).

Olson, S. (2020). *The Apocalypse Factory: Plutonium and the Making of the Atomic Age.* New York: W. W. Norton & Co.

"Onkyū Kaisei: Dōin Gakuto ni mo" ("Military Pension Reform: Will Also Apply to War-Mobilized Students"). (1958, January 29). *Asahi Shimbun.*

Osada, A. (Ed). (1959/1969). *Genbaku no Ko* (*Children of the Bomb*). Tokyo: Iwatani Shoten.

Ōta, Y., Mine, M., and Yoshimine, E. (2014). *Genshiya no Torauma* (*Trauma Amid Fields of Atom-Bombed Rubble*). Nagasaki: Nagasaki Shimbunsha.

Oughterson, A. W., et al. (1951). *Effects of Atomic Bombs: The Report of the Joint Commission for the Investigation of the Effects of the Atomic Bomb in Japan*, vols. 1–5. Oak Ridge, TN: United States Atomic Energy Commission.

Pacific War Research Society. (1972). *The Day Man Lost: Hiroshima, 6 August 1945.* Tokyo: Kodansha.

Pacific Wrecks. (No date). "North Field (Ushi Point Airfield)." Retrieved November 11, 2022, from Pacific Wrecks website, https://pacificwrecks.com/airfields/marianas/ushi/.

Pape, R. (1996). *Bombing to Win: Air Power and Coercion in War.* Ithaca, NY: Cornell University Press.

Peace Seeds. (2007, December 11). "Q & A About Hiroshima / The Atomic Bomb: (21) Why Was Giving Water to Victims of the Atomic Bomb Discouraged?" Retrieved June 3, 2023, from Peace Seeds website, https://www.hiroshimapeace media.jp/hiroshima-koku/en/exploration/index_20071211.html.

Perera, G. (1975). *Leaves from My Book of Life.* Boston: Private printing.

Plung, D. J. (2021, October 1). "The Impact of Urban Evacuation in Japan During World War II." *The Asia-Pacific Journal: Japan Focus.* Retrieved June 2, 2023, from APJJF website, https://apjjf.org/2021/19/Plung.html.

Postol, T. A. (1986). "Possible Fatalities from Superfires Following Nuclear Attacks in or near Urban Areas." In F. Solomon and R. Q. Marston (Eds.), *The Medical Implications of Nuclear War* (pp. 15–72). Washington, DC: National Academies Press.

Reed, B. C. (2020). *Manhattan Project: The Story of the Century.* New York: Springer.

Rhodes, R. (1986). *The Making of the Atomic Bomb.* New York: Simon & Schuster.

Rhodes, R. (1995, June 19). "The General and World War III." *New Yorker.* Retrieved February 22, 2020, from New Yorker website, https://www.newyorker.com /magazine/1995/06/19/the-general-and-world-war-iii.

Robertson, G. B. (2018). *Bringing the Thunder: The Missions of a World War II B-29 Pilot in the Pacific.* Wide Awake Books.

Rose, T. (2018, June) "Piecing Together a Nuclear Fireball." *Science & Technology Review,* 20–23. Retrieved November 14, 2023, from Lawrence Livermore National Laboratory website, https://str.llnl.gov/content/pages/2018-06/pdf /06.18.4.pdf.

Sakamoto, S. (1951/1969). "Remembrance of August 6, 1945." In A. Osada (Ed.), *Genbaku no Ko (Children of the Bomb)* (pp. 231–233). Tokyo: Iwatani Shoten.

Sand, J. (2003). *House and Home in Modern Japan: Architecture, Domestic Space, and Bourgeois Culture, 1880–1930.* Cambridge, MA: Harvard University Asia Center.

Sano, M. (1942). *Kōshiki Shin Kokumin Girei (Public Ceremony: Reverence of Subjects).* Tokyo: Sanseidō.

Schaffer, R. (1985). *Wings of Judgment: American Bombing in World War II.* New York: Oxford University Press.

Schiffer, H. F. (1953). "The Rosary of Hiroshima" (pamphlet). Washington, NJ: Blue Army of Our Lady of Fatima.

Schull, W. J. (1995). *Effects of Atomic Radiation: A Half-Century of Studies from Hiroshima and Nagasaki.* Hoboken, NJ: Wiley.

Seki, C. (1985). *Hiroshima Dai Ni Kenjo Ni-nen Nishi-gumi: Genbaku de Shinda Kyūyūtachi (Second Hiroshima Prefectural Girls' School, Second-Year West Class: My Classmates Who Died from the Atomic Bomb).* Tokyo: Chikuma Shobo.

Seki, C. (2015). *Hiroshima no Shōnen Shōjo-tachi: Genbaku, Yasukuni, Chōsen Hantō Shusshinsha (The Boys and Girls of Hiroshima: The Bomb, Yasukuni Shrine, Koreans).* Tokyo: Sairyūsha.

Sekimori, G. (Trans.). (1986). *Hibakusha: Survivors of Hiroshima and Nagasaki.* Tokyo: Kōsei Publishing.

Seraphim, F. (2006). *War Memory and Social Politics in Japan, 1945–2005,* Cambridge, MA: Harvard University Press.

Serber, R. (1992). *The Los Alamos Primer: The First Lectures on How to Build an Atomic Bomb.* Berkeley: University of California Press.

Sherry, M. (1989). *The Rise of American Air Power: The Creation of Armageddon.* New Haven, CT: Yale University Press.

Shirabe, R. (Kuo, A. F. [Trans.]). (2002). *A Physician's Diary of the Atomic Bombing and Its Aftermath.* Nagasaki: Nagasaki Association for Hibakusha's Medical Care [NASHIM].

Shirai, H. (1992). *Maboroshi no koe: NHK Hiroshima hachi-gatsu roku-nichi (Phantom Voice: NHK August 6).* Tokyo: Iwanami Shoten.

Shishido, K. (1972). *Hiroshima ga horonda hi: 27nen-me no shinjitsu (The Day Hiroshima Was Destroyed: The Truth Twenty-Seven Years Later).* Tokyo: Yomiuri Shimbunsha.

Shishido, K. (1991). *Hiroshima Gun Shireibu Hametsu (The Destruction of Hiroshima Army Headquarters).* Tokyo: Yomiuri Shimbunsha.

Shōno, N., and Iijima, S. (1975). *Kakuhōshasen to Genbakubyō (Nuclear Radiation and Atom Bomb Diseases).* Tokyo: NHK.

Siemes, J. (1945). "Postwar Debriefing Interview." In US Naval Technical Mission to Japan (Eds.), *Miscellaneous Targets: Atomic Bombs, Hiroshima and Nagasaki, Article 1: Medical Effects* (pp. 8–11). San Francisco: US Naval Technical Mission to Japan.

Snyder, C. R., Higgins, R. L., and Stucky, R. J. (1983). *Excuses: Masquerades in Search of Grace.* New York: Wiley-Interscience.

Stanford Research Institute and United States Federal Civil Defense Administration. (1953). *Impact of Air Attack in World War II: Selected Data for Civil Defense Planning,* vol. 2, *Economic Effects—Japan.* Washington, DC: United States Government Printing Office.

Supreme Commander for the Allied Powers (SCAP). (1945, September 19). SCAPIN (SCAP Memorandum for the Imperial Japanese Government) 33, "Press Code."

Supreme Commander for the Allied Powers (SCAP). (1945, December 15). SCAPIN (SCAP Memorandum for the Imperial Japanese Government) 448, "Abolition of Governmental Sponsorship, Perpetuation, Control, and Dissemination of State Shintō (*Kokka Shintō, Jinja Shintō*)."

Supreme Commander for the Allied Powers (SCAP). (1947). *Two Years of Occupation.* Washington DC: Department of the Army, Civil Affairs Division.

Swanberg, S. E. (2021, December). "Under the Influence: The Impact of Johannes A. Siemes, SJ's Eyewitness Report on John Hersey's 'Hiroshima.'" *Literary Journalism Studies, 13*(1 and 2), 131–161.

Sweeney, C. W. (1997). *War's End: An Eyewitness Account of America's Last Atomic Mission.* New York: Avon Books.

Tachikawa, K. (2007). *"Kyū Nihongun ni okeru horyo no toriatsukai; Taiheiyō Sensō no jōkyō wo chūshin ni"* ("POW Treatment by the Imperial Japanese Military, Focusing on Conditions in the Asia-Pacific War"). *NIDS Security Studies, 10*(1), 99–142.

Tado, S. (2010). *"Ma no seihin no o-sugata ni utarete"* ("I Was Struck by His Appearance of Utter Humility"). In *Arupe-shinpu no Reppuku wo Inoru Kai* (Eds.), *Arupe-shinpu kaisōki Dai-ni han* (*Memories of Father Arrupe*, vol. 2) (p. 34). Hiroshima: Private printing.

Tado, S. (2020). *Sora no tori, no no hana no yō ni: Kami no megumi ni ikasarete* (*Like a Bird in the Sky, and a Flower in the Field: Living Among God's Blessings*). Tokyo: Private printing.

Takemae, E. (Ricketts, R., and Swann, S. [Trans.]). (2002). *Inside GHQ: The Allied Occupation of Japan and Its Legacy.* London: Continuum.

"Three Hundred Eighty-Seven Thousand Deaths Confirmed in WWII Air Raids in Japan; Toll Unknown in Fifteen Cities: Survey." (2020, August 21). *Mainichi Shimbun.* Retrieved August 23, 2020, from *Mainichi Shimbun* website, https://mainichi.jp/english/articles/20200821/p.2a/00m/0na/018000c (dead link as of November 14, 2023).

Tibbets, P. W. (1998). *The Return of the Enola Gay.* Columbus, OH: Private printing.

Tomonaga, M. (2019). "The Atomic Bombings of Hiroshima and Nagasaki: A Summary of the Human Consequences, 1945–2018, and Lessons for *Homo sapiens* to End the Nuclear Weapon Age." *Journal for Peace and Nuclear Disarmament, 2*(2), 491–517.

Toyonaga, K. (2001). "Colonialism and Atom Bombs: About Survivors of Hiroshima Living in Korea." In T. Fujitani et al. (Eds.), *Perilous Memories: The Asia-Pacific War(s)* (pp. 378–394). Durham, NC: Duke University Press.

Tōyūkai. (No date). *"Tōkyōto no hibakusha kazu"* ("Hibakusha Numbers in Tokyo"). Retrieved June 5, 2023, from Tōyūkai website, https://t-hibaku.jp/soudan/toukei.html.

"Truman Reports, 'It Is an Atomic Bomb.'" (2006, September 1). *Air Force Magazine, 89*(9). Retrieved June 3, 2023, from *Air & Space Forces Magazine* website, https://www.airandspaceforces.com/article/0906keeperfile/.

Tsuchiya, K. (1975) *Setouchi no Kabutogani.* (*Horseshoe Crabs of the Seto Inland Sea*). Tokyo: Gakushū Kenkyūsha.

Tsukuda, A. (1995). *"50-nen mae no taimukapuseru"* ("A Time Capsule from Fifty Years Ago"). In *Hiroshima Ken Dōin Gakuto Giseisha no Kai* (Association for Hiroshima Prefecture Victims of Student War Mobilization) (Eds.), *Dōin Gakuto: Dōkoku no Shōgen* (*War-Mobilized Students: Wailed Testimonies*) (pp. 191–194). Hiroshima: *Hiroshima Ken Dōin Gakuto Giseisha no Kai.*

Tsuzuki, M. (1947). "Report on the Medical Studies of the Effects of the Atomic Bomb." In Atomic Bomb Casualty Commission (Eds.), *General Report* (pp. 66–111). Washington, DC: National Research Council.

Twenty-First Bomber Command. (1945, 5 April). "Monthly Activity Report." Guam: Headquarters, XXIst Bomber Command.

Ubuki, S. (2014). *Hiroshima sengoshi: Hibaku taiken wa dō uketomeraretekitaka (A History of Postwar Hiroshima: How Has the Atomic Bombing Experience Been Dealt With?)*. Tokyo: Iwanami Shoten.

"Ujina gaisenkan rekishi tsutaeru: Shi kyōdo shiryōkan kikakuten; shukushō mokei ya paneru" ("Telling the History of the Ujina Hall of Triumphant Return: Special Exhibit at City Museum of History and Traditional Crafts Shows Scale Model and Panel Displays"). (2017, July 10). *Chūgoku Shimbun*. Retrieved June 2, 2023, from *Chūgoku Shimbun*, Hiroshima Peace Media website, https://www.hiroshi mapeacemedia.jp/?p=73540.

United Nations War Crimes Commission. (Eds.). (1949). "Case No. 25, Trial of Lieutenant-General Shigeru Sawada and Three Others 1." In United Nations War Crimes Commission (Eds.), *Law Reports of Trials of War Criminals*, vol. 5 (pp. 1–26). London: His Majesty's Stationery Office.

"Uran genshi kaku no bunretsu: Saishōryō de kayaku 2-man ton ni hitteki" ("Fission of Uranium Nucleus: Tiny Amount Equivalent to Twenty Thousand Tons of Conventional Explosives"). (1945, August 16). *Asahi Shimbun*.

US Army Air Forces, Twentieth Air Force. (1945). "Mission Resume, Mission Number 325."

US Army Air Forces, Twentieth Air Force. (1945). *STARVATION: Phase Analysis of the Twentieth Air Force Strategic Mining Blockade of the Japanese Empire*.

US Army Air Forces, Twentieth Air Force. (1945). "Tactical Report: Mission No. Special."

US Army Signal Corps. (No date). *Atomic Bomb Footage: Tinian (1945)—Part 2* [Video]. Retrieved June 15, 2022, from the Naval History and Heritage channel on YouTube, https://www.youtube.com/watch?v=PxfxCSaeWmA.

US Naval Technical Mission to Japan. (Eds.). (1945). *Miscellaneous Targets: Atomic Bombs, Hiroshima and Nagasaki, Article 1: Medical Effects*. San Francisco: US Naval Technical Mission to Japan.

US Nuclear Regulatory Commission. (No date). "Lethal Dose (LD)." Retrieved March 2021 from Nuclear Regulatory Commission website, https://www.nrc .gov/reading-rm/basic-ref/glossary/lethal-dose-ld.html.

US Strategic Bombing Survey. (Eds.). (1946a). *Report 3: The Effects of the Atomic Bombs on Hiroshima and Nagasaki*. Washington, DC: United States Government Printing Office.

US Strategic Bombing Survey. (Eds.). (1946b). *Report 11: Final Report Covering Air-Raid Protection and Allied Subjects in Japan. Hiroshima and Nagasaki*. Washington, DC: United States Government Printing Office.

US Strategic Bombing Survey. (Eds.). (1946c). *Summary Report (Pacific War)*. Washington, DC: United States Government Printing Office.

US Strategic Bombing Survey. (Eds.). (1947a). *Report 14: The Effects of Strategic Bombing on Japanese Morale.* Washington, DC: United States Government Printing Office.

US Strategic Bombing Survey. (Eds.). (1947b). *Report 42: The Japanese Wartime Standard of Living and Utilization of Manpower.* Washington, DC: United States Government Printing Office.

US Strategic Bombing Survey. (Eds.). (1947c). *Report 54: The War Against Japanese Transportation, 1941–1945.* Washington DC: United States Government Printing Office.

US Strategic Bombing Survey. (Eds.). (1947d). *Report 90: Effects of Incendiary Bomb Attacks on Japan: A Report on Eight Cities.* Washington, DC: United States Government Printing Office.

US Strategic Bombing Survey. (Eds.). (1947e). *Report 92: Effects of the Atomic Bomb on Hiroshima, Japan*, vols. 1–3. Washington, DC: United States Government Printing Office.

Van Kirk, T. (1945, August 6). "Hiroshima Log of the *Enola Gay.*" Retrieved June 2, 2023, from Atomic Heritage Foundation website, https://ahf.nuclearmuseum.org/ahf/key-documents/hiroshima-log-enola-gay/.

Vogel, E. F. (1963). *Japan's New Middle Class.* Berkeley: University of California Press.

Walker, J. S. (1997). *Prompt and Utter Destruction: Truman and the Use of Atomic Bombs Against Japan.* Chapel Hill: University of North Carolina Press.

Wannier, M. M. A., et al. (2019, March). "Fallout Melt Debris and Aerodynamically Shaped Glasses in Beach Sands of Hiroshima Bay, Japan." *Anthropocene, 25.* Retrieved June 3, 2023, from Science Direct website, https://www.sciencedirect.com/science/article/abs/pii/S2213305419300074.

"War Department Called *Times* Reporter to Explain Bomb's Intricacies to Public." (1945, August 7). *New York Times.*

Watanabe, M. (2001). "Imagery and War in Japan 1995." In T. Fujitani et al. (Eds.), *Perilous Memories: The Asia-Pacific War(s)* (pp. 129–151). Durham, NC: Duke University Press.

Weaver, R. M. (1953). *The Ethics of Rhetoric.* Chicago: Henry Regnery Company.

Webb, R. (2020). "Strong Nuclear Force: The Fundamental Force of Nature That Holds Protons and Neutrons Together in the Atomic Nucleus." Retrieved June 2, 2020, from New Scientist website, https://www.newscientist.com/definition/strong-nuclear-force/.

Wellerstein, A. (2021). *Restricted Data: The History of Nuclear Secrecy in the United States.* Chicago: University of Chicago.

White, C. S., Bowen, I. G., and Richmond, D. R. (1963, June 11). "A Comparative Analysis of Some of the Immediate Environmental Effects at Hiroshima and Nagasaki." Eighth Annual Meeting of the Health Physics Society, New York City, NY.

"White House Press Release." (1943, April 22). *New York Times.*

"William Laurence, Ex–Science Writer for the *Times*, Dies." (1977, March 19). *New York Times.*

Winter, J. (1995). *Sites of Memory, Sites of Mourning; The Great War in European Cultural History.* Cambridge, UK: Cambridge University Press.

Wittner, L. S. (1971). "MacArthur and the Missionaries: God and Man in Occupied Japan." *Pacific Historical Review, 40*(1), 77–98.

Woodard, W. P. (1972). *The Allied Occupation of Japan 1945–52 and Japanese Religions.* Leiden, Netherlands: E. J. Brill.

World Nuclear Association. "Fukushima: Background on Reactors." (No date). Retrieved April 4, 2022, from World Nuclear Association website, https://world-nuclear.org/information-library/safety-and-security/safety-of-plants/appendices/fukushima-reactor-background.aspx.

World Population Review. (No date). "Tokyo Population." Retrieved January 3, 2020, from World Population Review website, http://worldpopulationreview.com/world-cities/tokyo-population/.

Yamane, S. (2021). *"Shōi dan no pika, makkura na sora, yaketa nioi Yahata dai kūshū no taikensha ga hajimete kataru riaru"* ("The Flash of the Incendiaries, a Black Sky, the Smell of Burning: A Survivor of the Great Yahata Air Raid Speaks for the First Time"). Retrieved November 13, 2022, from Fukuoka Fukabori Media Sasatto (*Yomiuri Shimbun*, Western Japan Office) website, https://sasatto.jp/article/entry-1308.html.

Yamashita, S. H. (2015). *Daily Life in Wartime Japan, 1940–1945.* Lawrence: University Press of Kansas.

Yamato Group. (No date). *"Sentaku no dai kaikaku"* ("The Great Reform in Laundry Technology"). Retrieved June 6, 2023, from Yamato Group website, http://www.yamato-gr.co.jp/ans/18-09/index.html.

Yamazaki, H., and Namakura, T. (2013). *"Chi'iki sozai wo katsuyō shita chigaku no gakushū: Taichi no naritachi no kyōzai to shite no Hiroshima derutā"* ("Geoscience Teaching Using Local Geological Materials (5): Hiroshima Delta as a Teaching Material on Formation and Change of Land"). *Hiroshima Daigaku Daigakuin Kyōikugaku Kenkyū Kiyō, 2*(62), 1–7.

Yoshida, Y. (2002). *Nihon no Guntai: Heishitachi no Kindaishi* (*Japan's Military: Modern History of Soldiers*). Tokyo: Iwanami Shoten.

Yoshioka, H. (2005a). "Forming a Nuclear Regime and Introducing Commercial Reactors." In S. Nakayama et al. (Eds.), *A Social History of Science and Technology in Contemporary Japan*, vol. 2, *Road to Self-Reliance, 1952–1959* (pp. 80–103). Melbourne, Australia: Trans-Pacific Press.

Yoshioka, H. (2005b). "Nuclear Power Research and the Scientists' Role." In S. Nakayama et al. (Eds.), *A Social History of Science and Technology in Contemporary Japan*, vol. 2, *Road to Self-Reliance, 1952–1959* (pp. 104–124). Melbourne, Australia: Trans-Pacific Press.

Young, L. (1998). *Japan's Total Empire: Manchuria and the Culture of Wartime Imperialism.* Berkeley: University of California Press.

Young, L. (2013). *Beyond the Metropolis: Second Cities and Modern Life in Interwar Japan*. Berkeley: University of California Press.

Zajtchuk, R. (Ed). (1989). *Medical Consequences of Nuclear Warfare* (*Textbook of Military Medicine, Part I*). Washington, DC: Office of the Surgeon General.

Zajtchuk, R. (Ed). (1994). *Military Dermatology* (*Textbook of Military Medicine, Part III*). Washington, DC: Office of the Surgeon General.

Zwigenberg, R. (2014). *Hiroshima: The Origins of Global Memory Culture*. Cambridge, UK: Cambridge University Press.

NOTES

EPIGRAPH

1. Miller and Spitzer, 1946, p. 111.

THE BOMBER

1. Krauss and Krauss, 2005, p. 151.
2. Beser, 1988, p. 96.
3. Sweeney, 1997, pp. 163–164.
4. Farrell, 2019, p. 246.
5. Laurence, 1946, p. 209.
6. Laurence, 1946, p. 209; Tibbets, 1998, pp. 209–210.
7. Correll, 2010, p. 75.
8. Sweeney, p. 162.
9. Tibbets had spent two years of his Army Air Forces career helping the design team at Boeing design and develop the B-29. This and other periods of his life are described in detail in his self-published 1998 autobiography. See Tibbets.
10. Tibbets, p. 198.
11. 509th Composite Group, 1945, p. 63.
12. Miller and Spitzer, p. 11.
13. Miller and Spitzer, p. 66.
14. Laurence, 1946, pp. 209–210.
15. Sweeney, p. 166. North Field had four runways by this point: Able, Baker, Charlie, and Dog. Each was some 2.5 kilometers long, and all were lined on both sides with paved hardstands, each of which was about the size of a baseball infield. The hardstands were essentially parking spots accommodating one B-29 each. There were some 265 hardstands on the field, about a dozen of which were used by the 509th Composite Group's special atomic-bomb-capable aircraft.

STANDING BY

1. Future Nobel Physics Prize winner Luis Alvarez was on board this aircraft, in charge of monitoring readings from the radiosondes. Knebel and Bailey, 1961, p. 249. See also Alvarez, 1987.
2. This aircraft was named *Necessary Evil* in the last few days of the war.

3. The sole exception was the ancient cultural capital of Kyoto, which had been removed from the target list by American decision-makers who had long since had an eye on winning postwar Japanese hearts and minds.

4. See Feis, 1966, p. 190. For a firsthand testimony discussion of scientific opposition to combat use of the bombs, see Alvarez, pp. 147–148.

5. For a firsthand testimony discussion of the Target Committee's process of choosing atomic bomb targets, see Groves, 1962, pp. 273–276. See also Malloy, 2008, pp. 134–135, et al.

6. See Rhodes, 1986, p. 703.

7. Tibbets, p. 82.

8. A special loading pit for Little Boy identical to the one at North Field was constructed on Iwo Jima.

9. Sweeney, p. 161.

THE BOMB

1. The average cost of each of the four atomic bombs built by the Manhattan Project was approximately six hundred million 1945 dollars each. Brookings Institution, 2002.

2. A group of Manhattan Project scientists who were led by James Franck and Glenn Seaborg at the Metallurgical Laboratory at the University of Chicago—and who included Robert Oppenheimer's right-hand theory man, Leo Szilard, at Los Alamos—was opposed to the immediate use of the new weapon against other human beings without a prior public demonstration of the weapon's power: (1) to give Japan a chance to surrender without first having to suffer its effects; and (2) to let the rest of the world in on a dialogue about whether these weapons should be used and what should be done with them in the future.

3. Olson, 2020, p. 35

4. Reed, 2020, p. 11.

5. See Olson.

6. Atomic Heritage Foundation, "Hiroshima and Nagasaki Bombing Timeline."

FAITH IN FINAL VICTORY

1. See Shirai, 1992.

2. Hiroshima Prefectural Government, 1976, pp. 30–31.

3. Drea, 1998, p. 162.

4. NHK was, and continues today to function as, Japan's public broadcasting corporation equivalent (in structure and scope of political and cultural influence) of the UK's BBC.

5. Hiroshima City (hereafter "Sensai"), 1971, vol. 2, p. 161. The girls were third-year students at Hijiyama, so fourteen to fifteen years old. See Shishido, 1991, p. 69.

6. See Shishido, 1972.

7. For a layout map of this bunker, see Hiroshima Jō, 2015, p. 9.

8. Hiroshima Jō, p. 10.

9. For documentation on the official prioritization of Japanese airpower to kamikaze operations by this point, see "Army-Navy Agreement on the Execution of Ketsu-Go Air Operation" (general order issued by IGHQ, July 13, 1945) in Japanese Self-Defense Agency Defense Research Center, 1972.

10. See Shishido, 1972, p. 149.

11. This civilian authority, under the direct purview of the prefectural governor, was formally known as the Hiroshima Prefectural Air Defense Observation Post Bureau. Under its jurisdiction across the prefecture were some thirty-three observation posts manned twenty-four hours a day by shifts of *Keibōdan* personnel (professional and also local volunteers). These were equipped with dedicated landline telephones connected directly to the Hiroshima Prefectural Office. See Hiroshima Jō, p. 43.

THE CASTLE

1. See Hyland, 2014. See also US Strategic Bombing Survey, 1947d, pp. 9–12. The main force carrying out the attack was the 58th Bombardment Wing of the Twentieth Air Force, arriving over the target at 0005 hours, August 6, 1945. There "64 aircraft dropped 490 tons of M69 incendiaries (and some normal high explosive bombs)." A third and last raid had been against urban concentrations in Nishinomiya, Hyogo Prefecture, on the outskirts of the metropolis of Osaka, over two hundred kilometers to the east. The all clear was sounded at 0430 hours. Mercifully, Chūgoku HQ decided not to set off sirens for this.

2. *Sensai*, vol. 1, p. 32.

3. Agricultural activity for the duration of the conflict had long since been legally limited by government decree to the production of rice and other staple crops. A comprehensive portrait of Japanese dietary conditions can be found in Yamashita, 2015.

4. "Specialized" or "normal" schools (as they were previously known) were teacher-training colleges. In this book, for the sake of clarity, I will refer to them as "teachers colleges."

5. See Mizukawa, 2019.

6. In its target planning, the US Army Air Forces also appreciated these waterways as natural firebreaks vis-à-vis incendiary attacks. See Office of Assistant Chief of Air Staff Intelligence, 1944, p. 14.

7. This is no longer the case, as centuries of landfill and land-reclamation projects extending far out into Hiroshima Bay have nearly doubled the dry-land acreage in the delta since then.

8. US Strategic Bombing Survey, 1947e, p. 335.

9. Nearly eleven thousand POWs from America, British Commonwealth countries, and the Netherlands died on these ships. Tachikawa, 2007, p. 102.

10. *Sensai*, vol. 1, p. 26.

11. Ubuki, 2014, p. 3.

WEATHER REPORT

1. Seki, 1985, p. 14.

2. The eastern Hiroshima Prefecture port of Onomichi is a best guess at the point where *Straight Flush*—and, fifty-odd minutes later, the Little Boy strike force—entered Honshu airspace. This is based on Japanese military and eye- and earwitness contact reports from August 6, when the strike force was detected passing over Matsunaga-chō, in the mountains behind Onomichi, and the latitude-longitude coordinates of the "IP" or "initial point" of the Hiroshima mission (the beginning point of a bomb run, from which a bomber would fly straight and level toward a target so a bombardier could aim better) indicates the nearby port of Mihara, according to 509th Composite Group, 1945, p. 65.

3. This execution of the captured Doolittle Raiders was known by US authorities but withheld from the American public until a White House press release on April 22, 1943. See "White House Press Release," 1943.

4. See Kita, 1997, p. 37. From February 1945, modifications to IJA legal directives for courts-martial dispensed with the need to have any judge advocate general or other legally qualified officers present when conducting a court-martial in the field. This essentially gave local field commanders carte blanche to summarily execute captured Allied airmen at their discretion.

5. See Martindale, 1998.

6. Mori, 2016, pp. 127–128.

7. See Cieslik, 1983.

8. Earlier in the war, even an American plane over Wake Island, more than three thousand kilometers from Tokyo, would set off sirens back in the Japanese Home Islands because protocol called for this when enemy aircraft penetrated Japanese—or Japanese-held—airspace anywhere in the empire (US Strategic Bombing Survey, 1946b, p. 35).

9. See US Strategic Bombing Survey, 1946b.

10. "Three Hundred Eighty-Seven Thousand Deaths," 2020. For evacuee estimates, see Plung, 2021.

11. See Miyamoto, 2005.

12. Pacific War Research Society, 1972, p. 151. "Because of Christians . . ." US Strategic Bombing Survey , 1946a, p. 21.

13. Marx, 1967, p. 159.

14. "Apprehension among Hiroshima populace that summer . . ." US Strategic Bombing Survey, 1946a, p. 21. Extensive quotable eyewitness accounts can also be found in Cieslik about the sleepless night of August 5–6 because of all the sirens going off at all hours. Cieslik's piece is chock-full of other details

about life in Hiroshima that summer under multiple daily American flyovers that never dropped bombs. See also Lifton, 1963, p. 464.

15. *Sensai*, vol. 1, pp. 30–31.

16. *Sensai*, vol. 4, p. 670.

17. Matsumura's testimony in Hiroshima Jō, p. 28. Hiroshima was one of six prefectural military districts under the administrative umbrella of the CMD.

18. Hiroshima Jō, p. 28.

19. Hiroshima Jō, p. 24.

20. Hiroshima Prefectural Government, 1976, p. 47.

21. Knebel and Bailey, p. 168.

22. The ground speed figure is based on navigator Van Kirk's flight log of the Hiroshima mission. See Van Kirk, 1945.

A SLOW MORNING

1. Tibbets, p. 226.

2. Two grades lower, four hundred students and four teacher chaperones were doing firebreak clearance between Zakoba-chō and Tsurumibashi (*Sensai*, vol. 4, p. 464).

INGRESS

1. Hiroshima/Nagasaki Editorial Committee, 1979, p. 351.

2. *Sensai*, vol. 4, p. 259.

3. See Atomic Heritage Foundation, "Warning Leaflets."

4. These accounts of crew activity on *Enola Gay* are based on Marx, pp. 163–164, and Knebel and Bailey, pp. 168–170.

5. Nishida Toshie's testimony in *Sensai*, vol. 2, p. 166.

6. In the headquarters of the 59th Army, also located in the Chūgoku HQ complex at Hiroshima Castle, the commanding general had sent his staff home after the last Imabari-related all clear with orders to rest up and report back for duty by ten thirty a.m. on August 6 (Shishido, 1972, p. 149).

7. US Strategic Bombing Survey, 1947e, vol. 1, p. 11.

THE BOMB RUN

1. Tibbets, p. 227.

2. US Strategic Bombing Survey, 1947e, p. 11.

3. These goggles—which resembled those used by welders—were specially built for the atomic-bombing missions. They employed full-extinction Polaroid lenses that allowed the passage only in the purple spectrum. (Purple light is not a medium for infrared heat radiation; thus it poses less danger for human retinas in intense light events.) Knebel and Bailey, p. 170.

4. Knebel and Bailey, p. 171.

5. The source of this alert has never been definitively determined.

6. There are lingering questions—most likely never to be solved—about who made this call, and whether or not it was ever made. Nevertheless, in postwar testimony, Furuta Masanobu, the night shift NHK announcer at Chūgoku HQ on August 5–6, insisted that the NHK office received such a call and that he broadcast the beginning of an emergency air raid alert that was cut short by Little Boy's explosion. See Akimasa, 2019. In *Phantom Voice*, Shirai insists this call was from Kure Naval Arsenal, which would make more sense, as they were the only ones who actually sounded an alarm as the Little Boy force began to penetrate Ōta Delta airspace.

7. Marx, p. 167; Knebel and Bailey, p. 172.

8. Physical details in Lee's testimony such as the angle to which she raised her head to watch this scene, as well as her eventually having her back to the city at the last moment that she was watching the plane, suggest that she was looking at the *Great Artiste*.

9. *Sensai*, vol. 3, p. 412.

10. Ōkura's exact words in Japanese were *"Iie, Hiroshima ga zenmetsu ni chikai jōtai desu"* (*Sensai*, vol. 2, p. 167).

COSMIC FIRE

1. See Broad, 2021.
2. Laurence, 1940.
3. "War Department Called *Times* Reporter," 1945.
4. "War Department Called *Times* Reporter," 1945.
5. See Groves, p. 325, and Laurence, 1946, p. xi.
6. See Marshall Foundation.
7. Wellerstein, 2021, p. 111.
8. Wellerstein, p. 119. See also Kirstein, 2009, p. 818. For additional bio info on Page as pioneer in the field of PR, see Arthur W. Page Society.
9. "William Laurence," 1977.
10. Hasegawa, 2005, p. 180.
11. Walker, 1997, p. 137.
12. Boyer, 1985, p. 3.
13. "Truman Reports," 2006.
14. See Harry S. Truman Presidential Library and Museum.
15. Boyer, p. 3.
16. By this point in the war, after Germany's surrender and a thorough on-site investigation of the facilities and progress of its nuclear research program by the Manhattan Project's Alsos field intelligence teams, the United States (and certainly anyone of Page's rank and higher involved with the War Department and the Manhattan Project) was well aware that the Nazis had been nowhere near even the most rudimentary stages of developing an atomic bomb. Although tangible intelligence on Japanese progress in nuclear research was still far less forthcoming, no one in Allied leadership suspected

that the Japanese had gotten further than the Nazis had in their own fission weapon work. See Groves.

17. Boyer, pp. 3–7.

THE BASIC POWER OF THE UNIVERSE

1. All forms of energy on the electromagnetic spectrum are mediated by photons—not just the spectrum's narrow band of visible light energy with which we are most familiar (and which, via ancient Greek, gives photons their name). The level of energy carried by a photon will determine where it falls on the spectrum, and therefore whether or not (usually not) we can see it, and whether or not it is potentially harmful to our bodies. At the high-energy end of the spectrum, we find gamma rays and X-rays, which are invisible to the naked eye but are indeed potentially harmful to our bodies, either through direct destruction of cells in high doses or through carcinogenic influence (typically DNA damage) at lower doses. At the lower-energized end of the spectrum are radio waves, which are also invisible but not harmful to our bodies in the normal doses in which we encounter them in our daily lives (despite what scaremongers may say about cell phones, Wi-Fi, etc.). Visible light, around the middle of the electromagnetic spectrum, is also usually harmless at the energy levels in which we encounter it in our daily lives, but in high-energy states (e.g., as encountered in a nuclear explosion), both it and the likewise usually benign radio waves can injure or destroy skin tissue and eyesight.

2. See BCcampus.

3. Any atoms heavier than hydrogen have multiple layers or shells of electrons orbiting their nuclei.

4. Rhodes, 1986, p. 209.

5. Rhodes, 1986, p. 209.

6. See Goodsell, 2005, p. 361.

7. Laurence, 1959, p. 24. The success of this experiment would not have been possible without the theoretical input of by then exiled Austrian Jewish physicist Lise Meitner, who was already in "Stockholm at this point, but was in almost daily postal communication with [chemist Otto] Hahn" (personal communication from Professor Mordecai Mac Low of the American Museum of Natural History and the University of Heidelberg).

8. As early as April 1943, Manhattan Project planners—in direct contradiction to General Groves' PR campaign 2.5 years later—were fully aware of the dangers of radiation involved with atomic bombs. A Manhattan Project training manual written for new scientists arriving for duty at Los Alamos contained the following passage confirming this: "Several kinds of damage will be caused by the bomb. A very large number of neutrons is released in the explosion. One can estimate a radius of about 1000 yards around the site of explosion as the size of the region in which the neutron concentration is

great enough to produce severe pathological effects" (Serber, 1992, p. 33). At the top secret decision-making level, these "pathological effects" were not considered particularly problematic, as "the physicists on the Manhattan Project had assumed that anyone close enough to the hypocenter of the explosion to have received significant amounts of radiation would have been killed by the blast or thermal effects of the bombs" (Neel, 1997, p. 5432).

9. So, yes, every time you eat a cheeseburger—or take a breath—you are accelerating the eventual and inevitable "Heat Death of the Universe" by turning matter into kinetic energy, but it will take a lot of eating and breathing yet before that really starts to become a serious problem many billions of years from now.

10. See Machleidt, 2014.

"VAPORIZED"

1. Jōhōji, 1981, p. 356. "The velocity of the shock wave is greater than the velocity of the sound in the air ahead of it. You don't hear the shock wave coming" (Serber, p. 36).

2. The Hiroshima Ginkō Shūkaijō, temporarily used as a Japanese Navy office facility in 1945, was a three-story reinforced-concrete building of modern (1936) construction located in Ōtemachi 2-chō-me. Postwar surveyors with the United States Strategic Bombing Survey were sufficiently impressed with the building to deem it "appreciably stronger" than American office buildings of similar use and age (US Strategic Bombing Survey, 1947e, vol. 2, p. 177).

3. US Strategic Bombing Survey, 1947e, vol. 2, p. 177.

4. The blast effects—from the impact initial shock wave until the subsiding of the blast winds—are estimated to have lasted anywhere up to twenty seconds. White et al., 1963, p. 63.

5. See White et al., p. 52, table 25. There does not appear to be any additional information regarding the fate of this lone survivor in the public record, but it seems likely that their radiation exposure would have eventually proved fatal.

6. See Serber, p. 38.

7. If this amount of TNT were stacked in packing crates on a plot of some two hundred eighty square meters, it would be approximately the height and volume of the Washington Monument.

8. Radio waves occupy the other end.

9. Brode, 1963, p. 10

10. See Tomonaga, 2019, et al.

11. Schull, 1995, p. 12.

12. This process of ionization changes atoms and molecules of substances that are supposed to be present in the cellular structure into substances that are not supposed to be there, often with catastrophically toxic consequences for both the cell (e.g., DNA) and its living host.

13. Spherical and other-shaped, near-microscopic glass globules of sand melted in the fireball can still be found all over the Hiroshima area. These are referred to by soil geologists as "Hiroshimaites." See Wannier et al., 2019.

14. Postol, 1986, p. 18.

15. Numerous eyewitnesses in Hiroshima likened the flash to something like an unimaginably bright magnesium flare; others described it as something like lightning, but tens or even "thousands" of times brighter.

16. See Postol, p. 18. A meteorological observatory in the Hiroshima waterfront district of Eba measured the initial shock wave from the explosion at over twice the speed of sound before this airspeed subsided to approximately the speed of sound within a second or so of detonation.

17. Serber, p, 38.

18. Jōhōji, p. 354. The three-second duration of hottest fireball phase (Butler, 1962, p. 483).

19. Hiroshima Prefectural Government, 1976, p. 88. See also Eden, 2006.

20. Jōhōji, p. 358.

21. Oughterson et al., 1951, vol. 5, p. 87.

ZHEN SU BING

1. See Chen, 2001, p. 182.

TSUCHIYA KEIJI

1. The best comprehensive history in English of the Manchurian/Mongolian settlement campaign of the 1930s and 1940s is probably Louise Young's *Japan's Total Empire*.

HURRY UP AND WAIT

1. See US Strategic Bombing Survey, 1947a, p. 21, et al.

2. Hiroshima Red Cross Hospital was founded in 1939 and still exists on the site. The Army Mutual Aid Hospital in the district of Minami-machi, just north of Ujina, was founded in 1942 and is the site of the present-day Hiroshima Prefectural Hospital. For a brief history of the hospital, see Hiroshima for Global Peace.

3. Surviving municipal and prefectural authorities (including police officials) staged an ad hoc regrouping—a sort of joint ad hoc city hall / prefectural office of civilian and bureaucratic authority at Tamon'in Temple on the west foot of Hijiyama on the night of August 6. See Junod, 1982, p. 332.

4. *Sensai*, vol. 1, p. 257.

5. Kaikōsha, 2021, p. 696.

6. See "*Hiroshima no kiroku*," 2000.

7. See "*Hiroshima no kiroku*," 2000.

8. By early 1943, a special Imperial Japanese Navy committee on nuclear research had concluded that neither their own country nor Germany or the

United States could spare war industry capacity for the extreme effort
necessary to develop a working nuclear bomb in time to use in the present
conflict. See Rhodes, 1986, p. 458.

9. The Ujina Line was a single-track railway constructed during the
militarization of the Hiroshima waterfront in the early twentieth century
for the primary purpose of moving troops and matériel between the national
railway (San'yō Line) depot at Hiroshima Station and the Army dis/
embarkation facilities at Ujina. The line was also within easy access of the
Army Clothing Depot in Danbara. See US Strategic Bombing Survey, 1946a,
p. 170.

10. Japan Broadcasting Corporation (NHK), 1981, p. 77. Within days, the
Akatsuki ferryboats had rigged up large rafts—up to five at a time—to tow
victims between different facilities in Hiroshima Bay. According to one
witness, up to seventy passengers would be loaded on each of these rafts,
each of which also had a "crew" of three soldiers supervised by one NCO. See
Japan Broadcasting Corporation (NHK), p. 83.

11. *Sensai*, vol. 1, p. 262.

12. *Sensai*, vol. 1, p. 262.

"MIZU … MIZU …"

1. *Sensai*, vol. 1, p. 266.

2. This building, officially known as the Ujina Hall of Triumphant Return
(*Ujina gaisenkan*) was built in 1938. See *"Ujina gaisenkan rekishi tsutaeru."*

3. *Sensai*, vol. 1, p. 27.

4. Aerial mine laying was a secondary mission of LeMay's B-29s from April
1945. See *Starvation* (US Army Air Forces, Twentieth Air Force, 1945), and
Hanley (2016).

5. For a detailed account of the Akatsuki recovery operations, see *Sensai*, vol. 1,
pp. 249–293.

6. During World War Two, the obstacle presented by superheated rubble meant
that it often took days for rescue and recovery personnel to be able to enter
urban areas destroyed by firestorms in the wake of incendiary raids. See
Postol, p. 44.

7. See Peace Seeds, 2007.

MISSION SHIFT

1. *Sensai*, vol. 3, p. 161.

2. *Sensai*, vol. 3, p. 161.

3. Second General Army commander Field Marshal Hata Shunroku had just
returned from a trip to Tokyo and was near Hiroshima Station when the
bomb exploded. Although he was technically the highest-ranking military
figure in Hiroshima in the aftermath of the bombing, his command HQ in
Futabayama had been almost completely wiped out, so he suggested that

Saeki—with his still relatively intact Akatsuki Command—be put in charge of rescue and recovery efforts for the city. See *Sensai*, vol. 1, pp. 203–204.

4. US Strategic Bombing Survey, 1947e, vol. 2, pp. 199–200.
5. Chūgoku Shimbunsha, 1974, p. 73.
6. The granite front steps of the building would become famous soon after the war for the "shadow" of a woman sitting there, waiting for the bank to open, that was scorched onto their surface by Little Boy's thermal rays. See Iwanami Shoten Editorial Staff, 2013, p. 48.
7. *Sensai*, vol. 1, p. 281.
8. *Sensai*, vol. 1, p. 279.

YOSHIJIMA

1. Nihon Chishi Kenkyūjō, 1978, p. 292.
2. A brief description of the Yoshijima Airfield / Kurashiki complex and its construction can be found in US Strategic Bombing Survey, 1947e, vol. 3, p. 335.
3. This was the same mobilization order that had summoned the Saitō Unit from Kōno'ura before noon on August 6.
4. Now that their homes or dormitories closer to Ground Zero had been destroyed, Chai and many other students had nowhere else to go at this point.
5. Burn victims—both from thermal radiation flash burns and flame burns (from burning structures)—composed approximately half of the total fatalities in both the Hiroshima and Nagasaki bombings. See Schull, p. 12.
6. See Arrupe, 1970/2004b, p. 43.
7. See Tsuzuki, 1947.
8. Hattori, 2010, p. 105.
9. Block and Tsuzuki, 1948, p. 417.
10. Hibakusha Tominaga Machiyo—older sister of Tominaga Chieko, whom we also met earlier in the text—experienced this firsthand when she attempted to assist in first aid for a badly burned classmate of Chieko back at their school. See Kurokawa, 1986. See also Seki, 1985, pp. 38–39. For detailed medical descriptions of atomic bomb burns and differing degrees of same, see Tsuzuki, 1947.
11. These are, of course, classic radiation sickness symptoms. See Oughterson et al., vol. 1; Schull; Hachiya, 1955; Akizuki, 2010; et al.
12. See Tsuzuki et al.
13. An exception was the witholding of relief for their agonizing thirst, on account of the restricted water-drinking policy.
14. See Oughterson et al., vol. 1, pp. 4–5.
15. See Hachiya.
16. This airstrip, which was expanded into a small municipal airport postwar, served as the heliport for President Obama's official visit to the city—specifically, to Hiroshima Peace Park—in May 2016.

EXPLAINING THE IMPOSSIBLE

1. The term "vacuum of meaning" is from, and used throughout, Viktor Frankl's seminal *Man's Search for Meaning*. See also Janoff-Bulman, 1992.
2. See Ōta et al., 2014.
3. Seki, 1985, p. 32, et al.
4. See Tsukuda, 1995, p. 191.
5. *Sensai*, vol. 4, p. 428. See also *Nagasaki City*, 1977, p. 216. In a report sent by Nagasaki prefectural governor Nagano Takeaki's office to western Japan military district authorities in Fukuoka after the August 9 bombing of Nagasaki, the parachute-attached radiosondes were theorized to have been some kind of electronic triggering mechanism for the new-type bomb that had just exploded over the city.
6. *Sensai*, vol. 4, pp. 668–670.
7. For detailed explorations of the Japanese state's use of mass communications in justifying its imperial expansion in prewar/wartime Japanese propaganda, see Young, 1998, and Kushner, 2007.
8. Havens, 1978, p. 21.
9. This phenomenon of the doggedly resilient will to continue the war paralleled the respective experiences of the British and German populaces under determined bombing campaigns.
10. *Sensai*, vol. 3, p. 407.
11. *Sensai*, vol. 3, p. 407.
12. *Sensai*, vol. 1, pp. 579–580.
13. Butow, 1954, p. 150.
14. Braw, 1991, p. 11.
15. *Asahi Shimbun*, August 7, 1945.
16. Butow, p. 151.
17. Braw, p. 16.
18. *"Uran genshi kaku no bunretsu,"* 1945. "Known since August 10 . . ." Butow, p. 152.
19. Atomic Archive, "Atomic Bombings." See also Tibbets, pp. 239–240.
20. Atomic Heritage Foundation, "Warning Leaflets."
21. Atomic Archive.
22. *Sensai*, vol. 5, p. 340.
23. See Akizuki et al.

THE BURN PITS

1. *"Hiroshima genbaku: Taiwanjin hibakusha ga shōgen,"* 2011.

GOING HOME

1. As I was able to confirm during a weeklong fieldwork trip to the country in December 2019, this is still the case in South Korea to this day.
2. See *"Hiroshima genbaku: Taiwanjin hibakusha ga shōgen."*

3. For additional details of the activities of such groups, see Toyonaga, 2001. One would suspect that the Japanese government—perhaps particularly the Ministry of Foreign Affairs—feared creating legal precedent for what might have been viewed as "reparations" for foreign victims of Japan's war.

4. Toyonaga, p. 382.

5. See *"Hiroshima genbaku: Taiwanjin hibakusha ga shōgen."*

6. Tsuchiya, 1975, p. 14.

7. *"Genbaku no Kioku: Hajimete uchiakeru kono omoi."* Although the cadet branch system of the imperial family was abolished in the postwar era, Takeda continued to be influential in cultural, political, and veterans group affairs, eventually becoming president of the Japan Olympic Committee in 1962—a role in which he was instrumental in seeing to the successful preparations and holding of the 1964 Tokyo Summer Olympic Games.

8. Horikawa, 2020, p. 363. The "First Repatriation Ministry" is what the Imperial Army officially became after November 1945 (the Imperial Navy became the "Second Repatriation Ministry").

9. *Sensai*, vol. 4, p. 462.

THE SUN SETS ON AKATSUKI

1. These reforms were stipulations of the School Education Law, which was passed by the Diet in a unanimous vote on March 27, 1947. See SCAP, 1947, p. 2.

2. See Hiroshima City,*"Genbaku kankei no ireihi nado no gaiyō."* The "period of high economic growth" is generally considered to have lasted from roughly 1955 until the collapse of the so-called Bubble Era in the early 1990s, with a brief interim hiccup resulting from the 1973–1974 oil crisis.

3. Lifton, 1968, et al.

4. See Becker, 1975, et al.

5. See Dower, 2000.

6. The concept of CORFing (Casting Off of Reflected Failure) was first proposed in Snyder et al., 1983, as a counterpart for the concept of BIRGing (Basking in Reflective Glory), first introduced in Cialdini et al., 1976.

7. Horikawa, 2020, p. 364.

8. Horikawa, 2020, p. 369.

9. Horikawa, 2020, pp. 366–367.

10. Kurokawa, 1976, p. 7

11. *"Hiroshima no kiroku,"* 2000.

GRAND BOULEVARDS

1. The literal meaning of *san'yō* is "the sunny side of the mountains."

2. For a historical analysis of the development and strategic importance of the Japanese national railway system, see US Strategic Bombing Survey, 1947c.

3. Nihon Chishi Kenkyūjō, p. 292.

4. As of the writing of this volume, construction is underway to connect this Super Express Line with Nagasaki finally.

5. See Bunce, 1955, p. 106.

6. While well-maintained school records that survived the bombing/firestorm make possible this exact tabulation of the number of schoolchildren working the firebreaks that day, such precise statistics were not maintained for the *Giyūtai* volunteers. For many of this latter group, participation in the work parties that morning was a last-minute, spur-of-the-moment matter.

7. Hamai, 2011, pp. 77–79.

8. Seki, 2015, p. 50. Kurokawa (neé Tominaga) Machiyo originally made the remark (which Tominaga repeated to me later) "Hiroshima is one giant cemetery."

"X" MARKS THE SPOT

1. The Honkawa (whose name means "the actual or main river") was once the main stream of the Ōta before the bulk of its flow volume was rerouted over the top of the city, then down along the western edge of the delta through what is now the Ōta River Spillway—which was one of the largest single civil engineering projects in Japanese history.

2. Horikawa, 2015, p. 21.

3. Hiroshima Prefectural Government, 2011.

4. This building survives today as a rest area and information desk facility for visitors to Peace Park.

5. These are also still extant.

6. Ba'ue, 2008.

7. At the convenience of the Allied occupation, both the Imperial Japanese Army and Navy continued to exist as organizations for several months after the war. Functioning in a sort of institutional limbo, they performed administrative, logistical, and other missions related to repatriation of overseas personnel, rubble clearing, etc., until they were dissolved by Allied decree in November 1945.

8. Until November 1945, city hall—even the mayor's office—was also used as a temporary storage facility for boxes of cremated remains. The practical need to alleviate this situation was also part of city hall's motive to construct a permanent municipal facility for this purpose, with the Jisenji Temple bone-collection point on Nakajima eventually becoming the location for this. See Horikawa, 2015, pp. 24–26.

9. Bodies in such circumstances were still being regularly uncovered in Hiroshima well into the 1950s and later (e.g., during the construction of the first Carp Stadium in Moto-machi).

10. To accommodate the remains of the vast numbers of ZTD evacuees who had perished on the western edge of the city, Zenhōji Temple in the Koi District

was also used as a drop-off point during the first few months of the postwar period. See Horikawa, 2015, p. 27.

11. According to the postwar testimony of Lieutenant Colonel Nomura Kiyoshi, one of Lieutenant General Yoshimura's Akatsuki Training Command staff officers, there was widespread burial of uncremated bodies in the early days after the bombing in the ZTD. At the time, this was primarily due to insufficient availability of pyre fuel (almost all of the wooden wreckage in the ZTD that might otherwise have augmented pyre building having been consumed by the firestorms of August 6–7) (*Sensai*, vol. 5, p. 430).

12. See Horikawa, 2015, p. 27. Such operations also took place at various Akatsuki aid facility sites on Ninoshima.

13. *Chūgoku Shimbun*, December 24, 1945. Letter to the editor from Mochizuki Yasuhiko demanding establishment of a more permanent and proper official ossuary. Quoted in full in Ubuki, pp. 12–13.

WHAT TO DO FOR THE DEAD

1. "normal fabric of community life . . ." US Strategic Bombing Survey (1946a), p. 6. See also Arayama, 2020.

2. Horikawa, 2015, p. 21.

3. Similar migrations of squatters from outlying areas, even from other prefectures—mostly people coming into the city as day laborers doing recovery work—were also simultaneously occurring in other parts of the city center, particularly on public lands along river embankments. These illegal settlements soon became known as "atomic ghettos" (*genbaku suramu*), and they plagued city redevelopment planning efforts for the former ZTD for decades, until the last of them were finally cleared by the 1970s and their inhabitants put up in public housing projects—mostly in the north of the city—purpose-built to accommodate this overflow. See Hiroshima City, 1985.

4. Several of my hibakusha informants also inhabited such dwellings in the early postwar period—one of them for nearly ten years after the bombing of Nagasaki.

5. See Winter, 1995.

6. Ubuki, pp. 12–13.

7. *Chūgoku Shimbun*, cited in Ubuki, pp. 12–13.

8. The acronym "SCAP" stands for "supreme commander for the Allied powers." Depending on the context, this could refer to the individual—that is, to General MacArthur himself—or to his Tokyo-based headquarters organization, which was tasked with coordinating the Allied occupation of Japan as a whole. In Japanese, SCAP and, somewhat more abstractly, the Allied occupation as a whole are almost always referred to as "GHQ" (General Headquarters), while "SCAP" in the context of the individual is inevitably referred to as Makkāsā—the imperfect phonetic Japanese rendering of "MacArthur." In this and the companion Nagasaki volume,

I will use "SCAP" when referring to the Tokyo headquarters organization and "Allied occupation (forces)" when referring to the presence and activities of these officers and soldiers locally and/or in the field, e.g., in Hiroshima, Nagasaki, etc. MacArthur will be referred to as "MacArthur."

9. See SCAP, September 19, 1945.

10. Seki, 2015, p. 47. GHQ censorship of bomb discourse was not as sweeping as people now assume it was. A translation of John Hersey's seminal *Hiroshima*, 1946, for example, became a massive bestseller in Occupied Japan in 1949 (Chūgoku Shimbunsha [1966], p. 40), with even Emperor Hirohito himself receiving a copy (Chūgoku Shimbunsha [1966], p. 42). See also Braw.

11. Hamai, p. 101.

12. Unlike Nagasaki, where prelates had been Japanese since the 1930s, the Catholic Diocese of Hiroshima—likely reflecting the influence of the Jesuits in that city—would not have a Japanese prelate until the 1950s.

13. Ubuki, p. 13.

14. Ubuki, p. 13. Today, this practice is observed throughout Japan every August 6 at eight fifteen a.m., although the earnestness and conformity with which it is done so have declined dramatically in recent years compared to my first experience of these events in the late 1980s. In Japan today, there are four other siren-accompanied national minutes of silence observed every year: at 11:02 a.m. every August 9, commemorating the atomic bombing of Nagasaki; at noon every August 15, commemorating Emperor Hirohito's surrender broadcast and the end of the war; at 11:58 a.m. every September 1, commemorating the Great Kanto Earthquake of 1923 (primarily to promote public disaster-prevention awareness); and, since 2012, at 2:46 p.m. every March 11, commemorating the 2011 earthquake, tsunami, and Fukushima nuclear disaster that ravaged northeast Japan.

15. Horikawa, 2015, p. 31.

BUILD IT AND THEY WILL COME

1. Hiroshima City, "The Hiroshima Peace Memorial City Construction Law and Commentary."

2. See Hiroshima City, 1985, pp. 56–57.

3. These hopes would prove unfounded. The atom-bombed cities of Hiroshima and Nagasaki remain special cases to this day, as they are the only Japanese municipalities to receive this generous treatment from the national government.

4. See Zwigenberg, 2014.

5. Braw, pp. 151–152

6. See Zwigenberg, pp. 49–52.

7. See Hamai, Zwigenberg et al.

8. Hamai, p. 76.

9. Chūgoku Shimbunsha (1966), p. 43.

10. Chūgoku Shimbunsha (1966), p. 43.
11. This was to have been built at the base of Mount Fuji and used as a site for patriotic rallies and ceremonies. See Jacquet, 2010.
12. See Ba'ue.
13. Kyōdō Tsūshin, 2021.
14. As of October 2021, 816 of the bodies identified and listed by Hiroshima City Hall by name have still not been claimed by next of kin, either because their family members also perished in the bombing or because they simply never knew the remains existed and were identified as such, having assumed that their loved ones had disappeared forever on August 6, 1945. See Kyōdō Tsūshin.
15. The park and an adjacent carbarn and siding depot for the 6, 8, and 9 Lines of the Hiroden streetcar system occupy what was once a rifle range for Hiroshima's IJA Fifth Division.
16. See Arayama.

THE MUTE MEMORIAL

1. SCAP, December 15, 1945. State Shintō definition: See Mullins, 2022, pp. 12–13. See also Wittner, 1971.
2. SCAP, December 15, 1945.
3. See Seki, 2015, p. 48. Memorial stone censorship was not so much strictly overseen and enforced by occupation authorities as it was left up to Japanese common sense. And the fact that the majority of the stones put up during the occupation were put up on school grounds, to commemorate casualties among their own faculties and student bodies and could thereby be considered "private" religious activity, in a sense, was another reason for relative censorial tolerance in such cases, as long as the words *genbaku* and *eirei* were avoided.
4. See Kurokawa, 1976.
5. Examples of these Occupation Era *tsuitō* stones include memorials that can today be seen on the grounds of Kokutaiji Prefectural High School in downtown Hiroshima, and Hiroshima Municipal Midori-machi Junior High School in Midori-machi, north of Ujina. See Kurokawa, 1976. For details on SCAP policy toward Shintō-inflected public war memorialization, see Creemers, 1968.
6. Ichijo became Hiroshima Municipal Funairi High School in the late 1940s. It still occupies the original location of the Ichijo campus in the south-central Hiroshima neighborhood of Funairi-chō.
7. Far below this inscription, close to the bottom of the plinth, "Hiroshima Ichijo Atom-bomb-bereaved Family Association" is carved in a much smaller, shallower, and different style of typeface. I believe there are two possible explanations for the existence of this inscription here: it was added as an afterthought when the stone was moved to its present location, now out from under the restrictions of occupation policy; or it was on the 1948 original, but placed inconspicuously like this so it could be hidden behind by

backdrop materials like bushes, flowers, or ornamental garden stones, with the intention that it would be exposed to public view once the occupation was over.

8. See NHK, 2011.

ICHIJO WORKSITE

1. "*'Kioku wo uketsugu,'*" 2018.
2. *Sensai*, vol. 4, p. 419.
3. *Sensai*, vol. 4, p. 419.
4. *Sensai*, vol. 4, p. 419.
5. *Sensai*, vol. 4, p. 419.

NOGUCHI KAZUKO

1. According to the National Militia Service Law (*Kokumin Giyū Hei'eki Hō*) of June 1945, passed after the formation of the *Kokumin Giyūtai* (armed home defense force mobilizing all men between the ages of fifty and sixty and all women between seventeen and forty not otherwise employed in essential war work) by the Koiso cabinet the previous March, the Army would have had the *Kokumin Giyū* people—including women, "if necessary"—fighting as militia infantry in the event of an Allied invasion.

ŌIWA KŌHEI

1. *Sensai*, vol. 4, p. 310.
2. Mullins, p. 118.
3. See Mullins.
4. This procedure was also followed by applicants to the Imperial Naval Academy on Etajima Island. It may be slightly misleading to refer to junior high schools here as being six-year programs—I have done so for clarity—when it is more precisely the case that, by the late war, schools known as "junior highs" (*chūgakkō* in Japanese) graduated students with "junior high" accreditation after four years, with students desiring "high school" accreditation (mostly students who wanted to go on to university or teachers college) staying on an additional two years in their junior high's higher-education programs.
5. *Hiroshima Kenritsu Itchū Hibaku Seito no Kai*, 1974, p. 5.

ITCHŪ WORKSITE

1. Interview with Dr. Sano Hitoshi, May 2018.
2. *Hiroshima Kenritsu Itchū Hibaku Seito no Kai*, p. 334.
3. "Hiroshima no koe: Imada Kōji-san."
4. *Sensai*, vol. 4, p. 328.
5. *Hiroshima Kenritsu Itchū Hibaku Seito no Kai*, p. 328.
6. *Hiroshima Kenritsu Itchū Hibaku Seito no Kai*, p. 13.
7. *Hiroshima Kenritsu Itchū Hibaku Seito no Kai*, p. 31.

DAI NI KENJO WORKSITE

1. Seki, 1985, p. 31.
2. Seki, 2015, p. 18.
3. Seki, 2015, p. 18. There was actually a third category of twelve-to-fourteen-year-old students under the Japanese school system at the time. These were attendees of what were called "higher primary" courses, two-year programs offered at selected elementary schools as a sort of junior high school substitute for students who wanted better prospects when they hit the job market at fourteen but whose families could not afford a normal full junior high program of four to five years.
4. *Sensai*, vol. 4, p. 371.
5. See Sakamoto, 1951/1969.
6. Sakamoto, p. 232.

TOMINAGA CHIEKO

1. Again, this is under the prewar Japanese education system, in which young men graduated from six-year junior high programs (four-year junior high programs plus two-year secondary education programs) at the age of eighteen or nineteen.
2. This footwear was very similar to what was marketed in the US in the 1970s and 1980s as "kung fu shoes."

ŌIWA EXPLOSION

1. This brief seismic shock was strong enough to be perceived as an "echo" reflection of Little Boy's shock wave off the earth's surface by the crew members of *Enola Gay* and the *Great Artiste*. This disturbance was felt after the initial and much stronger direct supersonic shock wave from the explosion had briefly buffeted the planes during their escape-maneuver egress runs.

NOGUCHI EXPLOSION

1. This is present-day Higashi Senda Park. The old Art Deco brick main campus administrative building—which was temporarily used as the office of the Chūgoku Administrative District (government of Japan late-war civilian bureaucracy administrative jurisdiction parallel to the CMD)—is still there, too.

WAKING UP IN HELL

1. Seki, 2015, p. 22.
2. Sakamoto, p. 232.
3. Sakamoto, p. 232.
4. Sakamoto Setsuko aside, the last firebreak site survivor from West Homeroom died on August 20, 1945. See Seki, 1985, p. 15.
5. Seki, 2015, p. 23.
6. Sakamoto, p. 232.

LD$_{50}$

1. *Hiroshima Kenritsu Itchū Hibaku Seito no Kai*, p. 13.
2. *Hiroshima Kenritsu Itchū Hibaku Seito no Kai*, p. 328.
3. This dust was probably pulverized mud mortar that had held the tiles in place on Itchū's traditional-style Japanese roof tiles.
4. *Hiroshima Kenritsu Itchū Hibaku Seito no Kai*, p. 31.
5. De Bary et al., 1958, pp. 198–200.
6. *Hiroshima Kenritsu Itchū Hibaku Seito no Kai*, p. 8.
7. See Kodama, 2005.
8. "4.6 grays" figure for LD$_{50}$ is from Zajtchuk, 1989, p. 28.
9. See Kodama.

REPRESENTATIVE OF THE ESTABLISHMENT

1. Seki, 1985, p. 29.
2. Seki, 1985, p. 44. By that afternoon, the undamaged portions of the teachers college / Dai Ni Kenjo had become an ad hoc official field hospital, with the classrooms turned into wards.

STACKING BODIES

1. *Sensai*, vol. 5, p. 456.
2. See the concept of "psychic closing off" as discussed by Lifton, 1968, pp. 31–34. Lifton also refers to this phenomenon as "psychic numbing." One of the anecdotes that Lifton provides is deserving of quotation in full: Lifton uses as an example an IJA NCO (likely Akatsuki personnel) assigned to mass cremations who said that "if we had been sentimental we couldn't have done the work. . . . We had no emotions. . . . Because of the succession of experiences I had been through, I was temporarily without feeling. . . ." A common Japanese idiom for this mental state is *oni (no) kokoro ni naru* ("have a demon's heart"), which describes an inability to experience empathy.

RESCUING REIKO

1. See *"Hiroshima no kiroku,"* 1998.
2. *Sensai*, vol. 4, p. 422. According to Hiroshima Meteorological Station records, the afternoon low tide for Hiroshima Bay and the Ōta Delta estuaries was at 1430 on August 6, which would have been just around the time the fires around Ōte-machi and Nakajima-honmachi subsided to the point where Yamazaki's foray into the ZTD would have been physically conceivable. See *Sensai*, vol. 3, p. 273, for tidal and other meteorological data for August 6.
3. *Sensai*, vol. 4, p. 422.
4. *Sensai*, vol. 4, p. 363. Takako and some fifty other fourth-year Kenjo girls were undergoing advanced combat nurse training at Second General Army HQ in preparation for the upcoming Allied invasion.

5. See *"Hiroshima no kiroku,"* 1998.

6. *Sensai*, vol. 4, p. 422.

THE BAMBOO GROVE

1. Two Itchū boys running from the same Zakoba-chō firebreak site ended up jumping into the water when their evacuation route led them to the Kyōbashi (they had been heading for the Miyuki Bridge—to get to their homerooms). These boys were rescued by an Akatsuki motor launch, only to die of their injuries/ARS by the next morning. See *Hiroshima Kenritsu Itchū Hibaku Seito no Kai*, pp. 302–303.

2. After consulting period maps, I believe this intersection was probably in Deshio-machi, occupying a point roughly equidistant from the northern tip of the Army Clothing Depot, the western tip of the Kasumi-chō Arsenal, and the southeastern foot of Hijiyama.

3. This would be the same aid station Ōiwa mentions in his testimony as the place where wounded people from—or passing through—Danbara were sent or carried by soldiers.

4. Seki, 1985, p. 22.

5. Sakamoto, p. 233. The time here can be confirmed as 1225 hours, as this was when the first US photoreconnaissance plane flew over Hiroshima to assess the bomb results; there would be others, sporadically, throughout the day and over following days. See Hiroshima Peace Memorial Museum, 2019, p. 4. Paul Tibbets, in his memoirs, confirms "two of our [i.e., 509th-assigned] photo planes" flying "over Hiroshima four hours after the bomb blast." Tibbets, p. 239.

6. Tibbets, p. 233.

7. Seki, 1985, p. 22.

8. A *kappa* is a mythical creature—sort of a cross between a frog, a turtle, and a leprechaun—in Japanese lore. It is supposed to possess magical powers and dwell in bulrushes and the like along rivers. Leaflike tufts ringing its otherwise bald head have something of the apparance of a monk's tonsure.

9. Tellingly, in Tominaga Chieko's first-year homeroom shot, taken on the same day, she and one other rebel are the only girls in the class without *kappa atama* haircuts.

10. The Kitakojis were/are a branch of the Fujiwara clan, a family of prestige and pedigree in Japan second only to that of the imperial household itself.

11. See Akikatso.

12. Two of my Korean Hiroshima hibakusha informants still remember playing in the precincts of this temple during their Niho childhoods.

13. Sakamoto, p. 233.

14. Seki, 1985, p. 24.

15. Seki, 1985, p. 24.

16. See Markus and Kitayama, 1991.

17. Seki, 1985, p. 25.
18. Seki, 1985, p. 25.

UNANNOUNCED GUESTS

1. *Sensai*, vol. 3, p. 279.
2. Seki, 1985, p. 61.
3. *Sensai*, vol. 4, p. 538.
4. See Sano, 1942.
5. *Sensai*, vol. 4, p. 534.
6. *Sensai*, vol. 4, p. 49.
7. Seki, 1985, p. 32.
8. Kurokawa, 1986, p. 93.
9. Kurokawa, 1986, p. 93.
10. Seki, 1985, p. 148.
11. Kurokawa, 1986, p. 94. It is possible that Ruriko was picked up by an Akatsuki truck on a lower stretch of Rijō Street and delivered to the hospital next door to the school.
12. Seki, 1985, p. 36.
13. Seki, 1985, p. 40. Although this was never brought up by Seki in either her written accounts or in her interviews with me, the gruesome possibility exists that, after six hours of clutching onto Hata's back, Michiko's and Hata's leaked blood and lymphatic fluid might have mingled and then dried, in effect gluing them together. This physical complication, rather than some on-the-spot acknowledgment of Hata-sensei's rank/importance by the Akatsuki personnel on the truck, might have been the determining factor in having the teacher's corpse brought back to the campus rather than its being left on the Red Cross lawn with Sakai Tamie.
14. Seki, 1985, p. 44.
15. Seki, 1985, p. 45.

RETURN TO DANBARA

1. Not to be confused with the teachers college / Dai Ni Kenjo campus.

FACING MONSTERS

1. See Lifton, 1968, et al.
2. See Ministry of the Environment.
3. The classic modeling of the concept of "symbolic universe" can be found in Berger and Luckmann, 1966.
4. Seki interview, December 2016.
5. Seki, 1985, p. 65.
6. Seki, 2015, p. 13.
7. The Makurazaki Typhoon the following month would destroy what was left of the building.
8. "tatami-floored tea ceremony classroom . . ." Seki, 1985, p. 35.

9. Seki, 1985, p. 168. See also *Hiroshima Ken Dōin Gakuto Giseisha no Kai*, 1995, p. 47.
10. Seki, 1985, p. 85.

FALLOUT

1. Zajtchuk, 1989, p. 14.
2. See Oughterson et al., vol. I, pp. 5–6.
3. Goodsell, p. 361.
4. The intended "product," in this case, being the strong-nuclear-force energy released by the shattering of nuclei.
5. See Alper, 1948.
6. Zajtchuk, 1989, p. 15.

THE ZAKOBA-CHŌ STONES

1. See Kitahara, 1984.
2. See US Strategic Bombing Survey, 1947a.
3. In wartime Japan, bereaved families were "the immediate recipients of . . . national honor (and consolation), both symbolically and materially, through government pension payments and a host of other benefits. The cult of the war dead thus combined the ideology of State Shintō (in terms of the shrines' role in ritually connecting the people with their nation's spiritual essence, the emperor) with the structures of a modern social welfare system" (Seraphim, 2006, p. 60).
4. "God term" is used here to mean a word that occupies a particularly exalted symbolic and emotionally powerful position within the belief system of its origin, representing core values the constituents of that belief system would consider figuratively or literally sacrosanct. For comprehensive explorations of the concept, see Weaver, 1953, and Burke, 1969.
5. NHK, *NHK Web Tokushū: Ikinokotte, sumimasen*. The number seven is significant in Buddhist cosmology because this is the number of upright steps the baby Buddha is supposed to have taken immediately upon his birth.
6. Sakamoto, p. 233.
7. Sakamoto, p. 233.
8. Seki, 2015, p. 21.
9. This rhetorical convention for "survivors' speeches" is something I also observed in dozens of Japanese veterans association gatherings (which were also attended by bereaved family members of war dead) in the early and mid-2000s.
10. There are no human remains buried here; the gathered souls of the students are supposed to be "at rest here."
11. This was the occupation-approved naming for Japan's war, which was far less sanguine and ancien régime than the wartime "Great East Asian War" name preferred by post-Occupation Japanese conservative / right-wing rhetors, but

which nevertheless conveniently elided the country's imperialistic embroilments in China and Southeast Asia.

12. Americans familiar with the Lost Cause sentiment of the Confederate monuments that still pepper the southern United States a century and a half after the Civil War should immediately recognize the operant psychology here.

13. After the war, the district of Zakoba-chō was renamed "Kokutaiji."

HIBAKUSHA OMERTÀ

1. Until the end of the 1946–1947 academic year, Itchū conducted classes in temporary barrackslike structures built on the campus of what is now Hiroshima Municipal Midori-machi Junior High. The following academic year, Itchū was absorbed into the short-lived Rijō Junior High, built over the ruins of the old Itchū campus. The 1948 national education reforms saw Rijō, in turn, dissolved to become the coed Kokutaiji High School, Tominaga Chieko's eventual alma mater.

2. Tōyūkai, *"Tōkyōto no hibakusha kazu."*

A WAR MEMORIAL IN A PEACE PARK

1. At least according to the interpretation of the Japanese government, any grievances related to colonial era and wartime Korean labor were considered legally settled by a treaty between Japan and South Korea—under rule, at the time, by a plutocratic military dictatorship—signed in 1965.

2. According to Seki Chieko (interview), this was Curtis LeMay's May 24–25 mass raid on the western half / Yamanote District of the capital, which had escaped incineration during the Great Tokyo Air Raid, which targeted the eastern Shita-machi industrial and commercial zone on March 9–10.

3. See Kurokawa, 1986.

4. Hata-sensei's teachers college had been absorbed into the new Hiroshima Prefectural Women's University by this time.

5. Seki, 1985, p. 241.

6. See Kurokawa, 1976.

7. Bank of Japan, *"Shōwa 40nen no 1-man-en no okane ni kansan suru to dono kurai ni narimasuka?"*

8. See *"Dō'in gakuto no tamashii yo yasukare,"* 1967. See also Hiroshima City, "Tour Site #42."

9. This is based on the author's firsthand observations of August 6 memorial activity at Peace Park in 2016, 2017, 2018, and 2019.

10. See Nakamae, 1953.

11. Seki, 2015, p. 82. Seki incorrectly states that this conference was held in 1956.

12. *Hiroshima Ken Dōin Gakuto Giseisha no Kai,* p. 94. *Hiroshima Ken Dōin Gakuto Giseisha no Kai,* p. 92.

13. Seki, 2015, p. 76. See also Seraphim, p. 61.

14. See Hewlett and Holl, 1989, especially p. 177.
15. See Naono, 2018. Germany has long since remunerated its own civilians for personal losses due to Allied bombing.

THE GADFLY

1. *Hiroshima Ken Dōin Gakuto Giseisha no Kai*, p. 89.
2. *Hiroshima Ken Dōin Gakuto Giseisha no Kai*, p. 96. This was Twentieth Air Force mission number 325, flown by 167 B-29s of the 58th Bombardment Wing, flying out of West Field, Tinian. Differing from its late-war, night-incendiary-bombing modus operandi, this particular mission was a daytime-precision operation with the aircraft targeting a specific limited area of industrial plants with standard five-hundred-pound M64 general-purpose (high-explosive) bombs. See US Army Air Forces, Twentieth Air Force, 1945, "Mission Resume, Mission Number 325."
3. *Hiroshima Ken Dōin Gakuto Giseisha no Kai*, p. 31.
4. See *"Onkyū Kaisei,"* 1958.
5. See Ministry of Health, Labor, and Welfare, 1969.
6. After 1978, their ranks were joined by Japanese executed by the Allies for war crimes. See Seraphim, p. 79.
7. *Hiroshima Ken Dōin Gakuto Giseisha no Kai*, p. 48.
8. *Hiroshima Ken Dōin Gakuto Giseisha no Kai*, p. 48.
9. See Okamoto, 2017.

"ATOMS FOR PEACE"

1. See Ōta et al.
2. See World Nuclear Association.
3. See Burnie, 2021.
4. Hewlett and Holl, p. 209.
5. Hewlett and Holl, p. 209.
6. Yoshioka, 2005b, p. 90.
7. See Gluck, 1985; Morris-Suzuki, 1998; Yoshida, 2002; et al.
8. See Yoshioka, 2005a, 2005b.
9. Yoshioka, 2005b, p. 115.
10. Zwigenberg, pp. 111–112.
11. There was a network of American cultural centers operating across Japan under the administration of the US Information Agency (a State Department global soft-power arm disbanded in 1999. See Zwigenberg, p. 122, for details on Nagaoka's unsuccessful opposition to the "Atoms for Peace" exhibit.
12. Nagaoka Shōgo quoted in Zwigenberg, p. 122.
13. Nagaoka Shōgo quoted in Zwigenberg, p. 122.
14. Zwigenberg, pp. 118–121.

15. This was under the old Buddhist ceremonial system for counting the passage of time, by which an event to be commemorated was counted as having occurred in "Year One." Similarly, in the old Japanese system for calculating people's ages, babies became "one year old" the moment they were born, and were thus "two years old" on the occasion of their first birthdays.

THE BRIGHT LIFE

1. See World Population Review.
2. Federal Civil Defense Administration, 1953, p. 27.
3. Young, 1998, p. 99.
4. Vogel, 1963, p. 71.
5. One reason for this is because of draconian prewar and wartime Japanese government national security policies restricting the dissemination of maps showing the precise locations of military, government, or key industrial facilities; even before the outbreak of hostilities, taking a photograph or making a sketch at the wrong place at the wrong time could result in on-the-spot arrest on espionage charges. See Fedman and Karacas, 2012.
6. Some of these spits of land are by now protruding considerably farther out into the bay, and a massive postwar civil engineering project to reroute several of the Ōta tributaries has completely altered the topography of the western third or so of the city, wiping out several of the neighborhoods that are sites of major 1945 activity in the narrative of this book.
7. Many Hiroshima districts once primarily occupied by craftsmen serving the castle community during the Edo period still bear the names of their various trades today. Nihon Chishi Kenkyūjō, p. 342.

HARMONICA HOUSES

1. Dedicated-use "bedrooms," as such, did not exist in traditional Japanese houses; they became part of the lived daily environments of most Japanese only with the increasing popularity of Western-style or mixed-Western-and-Japanese-style single-family residences from about the 1970s on.
2. The approximate location of the Yamaguchis' home can be viewed on Google Maps about 190 meters north-northeast of the Honkawa-chō streetcar stop, near the west foot of the Aioi Bridge.
3. For an informative graphic history of Japanese laundry technology, see Yamato Group, *"Sentaku no dai kaikaku."*
4. It is said that Japanese crime suspects know they are in serious trouble when the police come into their abodes with their shoes/boots still on.
5. Sand, 2003, p. 47.
6. See Sand, especially p. 50, for some useful analyses of *genkan* function and protocol.
7. US Strategic Bombing Survey, 1947b, p. 100.

8. Feis, p. 119.
9. See US Strategic Bombing Survey, 1947b.
10. See Ministry of Education, *Culture, Sports, Science, and Technology,* 1962.

THE BOY

1. The reader may recall that the burned-out shell of this building was one of the structures the Akatsuki Command began using as a temporary morgue from August 7, before mass cremations commenced the following day.
2. There were trainees from the Kamo Naval Medic School (*Sensai,* vol. 1, pp. 320–321).
3. The Yamate River was the western- and northernmost tributary stream of the Ōta Delta. It, the neighboring Fukushima River, and Fukushima—the delta islet both streams sandwiched—were obliterated during the postwar completion stages of the Ōta River Spillway. In their original configurations, downstream of the Fukushima islet, the Yamate and the Fukushima flowed together and formed a much larger waterway known as the Koi River. Downstream from the Fukushima islet, the Koi became the westernmost Ōta tributary in the delta. Like the smaller streams, this was essentially obliterated when it was widened, straightened, and renamed as the Ōta River Spillway. The geography-changing nature of this massive civil engineering project is frequently a cause of confusion when trying to cross-reference modern maps with Hiroshima hibakusha testimony of activity in the western reaches of the city/delta on and shortly after August 6.

THE MOTHERS

1. Neighborhood-level Japanese post office branches (both before and after privatization in the early twenty-first century) like the Sumiyoshi Bridge office have traditionally been operated as franchises, typically administered by local families, with ownership of the franchise license often passed along down generations to keep it in the family.
2. Residual radiation from this fallout precipitation likely killed both her and the Yamaguchis' youngest child, Shizue, some six decades later.

THE FISHING VILLAGE

1. Even now, whenever Yamaguchi opens the lid of her rice cooker at mealtime to scoop out rice, she always remembers that afternoon in the aid tent. She remembers to feel grateful—as she sees it (and as the approved Hiroshima narrative frames it)—for all the people who sacrificed their lives for the peace and prosperity Japan now enjoys, and she thinks that anyone who takes white rice for granted is disrespecting those sacrifices.
2. A sen was a denomination, under the old system of Japanese currency, valued at 1/100th of a yen. Until the 1950s—when Japanese currency became

exclusively yen-based—most small daily life purchases of food, transportation fare, cigarettes, etc., involved transactions in tens of sen.
3. Tado, 2020, p. 80.

BLACK-MARKET YAMS

1. SCAP, 1947, p. 13.
2. SCAP, 1947, pp. 12–13. A sizable portion of LARA-provided foodstuffs consisted of wheat flour; most Japanese at the time did not know how to prepare wheat flour to consume it. This "wheat infusion" of Japanese pantries had the long-term cultural effect of securing flour-based dishes a permanent niche in Japanese cuisine. The most famous of these is probably *okonomiyaki*, a sort of pancake-omelet hybrid; its name can be very loosely translated as "mix anything you want with this stuff and fry it up."
3. This did not come about merely as an act of largesse on the part of her older siblings; compulsory education in Japan was extended through three-year junior high as part of the 1948 reforms.

CHRISTIANIZING JAPAN

1. See Moore, 2011.
2. Wittner, p. 77.
3. Wittner, p. 77.
4. Wittner, p. 78.
5. Wittner, p. 78 (italics Wittner's).
6. The Confucianism-influenced formulation of State Shintō imposed on Japanese society from above by the new centralized, modern Japanese regime from the late nineteenth century was more a pragmatic, nation-building political innovation than it was any kind of religious awakening. See Bunce, p. 106.
7. State Department policy planner George Kennan—famous as the architect of America's postwar "containment policy" re: the Soviet Union—was one of the influential contemporary voices sounding the tocsin about the specter of Communism in Japan. See Moore, p. 124. See also Takemae, 2002, p. 377.
8. Wittner, p. 81.
9. Wittner, p. 81.
10. "President Truman . . . openly endorsed the dispatch of missionaries to Japan from the beginning of the Occupation. He approved MacArthur's support of American missionaries in Japan and the distribution of Bibles among the Japanese people; and he ordered officials in the Department of the Army to take control of the effort to send more missionaries to Japan" (Moore, p. 140).
11. "Spiritual vacuum" in postwar Japan (Moore, p. 43). See also Dower, 2010, p. 295.
12. Moore, pp. 6–10.
13. Moore, pp. 10–11.

14. For logistical support examples, see Moore, pp. 122–123, and Takemae, pp. 378–379.
15. Takemae, p. 378.

A NODE OF CHRISTIAN ACTIVITY

1. See Laures, 1954.
2. Laures, p. 231.
3. See Diehl, 2018.
4. The occupation of Nagasaki was in the purview of the American military, whereas the occupation of Hiroshima was under the administration of British Commonwealth troops (primarily Australian) headquartered in Kure.
5. Ishimaru, 1988, p. 11.
6. See Laures, p. 240.
7. This is the English name of the church, according to Hubert F. Schiffer, a Jesuit who was wounded by the bomb while he was in the Nobori-chō rectory. In Japanese usage, until the early-postwar period, the church was known as the *Nobori-chō Tenshu Kōkyōkai* (literally "Nobori-chō Church of God" [the Japanese word for the Judeo-Christian God/YHWH is *tenshu*, "lord/master" of "heaven"]). The name of the church rebuilt on the site is the Assumption of Mary Cathedral (aka Memorial Cathedral of World Peace) (Schiffer, p. 10).
8. See Catholic Bishops' Conference of Japan.
9. The wartime Jesuit Father Superior and vicar of Hiroshima, Hugo Lassalle, SJ, went on to become a world-renowned Western interpreter of Zen philosophy and practice in his emeritus years.
10. See Burke (1969), pp. 55–58.
11. See Nishimoto (2019). Two Italian nuns—who would have become enemy nationals after Italy's declaration of war against the Axis in October 1943—also avoided internment. An Irish nun at the convent would not have been at risk of internment, as the Republic of Ireland was neutral during the war.
12. The Miyoshi location of the Hiroshima Prefecture internment camp (*Sensai*, vol. 1, p. 24). Goossens stayed on with the Hiroshima vicariate after the war. A trained musician and composer, he helped found the Hiroshima Institute of Music, which eventually became the Elisabeth University of Music. See Mori, "Dutch POWs," and Luhmer, 1945.
13. See Siemes, 1945.
14. See Cieslik.
15. "goodwill . . ." See Siemes. Several of these priests and novitiates appear (both named and unnamed) in John Hersey's seminal *Hiroshima*.
16. Burke, 2004, pp. 19–20. Father Arrupe would eventually rise to the post of superior general of the Society of Jesus in 1965, during the turmoil of the Vatican II Council. During his tenure, he became a champion of the

"liberation theology" movement in the Church—a posture that won him few friends among conservatives in the Vatican, including future Pope John Paul II.

17. The Jōchi Catholic Settlement was a charitable community for the poor of Tokyo founded in 1931 by Father Hugo Lassalle. The community helped to familiarize newly arrived Jesuits with Japanese ways, and to give Sophia University students an opportunity to put the Jesuit men-and-women-for-others ethos and the sociology they had studied at school to practical charitable use. See Baeumler.

18. See Jésuites de la Province de L'Afrique Occidentale.

19. See Grogan, 2019, pp. 14–16, for a detailed account of Arrupe's arrest, confinement, interrogation, and release.

20. See Nishimoto et al.

21. See Gion Catholic Church.

22. Both Siemes' and Cieslik's testimonies make note of Laures' robust physique.

23. This characterization is based on Yamaguchi Sayoko's testimony about her personal acquaintance with Laures in the late 1940s and early 1950s.

24. See Siemes, Hersey et al.

25. The members of the party were Arrupe; two Korean novices, Chin Sungman and Kim Tegwan; and the German priests Laures, Klaus Luhmer, Helmut Ehrlinghagen, Laurenz Kruer, Friedrich Tappe, and Johannes Siemes. See "Foreign Jesuits Who Experienced the Atomic Bomb," 2019. After the war, Siemes provided influential testimony about the bombing to the US Strategic Bombing Survey and other Allied investigators.

26. In John Hersey's *Hiroshima*, several mentions are made of Kleinsorge going about his business in Nobori-chō and experiencing considerable anxiety about his conspicuousness as a foreigner and what he sensed (correctly or not) as an increasing, simmering xenophobia among Hiroshima's residents. In his *Sensai* testimony, Hugo Lassalle also notes experiencing similar anxiety about being a Westerner in Hiroshima as the war began developing to Japan's disadvantage. Father Johannes Siemes, in early-postwar testimony, reported of the apprehensive mood he shared with other Westerners in Hiroshima immediately after the explosion: "We did not want to go into town except under pressure of dire necessity, because we thought that the population was greatly perturbed and that it might take revenge on any foreigners which they might consider spiteful onlookers of their misfortune, or even spies." (See Siemes.)

27. See Siemes, Cieslik.

28. This is the extent of the dialogue recorded by the event's eyewitness chroniclers—Siemes and Cieslik. However, given the situation and what would have been Laures' natural inclination to use every exonerating qualification the Jesuits had in his attempt to save their necks from the

katana, he must certainly at some point have also mentioned that they were Catholic priests on a rescue mission from the Nagatsuka novitiate.

29. See Cieslik, Siemes, Hersey.

CONVERSION

1. Shōno and Iijima, 1975, pp. 158–170.

EPILOGUE

1. Laurence, 1946, p. 211.
2. Krauss and Krauss, p. 143. The flatbed truck was parked on the 509th's baseball field.
3. Sweeney, p. 174.
4. Tibbets refers to most of the ride home as resembling a "slumber party" (Tibbets, p. 236); Beser, p. 106.
5. Tibbets, p. 236.
6. Miller and Spitzer, p. 72.
7. Farrell, p. 170. The three assembly buildings for the bombs were on the northwest tip of the island, barely a stone's throw from the pounding surf and a quick truck ride over a coral-gravel-paved road leading to the bomb-loading pits (Farrell, p. 251).
8. Tibbets, p. 237.
9. Tibbets, p. 237.
10. My account of his reaction and movements at this time is based on a US Army Signal Corps silent-film record of the event. As of November 2022, this could be viewed as *Atomic Bomb Footage: Tinian (1945)—Part 2*. See US Army Signal Corps.
11. Beser, p. 101.
12. Beser, p. 131.
13. See Atomic Photographers.
14. See Keever, 2004.
15. Laurence, 1946, p. 227.
16. Laurence, 1946, p. 227.
17. See Laurence, 1945.
18. See Kristof, 1995.
19. See Yamane, 2021.
20. It would be another ten years before the people of Kokura would know how close their city had come to being wiped out. *See* Kitagome, 1955. This story broke in Japan after the publication of Truman's memoirs.

INDEX

ABOUT THE AUTHOR

M. G. SHEFTALL has lived in Japan since 1987. He has a PhD in International Relations/Modern Japanese History from Waseda University in Tokyo. Since 2001, he has been a professor of Modern Japanese Cultural History and Communication at the Faculty of Informatics of Shizuoka University—a campus in the Japanese national university system. Sheftall is married, with two adult sons, and makes his home in Hamamatsu, Japan.